The Gospel of The Holy Mother
Sri Sarada Devi

Recorded by

HER DEVOTEE - CHILDREN

SRI RAMAKRISHNA MATH
16, RAMAKRISHNA MATH ROAD,
MADRAS-600 004 :: INDIA

Published by
Adhyaksha
Sri Ramakrishna Math
Mylapore, Chennai-4

X-2M 3C-1-2012
ISBN 81-7823-001-1

Printed in India at
Sri Ramakrishna Math Printing Press
Mylapore, Chennai-4

PREFACE

'*The Gospel of the Holy Mother Sri Sarada Devi*', is the full translation of the Bengali work '*Sri Sri Mayer Katha*', parts of which have already come out in translation under other titles. This Math itself had published some important sections of it as early as 1940 under the title '*Conversations of the Holy Mother*', incorporated in her biography '*Sri Sarada Devi the Holy Mother*'. The present book, however, embodies the whole of the Bengali text. Most of the reminiscences and conversations of the Holy Mother, except what appears in the great work of Swami Saradeshananda, entitled '*The Mother as I saw her*', also published by this Math, are now available for the English reading public in one volume.

Recorded as it is by a large number of the devotee-children of the Mother, the present book reveals to mankind a great character that chose to remain outside public notice behind the Purdah and in the obscurity of the village of Jayrambati. Even under these conditions the great lady's greatness could not be obscured. Through the impressions and recollections of a large number of men and women of various stations in life, who came into contact with Sri Sarada Devi, her greatness emerges in the bright colours of Universal Motherhood, never before witnessed in so striking a manner in any personality we know of. Therefore, while the contents of this book are of special importance to the followers of Sri Ramakrishna, they can make an appeal to all who appreciate the great human value of motherliness.

The book is divided into three parts, as the translation has been done by three different persons. The reminiscences are of several people numbering 38. These recorders are both men and women, monastics and lay, and the reminiscences are of varying length and importance. But all the recorders were close to the Mother, some of them being very intimate with her as her personal attendants. It would have been possible to give greater perfection to the book, if we were able to give a few details at least about these recorders; but at this distance of time, it is not possible to gather precise information about most of them, except in the case of the few monastics who figure among them. So we have not given any biographical notes about the recorders.

It is hoped that the book will be appreciated by the general public, and especially by the devotees of Sri Ramakrishna.

Sri Ramakrishna Math
Madras PUBLISHERS
1-5-84

CONTENTS

	Page
1. Preface	iii
2. Introduction	vii

Recorded by

SECTION I

1. Sarayubala Devi	1
2. Swami Arupananda	73

SECTION II

1. Yogin-Ma	181
2. Smt. Kshirodbala Roy	190
3. Swami Santananda	212
4. Swami Santananda	220
5. Surendranath Sircar	222
6. Brahmachari Ashokakrishna	236
7. Prabodh Babu and Manindra	240
8. An anonymous lady devotee	255
9. Smt. Sailabala Chowdhury	263
10. An anonymous devotee	269
11. Srischandra Ghatak	278
12. Swami Ritananda	285
13. Smt. Susheela Mazumdar	290

14. An anonymous male devotee 300
15. Dr. Surendranath Roy 306
16. Swami Visweswarananda 309
17. Mahendra Nath Gupta 311
18. Swami Tanmayananda 314
19. Swami Parameswarananda 317
20. Dr. Umesh Chandra Datta 319
21. Nalinibehari Sarkar 322
22. Indu Bhushan Sengupta 325
23. An anonymous lady devotee 328
24. Prafulla Kumar Ganguli 330
25. An anonymous devotee 332
26. An anonymous lady devotee 334
27. An anonymous lady devotee 336
28. An anonymous devotee 337
29. An anonymous lady devotee 338
30. Jitendra Mohan Chowdhury 340
31. Lalitmohan Saha 342
32. Swami Maheswarananda 343
33. Sarayubala Sen 344
34. Priyabala Devi 345

SECTION III

1. Pravrajika Bharatiprana 349
2. Swami Ishanananda 374

INTRODUCTION

As these Conversations of the Holy Mother, now published under the title, *The Gospel of the Holy Mother Sri Sarada Devi*, are likely to fall into the hands of many who are not at all acquainted with her life, we think it is proper to add a short biographical account of hers as an Introduction to it. For, to understand the relevancy of these conversations, to grasp how they are revelatory of a great character through small incidents and talks that took place outside the public gaze, a knowledge of the facts of her life is an absolute necessity. Hence the following short life-sketch of hers is added to this book as an Introduction.

Early Life

Sri Sarada Devi the Holy Mother was the Divine Consort and first disciple of Bhagavan Sri Ramakrishna and thus an integral part of his spiritual self and of the saving message he delivered unto mankind. Unlike the spiritual counterparts of the past incarnations like Rama, Krishna and Buddha and some others, Sri Sarada Devi was born in a poor but cultured Brahmana family of Bengal in the village of Jayrambati in the Bankura District, situated about sixty miles to the west of Calcutta. Born on 22nd December, 1853, as the eldest daughter of Ramachandra Mukherjee and Shyamasundari Devi, her early girlhood was spent, as in the case of most girls of rural upbringing, in various domestic chores like caring for the younger children, looking after cattle and carrying food to her father and others engaged in work in the field. She had absolutely no schooling, though she learnt the Bengali alphabet and practised a little of reading and writing in later days by herself. But the domestic environment of a pious Brahmana family supplemented by the holy associations she had in later days imparted to her—to one with such high natural endowments as she—an education that was far more enlightening than instruction in the three R's.

Marriage

She entered into Sri Ramakrishna's life as his partner in it when she was aged only five. The strange marriage of Gadadhar of twenty three years of age with Sarada of five was part of a divine dispensation, and took place in a way that can only be described as Providential. When Gadadhar, as Sri Ramakrishna the Great Master used to be known in those days, was passing through the early phase of his spiritual adventure, his near and dear ones thought that marriage would have a resettling and stabilising effect on his mind, which had lost all interest in worldly affairs. But their search for a suitable bride met with failure every time they started on it, until Gadadhar himself came to their rescue. The relatives had kept their plans unknown to Gadadhar, as they feared a vehement protest from him; but upsetting all their worldly-wise calculations, Gadadhar himself came to the rescue of his disconcerted relatives. In an ecstatic mood, he declared: "Why are you searching for a bride here and there? She who is 'marked' for me is awaiting at the house of Ramachandra Mukherjee at Jayrambati." And that 'marked one' they found, was none other than Sarada Devi, the five year old daughter of Ramachandra Mukherjee and Shyamasundari Devi of Jayrambati.

There is a tradition of an incident of an earlier day indicative of the divinely ordained nature of this alliance. It was the occasion of a temple festival in the neighbourhood where quite a number of families from Kamarpukur and Jayrambati had gathered. Among them were young Gadadhar and infant Sarada. Some women folk on such occasions indulge in the pastime of pre-planning possible marriage alliances for the future. It seems when infant Sarada was asked whom she would marry, she pointed to the boy Gadadhar.

After the marriage, Sarada had occasion, when she was seven and again at thirteen and fourteen, to meet Gadadhar and be with him for a few days each time. Though on these occasions she had the happy experience of serving him, a really meaningful meeting between them took place only later, when she went to Dakshineswar to meet him under strange circumstances. Hearing the rampant rumour that the village gossips bandied about regarding Sri Ramakrishna's mental condition, young Sarada, now eighteen, felt much upset, and a sense of her duty to be by her husband's side to serve him in his ailment began to dominate her mind. So under the guise of a pilgrimage to the holy Ganga, she went with her father to Dakshineswar Temple at Calcutta, where the Master was then staying. Trudging most of the sixty miles to Calcutta, she arrived unannounced at Dakshineswar one night in March 1872, stricken with fever on the way, to boot.

The Mother at Dakshineswar

It was in every way a very strange meeting. Sri Ramakrishna had been passing through a mood of intense longing for God, and his spirit of renunciation of what he called 'Woman and Gold' was raging in his mind with the tempo of a whirl-wind. An ascetic in that mood is the last man one can expect to meet a situation of this type with composure. We expect him to flee the place or put on a very rude and cruel attitude of disregard. But the Master's response now was as unexpected as when the proposal for marriage was made. He extended a very warm welcome to his wife, made arrangements for her stay and medical treatment, and in every way behaved towards her as a devoted husband should do.

This great event took place in March, 1872. From now onward, with breaks of short intervals for visits to her mother at Jayrambati, Sarada Devi was by the side of Sri Ramakrishna at Dakshineswar and later at Cossipore till 1886 when death separated them in a physical sense. It was a period of training and discipleship, during which the Mother in her became more and more manifest making her ready to take up the leadership of the spiritual Movement that the Master inaugurated. She became the first and foremost of his disciples. This transformation was effected through her service of the Master and the practice of devotional disciplines he prescribed for her. It was a silent and profound process, about the details of which the world knows so little. The type of personality into which she was shaped through that training was one characterised by inexhaustible patience and peace, extreme simplicity combined with dignity, a non-turbulent but compelling spiritual fervour, a loving temperament that knew no distinction between friend and foe, and a maternal attitude of a spontaneous type towards all, that charmed and brought under her influence everyone who came near her.

She spent nearly the whole of the Dakshineswar period of her life of thirteen years, extending from 1872 to 1885, except when she went to Jayrambati periodically, in a small room in the northern side of the temple compound, called the Nahabat, from where she could get a view of the room in which the Master lived.

The ground floor of the Nahabat or Concert House was a small low-roofed octagonal room of less than 50 sq. feet in area, with a verandah four and a quarter feet wide surrounding it. Besides being her living room it served as her provision store, kitchen and reception room too—a surprising combination of functions for such a small enclosure. But so patient and long-suffering she was that what would have been impossible for others, was no problem to her. Several aristocratic women of Calcutta, fat and plumpy, would stand at the door of the Nahabat, and leaning forward, holding the door frame, would say: "Ah! what a tiny room for our good girl! She is, as it were in exile, like Sita." In later days the Holy Mother would, while recounting the experiences of her early days, tell her nieces, "You won't be able to live in such a room even for a day."

Appreciating the extreme inadequacy of her accommodation, a devotee by name Sambhu Mallick built in April 1874 a small house on a plot very near the temple for her to stay. She stayed there for about one year, but left it for the Nahabat when the Great Master fell ill with dysentery, as she wanted to be by his side for nursing him. After that, however, she never went back to that house.

Her life began every day at three a.m., and being a strict observer of the Purdah, she finished her ablutions in the Ganges long before daybreak when people began moving about. Till it was broad daylight, she spent her time in meditation and Japa. She never came out till about one p.m., when there would be no one round about. She would then sit out drying her long and luxuriant locks in the sun. In fact she lived so quietly and unobserved there that the temple Manager said once, "We have heard that she lives here, but we have never seen her." The Master appreciated her extreme reserve, but none the less felt anxious for her health, as continuous stay in that small room carried with it grave health hazards. The verandah round the room was also screened for making the place fit for a strict Purdah lady to live in. She used to stand behind the screen on the damp floor of her house and watch through holes in the screen the Master singing and dancing in ecstasy beyond the open northern door of the room. All this brought rheumatic pain in her legs. Afterwards, on the Master's advice, she began to go out of the room and meet the ladies of some known houses in the neighbourhood.

During the day much of her time was taken up with cooking

for the Master and devotees. Sri Ramakrishna's stomach was very delicate and could not stand the temple food. So Sri Sarada Devi prepared the diet for him and personally served it to him, coaxing him to take sufficient quantities of it. She also did the other personal services for the Master like cleaning his room, washing clothes, etc. The Master's mother was also staying at Dakshineswar in her last days, and Sarada Devi attended on her as well with meticulous care. Although in the earlier years her cooking work was limited, it gradually swelled to enormous proportions, as the number of the Master's devotees began to increase. Many of them stayed overnight or sometimes for a whole day with him. They had to be fed, and the Mother took upon herself that duty too. It is said that daily she made chapatis out of seven pounds of wheat flour, and prepared the condiments required for them. Besides, betel rolls for the Master and devotees were required, and countless were the rolls she prepared every day.

All through the day quite a large number of women devotees, who came to see the Master, made the Nahabat their first place of halt and spent much time in conversation. Some of them also stayed overnight with her in that small room. Besides attending to her household duties, she also spent hours in watching from the Nahabat the scenes of devotional fervour that went on in theMaster's room. During nights she spent long hours in meditation. Her whole time was thus occupied with acts of service of the Master and his devotees and with the practice of devotional disciplines. It was an ideal way of living in which work and worship went hand in hand, and led to a harmonious development of personality.

Spiritual and Secular Training

The Master took great care to help her in the development of her talents both in the secular and the spiritual fields of life. He taught her how to conduct herself with dignity and success in everyday life. While the Master gave her an all-round education, the emphasis of course was on the spiritual side. We do not know of the details of the spiritual practices she underwent, but we know that under the guidance of the Master she practised Japa and meditation with great intensity every day in the morning and at night. In an admonition given to her niece Nalini, she once gave a hint about the intensity of her practices amidst the discharge of the heavy duties of life. She said to Nalini, "What a lot of work I did when I was of your age! And yet I could find time to repeat my Mantra a hundred thousand times every day." That is indeed a tremendous performance by any exacting ascetic standard.

Beyond a few glimpses of this kind, we have little record of the Master's spiritual instructions to her and the way in which he imparted them. The Holy Mother seldom spoke on this subject to others. But we know for certain that the Master's teachings had a tremendous effect on her pure mind. To a disciple she gave a glimpse of her inner life in the following words: "During my days at Dakshineswar, I used to get up at 3 o'clock in the morning and sit in meditation. Often I used to be totally absorbed in it. Once, on a moonlit night, I was performing Japa, sitting near the steps of the Nahabat. Everything was quiet. I did not even know when the Master passed that way. On other days I would hear the sound of his slippers, but on this night, I did not. I was totally absorbed in meditation. In those days I looked different. I used to put on ornaments and had a cloth with red border. On this day the cloth had slipped off from my back owing to a breeze, but I was unconscious of it. It seems 'son Yogen' went that way to give the water-jug to the Master and saw me in that condition. Ah! the ecstasy of those days! On moonlit nights I would look at the moon and pray with folded hands, 'May my heart be as pure as the rays of the yonder moon!' Or 'O Lord, there is stain even in the moon, but let there not be the least trace of stain in my mind!' If one is steady in meditation, one will clearly see the Lord in one's heart and hear His voice. The moment an idea flashes in the mind of such a one, it will be fulfilled then and there. You will be bathed in peace. Ah! what a mind I had at that time! Brinde, the maid servant, one day dropped a metal plate in front of me with a bang. The sound penetrated into my heart. In the fullness of one's spiritual realization, one will find that He who resides in one's heart, resides in the heart of others as well—the oppressed, the persecuted, the untouchable and the out-caste. This realization makes one truly humble."

There is ample evidence to make one believe that she attained to exalted states of spiritual consciousness during this period of her life. But she was by nature so modest and unassuming that she would seldom speak to others of such facts of her life as might glorify her in their eyes. Sometimes certain happenings leaked out when any of her companions happened to be by her side. One such instance we come across in the account left by Yogin-Ma, of an exalted spiritual mood she witnessed personally in the Holy Mother. We give below her own words, a little abridged:

"When the Mother first came to Dakshineswar, she had not experienced Samadhi. Though she practised meditation and Japa every day with utmost devotion, we did not hear of her going into Samadhi at that time. On the other hand she even felt frightened at the sight of the Master's Samadhi in the days when she slept near him. After I had been acquainted with her for some time, she said to me one day, 'Please speak to the Master that through his grace I may experience Samadhi. On account of the constant presence of devotees, I hardly get any opportunity to speak to him about it myself.' I thought it was quite right that I should convey to him her request.

"Next morning Sri Ramakrishna was seated on his bed alone when I went to his room and, after saluting him in the usual way, I communicated the Mother's prayer to him. He listened to it, but did not give any reply. Suddenly he became very serious. When he was in that mood, no one dared to utter a word before him. So I left the room after sitting there silently for a while. Coming to the Nahabat, I found the Mother seated for her daily worship. I opened the door a little and peeped in. Strange to say, she was now giggling and the next moment weeping. This went on alternately for some time. Tears were rolling down her cheeks in an unceasing stream. Gradually she became very much withdrawn into herself. I knew she was in Samadhi. So I closed the door and came away.

"A long while after, I went again to her room. She asked me. 'Are you just returning from the Master's room?' I replied, 'How is it Mother, that you say you never experience Samadhi and other high spiritual moods?' She was abashed and smiled.

"After that event sometimes I used to spend the night with her at Dakshineswar. Though I wanted to sleep on a separate bed, she would never listen to it. She would drag me to her side. One night somebody was playing the flute outside. That brought on her a high spiritual mood. She was laughing at intervals. With great hesitation I sat in one corner of the bed. I thought that, being a worldly person, I should not touch her at that time. After a long while, her mind came to the ordinary state."

In later days, after the passing away of the Master, she had more frequent experiences of this exalted state. This will be dealt with in detail in the proper place. Suffice it to say here that soon after her contact with the Master, her mind, pure and disciplined as it was, attained to great heights of concentration and illumination. Ecstasies and visions are only the by-products of spiritual realization. They may or may not appear according to an aspirant's temperament. The essence of realization, however, consists in a transformation of the inner life, and not in any external manifestation. The Holy Mother was speaking from experience when she put this idea so beautifully in the following words: "What else does one obtain by realization of God? Does one grow a pair of horns? No, our mind becoms pure, and through that pure mind, comes enlightenment."

In conclusion it may be stated here that the training that the Master imparted to her did not exclude secular matters. especially the way of conducting oneself in everyday life. He instructed her that in arranging articles of domestic use, one must think out beforehand where particular things were to be kept. Those that were frequently required must be kept near at hand ana the others at a distance. When a thing was temporarily removed from a place, particular care should be taken to see that it was put back exactly in the same place, so that one might not fail to locate it even in darkness. He taught her also the way of rolling wicks, dressing vegetables, making betel rolls, cooking, and doing other items of domestic work. He instructed her that while travelling in a boat or a carriage she should always be the first to get in and the last to get out; for then only one could properly check whether all the luggage had been taken in or taken out. The secret of one's success in social relationships, he told her, depended entirely on one's capacity to adjust one's conduct according to time, place, circumstances and the nature of the people one had to deal with. Physically every one was made of flesh and bones, but the mind within was constituted in entirely different ways. So one should be very careful in selecting one's friends and associates. With some, one might mix freely, with others only a nodding acquaintance was advisable, and with still others it was better not to talk at all.

Thus the Master took pains to make the Holy Mother efficient in both spiritual and secular matters, and prepared her for the great mission that he was to entrust to her at the close of his life.

The Mother as a true Sahadharmini

By careful education he helped to make her a true Sahadharmini, a fellow-seeker in the quest for the higher values of life. It was the resuscitation of the Vedic ideal of the Pativrata,according to which man and woman got fused into a common ideal and purpose in life. The man and the woman, brought together as husband and wife, are like the two wheels of a vehicle moving together on a common track towards a common ideal. Dharma is that path of higher evolution, and the discharge of one's social and spiritual duties in the scripture-ordained way is the way of progress along it. The Sahadharmini of a spiritually oriented personage like Sri Ramakrishna must necessarily be one with that same outlook, if the objective of that ideal is to be fulfilled. It was because of this mutually complementary nature of their characters, that they have become perfect ideals of both the married state and the monastic values.

An examination of several incidents of the Master's life would amply prove that this idea was always in his mind. The extra-ordinary way in which their marriage was arranged has already been narrated. It is known from the Master's own statement that he had prayed to the Divine Mother to free Sarada from all bodily passions and make her a suitable mate for himself. It was found that this prayer was amply answered when, after Sarada's arrival at Dakshineswar, the Master pointedly put her a question: "Do you want to drag me down into Maya?" Sarada Devi's answer was equally prompt and to the point. She replied: "Why should I do so? I have come only to help you in the path of religious life." A noble answer indeed by a Pativrata and a true Sahadhar-mini! Only a woman of immaculate purity of mind could have given such a reply. There was no artifice in it, no hypocrisy or attempt to please anybody. It was the spontaneous expression of her lofty nature, of the lofty ideal of life that had unconsciously become hers as much as her husband's.

The seriousness and sincerity behind this challenging reply she proved before long when Sri Ramakrishna decided to subject himself to what may be called a fiery ordeal. His teacher Totapuri had told him, on knowing him to be married, that this was not much of a risk for him. For a sincere Sadhaka, an earnest aspirant struggling in the spiritual path, it is highly necessary to keep aloof from the company of women. But if and when he attains to realization, his moral purity will not be of the cloistered type based on difference, but on the apprehension of the one Self in man and woman alike—an apprehension which helps one to surmount the identification of the self with the body.

The Master therefore utilized the presence of Sarada Devi at Dakshineswar to allow her the right of a wife in the fullest sense as well as to test how far his Brahman-knowledge had raised him above the bodily sense. For a period of about six months this ascetic of ascetics had his wife sleep in his own room and the spiritual awareness of them both put to the acid test. They stood it wonderfully well. The Master's mind went only into deep Samadhi and was never assaulted by bodily passion. He also gave equal credit to Sarada Devi when he said: "Had she not been so pure, who knows whether I would not have lost my self-control? After marriage I had prayed to the Divine Mother, 'O Mother! Remove even the least trace of carnality from the mind of my wife.' When I lived with her, I understood that the Mother had really granted my prayer."

And as for the Holy Mother herself, we have her statement regarding her experiences of those memorable nights: "The divine state in which the Master used to be absorbed, passes all description. In an ecstatic mood, he would smile or weep, or at times remain perfectly still in Samadhi. This would sometimes continue throughout the night. In that divine presence, my whole body would tremble with awe and I would anxiously await the dawn. For I knew nothing of ecstasy in those days. One night his Samadhi continued for a very long time. Greatly frightened, I sent for Hriday. He came and began to repeat the name of the Lord in the Master's ears. When he had done this for a little while, external consciousness reappeared. After this incident, the Master came to know of my difficulty, and taught me the appropriate names that should be uttered in the ear in particular states of Samadhi. Thenceforth my fear was very much lessened, as he would invariably come to earthly consciousness on the utterance of the particular divine names. But even after this I sometimes kept awake the whole night, as there was no knowing when he would fall into Samadhi. In course of time he came to know of my difficulty. He learnt that even after the lapse of a considerable length of time I could not adjust myself to his Samadhi temperament. So he asked me to sleep separately at the Nahabat."

The Shodasi Pooja

Another memorable event in the life of this holy couple that took place about this time was the Shodasi Puja, in which the Master offered actual ceremonial worship to the Holy Mother, seating her on the pedestal of the Deity. It took place during her first visit to Dakshineswar when she stayed there continuously from March 1872 to October 1873, for more than a year and a half. Authorities differ about the exact date of this incident. According to some it was about a month and a half after the Mother's arrival at Dakshineswar; according to others it was one and a half years later. The latter is more likely. It took place on the night of Phalaharini-Kali Puja day, when the Divine Mother is worshipped as the consumer of the Karmas of the devotee. Arrangements for worship were made in the Master's room, and Sarada was requested to be present at the worship. After the Master had gone through the preliminary rites of worship, he beckoned to Sarada Devi to sit on the seat set apart for the Deity. He then invoked the presence of the Divine Mother in her with the Mantra: "O Divine Mother! Thou eternal virgin, the mistress of all powers, and the abode of all beauty! Deign to unlock for me the gate to perfection. Sanctifying the body and mind of this woman, do Thou manifest Thyself through her and do what is auspicious."

Then he went through all the procedures of a full ritualistic worship with sixteen ingredients. He first performed the Nyasa, which consists in touching the different parts of one's body with appropriate Mantras and identifying them in meditation with the corresponding parts of the Deity. After that he offered worship with sixteen items with appropriate Mantras. In the course of it he applied a red paint to the soles of Sarada Devi, put a vermilion mark on her forehead, put on her a new cloth, put a little of sweets and betel-leaf in her mouth, and performed the Arati (light-waving ceremony) before her. The bashful Sarada received all these acts of adoration without the least feeling of hesitation. The sense of identification with the Deity must have come on her. Both the Master and the Mother were in a state of ecstatic and semi-conscious absorption in the course of the worship, and by the time it came to an end they were in complete Samadhi in which the worshipper and the worshipped realised the identity of their being as Existence-Knowledge-Bliss Absolute. After a considerable length of time, when the second watch of the night had fairly advanced, the Master regained external consciousness. Then he resigned himself completely to the Divine Mother, and in a supreme act of consecration, offered to the Deity manifest before him, the fruits of his austerities, his rosary, himself and everything that was his. He then uttered the following Mantra: "O Goddess, I prostrate myself before Thee again and again—before Thee, the eternal consort of Siva, the three-eyed, the golden-hued, the indwelling spirit in all, the giver of refuge, the accomplisher of every end, and the most auspicious among all auspicious objects."

The significance of this rite in the lives of these two great personages can hardly be over-estimated. For Sri Ramakrishna it signified the final triumph of the spirit over the body, and the recognition of Divinity in all. It marked the successful conclusion of his spiritual strivings, and his establishment in the state of the 'divine man.' In the life of Sri Sarada Devi the Holy Mother, too, it had a deep significance. When Sri Ramakrishna, the Divine Incarnation of the age, invoked the presence of the Divine Mother in her, and worshipped her as such, she was elevated in truth and in reality from Sarada, the daughter of Ramachandra, to Sarada, the Holy Mother, the manifestation of the Eternal Mother of the Universe, for all humanity to worship. It has been already stated how the Master had from the time of his marriage been praying to the Mother of the Universe to divinise the person of his wife, and how her answer to a leading question he put to her as a test proved that the transformation was largely effected, and how she was a partner in life well-matched with him in all respects. And now by the performance of this rite of Shodasi Puja in which he identified the Deity with Sarada, and surrendered all his spiritual practices and their fruits to her, he virtually made her a participant of all his austerities and spiritual attainments. It is sometimes asked why the Holy Mother did not perform Sadhanas like the Master. She did perform much in this field, but the real answer is in the Shodasi Puja, by virtue of which the Holy Mother became a full sharer in the spiritual glory of the Master. As the spiritual counterpart of the great world-teacher Sri Ramakrishna, she had no need to re-enact the same scenes of the one common drama which they were together staging before mankind. She had other parts to play by way of fulfilling and supplementing the Master's work.

In another sense also the Shodasi Puja was a landmark in her life. It made her a vital part of Sri Ramakrishna's Mission.

In that rite the Master invoked in her the presence of the Divine Mother—the same Supreme Energy that was manifesting in him. Henceforth, just as in the Master's case, her body and mind became the venue of expression for that Energy. For the rest of her life she served the Master and helped in his Mission, and after his passing away, his mantle fell on her, and through a long period of spiritual ministry, she completed what he had left unfinished.

Relationship of Mutual Love and Respect

The Master's life combined in itself the highest ideals of the monastic life and those of the householders. The Master always taught men the gospel of renunciation of Kamini-Kanchana (translated literally as 'Woman and Gold', but meaning 'lust and greed') and had it not been for the advent of the Holy Mother into his life, he would have been taken to be only a hard-baked ascetic and nothing more. But his very cordial and affectionate relationship with the Mother, treating her as the first and foremost of his disciples and attendants, has lifted married life above the level of sex and made it a potent spiritual relationship. The crusader against 'Kamini-Kanchana', showed the highest consideration and respect to the Holy Mother. The welcome he extended to her on her first appearance was in itself an unexpected mark of cordiality. Not only was he particular about keeping her in comfort, he even thought of providing something for her future. Calculating the minimum amount required monthly for her maintenance as Rupees six, he had six hundred rupees deposited with the Zamindari Office of Balaram Bose, the interest of which was to go for her maintenance. He divined her liking to wear ornaments and spent three hundred rupees to have a pair of bracelets made for her. There is a tradition according to which Sri Ramakrishna had a vision of Sita at the Panchavati. He found her wearing a pair of bracelets with many tiny facets like diamonds. It was in imitation of these that he made for her gold bracelets which she wore till the last. Yogin-Ma, describing her appearance in those early days, says: "She wore a piece of cloth with broad red borders and put vermilion at the parting of her hair. Her thick black tresses almost touched her knees. She wore a gold necklace, a big nose ring, earrings and bracelets. Most of these were what Mathur Babu made for the Master when he practised spiritual disciplines assuming the role of a handmaid of the Divine Mother." It seems Manomohan's wife criticised her for wearing these ornaments while being the wife of a man of such great renunciation. Thenceforth she put aside most of them.

While receiving all her loving services, and moving with her in all frankness and child-like innocence, the Master always maintained an attitude of profound respect towards her as his spiritual counterpart and fulfiller of his life's Mission. This attitude was generally implicit, but sometimes expressed itself in striking little actions. One day the Holy Mother entered the Master's room with his meal. He thought it was his niece Lakshmi, and asked her casually to shut the door, addressing her as '*tui*', an expression meaning 'thou', but used with reference to juniors or inferior persons. When the Holy Mother responded, the Master felt very much embarrassed and said, "Ah! is it you? I thought it was Lakshmi. Please pardon me." But the Holy Mother tried to pacify him, saying there was nothing wrong in his addressing her like that. But the Master was not satisfied. Next morning he went to the Nahabat and said to the Holy Mother: "Well, I could not sleep all the night. I was so worried because I spoke to you rudely." Referring to this incident, she often said in later times, especially when some of her senseless relations behaved disrespectfully, "I was married to a husband who never addressed me as '*tui*'. Ah! how he treated me! Not even once did he tell me a harsh word or wound my feelings. He did not strike me even with a bunch of flowers!"

It will thus be seen that Sri Sarada Devi received from her husband all that a Hindu wife expects. But some may perhaps object, that she had no issue. Her own mother Shyamasundari Devi once lamented: "My Sarada has been married to an ascetic. She will never know the happiness of being addresed as 'mother'." The Master, who happened to hear it, remarked: "Your daughter will have so many children that she will be tired of being addressed day and night as 'Mother'."And countless indeed were her spiritual 'sons'and 'daughters'. She was the Sahadharmini,a companion in life, not of an ordinary man, but of the Incarnation of the age, who came to generate Bhakti and Jnana among men, and whose main teaching inculcated renunciation of lust and possessions. In conformity with his ideal, which was hers too, the children born of her were not physical but spiritual, and of these she had a countless number.

In the Passing of Events

The period of thirteen years that the Mother served the Great Master was inwardly characterised by her absorption in the Master's ideal and fusion of her life with his, and outwardly by her periodic migration from Dakshineswar to Jayrambati and back. During this period she went seven times to Jayrambati and back to Calcutta, a journey of about sixty miles, which she had often to make on foot. These visits were generally occasioned by ill health or for rendering assistance to her mother during the Jagaddhatri Puja. But as her services were very much needed by the Master, her stay at Jayrambati was perforce not very long. In 1874 her father died and her mother and brothers were reduced to poverty. The family had to be supported by her mother with wages earned by husking paddy, in which she was helped by her daugher Sarada also whenever she was at Jayrambati. After the performance of Jagaddhatri Puja was instituted in the family, their condition improved.

It was during one of these journeys to Calcutta that the Mother had to run the risk of facing some brigands after dusk. As she could not walk fast enough, the party she was accompanying had gone in advance, and she was left alone at about dusk half way across a solitary wilderness. A man who looked like a brigand and his wife converged on her path and halted her. In that precarious situation, the Mother, then a young woman of about twenty-four, did not lose her presence of mind. She addressed the couple as 'father'and 'mother' in a tone that roused the parental instinct in them and she narrated to them how she had been left in that helpless condition. The 'brigand' couple, reciprocated the filial confidence she put in them, and behaved in a very tender manner towards her. They took good care of her for the night, and enabled her to join her party in the morning.

During this period she once fell seriously ill. In 1875 she had a severe attack of dysentery, so severe that she was given up for lost. When all human remedies failed, as a last and desperate act of prayer and supplication for divine intervention, she resolved to perform the rite of Hatya before the Deity Simhavahini, according to which one observes the vow of starving unto death if no divine assistance comes. Within a few days of her fast, the Goddess is said to have revealed the name of some simple medicines, taking which she was cured. Some time after, she had a severe attack of malaria, with enlargement of the spleen, for which she was subjected to the curious countryside treatment of branding with a red hot iron in the region of the spleen—with what effect, no one knows.

It was on her fourth visit to Dakshineswar along with her mother in 1881 that she had to return the very next day owing to the rude behaviour of Hriday, nephew and care-taker of the Master. But the injured feeling of the Mother had instantaneous repercussion on Hriday. A few days after this, he indiscreetly worshipped with flowers the feet of a young daughter of Trailokyanath, the proprietor of the temple. As such an act of worship was supposed to be very harmful to the girl concerned, her father dismissed Hriday from the temple service, with the order that he should no more enter the temple precincts. This was a corroboration of the warning that the Master had given to Hriday, who had been for sometime past behaving discourteously towards him. He had told him that one might insult him (the Master) with impunity, but "dire consequences" would follow, if the Holy Mother were so treated.

The Mother stayed at Dakshineswar till about September 1885, when her happy days there ended with the transfer of the Master for treatment, first to Shyampukur in Calcutta, and afterwards to Cossipore, where he passed away in August 1886. While the men disciples arranged for the nursing and general treatment of the Master, the Holy Mother took upon herself the duty of preparing the diet of the Master and feeding him. Though for a Purdah lady like herself it was very inconvenient to stay in those places, she put up with everything with a sense of satisfaction derived from the feeling that she was of service to the Master, and she threw herself heart and soul into the work.

There are two incidents of importance recorded about the Holy Mother's experiences during her attendance on the Master at Cossipore. The Master was then lying in a weak and exhausted condition, unable to move without the assistance of others. But one day the Holy Mother saw him running out of the room. Startled, the Mother went inside the room to verify her observation, and she found the Master's cot empty. Shortly after, she found him returning. She made enquiries of him about this the next day. The Master at first made light of it, saying it was all the result of her heated brain. But when she pressed for an explanation, he informed her that Niranjan and some other disciples had gone to make palm juice from a date palm, that there was then a cobra on the palm, and that he went there in advance, using his higher powers, to drive away the cobra and protect them. This event, looking strange and miraculous, has to be accepted as it comes from the Mother's lips. It also raises interesting issues regarding the Master's ailment.

Another occurrence was her experience at Tarakeswar Siva Temple where she had gone to pray and seek Divine remedy for the Master's illness, which had been declared incurable by medical men. For two days she lay before the Deity without food or drink, supplicating for some remedy. During the night of the second day she was startled to hear a sound resembling the breaking of a pile of earthen pots at one blow. She woke up from her torpor, and the idea flashed in her mind: "Who is husband and who is wife? Who is my relative in this world? Why am I about to kill myself?" Freed from all personal attachments, her mind was full of an intense spirit of renunciation. She had another vision in which she saw that the image of Mother Kali was bent to one side. When she asked the Deity, "Mother, why do you stand like that?" she got the reply, "It is because of this (pointing to the Master's diseased throat). I also have it in my throat." All such experiences prepared her mind for the exit of the Master from his earthly sojourn, which took place on the 16th August, 1886. With the passing of the Master, this phase of the Mother's life came to a close.

After the Master's Passing: Pilgrimage to Vrindaban

The Master's demise brought about a drastic change in the Holy Mother's life. She reacted to his passing with extreme fortitude, exclaiming, "O Mother Kali! Have you left me!" She shed no tears, though her heart was heavy with the sorrow of separation. Soon after the cremation, she was removing her gold bracelets and tearing off the red border of her wearing cloth in order to be dressed in the pattern of a Hindu widow. Immediately she had a vision of the Master, telling her, "What are you doing? I have not gone away. I have only passed from one room to another." A reassuring experience indeed for her grief-stricken heart! All through life she wore her bracelets and a thin-bordered cloth in acceptance of the assurance of her experience that her Lord and Master is the Eternal Being, who never dies.

About a fortnight after the Master's Mahasamadhi, the Cossipore establishment was disbanded, and the Holy Mother had to shift to the house of Balaram Bose. As a measure for assuaging her grief and as a holy act in itself, she started, about two weeks later, on a pilgrimage with a party consisting of several disciples of the Master including Lakshmi-Didi and Golap-Ma. After visiting Banaras and Ayodhya, they halted at Vrindaban where they stayed for about a year. The stay was a very highly rewarding experience from the spiritual standpoint for the Holy Mother. The association of the place with the story of Radha's passionate grief in separation from her beloved Krishna brought home to her the similarity of her own situation after the Master's passing,and added a spiritual poignancy to the sorrow she was feeling in her heart from the bereavement. All her pent up feelings found expression as an upsurge of passionate longing for the Divine and in a torrential flow of tears that continued almost unremittingly during the early part of her life at Vrindaban. This mood in which love and grief blend in full harmony bringing about a gradual transformation of personality, continued for several days with her until she had a wonderful vision in which the Master appeared to her and said: "Why are you weeping so much? Here I am. Where have I after all gone? Only from one room to another." The experience assuaged her grief very much, as she began to feel the nearness of the Master more and more. The anguish of separation gradually turned into a sense of utter peace and radiant joy. Often she began to fall into exalted moods in which she would walk away over the sandy banks until her companions went after her and brought her back. Her temperament changed from that of an adult into that of a little girl of seven or eight.

Her life at Vrindaban was one of constant worship, meditation and spiritual experiences. She and Yogin-Ma would sit in meditation with such absorption that they ceased to be disturbed by flies that produced sores on their faces. She visited all the numerous temples in the place and also undertook the circumambulation of the whole area of Vrindaban involving a walk of several miles. At Radharamana's temple she prayed to the Deity: "O Lord, remove from me the habit of finding fault with others. May I never find fault with anybody." Her prayer was answered to the letter, and in later life one of the distinguishing features of her character was the complete absence of the fault-finding tendency. She maintained that this tendency only corrupted one without improving others.

She had several spiritual experiences during this time, though she never revealed them to anyone. But some of them could not escape the notice of her companions. Thus Yogin-Ma one day found her absorbed in Samadhi. Even repeating the Divine name in her ears several times had not the effect of bringing her to the body-consciousness. Then Swami Yogananda tried the same technique for some time, which brought her to a semi-conscious state in which she said, "I must eat something'—even as Sri Ramakrishna used to mutter in order to bring his mind to the worldly plane. She then partook of a little sweet as the Master would do. Even in taking betel rolls, she threw away the tip in the manner of the Master. Swami Yogananda put to her several questions in that mood, and received replies from her as if the Master himself were answering him. Afterwards she told her companions that the consciousness of the Master was upon her during that state. During this period she gave initiation to Swami Yogananda under the express command of the Master both to her and to the Swami. She gave the initiation in a highly exalted mood bordering on Samadhi. After visiting Haridwar and some other places, she along with the party returned to Calcutta by August 1887.

Life at Kamarpukur and after

The nine months following 1887 may be described as the dark period in the Holy Mother's life from the material point of view, although spiritually she was in an exalted mood. Now that the Master was no more, the Holy Mother could not stay on in Calcutta. She was a young widow of about thirty-three. Though the Sannyasin disciples of the Master and a few of the lay ones respected her, men at large had not yet come to recognise her spiritual status. She had therefore to go through all the difficulties which a young widow in her situation was bound to face. A few days after her return to Calcutta from her pilgrimage, she had to go to Kamarpukur to take her permanent residence there. The Master too had told her towards the close of his life: "After my time, you go to Kamarpukur and live upon whatever you get, be it mere boiled rice and greens, and spend your time in repeating the name of Hari." These words of his came to be literally fulfilled. She took her residence in the small cottage that had been assigned to the Master in the family campus. For her maintenance she had only some paddy which she could process into rice and eat without any condiments. For something to eat with rice, she had herself to dig the ground and grow some greens. She had absolutely no cash even to procure some salt. Ramlal, Sri Ramakrishna's nephew, who was legally her guardian, left her in utter neglect. It is said that he even positively contributed to her sufferings. The temple authorities had set apart a monthly pension of ten rupees to the Master which used to be paid to the Mother. But Ramlal, for reasons of his own, is supposed to have interfered and got it stopped. He even effected a partition, and assigning the Master's cottage to her, rid himself of all responsibilities.The other members of the family like Sivaram and Lakshmi-Didi were of no help to her, as they stayed at Calcutta with their uncle Ramlal who was the officiating priest at Dakshineswar. She had therefore to live alone in that hut. To add to the misery that neglect and loneliness caused, she became the butt of criticism of the village die-hards who vilified her as a 'merry widow' because she put on a red bordered cloth which custom strictly prohibited for widows. In the midst of these depressing influences, there were two factors that sustained her. One was the sympathy and support she got from Prasannamayi, an aged lady of the Laha family and a friend of Sri Ramakrishna when he was the boy Gadadhar of Kamarpukur. The other was the vision of the Great Master which she got now and then in difficult situations and the mood of spiritual exaltation in which she lived.

This state of affairs did not, however, continue for long. Her mother Shyamasundari Devi came to know of it, and through her son Prasanna Kumar, she remonstrated with Ramlal for the neglect of her daughter and also informed Golap-Ma of it. Golap-Ma at once took up the matter seriously, carried on a vigorous propaganda among the disciples of the Master, raised some funds, and invited the Holy Mother in the name of all the devotees of the Master to come to Calcutta and stay there. After some hesitation, arising from fear of public opinion attributing impropriety to a young widow staying amidst strangers, she finally arrived in Calcutta in April 1888 to the great joy of all the disciples and devotees.

It has to be pointed out that in the early days, several of the lay disciples attached no more importance to the Holy Mother than as the 'Wife of the Guru'. One is said to have actually remarked: "I know Sri Ramakrishna, but I know nothing of his wife." But hearing much from Yogin-Ma, Golap-Ma and Swami Yogananda about the highly exalted states of the Mother at Vrindaban, most of them veered round in their estimate of the Mother, and fully co-operated in the efforts made to provide for her stay at Calcutta.

From now (1888) onwards till her exit in 1920, the Mother stayed at Calcutta and Jayrambati alternately. She went to Kamarpukur also a few times in the early part of this period. At Calcutta she used to be accommodated at the houses of the devotees Balaram Bose or Mahendranath Gupta whenever her stay was short, and at rented houses when the stay was long. This arrangement went on until Swami Saradananda built the Udbodhan House as her Calcutta residence in 1909. She was attended upon by Swami Yogananda and Swami Trigunatita at first, and after Swami Trigunatita left India, Swami Saradananda took full charge of her responsibility. The lady disciples of the Master like Yogin-Ma and Golap-Ma kept company with her often.

It was a few months after her coming to Calcutta, that she went on another pilgrimage in April 1888 to Gaya accompanied by Swami Advaitananda. On this occasion she also visited Bodh Gaya, the place of the Buddha's enlightenment, where an event of great future significance took place. She saw there the well established monastery of Hindu Sannyasins, which provided the monks with good accommodation and food. The contrast between this and the poverty-stricken condition of her own 'children', the monastic disciples of the Master, evoked strong sentiments in her mind. About this incident she said as follows: "Ah! for this have I shed tears and prayed to the Master! And only through that this Math (Belur Math) came into existence now. When the Master left the body, the boys gave up the world and gathered together in a rented shelter for some days. Then they scattered about independently and went on roaming about here and there. Then I felt intensely sad and prayed to the Master, 'O Lord! You came, disported with a few and then went away. Should everything end with that? If so, what was the need for coming down and undergoing so many travails? I have seen in Banaras and Vrindaban many holy men who get their food by alms and move about from one place to another. There is no dearth of holy men of that type. I shall not be able to bear the sight of my 'sons', who have come out in your name, moving about begging for food. My prayer is, that those who leave the world in your name may never be in need of bare sustenance. They will all live together holding to your ideas and ideals, and the people afflicted by the worries of the world will resort to them and be solaced by hearing from them about you.

That is why you came. My heart is pained at seeing them wandering about.' "

Indeed a remarkable prayer for the monks, while she herself was in utter poverty and neglect! Her insight into the implications of the Master's advent too is profound and prophetic.

The Exalted State of the Mother's Mind

From the time of her return to Calcutta from Kamarpukur in 1888, her visits to that place were few, although she took care to see that the house that stood in the Master's name was kept in good condition. Her time was taken up by frequent visits to, and stay at, her paternal home at Jayrambati, and with disciples at Calcutta. Her companions Yogin-Ma and Golap-Ma noticed a great spiritual transformation in her after the Master's lifetime. Yogin-Ma noticed that she had become remarkably indrawn and was radiating an unearthly loveliness. During her stay at Calcutta in 1888, she saw the Mother in a state of Samadhi while meditating on the roof of Balaram Babu's house. About her experience in that state, the Mother said: "I found in that state that I had travelled into a distant country. I cannot describe the nature of the ecstatic joy I felt. When my mind came down from that exalted mood, I found my body lying there. I thought, 'How can I possibly enter into this ugly body?' I could not at all persuade my mind to do so. After a long while it did, and the body became conscious again."

Another day she was meditating in the house of Nilambar Mukherjee along with Yogin-Ma and Golap-Ma. After finishing her meditation, Yogin-Ma looked at the Mother and found her seated motionless as before, absorbed in meditation. It took a long time for her mind to come down to physical consciousness, and when it actually regained traces of it, she began to say, "O Yogin! Where are my hands and feet?" Yogin-Ma pressed her limbs and directed her attention to them in a loud voice, but it took much time for her to be conscious of the whole body.

Another vision she had was of Sri Ramakrishna getting down into the Ganga and his body dissolving into its sacred waters She found Narendra taking that water and sprinkling it everywhere This was a prophetic vision of what was to take place soon—of Narendra as Swami Vivekananda spreading the Master's universal message broadcast. The vision created a very vivid impression on her, for it filled her mind with a sense of purpose. She began to see that the Master lived in his Mission and that he worked through those whom he made his instruments in its fulfilment. Her own part in it began to dawn on her mind little by little.

It would thus be seen that after the Master's demise, in spite of various worldly difficulties, her mind was getting more and more detached from worldly concerns and was drifting towards Samadhi. So long as the Master was alive, serving him in every way filled her life with a meaning. But once he was no more, there was no other definite worldly purpose to hold her consciousness to the body, and Samadhi became a more frequent experience with her.Thus, it was the firm view of her close associates like Yogin-Ma that she would have given up her body soon in the absence of a worldly purpose, and her services in the great work of propagation of the Master's message would not have been available, had it not been for certain domestic entanglements that forced her mind back to the world

Radhu and her significance in the Mother's Life

The force that diverted her mind to the world was the entry of Radhu or Radhi, a niece of hers, into her life. To understand the nature of this connection, it is necessary to have some acquaintance with the domestic set up in the Holy Mother's paternal home at Jayrambati, with which she became intimately connected after she left Kamarpukur. That family consisted of her mother Shyama-sundari Devi and her four sons—Prasanna Kumar, Barada Prasad, Kali Kumar and Abhay Charan, who were all called 'uncles' (Mamas) by the devotees. Being the eldest of the family, the Holy Mother had much to do in her early days in the upbringing of these brothers of hers, and therefore there was a strong tie of affection uniting her with them. None of these brothers had any of the great spiritual qualities that distinguished the Holy Mother, but grew into just the ordinary men of the world, and some of them even represented an extreme type of worldliness. None of them except the last had enough talents to prosper in life. All of them and their children looked to the Mother for help, and on account of this, there was bitter rivalry among them for the Mother's favour. So in her later days at Jayrambati she was in the midst of this not very pleasant domestic environment on the one hand, and on the other, in the midst of her all-renouncing monastic attendants and highly devoted lay disciples. The picture of the Holy Mother in the midst of this contrasting environment is that of one living a life of utter detachment and renunciation, discharging at the same time whatever duties she had to perform to her kith and kin.

Among her brothers, the youngest Abhay Charan was the most talented, but in the end he became the cause of the devolution of heavy responsibilities on the Mother. He passed out of the Medical School, but died all of a sudden, leaving behind him his expectant widow who was a little unbalaced in mind. The brother made a dying request to the sister that she should take complete charge of his weak wife and her expected child, and she agreed. The child born of this 'mad aunt' was Radhu or Radhi, on whom the Mother pinned her affection, and who thus became that prop spoken of earlier, for sustaining her life in this world.

This interpretation of the Radhu episode is not any fanciful exaggeration by devotees. Antecedent events amply justify it. It was also the Mother's conviction. To quote her own words: "How the Master has entangled me through Radhu! After the passing away of the Master, I did not at all relish anything in life. I became utterly indifferent to worldly things and kept on praying, 'What shall I achieve by remaining in this world?' At that time I saw a girl ten or twelve years old walking in front of me dressed in red cloth. The Master pointed her out to me and said: 'Cling to her as a support. Many children (disciples) seeking instruction will come to you.' The next moment he disappeared. I did not see the girl anymore. Later on I was seated in this very place. At that time Radhu's mother was stark mad. She was dragging some rags tucked under her arms. I said to myself, 'Well if I do not look after this child, who else will take care of her? She has no father, and her mother is an insane woman.' No sooner had I taken the child in my arms than I saw the Master. He said 'This is the girl, cling to her as your support. She is Yoga-maya, the illusive power.' "

Radhu was born in 1900. From that time till 1920, the year of the Holy Mother's demise, she was the fulcrum on which the worldly life of the Holy Mother rested. After the above-mentioned vision the Holy Mother took charge of Radhu. She never allowed Radhu to be parted from her till a few days before her demise in 1920. She could neither eat nor sleep without Radhu, so strong was the bond of affection with which she came to be tied to this girl all of a sudden. She practically assumed the role of her mother, ousting the girl's own insane mother, the Chota-Mami, who made it the ground of her tirades against the Mother in later days. She became jealous of the Holy Mother when she found her daughter loving the Mother more than herself, and her insane imagination began to find various evil motives in the Mother's love for Radhu, as a result of which she began to behave to the Mother with a rudeness verging on persecution.

Radhu, too, proved, as she grew up, to be somewhat abnormal like her mother. Physically she was weak and mentally a moron. Though there was a simplicity and innocence about her, she was utterly lacking in understanding and discrimination. The Mother arranged for her marriage in 1911, but even after that she and her husband continued to be with the Mother. Her first confinement was a period of great anxiety for the Mother, as the girl was practically insane before and after the event.

The Mother in domestic and devotional setting

Besides Radhu and her insane mother, there were also Nalini and Maku, the two daughters of her brother Prasanna Kumar, who were also dependent on the Holy Mother. They stayed with her at the Jayrambati house, and often moved with her to Calcutta also, after Swami Saradananda built Udbodhan House in 1909 as the Calcutta residence of the Mother.

So in the scenario of the latter part of her life, which is meticulously depicted in these memoirs, one will find the Holy Mother amidst the circle of these relatives—her brothers described here as Mamas (uncles), their wives as Mamis (aunts), her nieces Nalini and Maku as Didis (elder sisters), and above all Radhu who is the central figure in this whole domestic set up. The selfishness of the brothers, the mutual jealousy of the nieces, Nalini's mania for ceremonial purity, the perversity of Radhu, and the insanity of Radhu's mother, all these together combine to produce a tangled domestic situation, in the intolerable atmosphere of which the Mother had to carry on her self-chosen duty without demur, sustained by her matchless patience, insight and power of detachment.

It is not that even some of her intimate associates did not feel the contradiction between her attachment to Radhu and other relatives, and the state of renunciation inculcated by the Master. Her very close friend Yogin-Ma was one such. She thought: "The Master was a man of such high renunciation and we see the Holy Mother behaving like a typical worldly-minded woman.

Day and night she is restless about her brothers, nephews and nieces. I don't understand it." Shortly after this doubt had arisen in her mind, she was one day meditating on the bank of the Ganges, when she saw in a vision the Master standing before her and saying, "Look there! Don't you see something floating on the Ganges?" She saw a new-born baby, entangled in its entrails, being carried along by the current. The Master then said to her, "Can anything ever make the Ganges impure? Can anything defile its waters? Regard her (the Holy Mother)too in the same way. Never have any doubt about her. Know that she and this (referring to himself) are identical."

In striking contrast to this domestic circle around her, were the numerous spiritual aspirants who had been gathering about her. Originally consisting of Golap-Ma, Yogin-Ma and some of the other women devotees of the Master, their numbers swelled with the addition of her own disciples whose number increased as her spiritual ministry gained momentum. Very senior Sannyasins of the older generation like Swami Yogananda, Swami Trigunatita and Swami Saradananda attended on her, besides several monastic disciples of her own. Countless numbers of initiation-seeking devotees also went to her both at Calcutta and at Jayrambati. They were all spiritual seekers who sought no worldly advantage from the Mother, but only an opportunity to offer her their service and whatever resources they had. It is a remarkable thing that the Holy Mother was able to satisfy both these types—her exacting and quarrelsome relatives on the one hand, and the devoted spiritual seekers on the other. In this sense she was really a *Bhukti-mukti-pradāyini*—a descriptive epithet for the Divine Mother, meaning granter of both worldly goods and spiritual emancipation. The unique spirituality of the Mother can be recognised only when one comprehends the inherent contradictions of the demands that these two situations made on her. One who is doting on an eccentric niece—how could such a person bestow unrestricted and absolute maternal love even on utter strangers, not to speak of one's disciples. and overwhelm them with the power and sincerity of it? This looks an insoluble mystery. But it is also a pointer to the lofty spiritual status of the Mother. None but one who is established in what is called Bhavamukha in the great Master's teaching, is capable of it. For it is the nature of worldly love that the more one loves one's kith and kin, the less becomes one's concern for others. But here the Mother's universal love stands undiminished even when it is diverted through diverse and contrary channels. The comprehensiveness and intensity of it is not at all affected by its bestowal on certain restricted circles also. These precious reminiscences about her vividly portray in variegated colours the scenes of the Mother pouring her astounding love on strangers, on criminals, on the rich, on the poor, on the sick and the suffering, on spiritual aspirants and on saints all alike, even while living amidst relatives with their exacting demands for worldly advantages.

Important Events of later Life

Let us resume the thread of the events of her life. During this period of her life from 1888 to 1920, her time was mostly divided between Jayrambati and Calcutta besides what she spent on short pilgrimages. Thus in April 1888 itself she went to Gaya and in November 1888 to the temples of Puri, both being places which the Master had not visited and to which he had advised her to go. In 1893 she performed the Panchatapa, an austere practice in which one has to subject oneself to the heat of five fires, these being four fires on the four sides with the hot sun above. In 1894 she again went to Banaras and Vrindaban. In November 1898 the first of her monastic attendants Swami **Yogananda, a disciple** of Sri Ramakrishna, as also her own youngest brother Abhay Charan passed away, to the great sorrow of the Holy Mother. In 1900 was born Radhu or Radharani who became the prop of her life thenceforth. In 1906 her mother Shyamasundari Devi passed away.

The year 1909 was a great landmark in the Holy Mother's life, because that year saw the opening of the Udbodhan House. Ever since Swami Saradananda took up the responsibility of the Holy Mother after the demise of Swami Yogananda, he was feeling the great inconvenience the Mother felt in being lodged in Calcutta in rented houses or in devotees' residences, especially because with the passing of time, her entourage increased in number. So, raising a loan, the Swami built a city house for her in the Baghbazar area. It was called Udbodhan Office, because the Udbodhan, the Bengali magazine of the Ramakrishna Order was published from there. In the upper storeys of the house the Mother and the ladies of her party stayed, while on the ground floor her monastic attendants and other disciples stayed. Swami Saradananda stayed in a room at the entrance as the 'gate keeper' of the

Mother. While the Mother stayed at Calcutta, Swami Saradananda met all the expenses of her and her party. When she went to her village home with the ladies, Swami Saradananda put one monastic in charge of her to look after her safety and convenience. He also sent substantial contributions of money, though the Mother herself was supposed to meet the expenses of her household in the village with contributions from disciples and devotees.

At Jayrambati she stayed at the houses of one or the other of her brothers, until Swami Saradananda built a separate cottage for her. The city folk could meet her at Calcutta easily, but such meetings could be very formal only. On the other hand when she was at her village home, she was readily accessible and mixed freely with the devotees. So, many preferred to meet her in the village. As their numbers increased, a separate establishment for her became necessary. The Ashrama at Koalpara, situated about five or six miles from Jayrambati, provided a mid-way resting place for the Mother on her journey to Jayrambati. The monastic disciples of the Mother who stayed there looked upon themselves as the out-post to guard and serve the Mother through manual labour, shopping, going on errands etc.

Pilgrimage to Rameswaram

Towards the end of February 1911, the Holy Mother started on a pilgrimage to Rameswaram, the trip being organised by Swami Ramakrishnananda, a direct disciple of Sri Ramakrishna and head of the Madras Centre. In spite of the language difficulty, she freely communicated with people and during her stay of a month in the city of Madras, gave initiation to several devotees. From Madras she went to Rameswaram where she was allowed the unusual privilege of entering the *sanctum sanctorum* and worshipping the Deity with her own hands. Returning from Rameswaram, she visited Bangalore towards the end of March, where also the President of that Ashrama, Swami Nirmalananda, extended a very hearty and respectful reception to her. Her stay at Bangalore created a great enthusiasm among the people. On her way back to Calcutta she halted at Rajahmundry for a holy bath in the Godavari. She reached Calcutta back on 11th April, 1911. One more pilgrimage she undertook, and that was her third visit to Banaras, extending from November 1912 to January 1913. She went with a fairly big party consisting of monks, devotees and some relatives.

Spiritual Ministry

Her life from 1888 up to her demise in 1920 was one of active spiritual ministry. The Master had commanded her to carry on the work he had started. Speaking on this point, she said: "I have received all these Mantras from the Master himself. Through these, one is sure to achieve perfection." In his last days at Cossipore, Sri Ramakrishna said to her feelingly: "Well, won't you do something? Am I to do all?" To this the Holy Mother replied, "I am but a woman. What can I do?" But the Master replied: "No, no, you have much to do." The Master's vision, in this respect was prophetic. She was his partner in life and in ideals, and he left her in this world to continue and add momentum to the work of spiritual regeneration of man that he had started.

Her spiritual ministry had begun, in a way, even during the life-time of the Master. Many of the women, who flocked to the Master, gathered round her and felt inspired by her. It is known that the Master himself asked his would-be Sannyasin disciple Sarada (Swami Trigunatita) to take initiation from her. But it is doubtful whether the initiation actually took place: but Swami Trigunatita was one of her earliest caretakers and attendants till he left for work in the West. Yogen, Swami Yogananda, another disciple of the Master, was initiated by her at Vrindaban according to the instruction given to her and Yogen by the Master himself in dreams.

During her stay at Jayrambati and Calcutta, the stream of initiation-seeking disciples increased from a trickle to a voluminous flow as time went on and the Master's name and message began to spread far and wide. She was very liberal in accepting disciples, without insisting too much on their competency, not because she could not assess the same, but because her motherly heart responded with sympathy and affection to whoever went to her calling 'Mother' and seeking refuge. In the ocean of her universal love, the relative statures of individual seekers had no meaning as far as their fitness to receive her blessings was concerned. Consequently the number of her disciples increased and many of them were not of any high standard of excellence. Referring to this, her companion Yogin-Ma once said: "Look at the Master's disciples. Each one of them is a spiritual giant. And look at your disciples, Mother." To this the Mother replied: "Is it to be wondered at? He picked up the best type, and with what care he selected them! And towards me he has pushed all this small fry, coming in their hundreds like ants! Don't compare his disciples with mine." Further she spoke to one disciple about the significance of her initiation: "Whatever I have to give, I give at the time of initiation. If you want peace immediately, practise the spiritual discipline prescribed. Otherwise you will achieve it only after the fall of the body." Another disciple protested against her liberality, saying that she was giving initiation sometimes even to boys of ten and twelve who might not even remember the Mantra, and that the number of these was so many that she hardly remembered them. Her reply to this was: "My child, the Master never forbade me to do so. He instructed me on many matters. Could he not have told me something about this as well? I give the responsibility of my disciples to the Master. Every day I pray to him, saying, 'Please look afer the disciples wherever they may be.' Further I received these Mantras from the Master himself. Through them one is sure to achieve perfection."

Once when she was badly ill a disciple noticed her getting up at 2.00 a.m. So he asked her whether she was not sleeping well. Her reply was, "How can I, my child? All these children come to me with much earnestness and take initiation, but most of them do not practise Japa regularly. Why regularly? They do not do anything at all. But since I have taken their responsibility, should I not see to their welfare? Therefore I do Japa for their sake and pray to the Master constantly, saying, 'Oh Lord! Awaken their consciousness. Give them liberation. There is a great deal of suffering in the world. May they not be born again!' "

How seriously she looked on her spiritual ministry, especially her work of initiation, is evident from her words quoted above. She practically assumed the spiritual responsibility of the disciple whom she initiated. Besides, it is believed that she took upon herself the sins of the disciples and vicariously suffered for them. Every disciple was a 'son' or a 'daughter' to her.

She was not very particular to observe any formal rituals when she gave initiation, although she generally gave it after her daily worship of the Master to previously fixed candidates. But often she overlooked all these conventions and initiated disciples at any hour and under any condition. There are instances of her initiating a lady, who was her intimate friend in her girlhood, while both were resting on a bed after lunch: of initiating another during the time of mourning which is considered as one of defilement; of still others on a verandah, beneath the eaves of a house, on an open meadow, or even in a railway yard with an umbrella to serve as roof and the rain water from a pit as purificatory water. It would look that she sometimes gave initiation as the result of an instantaneous impulse, as when she imparted a Mantra occasionally while standing, or when some one held her feet weeping with a heart yearning for initiation. Further there have been cases of devotees who had never seen even a picture of hers before, but on seeing her afterwards had recognised her as the 'human goddess' whom they had seen in dream affording them protection in critical situations of life. Some received initiation from her in dream, and found the Mantra given them tallying exactly with what she gave afterwards in the waking state.

An initiation took her only a very short time— a minute or two. This was so, not because she did it casually, but because her spiritual insight was so quick and unerring, resembling an inspiration. On this point she said once, "As soon as I want to impart a Mantra to some people, there arise in the mind such thoughts as, 'Give this' or 'Give that', whereas in other cases, it appears as though I know nothing, and nothing seems to come up. I keep on sitting. Then after some cogitation I visualise the Mantra. In the case of good aspirants, the Mantra springs up instantaneously."

It is said that the Great Master left the Holy Mother on earth to demonstrate the Motherhood of God. If one prefers, one can understand it in a theological sense, but it will be evident that if universal love is the nature of God, then that trait is amply exhibited by the Holy Mother in her remarkable life on earth. Her spiritual ministry too exemplifies this. Just as a mother's affection for an offspring is never inhibited by any weakness he may have, so the Mother too accepted all devotees who went to her for protection, irrespective of their merits. All were alike in the infinitude of her love —their comparative status in the moral and spiritual scales being obliterated in the very immensity of it.

Her Exit from the World

After her pilgrimages in 1911 and 1912, there are no major incidents to record in her life. She spent her days partly in Calcutta and partly at Jayrambati, engaging herself in active spiritual ministry.

From the end of 1919 her health declined fast. She was getting an intermittent fever, the seriousness of which was not at first recognised. All local treatment was at first tried, but as it had little effect, she was brought to Calcutta in a very emaciated condition. It was diagonised as Kala-Azaar (Black-water Fever) by doctors. There was no effective treatment for it in those days and she succumbed to it on 20th July 1920. Two remarkable happenings have to be recorded in connection with her last days. It has been mentioned that her attachment for Radhu was the main prop for her to sustain her physical life. Now it was noticed that a few days before her demise, she became entirely free from her strong bond of affection for Radhu. She, who could not till then remain in a place without Radhu by her side, now asked her not to come near her. On the other hand she wanted her to go to Jayrambati immediately. When Radhu's infant child went near her, she asked it to be carried away. When disciples and devotees pleaded with her on behalf of Radhu, she openly declared that she had completely taken her mind away from her. For Swami Saradananda and others, who knew the esoteric side of the Mother's personality, it was an indication that she was leaving her physical frame soon.

She was now fast sinking. Five days before her passing, an old devotee named 'Mother of Annapurna' was called into her room. When the lady expressed her fears about the future, the Mother remarked: "Why do you fear? You have seen the Master. But I tell you one thing—if you want peace of mind, do not find fault with others. Rather see your own faults. Learn to make the whole world your own. No one is a stranger. The whole world is your own." Perhaps this embodies her last message to the world also.

During the last three days she practically spoke nothing beyond calling Swami Saradananda to her side and saying: "Sarat, I am going. Yogin, Golap and the rest are here. You look after them."

Just before passing away, her face and body became dark and shrivelled, but to the astonishment of all, a great change took place after life was extinct. Her shrivelled form was found to relax, and her face swelled up and assumed a radiant hue. Her countenance seemed to resemble the face of the image of the Goddess Durga used in worship—mellow and golden in colour, with the expression of calmness and serenity writ large on it. This expression lingered on her face for a long time.

The body was taken in procession to the Belur Math compound where it was cremated on the bank of the Ganga. A small beautiful temple now stands on the site. Another temple with a monastery attached stands at Jayrambati, the place of her birth, to commemorate her life and doings.

In her the world found a unique figure in its history, who combined in herself the roles of a perfect wife, nun, mother and teacher at the same time. In the endless procession of the members of the human species on this planet of ours, the Holy Mother stands out as a unique example, whose utter innocence could melt even the hardest of hearts, who never looked at the fault of others, whose love never made any distinction between the deserving and the undeserving, in whose eyes the saint and the sinner were alike her precious children, whose wide heart held all humanity in its maternal embrace, and who considered it a privilege to labour and to suffer for even the least of them. If we cannot see here the face of the all-loving Universal Mother, of God the Redeemer, where else can we? Only we should have the sensitiveness to recognise that the subtle potency of love transcends the obtrusive display of power.

Holy Mother, 1898
First Photo

Jayrambati: A View

Amodar River

Holy Mother, 1898

Second Photo

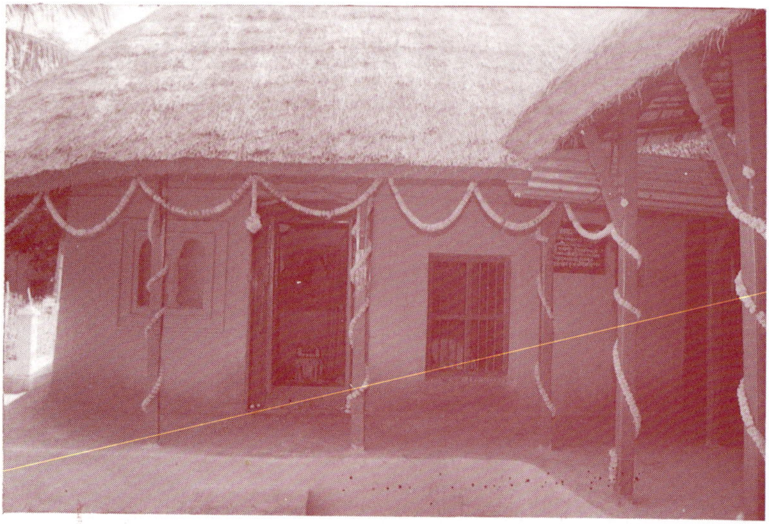

Holy Mother's House (old)

Holy Mother's House (new)

Sri Ramakrishna

Nahabat (left), where Holy Mother stayed for ten years,
and Sri Ramakrishna's Room (right).

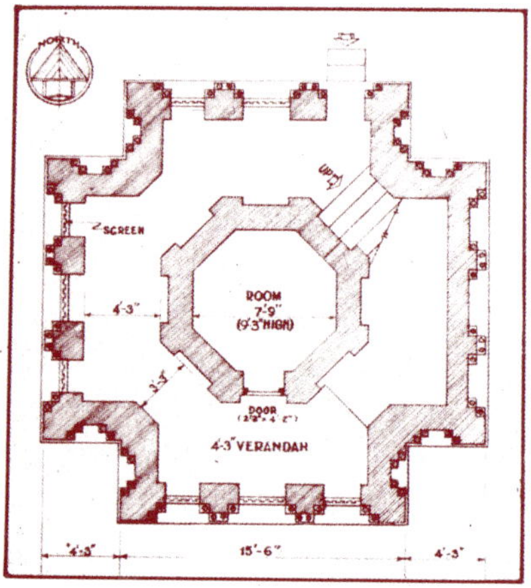

Ground plan of Nahabat

Nahabat

Holy Mother and Sister Nivedita
1898

Holy Mother, 1905

Holy Mother, 1905

Holy Mother at worship in Udbodhan Shrine

Udbodhan House

Gauri-Ma, Durga, Radhu, Holy Mother, Maku, Kusum, and Hari's Mother

Holy Mother and Radhu, 1918

Maku, her child and Holy Mother, 1918

Ganendranath and Asutosh
Nalini, Holy Mother, Radhu, Lakshmi

Shyamasundari Devi, Mother of Holy Mother

Swami Saradananda

Swami Yogananda

Yogin Ma

Golap Ma

Gauri Ma

Gopaler Ma

Holy Mother, 1913

Holy Mother, 1913

Holy Mother During Journey, 1913

THE GOSPEL OF SRI SARADA DEVI
THE HOLY MOTHER

SECTION I

Translated by

Swami Nikhilananda

THE GOSPEL OF THE HOLY MOTHER

FIRST SERIES

RECORDED BY SARAYUBALA DEVI

UDBODHAN OFFICE, CALCUTTA.

January, 1911

ONE Friday morning Sriman K—came to our home at Pataldanga in Calcutta and said: "We shall go to Baghbazar to-morrow afternoon to pay our respects to the Holy Mother. Please be ready at that time." Well, after all, I shall now have the good fortune to prostrate myself at the feet of the Holy Mother! Such was my exuberance of joy that I could hardly sleep during the night. I had been living in Calcutta for the last fourteen or fifteen years. And after such a length of time the Mother was gracious enough to afford me this opportunity to pay my respects to her.

Next day in the afternoon we hired a carriage, fetched Sumati from the Brahmo Girls School, and set out to the Holy Mother's house at Baghbazar. I can hardly describe the eagerness and fervour which I felt at the time of this pilgrimage. I reached her house at Baghbazar and found her standing at the door of the shrine room. She was standing with one foot at the door-sill and the other on the door-mat. There was no veil on her head. Her left arm was raised high and placed on the door, while the right one was hanging by the side. The upper part of her body was bare. She had been looking wistfully as if expecting somebody. As soon as I prostrated myself at her feet, she asked Sumati about me. Sumati introduced me as her elder sister. She had been visiting the Holy Mother for some time past. Then the Mother looked at me and said, "Look here, my child, how much I am troubled by these people here! My sister-in-law and her daughter, Radhu, are all down with fever. I do not know who will look after them and nurse them. Will you wait for a minute? Let me wash my cloth and come back." We waited and she returned after a few minutes. Then she offered us two handfuls of some sweets and asked me to share those with my sister. Sumati had to go back to her school. Therefore we could not stay for a longer time. We saluted her and took leave of her. The Mother said, "Come again." This interview of five minutes could not satiate the inordinate hankering of my soul. I returned home all the more thirsty.

12th February, 1911

When I went to the Udbodhan Office on this day, I found that the Holy Mother had gone to the house of Balaram Bose. I had not to wait long before she returned. As soon as I saluted her she asked me with a smile "Who has accompanied you to-day?" "One of my nephews," I replied.

Mother : How are you today? How is your sister? You did not come for a long time. I was anxious about you and thought you might not be doing well.

I was surprised because I had met her once only and that just for five minutes. But she had not forgotten us. My eyes were filled with tears of joy.

The Mother said with great tenderness, "You have come here, and I was feeling restive at the house of Balaram."

I was completely taken aback. My sister Sumati had sent two woollen caps through me for 'Khude', the baby nephew of the Holy Mother. I handed them over to her. She expressed much joy at these trifles. She sat on the bed and said, "Sit by me here." I sat by her side. The Mother said with great tenderness, "It seems, my child, as if I have met you many a time before, as if we know each other for a long time." "I do not know," said I, "I was here one day only for five minutes."

The Mother laughed and began to speak highly of the devotion and sincerity of mine and my sister's. But I do not know how far I deserve those compliments. Gradually many women devotees assembled. All of them looked wistfully and with great love at the smiling and compassionate face of the Mother. I had never seen such a sight before. My mind was feasting upon the spiritual joy, when someone reminded me that the carriage was ready for my return. The Mother at once left her seat and offered me some Prasada. She held these before me and said, "Eat these!" I felt shy of eating in the presence of others without sharing. The Mother said, "Why do you hesitate? Take these sweets." I accepted the offerings in my hand. I bowed down before her and took my leave. She said "Come again. Can you go down the steps alone, or shall I go with you?" She came with me as far as the staircase. I said, "I can go alone. You need not take trouble." The

Mother said in parting, "Come another day in the morning." I returned with a sense of fulfilment and thought, "What a wonderful love!"

14*th May*, 1911

No sooner had I prostrated myself before the Holy Mother today than she said, "It is fine that you have come. I was thinking all the time about you. Why did you not come all these days?"

Devotee: I was not in Calcutta. I was at my father's house.

Mother : What is the matter with Sumati? She has not come here for a long time. Is she very busy with her studies ?

Devotee: Her husband was not here.

Mother : Well, she goes to school. Do they follow the duties of the world?

Devotee: We do not know, Mother, what the world is and what our duty is. You alone know that.

The Mother smiled. "What a warm day!" she said, and gave me a fan. "Ah dear, you took a hurried meal and ran up here. Now lie down by my side."

A mat was spread on the floor. I hesitated to lie on her bed. But she said, "Why do you hesitate? Lie down! Listen to my words!" I could not help lying down. The Mother became drowsy and I lay silent. A few women devotees and two nuns arrived. One of the nuns was middle-aged while the other was young. The Mother said, with her eyes closed, "Who is there? Is it Gaurdasi?" The young nun said, "How did you know it, Mother?" The Mother said that she felt so. After a few moments she sat up. The young nun then said: "We had been to the Belur Math. Swami Premananda fed us sumptuously. When he is there, one cannot return from the Math without being fed thus." The Mother gently reprimanded some one of the party for not having put the vermilion mark on her forehead, such a mark being obligatory on every married woman if her husband is alive.

Gauri-Ma learnt about me from the Holy Mother and invited me to her girls' school. About sixty girls were attending the school. She asked me if I knew how to sew. I said that I could sew a little, and she requested me to teach that much to the students of the Ashrama.

With the permission of the Holy Mother, I visited the school of Gauri-Ma one day. Gauri-Ma was very loving to me, and requested me to go there every day for an hour or two and give the girls some lessons. I said, "It is absurd for me to be a teacher with my little training. If you insist, I can just teach them the simple alphabet." But Gauri-Ma was inexorable. I had to yield.

One day, after leaving the school of Gauri-Ma, I went to see the Holy Mother. It was then summer and I was quite tired. The Mother was seated in her room, surrounded by a group of women devotees. As soon as I prostrated myself before her, she looked at me and at once took a small fan from the top of the mosquito-curtain. She began to fan me so that I might be refreshed. Then she said anxiously, "Take off your blouse quickly so that the body may be cool." What an unprecedented love! She began to caress me before many devotees. I felt ashamed. All eyes were fixed upon me. Seeing her eagerness, I had to take off the blouse. The more I requested her to hand over the fan to me, the more she insisted with great tenderness, "That is all right! Be a little refreshed!" She brought a tumbler of water and some sweets. Watching me partake of them, she became happy. The carriage from the school had been waiting for me. So I had to take leave soon.

3rd August, 1911

This morning I went early to Baghbazar. I longed to be initiated by the Holy Mother to-day; so I took a few articles with me for the purpose. Gauri-Ma gave me the list of articles and she also accompanied me to the Holy Mother's place. When I arrived there, I found her absorbed in worship. She asked me by signs to take a seat. After the worship was over, Gauri-Ma broached the subject of my initiation. I had also spoken about it to her one day. I had taken some good bananas with me. She was very pleased to see the fruits and said, "Ah, I see you have brought many bananas." One of the monks present expressed his desire for them. Then she added, "Take that carpet and sit on my left." I replied. " I have not yet finished my bath in the Ganges."

Mother: That does not matter. It is enough if you have changed your clothes.

I sat by her side. I felt my heart palpitating. The Mother asked the others to leave the room and then said to me, " Now tell me what Mantra was revealed to you in dream."

Devotee : Shall I utter those words or write them down ?

Mother : You may tell them to me. . .

At the time of initiation the Holy Mother explained to me the meaning of the Mantra that I had received in dream. She at first asked me to repeat that Mantra and then communicated to me a new Mantra. I was instructed to repeat the first Mantra a few times every day, and then repeat the second and meditate.

I saw the Mother absorbed in meditation for a few minutes before she explained the meaning of the Mantra to me. At the time of initiation my whole body began to tremble. I began to weep, for which I could not divine any cause. The Mother put a big mark of red sandalpaste on my forehead. I gave her a few rupees for offering at the shrine. She handed over the money to Golap-Ma.

I noticed the Mother to be severely grave at the time of initiation. Then she left the seat of worship. She asked me to repeat the Mantra for some time and meditate and pray. I did as I was asked to do. As I bowed at her feet, she blessed me with the words, "May you attain devotion to God!" Even now I remember those words and pray to her, "Please remember your blessing. May I not be deprived of its effect!"

The Holy Mother was going to the Ganges for her bath. Golap-Ma accompanied her. I also joined the party, taking with me the towel and the cloth of the Mother. It was drizzling. After finishing her bath, the Mother gave the priest on the ghat a coin and a mango. As she made these offerings, she said, "I am giving you the fruit, but it is the *fruit* of the gift that belongs to you." Ah! the priest could hardly realize who made this gift! He could hardly understand the significance of those words! Nor can we, puny creatures, torn as we are by millions of petty selfish desires!

The Holy Mother changed her dress and gave me the wet cloth to carry. Golap-Ma headed the party while I walked behind. The Mother was between us. She carried some water of the Ganges in a small vessel and offered a little of it at every sacred banyan tree that stood along the way. There was a water-jar near the cistern close to the tap on the ground floor. The Mother washed her feet with that water and said to me, "There is mud on your feet. Wash it off." As I was looking for some water, she said, "There is water in the jar. Why do you not wash your feet with that ?" "You have touched that water. How can I use it?"[1] said I with some reluc-

[1] According to the Hindu custom, the water that has been touched by a revered person cannot be used for washing the feet.

tance. "Sprinkle a little over your head," replied the Mother. But I hesitated and said, "I cannot use that water." I took some water from the cistern in another jar and washed my hands and feet. She waited for me all the time. Then we went upstairs. She took some offered sweets and fruits in two leaf-plates, and asked me to sit by her. With great tenderness she fed me with the Prasada and also partook of it herself.

Gradually many women devotees arrived. I did not know them. They would take their meal at noontime at the Mother 's place. After the worship was over, we all sat for lunch. The Mother also occupied her seat. She took three morsels of food and then gave me some Prasada, which was also distributed among all others. The Mother now became her former self. She became jolly again. Since the time of initiation she had been altogether in a different mood, grave and introspective—a veritable goddess ready to grant favour and punish iniquity. I had been trembling with awe. I have seen her, later on, giving initiation to many devotees, but I have never again seen her in such a grave mood. Laughing and joking, she initiated many persons. They were also happy and satisfied. Goaded by curiosity, I sometimes asked the devotees how they found her at the time of initiation. One middle-aged widow once said in reply, "Just as we see her always. Nothing very particular. I had been initiated before by my family Guru. Afterwards I heard of the Mother and came to her for initiation. She at first asked me to repeat ten times the Mantra I had received from my family preceptor. Then she gave me initiation. She pointed out Sri Ramakrishna as my Guru and another deity as my Ishta. She instructed me to pray thus to Sri Ramakrishna: 'O Lord, please relieve me of all sins committed in this and in previous lives', and so on. I am greatly troubled now-a-days. Can you explain it? I cannot repeat the Mantra for more than half an hour. Someone, as it were, pushes me out of the seat. Do you also feel like that? I often think of asking the Holy Mother about it. But I cannot do so. You are so free with her. Has the Mother deceived me then?" I never wanted to know all these details. But as the lady spoke out all this very frankly, I said, "Please open your heart to the Mother. At first you may feel a little constraint. But it will be easy by and by. We also could not be so free with her at first. Even now she, at times, becomes so serious that we cannot approach her."

In the evening the women devotees took their leave of the

Mother one by one. She asked her nieces to meditate and pray. They were late, and she said in a tone of displeasure, "It is evening. Instead of meditating, they are gossiping!" Golap-Ma, Yogin-Ma and other devotees prostrated themselves at her feet. She blessed them all, laying her hand on their heads, or touching the chins, or kissing them. She bowed before the image of Sri Ramakrishna and then took her seat for meditation. After she finished her meditation, I took leave of her and returned home.

* * * *

I was not able to visit the Holy Mother for some days on account of the pressure of my school duties. No sooner had I saluted her today than she began to show her love for me in countless ways. Bhudev was reading the Mahabharata. He was a mere boy, and therefore could not read fluently. The Mother had her other duties also to attend to. It was almost evening. She said to Bhudev, pointing to me, "Give her the book. She will read it quite easily. The reading cannot be stopped without finishing this chapter." It was her order; so I began to read the Mahabharata. Never before had I read a book in her presence. At first I felt a sort of shyness, but somehow I finished the chapter. The Mother saluted the book with folded hands. We went to the shrine to witness the evening worship. The Mother took her wonted seat and soon became absorbed in meditation.

The Mother completed her Japa, uttering the name of God in a loud voice, and bowed down before the image of Sri Ramakrishna. The Prasada was then distributed to all. After this the conversation drifted to our daily duties. The Mother, referring to her own busy days at Jayrambati, said: "Always be engaged in some work or other. It is conducive to the health of both the body and the mind. In my early days at Jayrambati I was always busy with some work or other and would never visit my neighbours; for, people would blurt out at the very sight of me 'Dear me, Syama's daughter has been married to a lunatic!' I avoided meeting anybody in order to escape such criticism."

Just in the open square in front of the Holy Mother's house, there lived some people belonging to some parts of India outside Bengal. They earned their livelihood by hard manual labour. One of them had a mistress. They lived together. Once the mistress was seriously ill. Referring to her illness the Holy Mother said, "He nursed her with such great devotion! I have never before seen anything like it. He has shown a real spirit of service." She began to speak highly of the devotion of this man.

The idea of a mistress would certainly have made us turn up our noses in disgust. Ah, how often we fail to recognize goodness when veiled in an evil garb!

A poor up-country woman from the house across the street, came to the Holy Mother, carrying a sick child in her arms. She solicited her blessings. The Mother was gracious to that child. She said that the child would soon recover, and blessed it. Two big pomegranates and some grapes had been offered in the shrine. She handed over all these fruits to the poor woman, saying, "Give these to your sick child." The woman was overjoyed at this generosity of the Mother and repeatedly bowed down before her.

11*th February*, 1912

The moment I met the Holy Mother today and sat down after saluting her, she began to say with great sorrow, "Alas! Girish Babu is dead. Today is the fourth day. His relatives came here to invite me to go to their house. Is it possible for me to go there any more? What devotion for, and faith in, Sri Ramakrishna Girish had! Have you heard this incident? He begged Sri Ramakrishna to be born as his son. Sri Ramakrishna said in reply, 'Why should I care to be born as your son!' But who knows, my child, the inscrutable ways of the Lord! A son was born to Girish some time after the passing away of Sri Ramakrishna. A strange boy, indeed! Even when he was four years old, he would not exchange a word with anybody. People could know his mind only from his gestures. His parents looked upon him as Sri Ramakrishna himself. They kept apart everything belonging to him—his dress, plate, cup, glass, etc. Nobody else would use those things....

"One day the boy became extremely restive to see me. My picture was in the upper floor of the house. He dragged the whole household there, and uttering a cry, pointed out the picture to them. At first they did not understand him. Then they brought him to me. Though he was but a little child of four, he prostrated himself before me. Then he went to the first floor and began to pull his father by his cloth. He wanted that his father also should see me. Girish wept bitterly and said, 'I cannot, my darling, see the Holy Mother. I am a great sinner!' But the boy was inexorable. So Girish had to yield. He took the boy in his arm. With his whole body trembling and tears trickling down his cheeks, he came up and prostrated on the ground before me. He said, 'Mother, this boy has made me see your holy feet!' But the boy passed away when he was four years old.

"Once Girish and his wife were taking the air on the roof of their house. I had been staying then at the house of Balaram. The houses were near each other. I also went to the roof that day. I did not notice that Girish could see me from the roof of his house. His wife said to him, 'Look there, the Holy Mother is pacing on the roof of the house.' Girish at once turned his back on me and said to his wife, 'No, no, I cannot thus stealthily look at the Holy Mother. My eyes are vicious!' He at once came down from the roof. I heard this from his wife."

15*th June*, 1912

The Holy Mother was seated with a number of women devotees. I was acquainted with some of them. The Mother was very cheerful in their company. She welcomed me with a smile. I requested Gauri-Ma to bring from the library two books, the life of Sister Nivedita and the Indian lectures of Swami Vivekananda. I wished to read something from the life of Sister Nivedita. The Mother agreed and said, "Please read Nivedita's life. I also received a copy of the book the other day. But I have not yet looked into it." I felt a little shy to read the book in the presence of so many people. At the same time I was eager to read to the Mother the beautiful biography of the Sister written by Saralabala. So I obeyed her order. The Mother as well as the other devotees began to listen with rapt attention. Their eyes became moist on hearing of the wonderful devotion of Nivedita. Tears trickled down the cheeks of the Mother. Referring to Nivedita, she said, "What sincere devotion Nivedita had! She never considered anything too much that she might do for me. She would often come to see me at night. Once seeing that light struck my eyes, she put a shade of paper around the lamp. She would prostrate herself before me and, with great tenderness, take the dust of my feet with her handkerchief. I felt that she even hesitated to touch my feet." The thought of Nivedita opened the floodgate of her mind and she suddenly became grave.

Those present began to give their reminiscences of Sister Nivedita. Durga-didi said, "It is the misfortune of India that she passed away at such an early age." Another lady said. "She looked upon India as her motherland. She herself said so, many a time. On the day of the Saraswati Puja she would walk bare-footed, putting on her forehead the mark of the sacred ash of the sacrificial fire." I finished reading. The Mother now and then expressed her feelings towards the Sister. She said at last, "The inner soul feels for a sincere devotee."

It was the hour for afternoon worship. The Mother changed her clothes and sat on the carpet before the image of Sri Ramakrishna. She had made some flower garlands with her own hands to decorate the image. Rash Behari, a young Brahmacharin, had kept near the garland some sweets for offering. Ants gathered around the sweets. Some ants were seen also in the garlands. Mother said with a laugh, "See what Rash Behari has done! Sri Ramakrishna will be bitten by these ants." She removed the ants and tenderly decorated the image with the garlands. Seeing her thus decorate the picture of her husband with flowers before others, Surabala, her sister-in-law,[1] laughed. Later the Prasada was distributed to all.

One lady devotee said, "Mother, I have five daughters. I cannot find suitable bridegrooms for them. I am so anxious about it."

Mother: Why do you worry about their marriage? If you cannot find suitable husbands for them, please send them to the Sister Nivedita Girls' School. They will be trained there. They will be very happy in the school.

Another lady devotee: If you have faith in the Holy Mother, then do as she asks you to do. That will be for your good. If you listen to her, you will have no worry.

Needless to say, the mother of the five girls could hardly appreciate the advice.

Third devotee: It is very difficult to find suitable bridegrooms now-a-days. Many boys refuse to marry.

Mother: Yes, the boys have learnt how to discriminate. They are gradually realizing that the happiness of the world is transitory. The less you become attached to the world, the more you enjoy peace of mind.

---

[1] This is the crazy sister-in-law who figures so often in these conversations. She was the mother of Radhu.

It was quite late before I took leave of her that night.

* * * *

Another day I went to Baghbazar and found the Holy Mother resting after her lunch. She was gracious enough to request me to fan her. Suddenly I heard her speaking to herself: "Well, you all have come here. But where is Sri Ramakrishna?" I said in reply, "We could not meet him in this life. Who knows in which future birth we shall be able to see him? But this is our greatest good fortune, that we have been able to touch your feet." "That is true, indeed." was the brief remark of the Holy Mother. I was rather amazed at this confession. Very seldom would she speak of herself in such a way.

I could hardly realize at that time that people might possibly have their secrets to confide to the Holy Mother. I was a foolish girl, so I could not comprehend that. Therefore if I happened to miss her on entering her room, I would search the house for her; I could hardly wait for her to come. One evening two pretty young ladies had been taking the Holy Mother into their confidence in the northern porch of her room when I suddenly presented myself there, not finding her anywhere else. I heard the Mother saying to them, "Lay the burden of your mind before Sri Ramakrishna. Tell him your sorrows with your tears. You will find that he will fill up your arms with the desired object." I could at once understand that the ladies were praying to be blessed with children. They were abashed at the sight of me. My state of mind was even worse. But I was taught a great lesson that day. I took a vow that I would never again go to the presence of the Holy Mother without previously intimating my arrival. A few months later I again met those ladies in the house of the Holy Mother. I was glad to find that their cherished desire was going to be fulfilled soon.

Gauri-Ma was present there. In reply to our request, she gave us some of her reminiscences of Sri Ramakrishna. She said, "I had visited Sri Ramakrishna long before many devotees began to go to him. I saw Naren and Kali while they were quite young." It was evening. The conversation had to be cut short. Gauri-Ma took leave of the Holy Mother. I also had to go. As I was about to take leave of her, she called me to the porch and gave me some Prasada. She said, "Come again. You do not stay here long at a time. Come one morning at seven o'clock and have your noonday meal with us."

18*th September*, 1912

I was a little busy with some work in Gauri-Ma's Girls' School. Therefore I was not free to go to the Holy Mother according to my desire. It was an auspicious day when, one morning, I arrived at her place. She was getting ready to go to the Ganges for her bath. At the very sight of me she said with evident pleasure, "I am very glad you have come today. It is an auspicious day, being the birthday of Radhika. Wait here till I return from the Ganges." I expressed my desire to accompany her and she first agreed. It was drizzling and Golap-Ma sternly objected to my going, as I would be exposed to the rain. The Mother supported Golap-Ma and said, "Please wait here. I shall return presently." We often noticed her behaving like a gentle young girl. She would never press her views over those of others. As soon as she came to the street, the rain stopped. She returned home after finishing the bath and said, "Well the rain stopped as soon as I came out into the street. You also wanted to accompany me. I thought it would have been nice if you had come with me. You could have had a sight of the Holy Ganges." To tell the truth, I was not so eager for the Ganges as for her holy company. For, as we are involved in a thousand and one duties of the world, we can hardly find time to visit her. On those few days when we can fortunately go to her, we do not like to leave her presence even for a minute. Golap-Ma, however, heard the words of the Holy Mother and remarked, "What does it matter if she has not seen the Ganges! All desires will be fulfilled by touching your holy feet." I also nodded assent to these words. But the Mother said at once, "Do not say so! Ah, it is the Mother Ganges after all!" The Mother would seldom reveal her divine greatness through any word or deed. She would always act in such a way that people might take her to be an ordinary human being like themselves. Only on rare occasions would she, out of grace for some fortunate devotee, reveal her divine aspect. She entered the room, sat on the bed and said, "Look here. I have finished my bath in the Ganges!" I understood that she had come to know of my innermost desire of worshipping her lotus feet. I said to myself, "Thou art ever pure. It is not necessary for Thee to bathe in the Ganges to purify Thyself." When I sat at her feet with flowers and sandal-paste, she said, "Don't put any Tulasi leaves." I worshipped her feet with flowers and sandal paste. I bowed down to her. Afterwards she began to take her breakfast. She made me sit near and began to give me, with infinite love, half of every article of food she took. I ate the Prasada with great joy. As I was eating from the leaf plate, I was reminded of Saint Durga Charan Nag. I said to the Mother, "This leaf-plate often reminds me of Nag Mahasaya."

Mother: What wonderful devotion he had! Look at this dry leaf-plate. Who can eat it? But he had an exuberance of devotion, and would swallow the leaf which had touched the Prasada. Ah! what loving eyes he had! Slightly reddish and always moist with tears! His body was emaciated by hard austerities. He would come to see me. He could hardly climb the steps. His emotions would well up at the very sight of me. He would tremble like a leaf. He would stagger while walking. I have never seen such devotion in anybody.

Devotee: I have read in his biography that he gave up his medical practice and was absorbed, day and night, in his meditation on Sri Ramakrishna. One day his father said in an angry mood, "You are so indifferent to the world. What will be your fate? You will not have a piece of cloth to cover your body with! And you will have to eat frogs to satisfy your hunger!" There was a dead frog in the courtyard. Nag Mahasaya threw away the cloth that he had been wearing and ate the frog. Then he said to his father, "I have fulfilled your two prophecies. Please banish all your anxieties regarding my food and clothing and devote yourself to the thought of God."

Mother: What a wonderful devotion to his father! He did not make any difference between purity and impurity. This speaks of his high spiritual realization.

Devotee: Once, on a very auspicious day, he came home from Calcutta. The father reprimanded him and said, "You were in Calcutta near the Ganges. How foolish of you to have come home away from the Ganges on such an auspicious day! You should have stayed in Calcutta and taken bath in the holy river." But just at the auspicious moment of that day, all noticed water rising in a spout from the courtyard. Every place was flooded. Nag Mahasaya became mad with ecstasy and cried, "Come, Mother Ganges!" He sprinkled that water on his head. The people of his locality bathed in that water and felt as if they had bathed in the Ganges.

Mother: True, even the impossible becomes possible through devotion. Once I gave him a piece of cloth. He always tied it around his head. His wife also is very good and devoted. She came to see me the other day during the summer season. She is still alive.

At this time some devotees arrived and the conversation was stopped. They prostrated themselves before the Holy Mother. She asked me to prepare some rolls of betel leaves. I prepared two and handed them over to her. She ate one herself and returned the other to me. I left her again to prepare the rest of the betel leaves. The Mother, after a while, came to our room with two devotees. They started to help me and the work was over very quickly. The Mother separated a few leaves to make a present to them. She was very happy and said, "Ah! my good girls have finished their job so quickly."

The Holy Mother retired to the room of Golap-Ma on the second floor. I went there a few minutes later and saw that she was lying on the floor, resting her head on the door sill. So I could not step over the door-sill and enter the room. She looked at me and said, "Come in. It is all right!" She was always so free and informal. She raised her head from the sill and I entered the room. I sat by her side and began to fan her. She asked me various things regarding the school of Gauri-Ma. I gave her suitable replies. Just then the two women devotees came there. One of them began to dress the Mother's hair. She separated one or two grey hairs and tied them in the skirt of her cloth. She said, "I shall preserve them as a souvenir." The Holy Mother felt abashed and said with hesitation, "Why are you doing so? I have thrown away so much hair before." She went to the roof to bask in the sun. We also followed her. There were many clothes drying in the sun. She asked me to take them away to the room.

Later, when the worship was over, the Holy Mother asked me to make the necessary preparation for the noonday meal of the devotees. We all sat together for the meal. The Mother took a morsel or two. The Prasada was then distributed among us. The two women-devotees mentioned above were with us. One of them was old and had her husband. She had seen Sri Ramakrishna. The other one was her daughter-in-law.

The old lady said, "Sri Ramakrishna gave us many instructions. But we have carried out very few of them. Had we followed his advice, we would not have suffered so much in the world. We are attached to the world and are always running after this or that work."

The Mother said, replying, "One must do some work. Through work alone can one remove the bondage of work, not by avoiding work. Total detachment comes later on. One should not be without work even for a moment."

After the meal the Mother was resting for a while. She lay down on the bed. All the devotees were eager to do her some personal service. But she asked them all to take some rest. They all therefore went away to their respective places as they had various things to attend to. I remained there with an old widow who was a contemporary of Sri Ramakrishna. I was massaging the Mother's body. The widow sat by her side and began to narrate the various incidents of her family life. "Mother!" said she, "you always excuse my shortcomings but my people are so exacting." I asked her if she had seen Sri Ramakrishna. "Yes, dear," she replied. "I have seen him. He often visited our place. The Holy Mother was quite young at that time."

Devotee: Please tell us something about Sri Ramakrishna.

Widow: Not I. Ask the Mother to tell us something about him.

The Mother was resting with her eyes closed, so I did not ask her. After a while, the Mother herself said, "He who will pray to God eagerly will see Him. The other day one of our devotees, Tej Chandra, passed away. What a sincere soul he was! Sri Ramakrishna used to frequent his house. Some one had deposited Rs. 200 with Tej Chandra. One day he was robbed of that amount by a pick-pocket in the tram car. He discovered the loss after some time and suffered a terrible mental agony. He came to the bank of the Ganges and prayed to Sri Ramakrishna, with tears in his eyes, 'O Lord, what have you done with me!' He was not rich enough to make up that amount from his own pocket. As he was thus weeping, he saw Sri Ramakrishna appear before him and say, "Why do you weep so bitterly? The money is there under a brick on the bank of the Ganges." He quickly removed the brick and really found there a bundle of banknotes. He narrated the incident to Sarat (Swami Saradananda). Sarat said, 'You are lucky to get the vision of Sri Ramakrishna even now. But we do not see him.' Why should Sarat and others like him see him any more? They have had enough of him and all their desires have been fulfilled. Those who have not seen him with their physical eyes are most anxious for his vision. When Sri Ramakrishna was staying at Dakshineswar, Rakhal and other devotees were very young. One day Rakhal (Swami Brahmananda) came to Sri Ramakrishna and said that he was very hungry. Sri Ramakrishna came to the Ganges and cried out, 'O Gaurdasi, come here! My Rakhal is hungry.' At that time there was no refreshment stall at Dakshineswar. A little later a boat was seen coming up the Ganges. It anchored near the temple. Balaram Babu, Gaurdasi and some other devotees came out of the boat with some sweets. Sri Ramakrishna was very happy, and shouted for Rakhal. He said, 'Come here. Here are sweets. You said that you were hungry.' Rakhal became angry and remarked, 'Why are you broadcasting my hunger?' Sri Ramakrishna said, 'What is the harm?.. You are hungry. You want something to eat. What is wrong in speaking about it?' Sri Ramakrishna had a child-like nature."

Bhudev, the nephew of the Holy Mother, just then returned from school. He was having fever. The Mother asked me to arrange a bed for him. She was preparing to go to Balaram Babu's house to see his son who was suffering from an attack of dysentery. She finished the evening worship and offered me some Prasada. I said that I would eat it later on. She agreed and asked Nalini, her niece, to give me the Prasada later. A carriage was brought for her. She asked me to wait there till her return. Golap-Ma accompanied her. They returned after an hour. The Holy Mother was glad to see me and said, "I have come back quickly for you. Have you eaten the Prasada?" When I replied in the negative, she remarked, "Nalini, why did you not give her the Prasada as I had asked you?"

Nalini: I forgot to do so. I shall bring it presently.

Mother: You need not worry about it any more. I shall give her that Prasada myself. (*To me*) Why did you not ask for it yourself? This is your own home.

Devotee: I was not very hungry. Had I been so, I would have asked for it.

The Mother, shortly after, brought some sweets that had been offered in the shrine and gave them to me. I partook of them joyously. I prostrated myself before her and asked her leave. She said, "Come again, dear child. Durga! Durga! Shall I come with you to the ground floor? Can you go alone? It is night." I said, "I shall be able to go alone, Mother,". Still she began to repeat the name of God and accompanied me as far as the staircase. "You need not take any more trouble," I said "It will be easy for me to find the way."

* * * *

It was the Akshaya Tritiya—a very auspicious day with the

Hindus. I came to see the Holy Mother. The old lady with her daughter-in-law, mentioned before, was also there. She was about to give the Mother, as is the practice on such holy occasions, some fruits and a piece of sacred thread. The Mother interrupted her and said, "Why do you give these to me? Give them to Bhudev." Then in the course of her conversation she looked at us and said, "I bless you on this holy day that you may attain to liberation in this life. Birth and death are extremely painful. May you not suffer from them any more!"

* * * *

It was the day of the sacred Car Festival.[1] At seven o'clock in the morning I went to Gauri-Ma's Ashrama. She had invited me there for lunch. I had a desire to go to the Holy Mother from the school as soon as possible. We finished our meal at two o'clock. When Gauri-Ma and I came to the place of the Holy Mother, it was four o'clock. The Mother had been performing the evening service in the shrine room. We prostrated ourselves before her. Gauri-Ma took her aside and whispered something in her ears. I was asked to join them later on. I had taken with me a piece of silk cloth for her. I placed it near her feet and said, "Mother, will you kindly use it?" "O yes, darling," she said with a laugh. Just then some men devotees came to bow down before her. We retired to the porch. One devotee brought with him some hibiscus flowers and roses, a garland of jasmine, fruits and sweets. He placed these offerings near her feet and began to worship her. What a soul-enthralling sight! The Mother was seated quietly with a sweet smile playing on her lips. The garland was hanging round her neck. The flowers adorned her feet. After the worship was over, the devotee took a little from every fruit and sweetmeat and prayed to her to eat it. Gauri-Ma said with a laugh, "You are in the grip of a staunch devotee. You must eat a little of everything." The Mother also was laughing and said, "Not so much. I cannot eat so much!" She ate a little from every article of the offering. The devotee took the Prasada in his hand and touched his forehead with it. He beamed with an indescribable joy. He prostrated himself before the Mother and then came away. The Mother took off the garland from her neck and gave it to Gauri-Ma. The offered flowers were distributed

[1] A sacred festival when the Lord Vishnu at Jagannath is taken in procession in a chariot.

among the devotees.

As I have already stated, it was the sacred day of the Car Festival. Bhudev improvised a car for the occasion. Arrangements were made for taking the image of Sri Ramakrishna in this car. Gauri-Ma had an important engagement in the school, so she had to leave us. The conversation drifted to Gauri-Ma. The Mother said, "She devotes her energy to bring up the girls in the school. She nurses them when they are ill. She has no family of her own. Her motherly instinct has been finding expression through these girls. This is her last birth, therefore she has been passing through all these experiences."

The image of Sri Ramakrishna was taken in the car. The Mother from her bed looked at the image intently. She was very happy. The car with the image was taken down. The procession went along the streets and along the bank of the Ganges. The party returned after dusk. The women-devotees pulled the car in the porch of the upper floor. The Mother, her two nieces and I joined them. When the car was going along the street, the Mother remarked, "All cannot go to Puri to see the Car Festival.[1] Those who have seen Sri Ramakrishna in this car will realize God."

October, 1912

One morning, during the Durga Puja holidays, I went to visit the Holy Mother. I found her very busy. I sat near her. She sent for a devotee who had come from Ranchi. He had brought with him many flowers, fruits, a piece of cloth and a garland of linen flowers. He requested the Mother to wear the garland on her neck. As she did so, Golap-Ma took him to task, for the iron wire of the garland might hurt her. The Mother said tenderly, "No, I have put on the garland over my cloth." I had taken with me some fruits and sweets. The Mother asked me to offer them to the Lord. She ate a grape and said that it was very sweet.

The Mother had on her person the cloth which I had given her a few days ago. Pointing that to me, she remarked, "See, I have used it and now it is dirty." I was amazed to see this and thought what infinite tenderness the Mother had for even such an unfit devotee as myself.

[1]The popular belief is that by seeing the image of Vishnu in the car at Puri one realizes God.

Nalini, the Mother's niece, was in an angry mood. The Mother reprimanded her and said, "Women should not get angry so easily. They must practise forbearance. In infancy and childhood their parents are their only protection and in youth their husbands. Women are generally very sensitive. A mere word upsets them. And words also are so cheap now-a-days. They should have patience and try to put up with parents or husbands in spite of difficulties."

Radhu sat near us with her cloth pulled above her knees. The Mother reproved her and said, "Dear me! Why should a woman pull her cloth above her knees?" She cited a verse which says, "It is as good as being naked when the cloth is pulled above the knees."

Chandra Babu's sister came to see us. She asked me in the course of a conversation, "Is the husband of the Holy Mother still alive? Are these his children and daughters-in-law?" "Goodness gracious!" said I, "Have you not read the teachings of Sri Ramakrishna? He always exhorted people to renounce lust and gold." The lady was nonplussed and said, "Excuse me, I took them for her own children."

It was the time of the Durga Puja. The Mother had a bundle of new clothes before her. She separated the clothes intended for the husbands of her three nieces. She took a cloth in her hand and said, "G.—will put on this new cloth at the time of the Puja and go to the Belur Math."

After the noonday worship, we had our meal. The Mother was resting. I sat by her side and began to fan her. She said with great tenderness, "There is a pillow there. Bring it and lie down near me. I do not require any more fanning." I hesitated to use her pillow and brought one from Radhu's room. The Mother said with a smile, "This pillow belongs to Radhu's mother, that crazy woman. She will make a fuss. Please use my pillow. There is no harm in it." Then she said to Radhu, "Please come here and lie by your sister." The conversation drifted to the remarks of Chandra Babu's sister, narrated above. The Mother said, "Well, you could have easily replied that her husband is there in the shrine room, and that all of you are his children." I said, " All the men and women of the world are his children!" The mother laughed and remarked, "People come here with various selfish desires. Someone comes with a cucumber, offers it to Sri Ramakrishna, and prays for the fulfilment of selfish desires.

This is the nature of average people."

After a little rest we got up. A few women devotees were in the adjacent room. Two of them wore ochre robes. They prostrated themselves before the Mother. They brought some sweets for offering. We came to know they were the disciples of Siva-Narayan Paramahamsa of Kalighat. Their teacher was just then engaged in performing a grand sacrifice.

One of the nuns asked, "Is there any truth in image worship? Our teacher does not approve of it. He instructs people in the worship of the fire and the sun."

Mother : You should not doubt the words of your own teacher. Why do you ask me about it, when you have heard the opinion of your Guru in the matter?

The nun : We want to know your opinion.

The Mother refused to give any opinion. But the nun was stubborn and began to press for a reply. The Mother said at last, "If your teacher were an illumined soul—you have forced me to say—then he would not have made such a statement. From time immemorial innumerable people have worshipped images and thereby attained spiritual knowledge. Do you want to deny this fact? Sri Ramakrishna never cherished any such parochial and one-sided view. Brahman exists everywhere. The prophets and incarnations are born to show the way to a benighted humanity. They give different instructions suited to different temperaments. There are many ways to realize the Truth. Therefore all these instructions have their relative value. Take, for instance, a tree. There are birds perched on its branches. They have different colours, white, black, yellow, red, etc. Their sounds are also different. But we say that these are the sounds of the birds. We never designate a particular sound as that of birds and refuse to acknowledge other sounds as such."

The nuns desisted from argument after some time. They then inquired about the Calcutta address of the Holy Mother and said that they would like to see her again. After they had left, the Mother said, "It does not become a woman to argue like that. Even the wise could hardly realize the nature of Brahman by argument. Is Brahman an object of discussion?"

A few days after, the Mother was to leave for Banaras, and I might not meet her for some time. She was extremely kind to me when I took leave of her, and I was so overpowered by her love that I did not exchange a word with anyone that night.

31*st January*, 1913

The Holy Mother had returned from Banaras on 17 January. I went to her place one morning and found her absorbed in worship. After the worship was over, she left the seat and said, "I am glad to see you, my child. I was thinking of you and feared lest I should miss you again. We shall soon be leaving for our country home."

It was late in the morning. Radhu, her niece, was ready to go to the Christian missionary school of the neighbourhood. Golap-Ma came and said to the Mother, 'Radhu is now a grown-up girl. Why should she go to school any more?" She asked Radhu not to go to school. Radhu began to cry. The Mother said, "She is not quite grown-up. Let her go to school. She can do immense good to others if she gets education and learns some useful arts at the school. She has been married in a backward village. Through education she will not only improve herself but will be able to help others." So Radhu was allowed to go to school.

Annapurna's mother brought a girl with her to be initiated by the Holy Mother. She said, "Mother, this girl is pestering me to be taken to be initiated by you. I could not avoid her. Therefore I have brought her to you."

Mother: How will it be possible to give initiation to-day? I have already taken my breakfast.[1]

A.'s mother: But the girl is fasting. It does not matter at all if you have eaten anything or not.

Mother: Is she ready for initiation?

A's mother: Yes, Mother. She has come fully prepared for it.

The Mother agreed. After the initiation was over, Annapurna's mother began to talk about the girl and said, "She is not an ordinary girl. After reading about Sri Ramakrishna, she became eager for practising spiritual austerities. She cut her long hair, dressed herself as a man and set out on a pilgrimage. She went as far as Baidyanath, over two hundred miles from Calcutta. She entered a wood and was resting there when the Guru of her mother happened to pass that way. The Guru inquired where she was staying and informed her father. In the meantime she

---

[1] The general custom is that initiation is given before the teacher takes his or her meal.

was kept with the Guru. Later on, her father went there and took back the girl."

The Mother heard these words in silence and then remarked: " Ah! what devotion!" Other devotees present there, said, "Goodness gracious! Such a beautiful girl! How could she go out alone even with all her eagerness and devotion?" Nalini said, "It would surely have created a great scandal in our part of the country."

After the noonday meal all of us lay down to rest in the adjacent room. The Mother also requested her new disciple to rest for a while. She said that she was not in the habit of lying down during the day-time. I said that she should obey the order of the Holy Mother. She agreed but after a few minutes left the bed and went to the porch. The Holy Mother remarked, "She is restless. That is why she had left home." She asked the maid of the girl, "What is the occupation of her husband? Why does he not keep her near him?" "He gets a small salary," replied the maid, "besides, there is no one in his family. He cannot keep the girl alone in the house. Therefore she lives with her father. The husband visits the house of the father-in-law every weekend." Annapurna's mother said, "This girl says to her husband, 'You are not my husband. The Lord of the world alone is my lord.' " The Holy Mother kept quiet without giving any reply.

The women devotees were talking in the northern porch of the shrine room. That created a great deal of noise. The Mother told someone, "Go and ask them to talk in low tones. They are disturbing Swami Saradananda." There was no one in the room. I asked her a few questions regarding spiritual practices. The Mother said, "Do not make any distinction between Sri Ramakrishna and me. Meditate on and pray to the particular aspect of the Divinity revealed to you. Worship ends with absorption in meditation. Start here (the heart) and end here (the head). Neither Mantra nor scripture is of any avail; Bhakti or devotion alone accomplishes everything. Sri Ramakrishna is everything—both Guru and Ishtam. He is all in all."

Then the conversation drifted to Gauri-Ma and her disciple, Durgadevi. The Mother spoke highly of both. She said, "Listen, my child. Many may take the name of God after their minds have been hardened by the contaminating influence of the world. But he alone is blessed who can devote himself to God from very childhood. The girl is pure like a flower. Gaurdasi has moulded her character nicely. Her brothers tried their utmost to arrange for her marriage, but Gaurdasi took her from place to place and concealed her. At last she took her to Puri and made her exchange garlands with Jagannath and made her a nun. That is to say, she was married to Jagannath, the Lord of the Universe. Thenceforth she has been leading the life of a nun. Such a nice, pure girl! She has been well-educated. I have heard that she is preparing herself for a Sanskrit examination. I also heard from her many incidents of Gauri-Ma's early years and thus came to know that she also had to pass through a stormy life."

A little later four or five women devotees came. They offered the Holy Mother green cocoanuts and some other fruits. One of them was about to approach and touch her feet. The Mother said, "Please salute me from a distance." They offered her a few coins. She forbade them to do so. They then wanted some spiritual instruction. The Mother replied with a smile, "What shall I instruct you about? The words of Sri Ramakrishna have been recorded in books. If you can follow even one of his instructions, you will attain to everything in life." After they had taken leave, the Holy Mother said, "Where is that competent student who can understand spiritual instruction? First of all, one should be fit; otherwise, the instructions prove futile."

Annapurna's mother entered the room and said. "Mother, I saw you in a dream asking me to take your Prasada, which would cure me of my disease. But Sri Ramakrishna had forbidden me to eat the Prasada of anybody. Still I shall be glad if you will kindly give me a little of your Prasada." The Mother refused to do so, but the woman began to insist upon it.

Mother: Do you want to disobey Sri Ramakrishna?

A.'s Mother: Sri Ramakrishna's words were applicable so long as I made a distinction between him and you. But I now realize both of you to be identical. So please give me your Prasada.

The Mother had to yield. A little later we took leave of her.

Another day when I went to see the Holy Mother, she inquired about my husband. I said that he was not in very good health. She asked me to write a letter for her. She dictated it. After the noonday meal, the Mother had been resting for a while when a few women devotees came to her room. When the greetings were over, one of them said, "I have a nice goat. She gives four pounds of milk daily. I also keep three birds. I spend my time with these. I am now pretty old." I was reminded of the words of Sri Ramakrishna: "Mahamaya, the supreme power of cosmic illusion, makes us bring up a cat and thus forget God. This is how this world is going on." The Holy Mother simply nodded to the words of these devotees. Alas, what a great agony she had to bear for our sake! We did not allow her even to enjoy a little rest. We disturbed her with mere idle gossip. I took leave of her in the evening.

I went to see the Holy Mother again after many days. She had gone back to her country home on 26th February, and had returned to Calcutta in September, 1913, a few days before the Durga Puja. I visited her one afternoon and found a woman kneeling near her feet and begging with tears for initiation. The Mother was seated on her bedstead. She refused to comply with her prayer and said, "I have already told you that I would not be able to initiate you now. I am not well." The woman was insistent. The Mother felt annoyed and said, "You think only of yourselves. You are perfectly satisfied if you get the sacred Mantra. But you never think of the consequence." But the woman was inexorable. All of us felt disgusted. The Holy Mother at last asked her to come another day. Then the woman requested her to ask one of the monks to give her initiation.

Mother: Suppose they refuse?

Woman: What do you mean, Mother? They must obey you.

Mother: In this matter they may refuse to comply with my request.

Finding the woman unrelenting, the Mother said, "Well, I shall ask Khoka (Swami Subodananda.) He will initiate you." But the woman started insisting again and said, "I shall be happy to be initiated by you. You can certainly fulfil my desire if you like." She brought out ten rupees and said, "Here is some money. You may purchase the necessary articles for initiation." We all felt mortified at her impudence. At last the Mother was angry and said severely, "What? Do you mean to tempt me with money? You cannot coax me with these coins. Take them back." The Holy Mother immediately left the room. Being hard pressed by the woman, the Holy Mother at last agreed to initiate her on the sacred Mahashtami day. She soon took leave of us. The Mother now found some leisure to talk to me.

I came to see the Mother after two months and a half. She cried, "Oh! It is almost an age since I have seen you!" In the course of the talk I asked her about the woman whom she had consented to initiate.

Mother: She could not come here on the appointed day. I had said to her, "I am now ill. Let me be well and then I shall initiate you." My words came to be true. She could not come on the Mahashtami day as she herself fell ill. She came here many days later and was initiated.

Devotee: That is right. The words that are once uttered by you cannot but be fulfilled. We suffer as we go counter to your wishes. Many a time, you condescend to initiate people even while you are ill, and thus suffer all the more by transferring their sufferings to yourself.

Mother: Yes, my dear child. Sri Ramakrishna also used to say, "Otherwise why should this body have suffered at all?" The other day I was ill with an attack of diarrhoea.

My sister-in-law was with me. Referring to her, the Mother said, "A very nice and quiet girl. There is only one dish of vegetable. If that be not palatable, then the whole dinner is spoiled." She meant that I had only one sister-in-law in the family. My life could have been made unhappy if she had not been good to me.

February, 1914

I went to Baghbazar one morning with a basket of flowers. I offered it to the Holy Mother. She was exceedingly happy and began to decorate the image of Sri Ramakrishna with the flowers. Some of them were blue. She took these in her hands and said, "Ah, what a pretty colour! There was a girl at Dakshineswar named Asha. One day, she came to the temple-garden and picked a red flower from a plant with dark leaves. She cried, 'Dear me! Such a red flower on a plant with dark leaves! Goodness gracious! What a strange creation of God!' Sri Ramakrishna saw her and said, 'My dear child, what is the matter with you? Why are you weeping like that?' She could hardly utter a word. She was weeping incessantly. Sri Ramakrishna at last pacified her."

The Holy Mother was in an exalted mood and said, "Look at these flowers with a blue colour! How can one decorate God without such fine flowers!" She took a handful of them and offered them to the image of Sri Ramakrishna. A few flowers dropped at her feet before they were offered. She cried, "Dear me! How they have dropped at my feet before I could offer them to the Lord!" "It is very nice," I said. Then I thought, "To you Sri Ramakrishna may be a higher being; but we do not make any distinction between you and him."

A widowed lady came into the room. I asked the Mother about her. The Mother said, "She took initiation from me about a month ago. She had accepted another Guru before. She later felt that it was a mistake and came here for initiation. I could not convince her that all teachers are one. The same power of God works through them all."

We were resting after the midday meal and the talk turned to Kamarpukur. The Holy Mother said: "While I was quite young, the Master once came to Kamarpukur with stomach trouble. During the early hours of the morning he would wake up from sleep and tell us about the dishes I should prepare for his midday meal. I would follow his directions. One day I found that I had not a particular spice with which he wanted the vegetables flavoured. My sister-in-law (Sri Ramakrishna's elder brother's wife) asked me to cook without that spice. The Master heard those words and said, 'How is it? If you have not the spice, get it from the market. It is not proper to cook the curry without the spices necessary for it. I sacrificed the rich dishes of Dakshineswar temple and came here for the flavour of that spice, and you want to deprive me of that! That won't do.' My sister-in-law felt abashed and sent for the spice.

"The Brahmani (i.e. Yogesvari, the Sannyasini who instructed Sri Ramakrishna in Tantric practices) was then with us. The Master addressed her as mother, and I therefore looked upon her as my mother-in-law. I was rather afraid of her. She was very fond of red pepper. She used to cook her own dishes—all hot stuff. Often she offered me these preparations. I would silently eat them and wipe out the tears from my eyes. When she asked me how I liked them, I said in fear, 'Very nice!' My sister-in-law, however, would remark, 'Oh! they were very hot!' I noticed that the Brahmani was displeased at such remarks. She would say, 'Why do you say so? My 'daughter' approves of these dishes. Nothing can please you. I will not give you my curries any more."

The conversation again turned to flowers. The Mother said, "One day while living at Dakshineswar, I made a big garland of seven strands with some jasmine and *rangam* (Ixora). I soaked the garland in water in a stone bowl and quickly the buds turned into full blossoms. I sent the garland to the Kali temple to adorn the image of the Divine Mother. The ornaments were taken off from the body of Kali and She was decorated with the garland. Sri Ramakrishna came to the temple. He at once fell into an ecstatic mood to see the beauty of Kali so much enhanced by the flowers. Again and again he said, 'Ah! These flowers are so nicely set off against the dark complexion of the Divine Mother! Who made the garland?' Someone mentioned me. He said, 'Go and bring her to the temple.' As I came near the steps, I found some of the men devotees there—Balaram Babu, Suren Babu and others. I felt extremely bashful and became anxious to hide myself. I took shelter behind the maid, Brinde, and was about to go up the temple by the back steps. Sri Ramakrishna noticed this instantly and said, 'Don't try those steps. The other day a fisherwoman was climbing those steps and slipped. She had a terrible shock, fractured her bones and died. Come by these front steps.' The devotees heard those words and made way for me. I entered the temple and found Sri Ramakrishna singing, his voice trembling with love and emotion."

A few women devotees now entered the room and the conversation stopped. It was time for me to take leave. Again the Mother began to talk about God-realization. She said, "Do you know, my child, what it is like? It is just like a candy in the hand of a child. Some people beg the child to part with it. He does not care to give it to them. But he easily hands it over to another whom he likes. A man performs severe austerities throughout his life to realize God, but he does not succeed, whereas another man gets realization practically without any effort. It depends upon the grace of God. He bestows His grace upon anyone He likes. Grace is the important thing."

May 1914

That day the Holy Mother was coming to our Ballyganj home. All the necessary arrangements had been made from the previous day. A separate seat, a new set of white marble vessels, etc., had been purchased for her use. The whole night I couldn't sleep for joy at the thought of the Mother's coming. She was to come only by noon, but under the impression that her arrival was to be earlier, Sri Shokaharan had gone to her Baghbazar house early in the morning and was waiting there with the carriage. We also finished our household duties early and were ready to receive her. I spread the Holy Mother's seat, decorated all-around with flowers, sprinkled Ganges water all over the house, and made a garland of flowers. On either side of her seat two large bouquets spread their fragrance.

As the time of her arrival neared, we were on the lookout, in eager expectation. At last the blessed moment arrived. Hearing the sound of the carriage, we all went downstairs. As the carriage stopped, I beheld the Holy Mother's smiling face casting a compassionate glance on us. When she got down every one crowded round to take the dust of her feet. Seeing us all, her eyes were filled with tears of love.

Golap-Ma, the youngest aunt, Nalini-Didi Radhu and a few monks came with her. We led her upstairs, and after seating her, bowed down at her feet. The Mother said affectionately, "Have you all finished your meal?" With these words, she touched my chin endearingly. Till now I was too busy with the arrangements for the visit to think of meals or anything else. I now hurried downstairs to arrange for lunch.

Upstairs the gramophone was playing. Finding a little respite from work, I went up. Listening to the music of the machine, the Holy Mother was immensely pleased. "What a wonderful machine is this!" she said, bubbling with joy like a small girl. It was very hot. The Mother was reclining in the verandah on a mat. Near her all others were seated. In a stone pot iced water was kept, which the Holy Mother sipped now and then. Seeing me, she called, "Hullo, take a little ice water." I drank some as her Prasad and went to the kitchen.

After dusk, the offering to the Master was arranged in the next room. The Holy Mother came and asked Golap-Ma to make the offering but she declined. "You do it please. When you are here, why should I?" she said. So the Holy Mother sat down to make the offering. "How beautifully has everything been arranged!" she remarked. She was all praise for everything she saw and made us all immensely happy. Offering was over, and the Mother and the rest sat down to partake of the Prasad. The Holy Mother finished her meal first. She sat in an easy chair in the verandah and called to me, "Hullo, give me a betel roll." I was yet busy serving Golap-

Ma. Quickly I took a betel roll to her. Ashamed that she had to ask for the roll, I said to Sumati, "Could you not wait near the door with a betel roll? You saw how busy I was." A little later the Holy Mother came down. Taking a lamp, I also went with her.

It was time for departure. The Mother did not like to travel by car, as once a dog was crushed under her vehicle. But the distance was long and unless a car was used, she would reach her destination very late. So the Mother agreed to the devotees' request to use a car. She got ready, after making repeated Pranams to the Master. Blessing us all, she got into the vehicle.

* * * *

I saw the Mother one night. She was lying on her bed. Another woman was near her. She at once sat up in bed so that I might bow before her. In the course of conversation she said, "At the time of creation, people were born with the quality of Sattva, light. They had wisdom from their very birth. Consequently they at once realized the unreal nature of the world. They renounced it and practised austerity. They were liberated in no time. The Creator found that the purpose of His creation was going to be frustrated. These wise men, who were thus liberated, were unfit for the continuance of the play of the world. Then He again started the work of creation and mixed the qualities of Rajas (activity) and Tamas (inertia) with the Sattva. Thus His purpose was fulfilled." Then she cited a popular verse bearing on the theme of creation, and said, "In our young age we acquired these ideas from the country dramas. But now these have become rare."

Some of the young girls, relatives of the Holy Mother, were reading loudly from a book in another room. The Mother said, "Listen, how loudly they are reading! They have forgotten that there are many people on the ground floor."

Radhu's mother, the insane sister-in-law of the Holy Mother, entered the room and said, "Lakshmi-mani (Sri Ramakrishna's niece) is going to Navadvip on a pilgrimage. I wanted to go with her. But you have stood in my way." She left the room in a pique. The Mother said, "How can I allow her to go with Lakshmi? Lakshmi is a devotee. She would sing and dance with other devotees. She would not observe the distinction of caste and would dine with others. But Radhu's mother would not understand this. She hardly knows that the devotees need not observe caste rules among themselves. So she would come back and criticize the conduct of

Lakshmi before others. Have you met Lakshmi?"

Devotee: No, Mother.

Mother: She is in Dakshineswar. Visit her one day. Have you been to Dakshineswar?

Devotee: Yes, Mother, I have visited the place many a time. But I did not know that she had been living there.

Mother: Have you seen the Nahabat at Dakshineswar, where I used to stay?

Devotee: Yes, Mother, I have seen it from the outside.

Mother: When you visit the place another day, go inside the room. When I stayed there, my entire world consisted of that small room. Even the vessel containing fish was hung up. I had never seen water taps before. I came to Calcutta one day and entered a room where there was a tap. I opened the tap. Before the water rushed out, there came a hissing sound, like that of a snake, out of the tap. I was terror-stricken and ran from the room. I at once came to the other ladies of the house and cried, "There is a snake in that water pipe. It is hissing." They laughed and said, "There is no snake there. Do not be afraid. The hissing sound comes from the air being forced out by the rushing water." Then we laughed and laughed till our sides began to ache.

Saying this, the Holy Mother laughed heartily again. So sweet and innocent a laughter! I too could not hold back my laughter any more and thought, "So guileless is our Mother!"

Mother: Have you seen Sri Ramakrishna's birthday festival at Belur?

Devotee: No, Mother. I have never been to the monastery at Belur. I have heard that the monks who live there do not like a crowd of women in the monastery. Therefore I hesitate to go there.

Mother: Go there once and see the celebration of Sri Ramakrishna's birthday.

* * * *

It was evening when I went to Baghbazar to see the Holy Mother. She was kind enough to ask me to spread her small carpet on the floor and fetch her beads. She soon became absorbed in her meditation. Across the lane there was an open space. A few labourers lived there with their families. One of the male members began to beat a woman severely, probably his wife. Slaps and fisticuffs began to be showered upon her. Then he kicked her with such force that she was thrown to a distance with a child in her arms.

Then he started kicking her again. The Mother could not proceed with her meditation any more. Though she was extremely modest and would not usually talk even loud enough to be heard by people on the ground floor, she now came to the porch of the second floor, stood by the iron railing, and cried aloud in a tone of sharp reprimand, "You rogue! Are you going to kill the girl outright? I am afraid she is already dead!" Hardly had the man looked at her than he became quiet like the snake before its charmer, and released the woman. The sympathy of the Mother made the woman burst into loud sobs. We heard that her only fault was that she had not cooked in time. Afterwards the man became his old self again and wanted to be at peace with the woman. The Holy Mother saw this and came back to her room.

Some time later, the voice of a beggar was heard in the lane. He was crying, "Radha-Govinda! Glory unto God! Please be kind to the blind." The Mother said, "This beggar passes yonder lane almost every night. At first he would cry, 'Please be kind to the poor blind.' But Golap one day rightly said to him, 'Please utter that name, Radha-Krishna—the name of God. This will serve the double purpose of uttering the holy name and also of reminding the householders of God. Otherwise you will, day and night, think of your blindness alone.' Since then, the blind man, while passing through this lane, takes the name of God. Golap gave him a piece of cloth. He also gets alms in other forms."

* * * *

I went to Baghbazar one evening and heard the Holy Mother saying, "New devotees should be given the privilege of service in the shrine room. Their new zeal makes them serve the Lord carefully. The others are tired of service. Service, in the real sense of the word, is not a joke. One should be extremely careful about making His service perfectly flawless. But the truth is, God knows our foolishness and therefore He forgives us." One woman devotee was near her. I do not know if these words were directed towards her. The Mother was asking her to be careful in picking the right kind of flowers and in making sandal paste for the purpose of worship, as also in not touching any part of the body, cloth or hair while working in the shrine. "One must work in the shrine room with great attention," said she, "Offerings and the rest should be made the proper time."

* * * *

It was half-past eight in the evening when I came to the place of the Holy Mother. She was absorbed in meditation in the porch to the north of the shrine room. We waited for a while in another room. The Mother came there and said with a smile, "I am glad to see you, my child."

Devotee: I have brought my sister with me, Mother. Is Aratrika[1] (the evening service) over?

Mother: No. You may witness it now. I shall join you presently.

The evening service soon commenced. Many ladies sat in the shrine room and began to pray. After the worship was over, we prostrated before the image and came to the adjacent room to meet the Holy Mother. While we were at her place, we were unwilling to lose sight of her even for a moment.

A few minutes later, the Mother came to the room. An old lady was learning a devotional song from another. The Mother said, "I am afraid she may not be able to teach the song correctly. Ah, what a great singer the Master was! His voice was so sweet. While singing he would be one with his song. His voice is still ringing in my ears. When I remember it, other voices appear so flat. But Naren also had a melodious voice. Before leaving this city he came to see me and sang a few songs. While taking leave of me he said, 'Mother, if I can return as a man in the true sense of the term, I shall see you again; otherwise good-bye!' 'What do you mean, my child?' I cried. 'Well,' he replied, 'I shall soon come back through your grace.' Girish Babu also had a sweet voice."

Radhu came to the room and requested the Mother to lie down by her. She said, "You go and lie on the bed. These devotees have come from a distance. I should like to sit with them for a while." Radhu still insisted. I said, "Let us also go to your bedroom. You may lie there on your bed." The Mother asked us to follow her. The Mother lay on her bed and began to talk to us about various things. I was fanning her. She said after a few minutes, "It is now cool. Please do not take any more trouble." I rubbed her feet. An old lady was explaining to another about the six centres as described in Yoga. Golap-Ma forbade her to do so. But still she continued. The Mother heard her words and said to me with a smile, "Sri Ramakrishna with his own hands drew for me the pic-

[1] A form of worship in which the most important item is the waving of light and incense before the image.

ture of Kundalini and the six Yogic centres." I asked her if she still had the picture with her. The Mother replied, "No, my child. I had then no idea of the devotees coming to us. I have lost the paper."

It was eleven o'clock at night. We prostrated before her and took leave of her. The Mother sat on her bed and blessed us. She called me aside and said, "Spiritual progress becomes easier if husband and wife agree in their views regarding spiritual practices."

October-November, 1914

We had plenty of flowers at our Ballygunj home. The Holy Mother was always pleased with flowers. One day I gathered a large quantity of them and came to see her. I found her just ready for the worship. I arranged the flowers, and she sat on the carpet before the image. I forgot to keep aside some flowers for worshipping the feet of the Holy Mother. So I was sorry to think that it would not be possible for me to worship her that day. But I soon found out that she had anticipated my secret desire. She herself had separated some flowers on the tray. After the worship was over, she said to me, "Now, my dear child, I have kept those flowers in the tray for you. Bring them here." Just then a devotee came to see the Mother with a large quantity of fruits. She was very pleased to see him. She put a mark of sandal paste on his forehead and stroked him by touching the chin. I had never seen her express her affection for any man devotee in such a manner. Next she asked me to hand over a few flowers to him. He accepted them. I found his whole body trembling with devotional fervour. With great joy he offered those flowers at her feet and left after accepting the Prasada. She sat on the cot and invited me very tenderly to come to her. I worshipped her feet. With great love, she placed her hand on my head and kissed me. I was deeply touched by her blessings.

After a while I found her on the roof drying her hair. She invited me to come near her and said, "Take off the cloth from your head and dry your hair, otherwise it may affect your health." Golap-Ma came to the roof and requested the Mother to make an offering of food in the shrine room. The Mother came down from the roof. I also followed her after a while to the shrine room. Like a bashful young bride, she was saying to Sri Ramakrishna in a soft voice, "Come now; your meal is ready." Then she came to the image of Gopala and said, "O my Gopala, come for your meal." I was just behind her. Suddenly she looked at me and said with a smile, "I am inviting them all to their noonday meal." With these words, the Holy Mother entered the room where the food was offered. Her earnestness and devotion made me feel that the Deities, as it were, listened to her words and followed her to the offering room. I was pinned to the ground with wonder!

After the offering was over, we all sat together for our meal. Then the Mother asked me to rest for a while. A man came with a basket of fruits. The fruits were meant for offering. He asked the monks what he should do with the basket. They told him to throw it out in the lane. The Mother got up and went to the porch. She looked at the lane and said to me, "Look there. They have asked him to throw away such a nice basket! It does not matter for them in the least. They are all monks and totally unattached. But we cannot allow such a waste. We could have utilized the basket at least for keeping the peelings of the vegetables." She asked someone to fetch the basket and wash it. The basket was kept for some future use. I learnt a lesson from her words. But we are so slow to learn.

After some time a beggar came to the house and shouted for some alms. The monks felt annoyed and said rudely, "Go away now. Don't disturb us." At these words the Holy Mother said, "Did you hear their remarks? They have driven away the poor man. They could not shake off their idleness and give something to the beggar. He only wanted a handful of rice. And they could not take the trouble to do this bit of work. Is it proper to deprive a man of what is his due? Even to the cow we owe these peelings of the vegetables. We should hold these near her mouth."

Year 1917

I went to see the Holy Mother in the evening. I had been residing at our Baghbazar house at that time and I visited her almost every day. Finding her alone I narrated to her a dream and said, "Mother, one night I saw Sri Ramakrishna in a dream. You had been living then at Jayrambati. I saluted him and asked, 'Where is the Mother?' He said, 'Follow that lane and you will find a thatched cottage. She is seated in the front porch.' " The Holy Mother was on her bed. With great enthusiasm she sat up and said, "You are quite right. Your dream is true." "Is it, then, true?" I said in surprise, "I had the idea that your home at Jayrambati is a brick building. But in the dream I saw the earthen floor, thatched roof, etc., and therefore concluded that it was all illusory."

In the course of conversation regarding austerity for the realization of God, she said, "Golap-Ma and Yogin-Ma devoted a great deal of their time to meditation and the repetition of God's name. Yogin-Ma practised the greatest austerities. At one time she lived only on milk and fruits. Even now she spends much of her time in spiritual practices. The mind of Golap-Ma is hardly affected by external things. She does not even hesitate to eat cooked vegetables purchased from the market, which a Brahmin widow would never touch."

It was arranged to have devotional songs on the Goddess Kali sung that evening at the house of the Holy Mother. The monks of the Belur Math would take part in it. The music commenced at half-past eight in the evening. Many of the women devotees sat on the verandah to hear the music. I was rubbing oil on the Mother's feet and could hear the songs from the room. I had heard them many a time before. But that day those songs, coming from the mouth of the devotees, had a novel charm. They were full of power and thrill. My eyes became moist. They were singing now and then those songs which Sri Ramakrishna had himself sung. At such times the Holy Mother would cry out with enthusiasm, "Yes, Sri Ramakrishna would sing this song!" They commenced the song whose first line runs thus: "The bee of my mind has become fascinated with the blue lotus of the Divine Mother's feet!" The Holy Mother could not lie down any more. A few tear-drops trickled down her cheeks. She said, "Come, darling. Let us go to the verandah." After the singing was over, I saluted the Mother and returned home.

22nd July, 1918

It was half past seven in the evening when I arrived at the house of the Holy Mother. Only two months back she had returned from her village home, emaciated by a protracted attack of malaria. She greeted me with her usual smile and said, "It is a very warm day. Take a little rest and refresh yourself. What about your sister? Has she reached home?"

Devotee: Yes, Mother. I started after she had reached home.

Mother: Take this fan from Radhu, and rub this medicated oil on my back. There are heat-blisters all over my body.

As I started rubbing the oil, the bell rang for evening worship. The Holy Mother sat on her bed and saluted God with folded hands. Other devotees went to the shrine room to witness the worship.

The Mother said, "Everybody says regretfully, 'There is so much misery in the world. We have prayed so much to God, but still there is no end of misery.' But misery is only the gift of God. It is the symbol of His compassion."

That day my mind had been greatly troubled. Did she really know it and therefore address those words to me? The Mother continued, "Who has not suffered from misery in this world? Brinde, the woman devotee of Krishna, said to him, 'Who says that you are compassionate? In your incarnation as Rama you made Sita weep for you all through her life. And in this incarnation of Krishna, Radha has been weeping on your account. Your parents suffered extreme agony in the prison of Kamsa and cried day and night uttering your name. Then why do I repeat your name? It is because your name removes all fear of death.' "

Referring to a woman, the Holy Mother said, "People of that appearance are generally devoid of Bhakti, devotion to God. I have heard it from Sri Ramakrishna."

Devotee : Yes, Mother, I have read in the *Kathamrita*[1] that he used to say that people who are not frank cannot make real spiritual progress.

Mother: Oh, you are referring to that. He said those words in the house of a devotee named Narayana. A man had a mistress. She once came to Sri Ramakrishna and said with repentance, "That man ruined me. Then he robbed me of my money and jewels." Sri Ramakrishna was aware of the innermost contents of people's minds. But still he would like to hear about things from their own mouth. He said to that woman, " Is it true? But he used to give us tall talks about devotion." Then he described those traits which stand in the way of spirituality. In the end the woman confessed to him all her sins and was thus released from their evil effects.

Nalini: How is it possible, Mother? How can one be absolved from sin by simply expressing it in words? Is it possible to wash

---

[1] A book on Sri Ramakrishna's teachings in Bengali. Its English translation is known as the *Gospel of Sri Ramakrishna.*

away sin in this manner?

Mother: Why not, my dear child? Sri Ramakrishna was a perfect soul. Certainly one can be free from sin by confessing it to one like him. And one thing more, if at a certain place people talk of virtue and vice, those present there must take a share of those qualities.

Nalini: How is this possible?

Mother: Let me explain. Imagine a man confessed to you his virtue or vice. Whenever you think of that man you will remember his virtuous or sinful acts. And they will thus leave an impression upon your mind. Is it not true, my child?

Again the talk turned to human misery, affliction and worry. The Mother said, "Many people come to me and confide their worries. They say, 'We have not realized God. How can we attain to peace?' Thereupon the thought would flash in my mind: 'Why do they say so? Am I then a superhuman being? I never knew what worry was. And the vision of God,—it lies, as it were in the palm of my hand. Whenever I like it, I can have it.' "

I had read of the Holy Mother's dacoit father. Wishing to hear of it from her, I said: "Mother, I read about an episode in the book. You were once coming to Dakshineswar. Lakshmi-Didi and others were with you. You could not walk as fast as they. Seeing that night was approaching, you told them to go ahead and you were lagging far behind. At this time you met those who have come to be known as your dacoit father and mother."

Mother: It is not true that I was altogether alone. There were two other old women.[1] The three of us fell behind. Then seeing that man with silver wrist bands, shaggy hair, dark complexion, and a long stick in hand, I was terribly frightened. In those days dacoities used to take place in that area. The man understood that we were frightened and asked, "Hullo, where are you going?" I said, "To the east." The man responded, saying, "This is not the road, your path lies that way." Seeing that I did not proceed even then, he said, "Don't be afraid. There is a woman with me. She has fallen behind." Then I called him 'father' and took refuge in him. Was I like this in those days? How strong

[1] It is true that there were two other women with the Mother at the beginning. But the more accepted version says that when she was actually confronted by the dacoit, she was alone.

I was! I walked for three days at a stretch. I had walked around Brindavan and never felt tired.

Later the Holy Mother said: "Did you see the Nahabat at Dakshineswar? I used to stay there. The room was so low that at first I would knock my head against the upper frame of the door. One day, I got a cut on the head. Then I became accustomed to it. The head bent of itself as soon as I approached the door. Many stout aristocratic women of Calcutta frequently came there. They never entered the room. They would stand at the door and lean forward holding the jambs. And peeping in they would remark, addressing me, 'Ah, what a tiny room for our good girl! She is, as it were, in exile, like Sita.'" Turning to her nieces she continued, "You won't be able to stay in such a room even for a day." "True, aunt!" they ejaculated, "everything is different with you."

Devotee: I read in Gurudas Burman's book that finally they built at Dakshineswar a thatched house for you. The Master came there once, and because of heavy rain could not return to his own room.

Mother: What thatched house! It was just a small shed. All that is properly written in Sarat's book.[1] M's book also is good. He has recorded the Master's own words. What sweet words! I heard that there is so much material that there could be four or five parts more. He has now become old, would he be able to do all that? Selling the book, he seems to have got much money. I heard that he has kept aside all that money. For my house at Jayrambati, he gave nearly a thousand rupees (for the house Rs. 400 and for expenses Rs. 500). And every month he gives me ten rupees. If I stay here sometimes he gives twenty or twenty-five rupees. Earlier, when he was working as a teacher he used to give monthly two rupees.

Devotee: Is it Girish Babu who gave much money to the Math?

Mother: Not a large amount. It is Suresh (Surendra Nath) Mitra who gave regularly. But Girish, too, did give something. And he bore all my expenses at Nilamber Babu's house for a year and

---

[1] *Sri Sri Ramakrishna Lila-prasanga*, (Bengali) the authentic study of the life of Sri Ramakrishna; translated in English as 'Sri Ramakrishna the Great Master.'

a half. He has not given any large sum to the Math. And wherefrom could he give? He never had so much money. Earlier he was a wretch and used to move in bad company, running a theatre. He was a man of great faith and so obtained the Master's grace. The Master gave him salvation. In each Incarnation He liberates one wretch, like Jagai and Madhai in the Incarnation of Sri Chaitanya. The Master once said this also, that Girish was an aspect of Siva. What is there in money, my dear? The Master could not even touch money. His hand used to curl back when any metal contacted him. He used to say, "The world is an illusion. Ah, Ramlal, if I felt that the world was real, I would have covered your Kamarpukur with gold. But I know that it is all illusion. God alone is real."

Maku, her niece, said sorrowfully, "I could not settle myself at one place!" The Mother replied, "How is that? Wherever you live, you must feel quite at home. You think that you will be happy at your husband's place. How is that possible? He gets a small salary. How can you manage with such a pittance? You are staying with me. It is just like your father's place. Married girls sometimes live with their parents, don't they? Can't you practise renunciation a little?"

I requested the Mother to tell me something more about Sri Ramakrishna. "What the books say is not always correct", Mother said, "Ram's[1] book does not give a correct description of the *Shodasi Puja,* when the Master worshipped me."

She described the incident and said, "It was not at home, it was at Dakshineswar, in the Master's room, near the circular verandah, where the huge pitcher of Ganga water now stands. Hriday had made all the arrangements."

Yogin-Ma was then standing by the window, and was about to say something. The Mother said, "Come in. I seldom see you nowadays." Yogin-Ma laughed and entered the room. Her foot touched my body. As she was about to salute me with folded hands, I interrupted her and prostrated myself before her. "What is this, Yogin-Ma?" said I, "I am not even fit to take the dust of your feet. Why should you salute me if your foot touched my body?" In reply Yogin-Ma said, "Why not? A snake, whether big or small, is a snake all

---

[1] Ramachandra Datta, a householder disciple of Sri Ramakrishna.

the same. You are all devotees and therefore worthy of our respect." I looked at the Mother. The same compassionate smile lit her face. I took leave of her late at night.

28th July, 1918

It was evening when I visited the Holy Mother at her Baghbazar home. Just before evening service an elderly widow came and saluted the Mother by placing her head on the feet of the Mother. The Mother was greatly annoyed and said, "Why do you touch the feet with the head? I am not doing well at all. This sort of thing makes me worse." The Holy Mother washed her feet after the widow had left the place.

Later, while I was rubbing the Mother's body with medicated oil, the conversation drifted to Lalit Babu, a great householder devotee. I said, "He was at one time fatally ill. But I heard that he recovered through your grace."

Mother: He had many unfulfilled desires. He was very seriously ill with dropsy and was on the point of death. He said to me in a very plaintive voice. "Mother, I have a great desire to build temples and hospitals at Kamarpukur and Jayrambati. But this great desire is not going to be fulfilled." Ah, Sri Ramakrishna saved his life that time. Now he wants to carry out his plans. Let him try. He has bought a tank for me.

30th July, 1918

Swami Premananda, a disciple of Sri Ramakrishna, passed away in the evening. I went to see the Mother at dusk. The Mother said, "Come in, my child. Take your seat. Today my Baburam (Swami Premananda) has passed away. I have been weeping since morning." She again burst into tears. Continuing she said, "Baburam was dearest to my heart. The strength, devotion, rationality and all the great virtues were embodied in him. He was the very light of the Belur Math. His mother came from a family without any male heirs. So she inherited her father's property. She became a little proud of it. She herself confessed it to me and said, 'I had some gold ornaments and I thought of the world as a mere mud-puddle.' She left behind four children. The fifth one she lost before her own death."

After a while I saw the Holy Mother placing her head at the feet of the picture of Sri Ramakrishna hung on the southern wall of the room and uttering in a heart-rending voice, "Lord, you have taken away my Baburam!" I could hardly restrain my tears.

Golap-Ma was also seriously ill with blood dysentery. She was almost on her death-bed.

31*st July*, 1918

It was half past seven in the evening. The Holy Mother was seated in the shrine room. This day, too, her conversation turned on the late Swami Premananda. She said, "My child, in the body of Baburam there was neither flesh nor blood after his last illness. It was a mere skeleton." Chandra Babu came to the room and joined in our talk. He told the Mother that some devotees gave sandal-wood, butter, flowers, incense, etc., worth four or five hundred rupees for the cremation of the Swami's body. The Mother remarked, "Their money is, indeed, blessed. They have spent it for a devotee of God. God has given them abundantly and will give them more." Chandra Babu left the room.

"Listen, my child," she continued, "however spiritual a man may be, he must pay the tax for the use of the body to the last farthing.[1] But the difference between a great soul and an ordinary man is this: The latter weeps while leaving this body, whereas the former laughs. Death seems to him a mere play.

"Ah, my dear Baburam came to Sri Ramakrishna while he was a mere boy. Sri Ramakrishna used to make great fun with the boys. Naren (Swami Vivekananda) and Baburam would roll on the ground with side-splitting laughter. While living in the Cossipore garden, I was once climbing the steps, carrying a pitcher with five pounds of milk. I felt giddy and the milk spilt on the ground. My heels were dislocated. Naren and Baburam came running there and took care of me. There was a great inflammation of the feet. Sri Ramakrishna heard of the accident and said to Baburam, 'Well, Baburam, it is a nice mess I am now in. Who will cook my food? Who will feed me now?' He was then ill with cancer in the throat and lived only on farina pudding. I used to make it and feed him in his room in the upper storey of the house. I had, then, a ring on my nose. Sri Ramakrishna touched his nose and made the sign of the ring by describing a circle with his finger, in order to

[1] *i.e.,* undergo suffering and death incidental to the embodied state.

indicate me. He then said, 'Baburam, can you put her (making the sign) in a basket and carry her on your shoulder to this room?' Naren and Baburam were convulsed with side-splitting laughter. Thus he used to cut jokes with them. After three days the swelling subsided. Then they helped me to go upstairs with his meals.

"Baburam used to tell his mother, ' How little you love me! Do you love me as Sri Ramakrishna does?' 'How foolish!' she would reply, 'I am your mother, and I do not love you! What do you mean?' Such was the depth of Sri Ramakrishna's love. While four years old, Baburam would say, 'I will not marry, or else I will die.' When Sri Ramakrishna was suffering from cancer in the throat and could not swallow his food, he said one day, 'I shall eat later on in my subtle body through a million mouths.' Baburam, replying, said 'I do not care for your million mouths or your subtle body. What I want is that you should eat through this mouth and that I should see this gross body.' "

Golap-Ma had been suffering from an attack of blood dysentery. She was slightly better today. The doctor observed that it would take three months to be cured completely. The Holy Mother said, "Blood dysentery is not a simple disease. Sri Ramakrishna would often be down with that disease. It happened frequently during the rainy season. At one time he was rather seriously ill. I used to attend on him. A woman from Banaras had come to Dakshineswar. She suggested a remedy. I followed her directions and the Master was soon cured. The woman could not be seen any more. I never met her again. She had really helped me a great deal. I inquired about her at Banaras but could not find her. We have often seen that whenever Sri Ramakrishna felt the need, people would come of themselves to Dakshineswar and then disappear just as suddenly.

"I also suffered from dysentery, my child. The body became a mere skeleton. I would lay myself down near the tank. One day I saw my reflection in the water and noticed that all that remained of my body was only a few bones. I thought, 'Dear me! What is the use of this body? Let me give it up. Let me leave it here.' A woman came and said, ' Hallo, Mother! Why are you here? Come, let us go home.' She took me home."

Late at night, I took leave of the Holy Mother.

1st August, 1918

Today I found the Mother alone and therefore had a long talk with her. Our conversation drifted mainly to the monastic disciples of Sri Ramakrishna. Perhaps, on account of the passing away of Swami Premananda, the Mother had been continually thinking of these monks. Referring to them, the Holy Mother said, "Sri Ramakrishna accepted his disciples only after thoroughly examining them. What an austere life they led at the Baranagore monastery after his passing away! Niranjan (Swami Niranjanananda) and others often starved themselves. They spent all their time in meditation and prayer. One day these young monks were talking among themselves: 'We have renounced everything in the name of Sri Ramakrishna. Let us see if he would supply us with food if we simply depend upon him. We will not tell anybody about our wants. We will not go out for alms!' They covered their bodies with sheets of cloth and sat down for meditation. The whole day passed. It was late at night. They heard somebody knocking at the door. Naren left the seat and asked one of his brother monks, 'Please open the door and see who is there. First of all, notice if he has anything in his hand.' What a miracle! As soon as the door was opened, it was found that a man was standing there. He had brought some delicious food from the temple of Gopala on the bank of the Ganges. They were exceedingly happy and felt convinced of the protecting hand of Sri Ramakrishna. They offered that food to Sri Ramakrishna at that late hour of the night and partook of the Prasada. Such things happened many a time. . . . Now the monks do not experience any such difficulty. Alas! What hardship Naren (Swami Vivekananda) and Baburam (Swami Premananda) passed through! Even my Rakhal (Swami Brahmananda), who is now the President of the Ramakrishna Mission, had to cleanse the pots and kettles, many a day. At one time Naren was travelling as an itinerant monk towards Gaya and Varanasi. He did not get any food for two days and was lying down under a tree. He found a man standing near with delicious food and a jar of water in his hands. The man said, 'Here is the Prasada of Rama. Please accept it.' Naren said, 'You do not know me, my good friend. You have made a mistake. Perhaps you have brought these articles for someone else.' The man said with the utmost humility, 'No, revered sir. I have brought this food solely for you. I was enjoying a little nap at noontime when I saw a man in dream. He said: Get up quickly; a holy man is lying under yonder tree; give him some food. I dismissed the whole thing as a mere dream. Therefore I turned on my side and again fell asleep. Then I again dreamt of the man, who said, giving me a push: I am asking you to get up and still you are sleeping! Carry out my order without any more delay. Then I thought that it was not an illusory dream. It was the command of Rama. Therefore in obedience to His command I brought these articles for you; sir.' Naren realized that it was all due to the grace of Sri Ramakrishna, and cheerfully accepted the food.

"A similar incident happened another day. Naren was travelling in the Himalayas for three days without any food. He was about to faint when a Mussulman Fakir gave him a cucumber. It saved his life that time. After his return from America, Naren was one day addressing a meeting at Almora. He saw that Mussulman seated in a corner. Naren at once went to him, took him by the hand, and made him sit in the centre of the gathering. The audience was surprised. Naren said, 'This gentleman saved my life once.' He then narrated the whole incident. He also gave the Fakir some money. But at first he refused to accept the gift. He said, 'What have I done that you are so anxious to make me a gift?' Naren did not yield and pressed some money into his pocket.

"Naren took me to the Belur Math at the time of the first Durga Puja festival, and through me gave twenty-five rupees to the priest as his fee. They spent fourteen hundred rupees on that auspicious occasion. The place became crowded with people. The monks worked hard. Naren came to me and said, 'Mother, please make me lie down with fever.' No sooner had he said this than he was down with a severe attack of fever. I thought, 'Goodness gracious! What is this? How will he be cured?' 'Do not be anxious, Mother,' said Naren, 'I have myself begged for this fever. My reason is this. These boys are working hard. But if I see the slightest mistake, I shall fly into a rage and abuse them. I may even give them slaps. It will be painful to them as well as to me. Therefore I thought it would be better to lie down with fever for some time.' When the day's function was over, I came to him and said, 'Dear child, the work is over now. Please get up.' Naren said that he was all right and got up from bed.

"Naren brought also his own mother to the Math at the time of the Durga Puja. She roamed from one garden to another and picked chillies, egg-plants, etc. She felt a little proud, thinking that it was all due to her son, Naren. Naren came to her and said, 'What are you doing there? Why do you not go and meet the Holy Mother? You are simply picking up these vegetables. May be, you are thinking that your son has done all this work. No, mother. You are mistaken. It is He who has done all this. Naren is nothing.' Naren meant that the Math was founded through the grace of Sri Ramakrishna. What great devotion! . . . . My Baburam is dead! Alas! who will look after the Durga Puja this year? "

6th August, 1918

When I went to-day to see the Holy Mother, I found her in the porch, absorbed in meditation. Some time after, five or six women devotees came to her to pay their respects. They prostrated themselves before the image of Sri Ramakrishna in the shrine room. The Mother asked them about themselves. Nalini introduced them. One of them had come to Calcutta for treatment. The doctor had diagnosed her trouble as tumour in the abdomen. He had asked her to be operated. She was extremely nervous about the operation. The Holy Mother did not allow any of them to touch her feet. I do not know the reason. They begged her again and again to let them take the dust of her feet. The Mother firmly asked them to bow to her from a distance. They pointed to the sick girl and said, " Please bless her so that she may be cured. May she be able to pay her respects to you again." The Mother answered them, saying, "Bow down before Sri Ramakrishna and pray to Him sincerely. He is everything." The Holy Mother appeared to be restive and said to them. " Good-bye, my children. It is getting late for you."

After they had left, the Mother said, "Please sweep the room and sprinkle it with Ganges water. It is now time for food-offering for the Lord." Her order was at once carried out.

She lay down on the bed and gave me a fan, saying, "My child, please fan me a little. The whole body is burning. My salutations to your Calcutta! People come here and lay before me the catalogue of their sorrows. Again there are others who have committed many sinful acts. There are still others who have procreated twenty-five children! They weep because ten of them are dead! Are they human beings? No! They are veritable beasts. No self-control! No restraint! It is therefore that Sri Ramakrishna used to say, ' One seer of milk mixed with five seers of water! It is so difficult to thicken such milk. My eyes have become swollen by constantly blowing the fire to keep it burning. It is such a hard job to thicken such milk! Where are my sincere children who are ready to renounce everything for God? Let them come to me. Let me talk to them. Otherwise life is so unbearable.' These words are so true. Fan me, dear. People have been streaming here today since four o'clock in the afternoon. I cannot bear the misery of people any more.

" The wife of Balaram also came here today. She is the sister of my Baburam. She wept bitterly for him. She said, 'Is he just an ordinary brother?' True, he was like a god."

14th August, 1918

I found the Holy Mother engaged in conversation with a widow, the sister of Dr. Durgapada Babu. The doctor's sister had become widowed at an early age. There was some trouble regarding the property left by her husband. She could not secure the probate of the will. They were talking about these things, and at last the Holy Mother said to the widow, "As you have no right to sell the property, I would advise you to place it under the care of a good man. A worldly-minded person can never be trusted in money matters. Only a real monk can resist the temptation of money. Please do not worry so much, my child. Let the will of God be done. You have been following the right path. The Lord will never put you to any difficulty. You want to leave now? All right but write now and then, and come again."

After the widow had left, Shyamadas, the Ayurvedic physician, came to see Golap-Ma. The Holy Mother waited a while for him, but when she found that he had left, she lay down on her bed and, looking at me, said, "Now do your duty." I began to rub her body with the medicated oil. The Mother said, "The sister of Girish Ghosh was very fond of me. She would always keep apart for me a little of all the articles of food she cooked at home and send them here. A Brahmana would bring them, and she would sit by me as I ate them. Her love for me was deep. She had been married in an aristocratic family and owned considerable wealth; but her relatives had squandered away the money. Atul, the brother of Girish, started business with five thousand rupees. Besides, she had had to spend a large amount of money for her husband's illness which lasted for a year. In her will she expressed her desire to leave a hundred rupees for me. While alive, she was ashamed to give me this amount. She thought one hundred rupees was too small an amount! After her passing, her brother came here and gave it to me. She had come to see me on the day previous to the Durga Puja. As long as she stayed, she never left me even for a second. I had planned to go to Banaras immediately after the Durga Puja. I was a little busy arranging my things and was moving from room to room. At last she said, 'May I take your leave now?' I was a little absent-minded and said, 'Yes, go.' She hurried down the stairs. As soon as she left, I said to myself, 'What a foolish thing have I done! Did I say to her: Go![1] Never before did I say such a thing to anybody.' And, alas, she never came back.[2] I do not know why such words came out of my mouth."

* * * *

I went to the Udbodhan Office in the evening. The Mother was lying in bed. Radhu also was lying by her side on another mat and was pressing her to tell a story. The Mother requested me to tell one instead. I was in a quandary. I did not know what to say. I knew the story of Mirabai, the great Vaishnava saint. I narrated it. As I recited the song of Mirabai which ends in the line, "God cannot be realized without love," the Mother cried out in an exalted mood, "Yes, it is very true. Nothing can be achieved without sincere love." But Radhu did not appreciate the story very much. Sarala at last came to my rescue. She told a story from the fairy tales. That pleased Radhu. The Holy Mother was very fond of Sarala. She had to nurse Golap-Ma who was ill, and so left the room after a while. Then Radhu asked me to massage her feet, but she was not pleased with my doing and requested me to give her a harder massage. The Mother said, "Sri Ramakrishna taught me the art of massaging by massaging my own body. Let me see your hand.' I stretched out my hand towards her. She showed me how to massage. Radhu fell asleep very soon. The Mother said, "The mosquitoes are biting my feet. Please pass your hand gently over them." She was quiet for a while and then said, "This year is a very bad one for the Belur Math. Baburam, Devavrata and Sachin have passed away."

[1] The Indian custom is that anyone taking leave should be told, "Come again." It is very inauspicious to say 'Go' to anybody.

[2] She passed away that very night.

I had heard that Swami Brahmananda had seen a disembodied form some days before the passing away of Devavrata Maharaj. I asked her about the incident. The Mother said, "Please talk softly, my child; otherwise they will be frightened. Sri Ramakrishna also often saw many such spirits. One day he had been to the garden-house of Benipal with Rakhal (Swami Brahmananda). He was strolling in the garden when a spirit came to him and said, 'Why did you come here? We are being scorched. We cannot endure your presence. Leave this place at once.' How could it stand his purity and blazing holiness? He left the place with a smile. He did not disclose this to anybody.

"Immediately after supper he asked someone to call for a carriage, though it had been previously arranged that he would spend the night there. A carriage was brought and he returned to Dakshineswar that very night. I heard the sound of the wheels near the gate. I strained my ears and heard Sri Ramakrishna speaking with Rakhal. I was startled. I thought, 'I do not know if he has taken his supper. If not, where can I get any food at this dead of night?' I always used to keep something in the stores for him, at least farina. He would ask for food at odd hours. I had been quite sure of his not coming back that night and so my store was empty. All the gates of the temple-garden were barred and locked. It was one o'clock in the morning. He clapped his hands and began to repeat the names of God. The entrance gate was opened. I was thinking anxiously what to do about his food in case he was hungry. He shouted to me, 'Don't be anxious about my food. I have had my supper.' Then he narrated to Rakhal the story of the ghost. Rakhal was startled and said, 'Dear me! It was really wise of you not to have told me about it at that time. Otherwise my teeth would have been set on edge through fear. Even now I am seized with fear.'" The Mother ended the story with a hearty laugh.

Devotee: Mother, those spirits must have been foolish. Instead of asking him for their liberation, they told him to go away.

Mother: They will, no doubt, be liberated. His presence cannot be in vain. Once Naren (Swami Vivekananda) liberated a disembodied spirit in Madras.

I narrated one of my dreams to the Mother. I said, "Mother, I once dreamt that I was going to some place with my husband. We came to a river, the other bank of which could not be seen. We were going by the shady track along the river when a golden creeper so entwined my arms that I could not free them from it. From the other side of the river came a dark-complexioned boy with a ferry-boat. He said, 'Cut off the creeper from your arm and then only will I take you across the river.' I cut off almost the whole creeper but the last bit I could not get rid of. In the meantime my husband also disappeared. In despair I said to the boy, 'I cannot get rid of this bit. You must take me to the other side.' With these words I jumped into the boat. It sailed and my dream vanished."

The Mother said, "The boy whom you have seen is none other than Mahamaya, the great cosmic Illusionist. She took you across the waters of the world in that form. Everything, husband, wife, or even the body, is only illusory. These are all shackles of illusion. Unless you can free yourself from these bondages, you will never be able to go to the other shore of the world. Even this attachment to the body, the identification of the self with the body, must go. What is this body, my darling? It is nothing but three pounds of ashes when it is cremated. Why so much vanity about it? However strong or beautiful this body may be, its culmination is in those three pounds of ashes. And still people are so attached to it. Glory be to God!

"Once I spent a couple of months at Kailwar in the district of Arrah. It is a very healthy place. Golap-Ma, Baburam's mother, Balaram's wife and others were with me. The country abounded in deer. A herd of them would roam about in the form of a triangle. No sooner had we seen them than they fled away like birds. I had never before seen anything running so swiftly. Sri Ramakrishna would say, 'Musk forms in the navel of the deer. Being fascinated with its smell, the deer run hither and thither. They do not know where the fragrance comes from. Likewise God resides in the human body, and man does not know it. Therefore he searches everywhere for bliss, not knowing that it is already in him.' God alone is real. All else is false. What do you say, my child?"

The Holy Mother had nettle-rash all over her body. She said, "I have been suffering from this ailment for the last three years. I do not know for whose sins I have been suffering in this body. Otherwise how is it possible for me to get any disease?"

I went to see the Mother one evening and found that a number of girls from the Nivedita School had come. Among them were two girls from South India. When Mother learnt that they knew English, she said, "Let me see. Come on, translate this into

English—'I shall now go home.' " One of them did it. Mother said again, "'What will you eat at home?'—how will that be in English?" Hearing the translation, Mother laughed heartily with joy. She asked them, "Can you sing?" When they answered in the affirmative, she asked them to sing a South Indian song. They began singing and Mother was delighted.

22nd August 1918

It was evening when I went to see the Holy Mother. She was lying on a mat on the floor near her couch. I prostrated myself before her and asked her in the course of our conversation, "Mother, it is a long time since I had been to our home at Kalighat. Should I go there now?"

Mother: Why don't you stay here for a few days more? Once you go to Kalighat you will not be able to come here so frequently. If you fail to come for one day, I become very anxious. You were not here yesterday. I was worried to think that you might be unwell. If you had failed to come today, I would have sent someone to inquire about you. But if your husband be ailing, if you think that he wants your presence there, then you will have to go to Kalighat.

When I told her that there was no such difficulty, and that all I feared was popular criticism for staying too long with my sister, she asked me not to mind it and advised me to stay on at Calcutta for a month more.

A Brahmacharin came up and said to the Mother that a certain woman devotee wanted to see her. The Mother was very tired and lay on her bed. She was evidently annoyed and said, "Dear me! I am to see another person! I shall die!" She sat on her bed. A little later, a well-dressed lady entered the room and bowed down to her, touching the Mother's feet with her head.

"You could salute from a distance," said the Mother. "Why do you touch the feet?" The Mother asked her about her welfare.

Devotee: You know Mother, that my husband has been ailing for some time past.

Mother: Yes, I have heard of that. How is he now? What is the trouble with him? Who is treating him?

Devotee: He has been suffering from diabetes. His feet have swollen. The doctors say that it is a dangerous disease. But I do not care for their opinions. You must cure him, Mother. Please say that he will be cured.

Mother: I do not know anything, my child. The Master is everything. If he wills, your husband will be all right. I shall pray to the Master for him.

Devotee: I am now very happy, Mother. Sri Ramakrishna can never disregard your prayer.

She began to weep, putting her head on the feet of the Holy Mother.

The Mother consoled her and said, "Pray to the Master. He will cure your husband. What is his diet now?"

Devotee: He takes Luchi and such other things as are prescribed by the physician.

She soon took leave of the Holy Mother and went to see Swami Saradananda.

"I am burning day and night with the pain and misery of others," said the Mother, and took off the cloth from her body. I was about to rub her body with the medicated oil when a relative of the lady devotee who had just left, entered the room to salute her. She had to get up again. No sooner had she left the room than the Holy Mother lay down again and said, "Let anybody come. Whoever he may be, I am not going to get up again. What a trouble it is, my child, to get up again and again with my aching feet! Besides, I feel the burning sensation on my whole back due to the rashes. Please rub the oil well."

As I was rubbing the oil, the talk turned on the lady who had left. The Mother said, "Her husband is so dangerously ill. She has come here to pray to God for his recovery. Instead of being prayerful and penitent, she has covered herself with perfumes. Does this become one who comes to a shrine? Ah! Such is the nature of your modern people!"

As I was going to take leave of her, the Mother asked someone to give me Prasada.

23rd August, 1918

I went to see the Mother in the evening. Referring to a woman devotee, she was saying, "She imposes very strict discipline upon her daughter-in-law. She should not go to such excess. Though she has to keep an eye upon her, she should also give her a little freedom. She is only a young girl. Naturally she likes to enjoy some nice things. If the lady becomes overstrict, she may go away from her or even commit suicide. What can she do then?"

Looking at me, she said, "She had painted her feet a little. Is it a crime to do so? Alas! She cannot even see her husband. The husband has become a monk. I saw my husband with my own eyes, nursed him, cooked for him and went near him whenever he permitted me. At other times, I have even stayed in the Nahabat for two months at a stretch without moving out. I bowed down to him from afar. He used to say, 'Her name is Sarada. She is Saraswati (Godess of Learning). That is why she loves to adorn herself.'[1] He had told Hriday, 'See how much money is there in your box. Have a pair of nice gold armlets made for her.' He was ill then; still he arranged to get the ornaments made for me for Rs. 300. And mind you, he himself could not touch money.

"After the Master's passing away, I was at Kamarpukur. I was to come here to Calcutta, but many people began to object, 'Oh dear, will you go and stay among those youthful boys!' But I made up my mind that I would stay here only. Still one has to respect what society says. So I asked many people. Some began to say, "Certainly you can go. They are all your disciples." I merely listened. There was an old widow (Prasannamayi of the Lahas) in our village. People used to respect her as a wise and pious person. Later I went and asked her opinion. She replied, 'Why, you may certainly go. They are your disciples, like your own children. What is there in this to ask? Of course you can go.' Hearing that, all approved of my moving to Calcutta. And so I came. Ah, for my sake, out of devotion for their Guru, they cherish even a cat from Jayrambati.

"My mother used to lament, 'Oh, I gave my daughter in marriage to such a mad son-in-law. She could not set up a household, nor have children. She could not even hear herself called 'mother'.' One day the Master heard this and said, 'Oh mother! Don't grieve on that account. You will see that your daughter will have so many children that she would be tired of hearing the cries of 'mother, mother' from them.' What he said has literally come to pass, my dear."

A little later, as night approached, I took leave of her and came away.

---

[1]On another occasion, Sri Ramakrishna had told Golap-Ma: "She (Holy Mother) is Sarada—Saraswati. She is born to bestow knowledge on others. She has hidden her beauty lest people should look upon her with impure eyes and thus commit sin."

Another evening it was raining heavily. I had a rain-coat on but still my clothes got wet at the edges. When I went to the Holy Mother, she burst out laughing at the strange appearance I presented in the rain-coat. But when she felt my wet clothes as I made Pranam, she was immediately anxious. "Oh, you have got wet. Change your clothes quickly. Take Radhu's clothes," she said. "There is no need to change clothes, Mother. I am not at all wet. Just see!" I assured her. The Holy Mother examined me closely and was satisfied.

The topic of conversation now turned to Jayrambati.

Mother: At one time a terrible famine devastated Jayrambati.[1] People without number would come to our house for food. We had a store of rice from the previous year's produce. My father made Khichuri, cooking that rice and pulse together. The Khichuri used to be kept in a number of pots. All the members of the family would take only that Khichuri. The starving people would also eat the same. My father would, however, say, "A little plain rice of good variety shall be cooked for my daughter Sarada (the Holy Mother). She will eat that." Sometimes the starving people would come in such large numbers that the food would not be sufficient for them. Then new Khichuri would be cooked, and when the hot stuff was poured in large earthen pots, I would fan and make it cool. People with hungry stomachs would be waiting for it. One day a low class girl came there. She had shaggy hair and blood-shot eyes like those of a lunatic. She saw the rice polishings soaking in a tub for the cattle and at once started eating it. We said to her, "There is Khichuri inside the house, go and eat it." But she was too impatient to wait. Is it a joke to bear the agony of an empty stomach? As soon as one takes a body, one takes on hunger and thirst also. This time at home when I was ill, one night I was so hungry! Sarala and all others were sleeping. Ah! They had toiled so long and slept. Could I wake them again? Never. So, lying down I felt all around. There was some parched rice in a dish and a few biscuits near the pillow. I was immensely happy. I ate that and drank water which was nearby in a pot. I was so hungry that I was not at all aware of what I ate.

Saying this she began to laugh and continued, "I had high fever

[1] In the year 1864. The Holy Mother was eleven years old then.

that time. What severe illness did I have at Koalpara! I was unconscious, calls of nature had to be answered in bed only. That time Sarala and others served me in a spirit of dedication. (*In a weeping voice*) So I wonder if I have to suffer like that again! That time I was cured by Dr. Kanjilal's medicine. Oh! What a burning sensation all over the body! Sarat also came to serve me."

A little later I asked her, "Mother, why did you write to us from Jayrambati not to mix with that lady devotee?" "Her path is different," she replied, "She is not of this (The Master's) path."

Next day when I went to the Holy Mother, she was sitting in the verandah telling her beads. The Mother welcomed me, finished her Japa and touching the rosary to her forehead, put it away. At that time the area in front of Mother's house was vacant. Some labourers were living in huts towards the west of it. Referring to them she said, "They have laboured the whole day and are now sitting free from worry. The poor are indeed blessed." The words of Christ in the Bible occurred to me. Today I heard the same words from the Holy Mother also. A little later we came back to the room. The Mother laid herself down on her bed. Earlier in the morning, I had sent her some powder for her prickly heat. The Mother said, "I applied the powder you sent. The prickles are much less now. In this place it is more. Please apply there. Itching also is much reduced. Sarat also is suffering from severe prickly heat. Ah! If only some one would apply the powder on him also!" I said, "Oh, no, who will dare tell him of this matter? These things are used by fashionable people!" Hearing this the Holy Mother began to laugh.

The rheumatism in the Mother's knee had increased. Yesterday a devotee's two children had given her electric treatment which benefited her. They came today too. The younger aunt said, "My rheumatism also has increased from yesterday. I also will apply the battery." The Holy Mother heard it and said laughing, "Give it to her by all means." The two mischievous fellows quickly arranged their instruments and touched her feet with the wires. And what a shout it brought from the younger aunt! "Oh God, I am dead," she exclaimed, "My whole body is in jitters. Let me go, let me go." Everybody laughed hearing her cries.

Another day I had been to the Holy Mother's place, when a monk came and prostrated before her. He said, "Mother, why does the mind become so restless every now and then? Why can't I constantly meditate on you? Many worthless thoughts disturb my mind. Useless things we can easily obtain if we simply want them. Shall I never realize the Lord? Mother, please tell me how I can attain peace. Nowadays seldom have I visions. What is the use of this life if I cannot realize Him? It is better to die than to lead such a worthless life."

Mother: What are you talking of, my child? Do not even think of such things. Can one have the vision of God every day? Sri Ramakrishna used to say, "Does an angler catch a big carp every day the moment he sits with his rod? Arranging everything about him, he sits with the rod and concentrates. Once in a while a big carp swallows the hook. Many a time he is disappointed. Don't relax the practices for that reason. Do more Japa.

Yogin-Ma: Yes, that is true. The Name is identical with Brahman. Even if the mind be not concentrated at the outset, you will succeed ultimately.

Monk: Please tell me, Mother, how many times I should repeat the Name. That may help me to get concentration.

Mother: Ten thousand times, or even twenty thousand times or as many times as you can.

Monk: One day, Mother, I was kneeling in the shrine and weeping, when I suddenly saw you standing by my side. You said to me, "What do you want?" "I want your grace, Mother," I replied, " as you bestowed it on king Suratha."[1] Then I added, "No, Mother, that was done by you as Durga. I do not care for that form. I want to see you as you are at present." With a smile you disappeared. My mind became all the more restless. Now nothing satisfies me. Often I think, "If I cannot realize Her, then what is the use of this life?"

Mother: Why are you so restless, my child? Why don't you stick on to what you have got? Always remember, " I have at least a Mother, if none else." Do you remember those words of Sri Ramakrishna? He said he would reveal himself to all that take shelter under him,—reveal himself at least on their last day. He

[1] The reference is to the story contained in the *Devīmāhātmya,* a great devotional text of the Mother cult, in which a king named Suratha and a merchant named Samadhi, both exiles from home and country, worship the Divine Mother and receive Her grace.

will draw all unto Him.

Monk: I have been staying with a householder who is a great devotee. His wife comes from a very aristocratic family. She spends much money for me.

Mother: Ask her not to spend much money for you. The money of the devoted householders is for the benefit of the monks. Their money enables the monks to stay at a place for four months together during the rainy season. It is very inconvenient for the monks to go out (at that time) for begging.

The monk prostrated himself before the Mother and left the room.

3rd September, 1918

I was in indifferent health for a few days. When I felt better, I went to see the Holy Mother one evening. In the course of conversation the Mother began to speak of Sri Ramakrishna.

Mother: (*To me*) What a good time we had yesterday! Sarala read about Sri Ramakrishna. How fine his teachings were! How could we know then that things would take this turn! What a great soul was born! How many people are illumined by his words! He was the embodiment of Bliss itself. All the twenty-four hours of the day were spent in devotional music, merriment, laughter, teaching and story-telling. So far as I remember, I never saw him worried by anything. Often he would tell me nice words of advice. If I had known how to write, I would have noted them down. Well, Sarala, please read something today.

Sarala began to read from the *Kathamrita*, the Bengali original of the *Gospel of Sri Ramakrishna*.

"Do you notice those words," said the Mother. "which he addressed to Rakhal's father,—'A good apple tree begets only good apples'? In this way he would satisfy him. When he would come to Dakshineswar, Sri Ramakrishna would carefully feed him with delicious things. He was afraid lest he should take his boy away. Rakhal had a step-mother. Whenever she came there, he would say to Rakhal, 'Show her everything. Take good care of her.' "

Sarala was now reading about Brinde, the maid-servant. The Mother said, "She was by no means an easy woman. A fixed number of luchis was set aside for her tiffin. She would be extremely abusive if anything was found wanting. She would say, 'Look at these sons of gentlemen! They have eaten my share also. I do not get even a little of sweets.' Sri Ramakrishna was afraid lest those words should reach the ears of the young devotees. One day, early in the morning, he came to the Nahabat and said, 'Well, I have given to others Brinde's luchis. Please prepare some for her. Otherwise she would indulge in abuses. One must avoid wicked persons.' As soon as Brinde came, I said to her, 'Well, Brinde, there is no tiffin for you today. I am just preparing luchis.' She said, "That's all right. Please do not take the trouble. You may give me raw food-stuffs.' I gave her flour, butter, potato and other vegetables."

After finishing a chapter, Sarala went away to attend on Golap-Ma who was ill.

The Holy Mother began to speak in a low voice: "Sri Ramakrishna spoke about nothing but God. He used to tell me, 'Do you notice this human body? Today it is and to-morrow it is not. And coming to this world it suffers no end of misery and pain. Why should one worry about taking another birth? God alone is eternally true. If one can call on Him, it is good. Taking a body one has to suffer from its accompanying troubles!' The other day Bilas said to me, 'Mother, we have to be always very alert. We always tremble with fear lest we should think any unholy thought.' That is very true. A monk is like a bleached cloth, and the householder is like a black one. One does not notice the spots in a black cloth so much, but even a drop of ink looks so prominent on white linen. The monk's life is always beset with dangers. The whole world is engrossed in lust and gold. The monk must always practise renunciation and dispassion. Therefore Sri Ramakrishna used to say, 'A monk must be always alert and careful.' "

In the meantime Harihar Maharaj came to the shrine for offering food. Pointing to him, the Mother said to me, "Look at this child who has renounced the world. He has left everything behind in the name of Sri Ramakrishna. The worldly men beget children without number, as if that is their only duty in this world. Sri Ramakrishna used to say, 'One must practise self-control after the birth of one or two children.' I have heard that the Englishman begets children according to the amount of his property. After the birth of the children they want, the husband and wife live separately, each one busy with his or her own work. And look at our race!"

The Mother continued with a smile, "Yesterday a young

woman came to see me. She had a lot of children, some hanging from her back and some clinging to her arms. She could hardly manage them. Can you imagine what she told me? She said, 'Mother I do not at all enjoy this worldly life.' I said, 'How is that, my child? You have got so many young ones!' She replied, 'That is the end of it. I will not have them any more.' I said, 'It would be well if you could carry out your intention.'" The Mother began to laugh.

Devotee: Well, Mother, according to our Hindu conception, the husband is our most adorable Guru. The scriptures say that by serving him one can go to heaven, and even be united with God. Now if a wife, somewhat against the will of the husband, tries to practise self-control through prayer and spiritual pursuits, is she committing a sin?

Mother: Certainly not. Whatever you do for the realization of God cannot have any sinful effect. Self-control is absolutely necessary. All the hard disciplines enjoined upon Hindu widows are meant to help them practise self-control.

All the acts of Sri Ramakrishna were directed to God alone. He once performed the Shodasi Puja, making me the object of worship. I asked him what I should do with the bangles, the clothes and other articles of worship. After a little thought he said that I could give them all away to my mother. My father was then alive. Sri Ramakrishna said to me, "When you present your mother with these articles, don't think that she is an ordinary human being. Think of her as the direct embodiment of the Divine Mother of the Universe." I acted accordingly. That was the nature of his teaching.

4th September, 1918

The Mother was seated on her meditation carpet, counting beads. The evening service was over. A sister-in-law of the Mother came there and said to her, "Please set my mind right. I am full of worries. I do not wish even to live for a day. I shall make a will and leave all my property to you. After my death, you execute my will." The Mother laughed and said, "When are you going to die?" Suddenly she became grave and reprimanded her for her foolish thoughts, which she attributed to a heated brain and idle life.

Looking at me, the Mother smiled and said: "Do you notice,

my child, the inscrutable play of Sri Ramakrishna? Look at my own relatives! See the evil company I am in! One is already mad and this one also is verging on insanity. And look at the third one (Radhu)! How much care I took to train her up, but all to no effect! She does not have the slightest trace of wisdom. Look there. She is standing in the porch, leaning against the railing and wistfully looking forward to the return of her husband. She is afraid that her husband may enter the house where that music is going on. Day and night she has been trying to keep him within her sight. What an inordinate attachment! I could never dream that she would be so much attached."

The woman relative of the Mother left the place with a sorrowful air and lay down on her bed.

Mother: My child, you have been extremely fortunate in getting this human birth. Have intense devotion to God. One must work hard. How can one achieve anything without effort ? One must devote some time for prayer even in the midst of one's household duties. What shall I say about myself, dear? In those days, at Dakshineswar, I used to get up at 3 o' clock in the morning and sit in meditation. Often I used to be totally absorbed in it. Once, on a moonlit night, I was performing Japa, sitting near the steps of the Nahabat. Everything was quiet. I did not even know when the Master passed that way. On other days I would hear the sound of his slippers, but on this day, I did not. I was totally absorbed in meditation. In those days I looked different. I used to put on ornaments and had a cloth with red borders. On this day the cloth had slipped off from my back owing to the breeze, but I was unconscious of it. It seems 'son Yogen' (Swami Yogananda) went that way to give the water-jug to the Master and saw me in that condition. Ah! The ecstasy of those days! On moonlit nights I would look at the moon and pray with folded hands, 'May my heart be as pure as the rays of yonder moon!' Or, 'O Lord, there is a stain even in the moon, but let there not be the least trace of stain in my mind!' If one is steady in meditation, one will clearly see the Lord in one's heart and hear His voice. The moment an idea flashes in the mind of such a one, it will be fulfilled then and there. You will be bathed in peace. Ah! What a mind I had at that time! Brinde, the maidservant, one day dropped a metal plate in front of me, with a bang. The sound penetrated into my heart. In the fullness of one's spiritual realization, one will find that He who resides in one's heart, resides in the hearts of others as well—the oppressed, the persecuted, the untouchable and the outcast. This realization makes one truly humble.

Let my sister-in-law, who complains of mental worry, do likewise. Let her get up from bed at 3 o'clock in the morning and sit in the porch adjoining my room for meditation. Let me see whether she can still have any worry of mind. She will not, however, do that, but only talk about her troubles! What is her suffering? I never knew my child, what mental worry was. But now I have been suffering day and night because of my relatives. It was an unlucky time when this sister-in-law came to our family; all my sufferings are due to my efforts to bring up her daughter Radhu. Let them all go away. I do not want anybody. Just look at these girls. They never listen to me. Such disobedient women!

Golap-Ma: Just see how they decorate their bodies! They think that is how they will get the love of their husbands.

Mother: Ah! how kindly Sri Ramakrishna treated me! Not even one day did he utter a word to wound my feelings. He would tell me, "One should always be active. One should never be without work. For when one is idle, all sorts of bad thoughts crop up in one's mind." One day he gave me some hemp and asked me to prepare some string suspenders with it. He said he wanted them to hang the pots of some sweets etc. for his young disciples. I made the suspenders accordingly, and with the fibre that was left, stuffed a pillow. I used to lie down on a stiff mat under which I spread some hessian, and placed that pillow under my head. Now you see all these beds and mattresses, but even at that time I used to sleep as well as I do now. I don't feel any difference, dear. People call me 'goddess,' and I too am led to think so. Or how could you explain all the strange things that have happened in my life? Yogin and Golap know much of this. I should but think, 'Let this happen' or 'I shall eat this', the Lord somehow fulfils these.

Ah, my dear! Those were unforgettable days in Dakshineswar! Sri Ramakrishna would sing and I would stand for hours together and watch the scene through the hole in the screen of plaited bamboo chips that surrounded the verandah of the Nahabat. I would salute him with folded hands from afar. Those days were indeed full of bliss! People streamed in throughout the day, and religious talks went on continuously.

My child, this mind is just like a wild elephant. It races with the wind. Therefore one should discriminate all the time. One should work hard for the realization of God. What a wonderful mind I had at that time! Somebody used to play on the flute at Dakshineswar. As I listened to the sound, my mind would be extremely eager for the realization of God. I thought the sound was coming directly from God, and I would enter into Samadhi. I experienced the same ecstasy at Belur also. The place was then very peaceful and I was constantly in a mood of meditation. Therefore Naren (Swami Vivekananda) intended to build a house there for me. The land on which this house stands was given by Kedar Das. But now the price of land has soared high; it is impossible to purchase a place now. All this has been done through the grace of God.

Just at that time, Maku, her niece, entered the room, with her child in her arms, and left the boy there, saying, "Mother, what shall I do? He does not sleep at all." The Mother said, "The child has the quality of Sattva, therefore he does not sleep."

The Mother had been suffering terribly from the pain caused by nettle-rash. At her bidding I rubbed her with medicated oil.

* * * *

One day the Mother was sitting in the northern verandah. A young man was speaking with her. He bowed low before the Mother and placing his head on her feet, said, "Mother, I have suffered much in the world. You are my Guru, you are my Ishta (Chosen Ideal)—and I do not care for anything else. Really, Mother, I feel too ashamed to speak to you about all the evil deeds I have committed. Yet, it is only your grace that has saved me." The Mother lovingly placed her hand on his head and said, "A son is always a son to the mother." The boy replied, "True, Mother. But because I have received so much of your grace, may I never imagine that your grace can be so easily available."

19th *September*, 1918

It was nearly 8.30 p.m. A mat had been spread on the floor near the Mother's bed, and she was about to lie down. No sooner did I enter the room, she said, "Come dear, come. Sit near me. Sarala, give her some refreshments. After a whole day's toil, my child has come here." I protested, but the Mother insisted saying, "One should take proper care of one's health." Then she mentioned her nettle-rash and said, "What to make of this, dear? People suffer from it and become well again; but once I catch it, it doesn't leave me. Sri Ramakrishna used to say that all sorts of people would come with their ailments, afflictions, sins and troubles and touch him, and all those things would take refuge in his body. It is true, my child; it may be the same case with me." The conversation then turned to Sri Ramakrishna.

Mother: Once when Sri Ramakrishna was lying ill at Cossipore, a few devotees brought some offerings for Mother Kali of Dakshineswar temple. On hearing that the Master was at Cossipore, they offered all the things they had brought before a picture of the Master, and then partook of the Prasada. On hearing about this Sri Ramakrishna remarked, "All these things were brought for the great Mother of the Universe. And they have offered them all here (meaning himself)!" I was frightened very much at this and thought, "He is suffering from this dangerous disease. Who knows what might happen?" What a calamity! Why did they do it?[1]

The Master too was referring to this incident again and again. Afterwards at a late hour in the night he said to me, "You will see how in course of time I will be worshipped in every house. You will see everyone accepting this (meaning himself). This is surely going to happen." This was the only day I heard him using the first personal pronoun with reference to himself. Usually he would speak of himself not as 'I' or 'me', but as the 'case belonging to this', pointing to his body.

After the Master's passing, there was a quarrel as to who should get possession of some of the valuable things like his woollen wrap-

[1] It is sacrilegious to offer to a man the gifts that are meant for the Deity, and hence this fear that it may bring about some misfortune. Sri Ramakrishna also seems to show this feeling at first in his mood as a humble devotee, but the subsequent part of the conversation would show that worship of him is not improper if one understands his Divine aspect. It is indicative of the alternating moods of a devotee and of the Divinity that used to be on him.

per, shawl and other garments. After all, it is the devotees who would look upon them as invaluable possessions and preserve them for all time. And it was they who finally gathered them in a box and kept them in the drawing-room of Balaram Babu's house. But, O my daughter, who knew the Master's will! In Balaram Babu's house a servant stole away most of the things, and either sold them or disposed of them in some other way. It was not proper to keep such things in the drawing-room of a house. They ought to have been kept in the inner apartments of the house. What was left of those garments and other things of the Master, is now being preserved at the Belur Math.

My father-in-law (*i.e.* Sri Ramakrishna's father) was a pious and spirited Brahmana. He never received gifts from anyone. He even prohibited his people from accepting any gift brought to his house in his absence. But as regards my mother-in-law, if anyone made a private gift to her she would accept it, cook it, offer it to the Deity, and then give it to others as Prasada. My father-in-law used to get angry if he happened to know of it. He possessed a burning devotion. That was why the Master was born in his family.

A woman named Hari Dasi wanted to go on a pilgrimage to Navadvip. She did not, however, actually reach there, but stopped at Kamarpukur. She loved me very much. She was a woman of great faith. She kept with her some dust gathered from the Master's birth-place and would remark, "This itself is my Navadvip. Gauranga himself was born here. Why should I then go to Navadvip?" What a tremendous faith!

After the Master's passing, a Sadhu, hailing from Orissa, was staying at Kamarpukur. I used to give him rice, pulses and other necessaries. I used to visit him both morning and evening and ask, "Revered sir, how do you do?" Ah, with what great difficulty I built a thatched hut for him! Every day the sky would be overcast with clouds, and it would seem as if it were going to rain just then. I would therefore pray with folded hands, "O Lord, wait a while, wait a while. Let me finish the cottage, and then let it rain in torrents if necessary." The people of the village helped me in the work by giving timber, straw and other necessary materials. Somehow the cottage was completed, but unfortunately it so happened that a few days after, the Sadhu passed away in that cottage.

Sri Ramakrishna used to say that his body had come from Gaya. When his mother passed away, he asked me to offer Pindam (funeral cakes) at Gaya. I replied I was not entitled to perform those rites when the son himself was alive. The Master replied, "No, no, you are entitled to do it. Under no circumstances can I go to Gaya. If I go, do you think it will be possible for me to return?"[1] So I did not want him to go there. And later on I performed the rites at Gaya.

28th September, 1918

It was morning when I went to the Udbodhan office. The Holy Mother was peeling fruits for worship. As soon as her eyes fell on me, she said, "I am so glad to see you here. It is the day of the Bodhan.[2] (I had entirely forgotten about it). Please arrange these flowers for the worship of Sri Ramakrishna, and keep the fruit tray on this side." I obeyed her orders. I then combed her hair. While combing, a number of her hairs came out. The Mother said, "Here they are! Preserve these." I felt myself really blessed. I had a strong desire for some of her hair.

Shyamadas Kaviraj, the celebrated physician, came to examine Radhu. When the examination was over, the Mother asked Radhu to bow before the physician. Radhu did as she was asked. After the physician had left the place, someone inquired, "Is the physician a Brahmana?"

Mother: No, he is a Vaidya.

Devotee: Why, then, did you ask Radhu to bow down before him?

Mother: Why should I not do so? The physician is so full of wisdom. He is equal to a Brahmana. To whom should one bow down if not to him? What do you say, my child?

---

[1]Tradition has it that the birth of Sri Ramakrishna was heralded by the vision his father had at Gaya of the Deity, who announced that He would be born as his son. Hence the spiritual association he had with Gaya was likely to overwhelm him if he went to that place.

[2]The day previous to the commencement of the Hindu festival of the Durga Puja.

30th September, 1918

It was the sacred day of the Mahashtami.[1] My sister and I arrived at the Udbodhan Office early in the morning. After a while, a few women devotees brought some flowers. They worshipped the Holy Mother and went to the Ganges for their bath. The Mother asked me, "Will you stay here today? It is the day of the Mahashtami." I answered in the affirmative. A few moments later, Revered Sarat Maharaj (Swami Saradananda) came there to salute the Mother. We retired into the next room. The Mother was seated on her bed, with her feet resting on the ground. Many devotees came and bowed before her.

Later on, we went to take our bath in the Ganges in the company of Maku and other women devotees. The Mother said she would finish her bath at home, as rheumatism prevented her from bathing in the Ganges every day. After returning we saw many women devotees worshipping the Holy Mother. Many of them brought new clothes as offerings. After the worship, they wrapped the body of the Mother with the clothes, as they do for the image of Kali at Kalighat. Then she laid the clothes aside, one by one. To some devotees the Mother would say, "It is a nice piece of cloth."

A Brahmacharin came to the room and said that the men devotees would come now to bow down before the Mother. What an impressive sight! With flowers, full-blown lotuses and Bel leaves in their hands, they came there one by one, and after worship and salutation, went away. Some time passed in this manner. The members of Balaram's family came and worshipped the Holy Mother.

I was the last to go to her. After the worship I wrapped her body with a cloth, when she said suddenly, "I will wear this cloth, as today I must put on a new one." She at once put on the cloth given by me. This brought tears in my eyes. After all it was an ordinary piece of cloth. There were so many costly clothes around her. I was the poor daughter of the Mother. Her excessive affection for me made me bashful. The Mother said, "What a fine border this cloth has!"

A woman dressed in an ochre robe worshipped Mother and placed two rupees near her feet. The Mother said, "Goodness!

---

[1]The second day of the Durga Puja which is considered very auspicious by the Hindus.

Why should you do that? You have put on the ochre robe. You have Rudraksha beads on your arm." The Mother asked her about her spiritual teacher. In reply the woman said that she had not been initiated. "Without initiation," said the Mother, "and without any spiritual realization, you have put on this sacred robe. This is not proper for you. The robe you have put on is very holy. I was about to salute you with folded hands. All will bow down at your feet. You must acquire the power to assimilate the honour." The woman said, "I have a desire to be initiated by you."

Mother: How is it possible?

But the woman insisted. Golap-Ma supported her. The Mother seemed to yield a little. She said, "We shall think about it."

Gauri-Ma came with the girls of her Ashrama. They all worshipped the Mother, took Prasada, and went away.

After finishing the worship in the shrine room, Bilas Maharaj came there and whispered to the Holy Mother, "I do not know, Mother, if Sri Ramakrishna has accepted the food-offering to-day. An impure leaf, carried by the wind, dropped on the food. Why was it so? Many devotees brought offerings from home. I do not know what has happened." The Mother asked if he had sprinkled the water of the Ganges over the food. He answered in the affirmative and went away. I felt troubled in mind to hear this.

The worship of the Holy Mother went on in the same way. No sooner had one heap of flowers and Bel leaves been removed, than a fresh pile was formed near her feet.

It was the time of the noonday worship, when a party of three men and three women from a distant part of the country came to pay their respects to the Holy Mother. They were very poor, all their possessions consisting of one piece of cloth each. They had begged their passage to Calcutta. One of the party—a man devotee—was having a private talk with the Mother. There seemed to be no end to the conversation. The time for the noonday worship was passing, and the Mother must perform it. The inmates of the Udbodhan Office became annoyed. One of them said to the devotee in unmistakable language, "If you have anything more to say, you had better come downstairs and talk to the monks." But the Mother declared with some firmness, "It does not matter if it gets late. I must hear what they have to say." She continued to listen to him with great patience. In a whisper she gave him some instructions. Then she sent for his wife as well. We inferred that they must have experienced something in dream. Later on we came to learn that they had received some sacred Mantra in dream. After about an hour they took leave of the Mother. The Mother said, "Alas, they are very poor! They have come here with great hardship."

After the noonday worship, we had our meal. The Holy Mother now wanted to have a little rest, and we retired into the adjoining room.

It was four o'clock in the afternoon. After the worship in the shrine, Rashbehari Maharaj said, " A European lady has come to pay her respects to you. She has been waiting for a long time." The Mother asked him to bring the lady to her. As she bowed down before the Mother, the latter clasped her hand as one does in shaking hands. The words of the Mother, that one should behave according to time and circumstance, were verified in this instance. Then she caressed the lady by touching the chin. The latter knew Bengali and said, "I hope I have not inconvenienced you by this visit. I have been waiting for a long time downstairs to see you. I am in great difficulty. My only daughter, a very good girl, is dangerously ill; so I have come here to crave your favour and blessings. Please be gracious to her, so that she may be cured. She is such a nice girl. I praise her because one seldom finds nowadays a good woman among us. I can vouch that many of them are wicked and evil-minded; but my daughter is of quite a different nature. Please be kind to her."

Mother: I shall pray for your daughter. She will be cured.

The European lady was much encouraged by this assurance from the Holy Mother and said, " When you say that she will be cured, she *shall* be cured. There is no doubt about it." She spoke these words thrice with great faith and emphasis. The Mother, with a kindly look, said to Golap-Ma, "Please give her a flower from the altar. Bring a lotus." Golap-Ma brought a lotus with a sacred Bel leaf. The Mother took the lotus in her hand and closed her eyes for a few moments. Then she looked wistfully at the image of Sri Ramakrishna and gave the flower to the lady, saying, "Please touch your daughter's head with it." She accepted the flower with folded hands and bowed down before the Mother.

"What shall I do with the flower after that?" she asked.

Golap-Ma: When it is dried, throw it into the Ganges.

Lady: No, no! This belongs to God. I cannot throw it away. I shall make a bag out of a new piece of cloth and preserve the flower in it. I shall touch my daughter's head and body every day with it.

Mother: Very well, do that.

Lady: God is the supreme Reality. He exists. I want to tell you something. A few days ago, my baby was bed-ridden with fever in the house. With great fervour I prayed to God, "O Lord! I believe in Your existence, but I want an actual demonstration." I wept and laid my handkerchief on the table. After a long time I was surprised to find three sticks in its folds. I gently touched the body of the baby thrice with the three sticks. Soon it was cured of the fever.

As she narrated the incident, tears trickled down her cheeks. She said, "I have taken much of your valuable time. Please forgive me." "No," said the Mother. "I am greatly pleased to talk to you. Come here again on Tuesday." The lady bowed down and took leave of her.

When I went to the Mother a few days after, I learnt that the European lady went to see her on Tuesday. The Mother had shown her special favour and initiated her. Her daughter, too was cured of her illness.

24th March, 1920

The Holy Mother had been staying in her country home at Jayrambati. After about a year she returned in spring to Calcutta. She was extremely unwell, having been in the grip of malarial fever for a long time. I prostrated myself before her and she blessed me by placing her hand on my head. She asked me how I was. I offered her a little money and she accepted it. At the sight of her emaciated body, I lost all power of speech. I looked at her face wistfully and thought, "Alas, how pale and weak her body is!" My sister's maidservant was with me. She was about to touch the Mother's feet in salutation, but she said to her, "You may bow from a distance." The maid bowed from near the door-step and went away.

The Mother was so weak that she felt it painful even to utter a word. I was seated on the floor. In the meantime, Rashbehari

Maharaj came up and requested the Mother not to strain herself by talking; but the Mother now and then asked me about various things. I gave her very short replies. Then Radhu came with her child. I took him in my arms and gave him some cash as a present. Radhu insisted on his not accepting it. The Mother said, " What is this, Radhu? She is your sister. Why should you not accept the present when she gives it with so much love?" The Mother accepted the money herself. She felt so sorry for the sufferings of the child caused by his mother's and grandmother's negligence. Radhu protested in bitter words. The Mother said, "There is no use talking to her," and kept quiet. After a while Sarala and a few women devotees came there to see the Mother. She was lying in bed. She began talking with them.

30*th March*, 1920

I went to pay my respects to the Holy Mother after five or six days. She had had no fever for the previous two or three days, but she was much worried on account of Radhu and her incapacity to look after her little child. Moreover, today Radhu's hand had bumped against an iron railing and with the swollen hand dressed in a dirty linen soaked in castor oil, she came to the Mother's room to consult Dr. Kanjilal who had come to examine the Mother.

After Radhu's hand was properly dressed, the Mother lay down on her bed and asked me to rub her feet. While rubbing I asked her whether I could question her about something and if it would inconvenience her.

The Mother said, "No, not at all. Speak what you have to." I spoke to her about some experience I had, and at this the Mother remarked, "Ah, my daughter, can one experience such delight every day? Everything is real. Nothing is untrue. The Master is all—He is Prakriti, He is Purusha. Through Him you will achieve everything."

Disciple: Mother, one day while doing Japa with great concentration, a long period of time passed quite unobserved. I had therefore to get up for attending to my household duties without carrying out the other items of spiritual practices that you had instructed me to do. Was it wrong on my part to have done so?

Mother: No, no. There is nothing wrong in it.

Disciple: Someone told me that while meditating at the dead of night, he hears a mystic sound. Generally he experiences it as coming from the right side of the body; sometimes, (when the mind comes to a slightly lower plane), it comes also from the left side.

Mother: (*after thinking a while*) Indeed, the sound comes from the right side. Only when there is body-consciousness it comes from the left side. Such things happen when the power of the Kundalini is awakened. The sound that comes from the right side is the real one. In time the mind itself becomes the Guru. If one is able to pray to God and meditate on Him for even two minutes with full concentration it is very good.

I did not feel inclined to question the Mother on the significance of 'body-consciousness', for the Mother was not doing well.

I was about to take leave. Instantly the Mother raised her head from the pillow and said, "Well, my daughter, I have raised my head." She did so, because it is not the custom for a devotee to bow down to one lying. When I bowed down, she said, "Come again. Come a little earlier in the evening. Can't you finish your household duties a little earlier and come?"

Then taking the name of Durga as a prayer for my safety, she bade me adieu. Even after I had come to the verandah I heard her uttering the name of Durga in a compassionate tone. What an unbounded love! So long as we were by her side, we forgot all the sorrows and sufferings of worldly life.

* * * *

The Mother's illness showed no signs of abatement. Her body was getting weaker and weaker. I went to see her one afternoon. She was about to go for her evening wash. She asked me to help her to get up. She said. "I am getting fever very often and the body has become very weak."

* * * *

Another day, when I visited the Mother. I heard the monks telling her, "Mother, after your recovery this time, we will not allow anyone to receive initiation from you. You have to undergo a lot of suffering by taking upon yourself the sins of your disciples." The Mother smiled softly and said, "Why, my dear children? Did Sri Ramakrishna come only to eat *rasagollas*?" That silenced all. O Mother! How much indeed did you express in those few words: ignorant that we are, how little could we understand!

This reminded me of another episode. A woman from a respectable family had fallen on evil ways. But perhaps due to some merit of previous life, she fortunately came in contact with a holy man. Under his guidance, she realized her mistake and became repentant. He advised her to visit the Holy Mother.

One day she came to meet the Mother at the Udbodhan Office. She felt shy to enter the prayer-hall. So standing near the doorstep, she confessed to the Mother all her dark past, and said, "O Mother. what will be my fate? I am not even fit to enter this holy shrine to meet you." The Mother herself went forward and embracing the woman, told her lovingly, "Come, child, come inside. You have understood what is sin, and you are also repentant of your deeds. Come, I shall initiate you. Surrender everything at the feet of Sri Ramakrishna. Why should you fear?"

Accepting the sins and afflictions of mankind on her own shoulders and raising the 'fallen', it is only the all-compassionate Mother, who can smilingly say, "Why! Did Sri Ramakrishna come only to eat *rasagollas*?"

14th April, 1920

The evening Aratrika (vesper service) in the shrine was over. The Mother had fever. Rashbehari Maharaj was rubbing her hands and Brahmachari Varada her feet. They were taking her temperature, and the Mother was lying with her eyes closed. I stood by her side. Once the Mother asked, "Who is there?" Rashbehari Maharaj replied to her in a low voice. I heard that the temperature was 100.1 degrees.

Sister Sudhira was giving a treat to the girls of the Nivedita School, as it was the (Bengali) New Year's day. So Sarala, the disciple who was attending on the Mother, had gone to the school. The Mother asked Brahmachari Varada to bring Sarala from there; for, she had to feed Radhu's child. It was not yet time to feed the child but as he was weeping, Radhu wanted to feed him just then. The Mother tried to dissuade her. This only enraged Radhu who began to abuse the Mother. She said, " May you die, and I shall light your funeral pyre!" We were deeply pained to hear this. The Mother was so badly ill, and Radhu was abusing her in such a fashion at that time! Radhu, however went on shouting out many more abusive words. Such conduct on her part had become quite frequent. The Mother, who had unbounded patience, would put up with such behaviour on all occasions. But this time, due to her protracted illness she too got annoyed and remarked, "You will realize the consequences of this afterwards! What a sad plight you will be in after my death, you will understand! I do not know how many kicks and thrashings with broom-stick are in store for you!"

At this Radhu became still more irritated and abusive. After a time Sarala arrived and fed the child. The experience of that day cast a gloom over my mind. The Mother asked me to rub her feet.

Just then Rashbehari Maharaj entered the room and began to fix up the mosquito netting. So I took leave of her and the Mother said by way of bidding farewell, "Come." This was the last command and the last word that I heard from her.

I had to return to my Kalighat residence. Afterwards for several days I could get no opportunity to visit her, due to the illness of many at home and other difficulties. I used to get regular information about her health, and came to know that she was sinking day by day. At the earliest opportunity I went to see her, my heart filled with the fear that we were to lose our most precious possesion in life very soon. I was, however, still hoping against hope.

THE GOSPEL OF THE HOLY MOTHER

SECTION I

CONVERSATIONS: SECOND SERIES

(RECORDED BY SWAMI ARUPANANDA)

JAYRAMBATI

1st February, 1907, 8-30 *a.m.*

UNCLE Varada said to me, "The Mother has sent for you."

I went inside the inner apartment and found the Holy Mother standing at the door of her room waiting for me. As I saluted her, she asked, "Where do you come from?" I told her the name of the district of my native village.

Mother: I suppose you are now reading the teachings of the Master.

I did not reply to these words. She spoke to me as if we had known each other for a long time. I still remember her tender and affectionate look.

Mother: Do you belong to the Kayastha caste?

Disciple: Yes.

Mother: How many brothers have you?

Disciple: Four.

Mother: Sit down and take some refreshments.

With these words the Mother spread a small carpet on the floor of the verandah and gave me some luchis and sweets that had been offered in the shrine on the previous night.

I told the Mother that I had walked all the way from Tarakeswar on the previous day, spending the night in the village of Deshra, to the northwest of Jayrambati, in the house of a young man whom I had met at the railway station of Haripal. The Mother listened to all this and said to me, after I had finished my refreshments, 'Don't bathe now; you have walked a great deal.' Then she gave me a betel leaf to chew.

She sent for me again after the noonday worship. After the offerings were over, she first of all served me food. She served it with her own hands, on a Sal leaf, on the porch of her room. "Eat well, and, remember, don't feel shy!" she said to me as I was enjoying the meal. Afterwards she gave me a betel leaf.

I went to the Holy Mother again at three or four o'clock in the afternoon and found her kneading dough for bread. She was seated on the floor, facing the east, her legs stretched out in front of her. The oven stood near her. Casting a benign glance upon me, she said, "What do you want?"

Disciple: I want to talk to you.

Mother: What do you want to talk about? Sit down here.

She gave me a seat.

Disciple: Mother, people say that our Master is God Eternal and Absolute; what do you say?

Mother: Yes, he is God Eternal and Absolute to me.

As she had said 'to me', I went on, "It is true that to every woman her husband is God Eternal and Absolute. I am not asking the question in that sense."

Mother: Yes, he is God Eternal and Absolute to me as my husband, and in a general way as well.

Then I thought that if Sri Ramakrishna were God Eternal, then she, the Holy Mother, must be the Divine Power, the Mother of the Universe. She must be identical with His Divine consort.She and he are like Sita and Rama, Radha and Krishna. I had come to the Holy Mother, cherishing this faith in my heart. I asked her, "If that be the case, then why do I see you preparing bread like an ordinary woman? It is Maya, I suppose, is it not?"

Mother: It is Maya, indeed! Otherwise, why should I fall into such a state? But God loves to sport as a human being. Sri Krishna was born as a cowherd boy and Rama as the child of Dasaratha.

Disciple: Do you ever remember your real nature?

Mother: Yes, I recall it now and then. At that time I say to myself, "What is this that I am doing? What is all this about?" Then I remember the house, buildings and children (*pointing with the palm of her hand to the houses*) and forget my real self.

I used to visit the Mother almost daily in her room. She would lie down on her bed and talk to me, with Radhu lying asleep by her side. An oil-lamp would cast a dim light in the room. On some days a maidservant rubbed her feet with medicated oil for rheumatism.

One day she said to me in the course of conversation, "Whenever the thought of a disciple comes to my mind and I yearn to see him, then he either comes here or writes a letter to me. You must have come here prompted by a certain feeling. Perhaps you have in your mind the thought of the Divine Mother of the Universe."

Disciple: Are you the Mother of all?

Mother: Yes.

Disciple: Even of these birds and animals?

Mother: Yes, of these also.

Disciple: Then why should they suffer so much?

Mother: In this birth they must have these experiences.

One evening I had the following conversation with the Holy Mother in her room.

Mother: You all have come to me, because you are my own.

Disciple: Am I your 'own'?

Mother: Yes, my 'own'. Is there any doubt about it? If a man is the very 'own' of another, they remain inseparably connected in the successive cycles of time.

Disciple: All address you as *Apani*,[1] but I could not do so. The word *Tumi* comes spontaneously and naturally.

Mother: That is good, indeed. It denotes an intimate relationship.

In the course of our talk I said to her, "You must have taken the responsibilities of those whom you have initiated with the sacred Mantra. Then why do you say when we request you to fulfil a desire, 'I will speak to the Master about it?' Can't you take our responsibility?" I had as yet not felt the urge to be initiated. Hence this question.

Mother: I have, indeed, taken your responsibility.

Disciple: Please bless me, O Mother, that I may have purity of mind and attachment to God. Mother, I had a classmate in school. I would have been happy if I could bestow upon Sri Ramakrishna a fourth of the love which I cherished for my chum.

Mother: Ah me! That is true, indeed! Well, I shall speak to the Master about it.

Disciple: Why do you only say that you will speak to the Master? Are you different from him? My desire will certainly be fulfilled by your blessings alone.

---

[1] *Apani*—There are three words in Bengali by which one can address another. *Apani* is used when a person addresses his superior entitled to respect. *Tumi* is used to address an equal and is a term of intimacy and endearment. *Tui* is used to address inferiors, servants, etc.

Mother: My child, if you can get perfect knowledge through my blessings then I bless you with all my heart and soul. Is it ever possible for a man to free himself unaided, from the clutches of Maya? It was for this that the Master performed spiritual austerities to the utmost extent and gave the results thereof for the redemption of mankind.

Disciple: How can one love Sri Ramakrishna without seeing him?

Mother: Yes, that's true. Can one ever have intimate relationship with a mere airy being!

Disciple: When shall I have the vision of the Master?

Mother: You shall certainly see him. You shall see the Master at the right time.

One day the Mother lay on her bed while Kamini, the maid, was rubbing her knee with some medicated oil for rheumatism. The Mother said to me, "The body is one thing and the soul another. The soul pervades the whole body; therefore I have been feeling the pain in my leg. If I should withdraw my mind from the knee, then I would not feel any pain there."

Referring to initiation by Mantra, I said to her, "Mother, what's the need of taking the Mantra from a teacher? Suppose a man does not repeat his Mantra; will it not do for him if he simply repeats, 'Mother Kali, Mother Kali'?"

Mother: The Mantra purifies the body. Man becomes pure by repeating the Mantra of God. Listen to a story. One day Narada went to Vaikuntha to see the Lord and had a long conversation with Him. Narada had not, at that time, been initiated. After Narada left the place, the Lord said to Lakshmi, "Purify the place with cow-dung." "Why, Lord?" asked Lakshmi. "Narada is your great devotee. Why, then, do you say this?" The Lord said, "Narada has not, as yet, received his initiation. The body cannot be pure without initiation."

One should accept the Mantra from a Guru at least for the purification of the body. The Vaishnava, after initiating the disciple, says to him, "Now all depends upon your mind." It is said. "The human teacher utters the Mantra into the ear; but God breathes the spirit into the soul." Everything depends upon one's mind. Nothing can be achieved without purity of mind. It is said, "The aspirant may have received the grace of the Guru, the Lord and the Vaishnava; but he comes to grief without the grace of 'one'." That 'one' is the mind. The mind of the aspirant should be gracious to him.

Talking of her mother, the Holy Mother said, "My mother used to be highly pleased when any one of the devotees came to our place. She would exclaim, 'Ah! my grandchild has come!' She would look after them with great attention. She looked upon this family of devotees as her own flesh and blood."

Continuing, the Holy Mother said, "When the Master passed away, I also wanted to leave my body. He appeared before me and said, 'No, you must remain here. There are many things to be done.' I myself realized later on that this was true; I had so many things to do. The Master used to say, 'The people of Calcutta live like worms squirming in darkness. You will guide them.' He said that he would live for three hundred years in a subtle body, in the hearts of the devotees. He further said that he would have many devotees among white people.

"After the passing away of the Master, I was at first greatly frightened, for I used to put on a Sari with thin red borders and wear gold bangles on my wrist, which made me afraid of people's criticism.[1] I was then at Kamarpukur. Sri Ramakrishna started appearing often before me. Then I gradually got rid of that fear. One day the Master appeared before me and asked me to feed him with Khichuri. I cooked the dish and offered it before Raghuvir[2] in the temple. Then I mentally fed the Master with it.

"Harish was then staying at Kamarpukur for a few days. One day, when I was entering the house after visiting a neighbour, he began to chase me. He was then in a distracted state of mind. He had lost his senses on account of his wife. There was then no one else in the house. I did not know where to go, and ran quickly behind the barn. He would not, however, leave me. I ran and ran round it seven times till I got exhausted. Then my true self came out. I threw him to the ground, pressed my knee on his chest, drew out his tongue and slapped him hard on the cheeks

---

[1]Hindu widows, according to traditional custom, are required to put on a white Sari without any border and to give up all ornaments. The Mother at first wanted to follow this custom of Hindu widows, but Sri Ramakrishna appeared in a vision and told her not to do so, as he was not really dead.

[2]The tutelary Deity of Sri Ramakrishna's family at Kamarpukur.

until my fingers became red with slapping. He began to gasp for breath." [1]

The talk turned to Yogen Maharaj (Swami Yogananda).

Mother: None loved me as did my Yogen. Should anyone give him some money, he would keep it aside, saying, "It will be useful for Mother when she goes on pilgrimage." He would be always near me. The other monks would sometimes tease him for staying in this household full of women. He would ask me to address him as Yogā. Before passing away, he said, "Brahma, Vishnu, Siva, and Sri Ramakrishna—they have all come, Mother, to take me."

About herself she said, "Balaram Babu used to refer to me as the 'great ascetic, the embodiment of forbearance.' Can you call him a man, who is devoid of compassion? He is a veritable beast. Sometimes I forget myself in compassion. Then I do not remember who I am."

Finally the Holy Mother said to me, "I feel very free with you. See me in Calcutta and stay with me."

At that time I lived with my people, though I had been cherishing an intense desire to embrace the monastic life. I said to

---

[1] Harish was a devotee of Sri Ramakrishna who used to frequently visit the Baranagore monastery of the Ramakrishna Brotherhood at its early inception. It is said that his wife, afraid of his tendency towards a life of renunciation, sought to deter him from it with drugs and charms, which eventually made his mind deranged. In this deranged condition he once visited Kamarpukur, and the Mother, coming to know his condition, wrote to the Math, asking that some one should come and take him away. Accordingly Swamis Saradananda and Niranjanananda started for this purpose. It was just before their arrival that the above mentioned incident took place. The Mother's words, "Then my true nature came out," is given a mystical meaning by many. They believe that the Mother, being a manifestation of the Divine Devi, could take any form she wanted. In this instance, the consciousness of Bagala, one of the Mahavidyas, must have been on her, as Bagala is said to have killed an Asura in the same manner as the Mother now punished Harish. This punishment had a salutary effect on Harish. He fled to Vrindavan, and gradually his mental equilibrium was restored. Apart from these mystical implications, this incident, together with that of the 'dacoit father', reveal certain most unsuspected features of the Mother's human character and personality also.

myself, "Perhaps in future it will be possible for me, through her grace, to be a monk and live near her."

When I was in Jayrambati, Radhu's mother, Surabala, was mentally deranged. She had taken to her father's house all the jewellery of her daughter Radhu. Taking advantage of her insane condition, her father snatched away all the jewellery. That made her even more distracted. On her return to Jayrambati, Radhu's mother wept in the temple of Simhavahini, praying for the jewellery. It was dusk. I was talking to the Holy Mother in her room when suddenly, she said to me, "My child, I must go now. That crazy sister-in-law of mine has none else to call her own but me. She is weeping before the Deity for the jewellery." With these words, the Mother left the room. But I could not hear any sound of weeping, nor was it possible to do so at such a distance; yet she had recognized the voice. She returned with Radhu's mother. The latter said to her, "O sister-in-law, you have put away my jewellery. You have deprived me of it." The Mother said, "Had these ornaments belonged to me, then I would have thrown them away at once like the filth of a crow." Referring to Radhu's mother, she said to me, laughing, "Girish used to say that she was my mad companion."

At first I used to hesitate to address the Holy Mother as "Mother". My own mother had died during my childhood. One morning the Holy Mother sent me to a certain person on an errand. As I was about to leave, she asked me, "What will you say to him?" I said, "Why? I shall say to him, 'She asked me to tell you, etc.' " "No, my child," said the Holy Mother, "tell him, 'The *Mother* asked me to tell you.' " She emphasized the word '*Mother*'.

One morning I was reading aloud to the Mother and a few devotees on the porch of her room. I was reading a life of Sri Ramakrishna entitled *Ramakrishna Punthi* written in verse. In the chapter on her marriage with Sri Ramakrishna, the author eulogized her greatly and referred to her as the 'Mother of the Universe.' As I read that passage, the Mother left the porch. A few minutes earlier I had read to her some pages from the *Udbodhan*, in which had been published a portion of the Kathamrita by M.[1] No one else was present then. I had been reading the following passage:

Girish: I have a desire.

---

[1] Mahendra Nath Gupta, the author of the *Kathamrita* translated into English as *The Gospel of Sri Ramakrishna*.

Master: What is it?

Girish: I want love of God for the sake of love.

Master: That kind of love is possible only for the Isvarakotis. Ordinary men cannot achieve it.

I asked the Holy Mother, "What does the Master mean by that?"

Mother: The Isvarakotis have all their desires fulfilled in God (*Pūrṇa-Kāma*). Therefore they have no worldly desires. Love for the sake of divine love is not possible so long as a man has any desire.

Disciple: Mother, do your own brothers belong to the same level as these Isvarakotis?

I thought that as they were her brothers, they must have the same spiritual capacities as the monastic disciples of Sri Ramakrishna. At this the Mother simply looked scornfully, as if she were going to say, "What a comparison! What can one achieve by simply being my brother! To be the intimate disciple of the Master is quite a different thing!"

One morning, the Holy Mother was assisting in husking paddy. It was almost her daily job. I asked her, "Mother, why should you work so hard?" "My child," said she in reply, "I have done much more than is necessary to make my life a model."

One night, all were asleep in the house of the Holy Mother when the husband of Nalini, a niece of the Holy Mother, arrived unexpectedly with a bullock cart to take Nalini to his house. Nalini had returned from her husband's place and did not want to go back. Hearing of her husband's intention, Nalini shut the door of her room and threatened suicide if her husband forced her to go back with him. The Holy Mother, however, assured her that she would not have to go back with her husband and she opened the room. There was confusion in the family for the whole night and the Holy Mother sat through the night on the porch of Nalini's room. She put out the lamp at dawn and repeated to herself, "Ganga, Gita, Gayatri, Bhagavata, Bhakta, Bhagavan, Sri Ramakrishna, Sri Ramakrishna!"

One day the Holy Mother sent me with an old servant of the family to Pagli's (the mad sister-in-law's) father to persuade him either to come to Jayrambati or to return the ornaments he had taken from his daughter. After a great deal of persuasion he accompanied us but did not bring the ornaments with him. The Mother begged him to return them and thus free Pagli from her mental agony but the greedy Brahmana turned a deaf ear to her request.

I intended to return home on the day before the Sivaratri, as I wanted to attend Sri Ramakrishna's birthday celebration at Belur Math, which came off two days after the Sivaratri. I told the Mother about it. She asked me to go to Kamarpukur first. I had left home with a great yearning to see the Holy Mother alone, and in my eagerness I had forgotten to take my umbrella or an extra piece of cloth. At the request of the Mother, I agreed to visit the birth-place of the Master. She gave me a fresh piece of cloth to put on, and asked me to take it with me.

Mother: Have you any money with you? You will require carriage hire. Take the money from me.

Disciple: I have money with me. I have not to take it from you.

Mother: Write to me after you reach home. Ah, I could not feed my son properly. I could not prepare anything good for him. This was because this time there was great confusion in the family on account of Nalini and Pagli.

I prostrated myself before her and set out with tears in my eyes. The Holy Mother accompanied us for some distance and then watched us till we were out of sight. I could not refrain from weeping out of devotion for her, till I had reached Kamarpukur.

After my arrival at Kamarpukur, I was shown the room where the Holy Mother had lived. There I saw a picture of the Mother, which made me still more restless to see her again. Next day M. and Prabodh Babu went to Jayrambati via Kamarpukur, halting at the latter place for a few hours. In the evening, Lalit Babu, a disciple of the Mother, arrived there, dressed in turban, trousers and long toga. He was on his way to Jayrambati. As it would be difficult for me to go from Kamarpukur to Calcutta alone, some devotee suggested that I might revisit Jayrambati and go to Calcutta in the company of Lalit Babu. So I went with him to Jayrambati once again, and said to the Mother, "I am here again." The Mother was greatly pleased and said, "That's very good. You can go to Calcutta with Lalit."

After the Sivaratri festival was over, the devotees sat down for their meal. They were served some Prasada on leaf-plates. I asked them what it was. They said that it was the Prasada of the Holy Mother. I also partook of it. Later on, I said to the Mother, "They all enjoyed your Prasada. But you never offered it to me."

"My child," said the Mother, "you never asked for it. How could I suggest it?" What great humility!

The next day, Lalit Babu was sent in a palanquin to get Radhu's ornaments from her grandfather. Lalit posed as a Government official and carried a letter with him supposed to have been written by a high police officer of Calcutta. The Holy Mother asked M. to accompany Lalit Babu lest the latter, a young man, should use insulting language when speaking to the old Brahmana. However, he succeeded in bringing Radhu's grandfather with the ornaments to Jayrambati in the afternoon. At about two o'clock in the morning, we heard that the Mother was spending a sleepless night. She was feeling nervous. M. and I entered the inner apartments. While all were looking for medicines, I asked Mother the cause of her ailment. She said, "After they had left to fetch the ornaments, I felt worried and feared that they might insult the old Brahmana. That made me nervous." I was amazed to see the compassion of the Mother for the Brahmana who was at the root of all these troubles.

The next afternoon I left with the party for Calcutta. The Mother had told Lalit Babu about me, "He is very devoted to God. Please take him with you." We all prostrated ourselves before the Mother. Her eyes became filled with tears. She was moved to tears as she accompanied us to the outer gate of the house. At Vishnupur, on our way to Calcutta, M., Prabodh Babu and others visited the shrine of Mrinmayi, an aspect of the Divine Mother. But Lalit Babu and I directly went to the Railway Station and boarded the train. M. sent Prabodh Babu to request us also to visit the shrine, but we did not care to see Mrinmayi (lit. made of earth) as we had seen Chinmayi (a living Goddess). I arrived at the Belur Math and after witnessing Sri Ramakrishna's birthday festival, returned home.

Udbodhan Office, Calcutta
Year 1907

Next winter I came to Calcutta to pay my respects to the Holy Mother. On the first day I went to see her, she was still staying at the house of Balaram Bose, but by the time of my second visit, she had shifted to her newly constructed house in Calcutta (*i.e.,* the Udbodhan Office). On entering the house, I saw Doctor Kanjilal reading a newspaper. In answer to my query he said, "The Mother had an attack of pox. She has not yet completely recovered. You may see her after two weeks." I had not been aware of her illness. Swami Saradananda said to me, "Come tomorrow, you may see her then. Also take your meal here." When I went the next day, the Mother showed me the pox marks. Most of them had disappeared. Through her blessings and the arrangement made by Swami Saradananda, I was staying at the Belur Math. On being informed of this, the Holy Mother remarked, "That's good. He has fallen a victim to the influence of monastic life. Live in the Belur Math. May you get love for the Master! You have my blessings."

I used to take milk for the Mother now and then from the Belur Math. That would also give me the opportunity to pay my respects to her. One day, while entering her house with milk, I saw her preparing betel-rolls assisted by Nalini, her niece. Seeing me, Nalini was about to leave the room. The Mother checked her and said, "Don't go away. He is my child. Sit here." In the course of conversation, she referred to the relatives of Maku's husband (Maku was another niece), and said, "I have to take special care of them, otherwise they feel offended . But you are my children. You are satisfied with whatever I do for you. You do not mind if I cannot always show you attention. But those relatives feel very much offended if I do not give them the best of everything, or if I fail in the least in attending to them." After a while I asked her, "Mother, how does one get purity of mind and yearning for God?"

Mother: Oh! You will certainly have these. As you have taken refuge in the Master, you will achieve all. Pray to him sincerely.

Disciple: I can't do it. Please do pray for me.

Mother: I always pray to Sri Ramakrishna to make your mind pure and holy.

Disciple: Yes, Mother, I shall have everything if you but pray for me.

After a few months I was sent to Ghatal, not very far from Jayrambati, to give relief to the flood-stricken people of that place. I took leave for three days and visited the Holy Mother at Jayrambati on the occasion of the Jagaddhatri Puja. Atul was with me. This was his first visit to the Mother. We went to Jayrambati via Kamarpukur and as soon as we reached her house, Ashu Maharaj, an attendant of the Holy Mother, said, "It is nice that you have come. The Mother has been sad because of not seeing any devotee for some time past." The Mother asked us to stay for meal and fed us sumptuously. Early next morning we had to return to the relief work. While taking leave of the Mother, I said to her, "I shall come again." Atul said, like a school-boy, "Please remember."

JAYRAMBATI

16th December, 1909

After finishing the relief work at Ghatal, I again returned to Jayrambati. On reaching the house of the Holy Mother in the evening, I found her seated on the porch applying medicine to her leg. She was suffering from rheumatic pain in her knees.

Disciple: What is this medicine ?

Mother: Someone suggested this leaf. Have you been starving the whole day?

Disciple: No, but I have not taken any food on the way.

Mother: Why did you not buy some refreshments? There are stores on the way.

I had with me only a rupee which I had saved for my return journey to Belur Math. However, I did not tell her about it. She served me with a hot meal which I ate heartily. The Mother said to me, "The Master will get a great deal of his work done through you. You went to Ghatal, distributed so many things and a great number of people were benefited. When the work is over, at the right time, the Master will gather his child back to his bosom."

Disciple: Mother, why do I not see him?

Mother: You will see him, son, you will see him at the right time. Lalit (a disciple of the Mother) would never ask: 'Why do I not see him?' He firmly believed that since the Master was his very own, sooner or later, he was certain to see him.

Disciple: Mother, please look after my welfare. Please bless me that I may develop pure devotion.

Mother: Yes, dear child, you will be endowed with pure devotion.

She gave me a blanket and asked me to use it during the night. I asked her, "Whose is this blanket?" She said, "It is mine. I use it myself."

18th December, 1909

Mother was preparing betel-rolls in the verandah of her room. It was nearly 9 a.m. I was eating puffed rice. I said to her, "Mother please do not detain me this time for long."

Mother: If you don't want to stay, you can come with me. When the time comes (i.e. death), all have to go.

Disciple: Please remember your promise, Mother.

Mother: I have already said, I will come and carry you along with me.

Disciple: Please take me with you this time. Next time I will accompany the Master when he comes.

Mother laughed and said, "Well, I am not coming again!"

Disciple: Whether you decide to come or not, I will certainly come back to this world. I have a desire to come.

Mother: Most probably, you wouldn't want to return when the time comes. What is there in this world, my child? Tell me at least one thing that is worth-while! That is why Sri Ramakrishna was satisfied with the most ordinary dishes. Whenever I would offer him Sandesh (a kind of sweetmeat), he would say, "What is so special in it? It is just the same as a lump of clay."

Disciple: Why do you cite the example of Sri Ramakrishna? He is beyond all comparison.

Mother: Exactly so. Will there ever be anyone really like him?

At this point, Uncle Varada came to read the letters to her. One of the letters was from my brother, requesting the Mother to persuade me to return home. Though short, the letter was written in a good style and contained beautiful sentiments. The Mother said, "Ah! what a nice letter!" Then she said, addressing me, "Why don't you return home? Live in the world, earn money and bring up a family." She was testing me. "But, Mother, " said I, "please do not say that."

Mother: So many people are leading worldly lives. If you do not feel inclined, you need not do it.

I began to weep. The Mother then said to me with great tenderness, "My child, please do not weep. You are a living God. Who is able to renounce all for His sake? Even the injunctions of Destiny are cancelled if one takes refuge in God. Destiny strikes off with her own hand what she has written about such a person. What does a man become by realizing God? Does he get two horns? No. What happens is, he develops discrimination between the real and the unreal, gets spiritual illumination and goes beyond life and death. God is realized in spirit. How else can one see God? Has God talked to anybody devoid of ecstatic fervour? One sees God in spiritual vision, talks to Him, and establishes relationship with Him in Spirit."

Disciple: No, Mother. There is something else besides. One gets a direct vision of the Atman.

Mother: That Naren (Swami Vivekananda) alone had. The Master kept with himself the key to Naren's liberation. What else is spiritual life besides praying to the Master, repeating his Name, and contemplating on him? (*With a smile*) And the Master? What is there after all in him? He is our own eternally!

Disciple: Mother, please see that I realize the right thing— Just that Sri Ramakrishna is *our own*!

Mother: Must I repeat it? (*Firmly*) You will certainly realize it. Certainly.

* * * *

19*th December*, 1909

I was talking to the Mother in her room. She was lying on her bed. The conversation drifted to the Vedanta. I said to her, "Nothing exists in the world except name and form. It cannot be proved that matter exists. Therefore the conclusion is that God and such other things do not exist."

My idea was that such things as the Master and the Holy Mother were also illusory. She at once understood my thought and said, "Narendra once said to me, 'Mother, the knowledge that disregards the lotus feet of the Guru is nothing but ignorance. What is the validity of knowledge if it proves that the Guru is naught? Give up this dry discussion, this hodgepodge of philosophy. Who has been able to know God by reasoning? Even Siva and sages like Suka and Vyasa are like big ants at the most."[1]

---

[1] The reference is to an illustration given by Sri Ramakrishna: "Men often think they have understood Brahman fully. Once an ant went to a hill of sugar. One grain filled its stomach. Taking another grain in its mouth, it started homeward. On its way it thought, 'Next time I shall carry home the whole hill.' That is the way shallow minds think. They don't know that Brahman is beyond one's words and thought. However great a man may be,

Disciple: I want to know. I understand a little too. How can one stop reasoning?

Mother: Reasoning does not disappear as long as one has not attained to perfect knowledge.

I asked her about Japa and other spiritual practices. The Mother said, "Through these spiritual disciplines the ties of past Karma are cut asunder. But realization of God cannot be achieved without ecstatic love (Prema Bhakti) for Him. Do you know the significance of Japa and other spiritual practices? By these, the dominance of the sense organs is subdued."

Referring to Lalit Chatterjee who had been dangerously ill, the Mother said, "Lalit used to give me great financial help. He would take me out in his carriage. He gives much for the Divine service in the shrines at Dakshineswar and Kamarpukur. My Lalit has a heart worth a million rupees! There are many who are miserly in spite of their wealth. The rich should serve God and His devotees with money, and the poor worship God by repeating His Name."

Referring to ecstatic love, the Mother said, " Did the cowherd boys of Brindavan get Sri Krishna as their "own" through Japa or meditation? They realised Him through ecstatic love. They used to say to Him, as to an intimate friend, 'Come here, O Krishna! Eat this! Take this!' "

Disciple: How can one yearn for God without seeing the manifestation of His love?

Mother: Yes, it is possible. There lies the grace of God.

JAYRAMBATI

31*st December*, 1909

It was about nine in the morning. The Holy Mother had been preparing betel-rolls when I came to see her. Soon we were engaged in conversation.

Disciple: Mother, I have seen and heard so much; still I cannot recognize you as my 'own mother'.

---

how much can he know of Brahman? Sukadeva and sages like him may have been big ants; but even they could carry at the utmost eight or ten grains of sugar!" — *The Gospel of Sri Ramakrishna,* (Madras: Sri Ramakrishna Math, 1980) Vol. I, p. 102.

Mother: If you do not think of me as your 'own', how is it that you come here so often? You will know your 'own mother' in proper time.

After a while I said to her, referring to my parents and brothers, "My parents brought me up. I do not know where they are now (after their death), or how they live. Please give your blessings that my brothers may have good tendencies."

Mother: Do most people ever want God? There are so many people in this very family; but do all want the Lord?

After a few minutes she said to me, "Don't marry. Don't enter worldly life. What should you fear if you are a celibate? Wherever you may live, you will be free."

Disciple: But, Mother, I have fear.

Mother: No, have no fear. All depends upon the will of the Master.

Disciple: The mind is the whole thing. If it be in a pure state, it does not matter where I live. Please see, Mother, that my mind always remains pure.

Mother: May it be so!

2nd January, 1910

It was the birthday of the Holy Mother. A few days before, Prabodh Babu had come to Jayrambati and given five rupees to the brothers of the Holy Mother for special worship on her birthday. The Mother said to them, "You need not do anything special today. I shall wear a new cloth; the Master will be worshipped with a sweet-offering and I shall partake of it later on. That is all for this occasion."

After the worship in the shrine, the Holy Mother sat on her couch with her feet hanging down. She had put on a new piece of cloth. Prabodh Babu offered some flowers at her feet. I stood on the porch near the door. The Mother said to me, "What! Won't you offer some flowers? Here they are. Take them." Then I also offered flowers at her feet. We enjoyed a sumptuous feast at midday and afterwards Prabodh Babu left for Calcutta; but as I was indisposed, I remained at Jayrambati.

5th January, 1910

In the course of a conversation, the Mother said, "Can you tell me if anyone could bind God? Mother Yasoda could and also the cowherd boys and milkmaids of Brindavan could, because He Himself allowed them to do so.

"As long as a man has desires, there is no end to his transmigration. It is the desires alone that make him take one body after another. There will be rebirth for a man if he has even the desire to eat a piece of sweetmeat. It is for this reason that a variety of food-stuffs are brought to Belur Math. Desire may be compared to a minute seed. It is like a big banyan tree growing out of a seed, which is no bigger than a dot. Rebirth is inevitable so long as one has desires. It is like taking the soul from one pillow-case and putting it into another; only one or two out of many men can be found who are free from all desires. Though one gets a new body on account of desires, yet one does not completely lose spiritual consciousness if one has to one's credit merits from previous **births.**

"A priest in the temple of Govinda in Brindavan used to feed his mistress with the food-offerings of the Deity. As a result of this sin, he got the body of a ghoul after his death. But he had served God in the temple. As a result of this merit, he one day appeared before all in his own physical body. It was possible for him to do so on account of his past good actions. He told people the cause of his inferior birth and said to them further, 'Please arrange a religious festival and music for the redemption of my soul from this state. That will free me.'"

Disciple: Is it possible to be freed from such states through religious festivals and music?

Mother: Yes; that is enough for the Vaishnavas. They do not perform such obsequies as Sraddha and so forth.

Once I visited the image of Jagannath at Puri at the time of the Car Festival. I wept in sheer joy to see so many people having a view of the image of the Deity. 'Ah,' I said to myself, 'it is good. They will all be saved.' But later on I realized that it was not so. Only one or two who were absolutely free from desires could attain liberation. When I narrated the incident to Yogin-Ma, she corroborated this by saying, 'Yes, Mother, only people who are free from desires attain liberation (Mukti).'

* * * *

One morning, while taking my breakfast on the verandah of the Holy Mother's room, I asked her, "Mother, will I have to be initiated into Sannyasa if I am to live in Belur Math?"

Mother: Yes, my child.

Disciple: But, Mother, the monastic life begets a terrible vanity.

Mother: Yes, that is true. A monk may become very vain. He may think, 'See, he does not respect me. He does not bow down before me, and so on.' (*Pointing to her own white cloth*)[1] One should rather live thus (meaning possessed of inner renunciation). Gaur Siromani[2] took to the monastic life in his old age when his sense-organs had become dull. Is it possible, my child, to get rid of vanity—vanity of beauty, vanity of virtue, vanity of knowledge and vanity of a holy life?

The Holy Mother exhorted me to make ready for the life of renunciation. "Go home," said she, "and tell your brothers once and for all, 'I will not accept any job; I need not be a slave to anyone, now that my mother is no more. I will not do anything of that sort. You be happy with your householder's duties.' "

The Mother and I were engaged in conversation in the evening.

Disciple: Mother, one gets spiritual realization at any time if the grace of God descends on him. Then he does not have to wait for the right time.

Mother: That is true; but can the mango which ripens out of season be as sweet as the one which ripens in the month of Jaishtha, that is, the proper season? Men are trying to get fruits out of season. You see, nowadays one gets mangoes and jack-fruits even in the month of Asvin (autumn). But these are not as sweet as those found in the proper season. This is also true of the efforts that lead to God-realization. Perhaps you practise some Japa and austerities in this life; in the next life you may intensify the spiritual mood and in the following life you advance further.

Referring to one's attaining spiritual realisation suddenly, the Mother said, "God has the nature of the child. One man does not ask for it, yet He gives it to him, whereas another man asks for it and God will not give it to him. It is all His whim."

* * * *

[1] The white cloth is the symbol of the householder whereas the monks put on ochre clothes.

[2] He was an outstanding holy man of the Vaishnava sect. He visited the Holy Mother in Brindavan.

Another day while the Holy Mother was seated on her porch preparing betel-rolls, I said to her, "In future, how many will practise spiritual disciplines to propitiate you!" Mother said with a smile, "What do you say! All will say, 'Ah, the Mother had such a gout, she used to limp like this!' "

Disciple: You may say that.

Mother: That's good. That is why the Master used to say when he was lying ill at the Cossipore garden, "Those who came to me expecting some earthly gain have disappeared, saying, 'Ah, he is an Incarnation of God! How can he be ill? This is all Maya.' But those who are my 'own', have been suffering a great deal in seeing this misery.'.......

UDBODHAN OFFICE, CALCUTTA

On the day previous to my initiation I said to the Holy Mother, "Mother, I want to be initiated." Mother said, "Have you not been initiated yet?" I answered in the negative. "I thought that you had been initiated," she said. After initiating me, she blessed me, saying "May your body and mind become pure by repeating the name of God!"

Disciple: What is the need of repeating the Mantra with the fingers? Is it not enough to do so mentally?

Mother: God has given the fingers that they may be blessed by repeating His Name with them.

25th September 1910

The Mother was engaged in a conversation with me in the morning.

Disciple: Mother, if there exists some being called God, why is there so much suffering and misery in the world? Does He not see it? Has He not the power to remove it?

Mother: The creation itself is full of misery and happiness. Could any one appreciate happiness if misery did not exist? Besides, how is it possible for all persons to be happy? Sita once said to Rama, "Why don't you remove the suffering and unhappiness of all your subjects? Please make all the inhabitants of your kingdom happy. If you only will, you can easily do it." Rama said, "Is it ever possible for all persons to be happy at the same time?" "Why not?" asked Sita, "Please supply from the royal treasury the means of satisfying everyone's wants." "All right," said Rama,

"Your will shall be carried out." Rama sent for Lakshmana and said to him, "Go and notify everyone in my empire that whatever he wants he may get from the royal treasury." At this the subjects of Rama came to the palace and told their wants. The royal treasury began to flow without stint. When everyone was spending his days joyously, through the Maya of Rama the roof of the building in which Rama and Sita lived, started to leak. Workmen were sent for to repair the building. But where were workmen to be had? There was not a labourer in the kingdom. In the absence of masons, carpenters and artisans all buildings went out of repair, and work was at a standstill. The subjects of Rama informed the king of their difficulties. Finding no other help, Sita said to Rama, "It is no longer possible to bear the discomfort of the leaking roof. Please arrange things as they were before. Then all will be able to procure workmen. Now I realize that it is not possible for all persons to be happy at the same time." "Let it be so," said Rama. Instantaneously all things were as before and workmen could once more be engaged. Sita said to Rama, "Lord, this creation is your wonderful sport!"

No one will suffer for all time. No one will spend all his days on this earth in suffering. Every action brings its own result. and one gets one's opportunities accordingly.

Disciple: Is everything then due to Karma?

Mother: If not, to what else? Don't you see the scavenger carrying the tub on his head?

Disciple: Whence does one first get the propensity which leads him to an action, good or bad? You may say, as an explanation of the propensities of this life, that they are due to the actions of the previous life, and the propensities of that life to the preceding one. But where is the beginning?

Mother: Nothing can happen without the will of God. Not even a blade of grass can move. When a man passes into a favourable time, he gets the desire to contemplate on God. But when the time is unfavourable, he gets all the facilities for doing evil actions. Everything happens in time according to the will of God. It is God alone who expresses His will through the actions of man. Could Naren (Swami Vivekananda) by himself have accomplished all those things? He was able to succeed because God worked through him. The Master has predetermined what he is going to accomplish. If anyone surrenders himself totally at his feet, then the Master will see that everything is set right. One must bear with everything, because everything is determined by actions (Karmas). Again, our present actions can counteract the effect of past actions.

Disciple: Can action ever cancel action?

Mother: Why not? If you do a good action, that will counteract your past evil action. Past sins can be counteracted by meditation, Japa and spiritual thought.

I had heard that a boy in the Mirzapur Street was possessed by a ghost. Some members of the Udbodhan Office had visited the boy yesterday. I asked the Mother, "How long does one live in the spirit body?"

Mother: All people, excepting highly evolved souls, live in the spirit body for a year. After that, food and water are offered in Gaya for the satisfaction of the departed souls and religious festivals are arranged. By these means the souls of the departed are released from their spirit body. They go to other planes of existence and experience pleasure or pain, and in course of time, are born again in human forms according to their desires. Others attain salvation from those planes. But if a person has some meritorious action to his credit in this life, he does not lose spiritual consciousness altogether in his spirit body.

Here the Mother referred to the spirit of the Vaishnava priest of the Govindaji temple in Brindavan.

Disciple: Is it possible for one to attain to a higher state if one's Sraddha ceremony is performed in Gaya?

Mother: Yes, that is true.[1]

---

[1] In this connection I am reminded of another incident. The Holy Mother was in Banaras. I had left a day or two before for Gaya to perform the Sraddha ceremony for my dead ancestors. I had said to the Holy Mother before my departure, "Mother, please give your blessings that my ancestors may attain heaven." On the very night of the day I offered food and drink in Gaya for the gratification of my departed ancestors, Bhudev, the Mother's nephew, who had accompanied her to Banaras saw the Holy Mother in a dream, engaged in Japa, with a crowd of people around her, saying, "Please give me salvation! Please give me salvation!" The Mother sprinkled over them the holy water kept in a jar and said, "Go away, you are saved!" Then they departed in great happiness. Then another man appeared. The Mother said to him, "I cannot continue like this any longer." He begged of her a long time and at last received her grace. The next day Bhudev

Disciple: Then what is the necessity of spiritual practices?

Mother: These dead souls, no doubt, attain to a higher state and live there for some time, but afterwards they are again born in this world according to their past desires. After their birth in a human body some of them obtain salvation in this life, whereas others take inferior births to reap the results of their Karma. This world is moving around like a wheel. That indeed is the last birth in which one gets rid of all desires completely.

Disciple: You just referred to the dead souls attaining to a divine state. Do they go there by themselves or does someone lead them?

Mother: No, they go by themselves. The subtle body is like a body made of air.

Disciple: What happens to those for whom no Sraddha ceremony is performed in Gaya?

Mother: They live in the spirit body until some fortunate ones born in their family perform the Sraddha ceremony in Gaya or some other forms of obsequies.

Disciple: We hear of ghosts and spooks. Are they the attendants of Siva or simply spirits? Or are they the spirits of dead people?

Mother: They are the spirits of the dead. The spirit attendants of Siva belong to a special group. One must live very carefully. Every action produces its results. It is not good to harass others or use harsh words towards others.

Disciple: Mother, a margosa tree does not produce a mango, nor does a mango tree produce a margosa fruit. Everyone reaps the result of his own Karma.

Mother: You are right, my child. In course of time one does not feel even the existence of God. After attaining wisdom (Jnana) one sees that gods and deities are all Maya. Everything comes into existence in time and also disappears in time.

* * * *

---

narrated this dream to the Holy Mother and she said in reply. "R— has gone to Gaya to perform the Sraddha ceremony of his ancestors. Therefore all these people have obtained their salvation." In fact, while offering oblations for my departed ancestors with great sincerity, I had also offered food and drink for the salvation of all persons whose names I could remember at that time. I had prayed for the salvation of all of them.

UDBODHAN (PRAYER-HALL)

It was morning and we were talking with the Holy Mother.

Mother: After Sri Ramakrishna passed away, while staying alone at Kamarpukur, I thought within myself, "I have no children. There is no one in this world whom I can call my *own.* What will happen to me?" Then the Master appeared to me and said, "Well, you want a son. I have given you so many jewels of sons. And in course of time you will hear many many more people addressing you as Mother."

While I was going to Brindavan, I saw the Master look at me through the window of the railway carriage and say, "You have the gold amulet with you. See that you do not lose it."

I had tied his amulet on my arm. I used to worship it. Later I gave it to the Belur Math. They worship it there.

Devotee: That amulet, it seems, was lost this year on the Master's Tithi Puja day. Along with flowers and Bel leaves, that also was thrown into the Ganges, unknowingly. When water receded at the ebb tide, Ram Babu's son found it while playing there and brought it back.

Mother: It is his amulet. It must be preserved carefully.

The talk turned to Belur Math.

Mother: Of a truth, I always saw as though the Master lived on the land on the other side of the Ganga (that is, opposite to Dakshineswar)—in a cottage just where the present monastery and plantain trees are. (At the time there was no Math). After the new land was purchased for the Math, Naren took me there one day. He showed me each and every part of it and said, "Mother, now you can move about in your own place at will without any restraint."

At Bodh Gaya I saw the Math of that place with so much of property. There was no dearth of any commodity there. I used to weep and pray to the Master: 'Oh, Master, my children have no place to stay, nothing to eat. They go wandering from door to door. If only they could have a place like this to stay!' And so by the grace of the Master this Math came up.

One day Naren came and said, "Mother, just now I offered one hundred and eight Bel leaves to the Master, so that we could have a piece of land for the Math. That Karma can never go without its fruit. One day it will certainly happen that way."

At night after food I went to bring the betel-rolls and heard these words from the Holy Mother: "Naren said, 'Mother, nowadays everything of mine is flying away. I see that every thing flies away.'" The Mother smilingly continued, "I said, 'Please take care. Don't send me also flying.' At that Naren answered, 'Mother, if I were to send you flying, where shall I remain? That Jnana which makes nothing of the lotus feet of the Guru is surely Ajnana. If the Guru's lotus feet are slighted, where is the basis for Jnana?'"

Having said this, she continued, "After knowledge dawns, God and all else vanish into nothing. Mother, Mother—in the end my Mother pervades the whole universe. Everything becomes One. This is the simple truth."

* * * *

UDBODHAN (PRAYER-HALL)

The Holy Mother was sorting Bel leaves for the daily worship, when I showed her one of the photographs of her that had been printed recently. I asked if it was a good likeness of hers.

Mother: Yes, this is a good picture, but I was stouter before it was taken. Yogen (Swami Yogananda) was very ill at that time. Worrying about him, I became emaciated. I was very unhappy then. I would weep when Yogen's illness took a turn for the worse and I would feel happy when he felt better. Mrs. Sarah Bull took this photograph. At first I did not agree to it; but she insisted and said, "Mother, I shall take this picture to America and worship it." At last the picture was taken.

Disciple: Mother, that photograph of Sri Ramakrishna which you have with you is a very good one. One feels it when one sees the picture. Well, is that a good likeness of the Master?

Mother: Yes, that picture is very, very good. It originally belonged to a Brahmana cook. Several prints were made of his first photograph. The Brahmana took one of them. The picture was at first very dark, just like the image of Kali. Therefore it was given to the Brahmana. When he left Dakshineswar for some place—I do not remember where—he gave it to me. I kept the photograph with the pictures of other gods and goddesses and worshipped it. At that time I lived on the ground floor of the Nahabat. One day the Master came there and at the sight of the picture he said, "Hallo, what is all this?" Lakshmi and I had been cooking under the staircase. Then I saw the Master take in his hand the Bel leaves and flowers kept there for worship, and offer them to the photograph. He worshipped the picture. This is the same picture. That Brahmana never returned; so the picture remained with me.

Disciple: Mother, did you ever see the face of the Master to be pale at the time of his Samadhi?

Mother: Why, I don't remember to have seen it so. On the other hand, I always saw a smile on his face in his ecstatic mood.

Disciple: It is possible to have a smile during the state of emotional ecstasy (*Bhāva Samādhi*); but regarding the photograph of his sitting posture, the Master had said that it was a picture of a very exalted state. Is it possible to have a smile in that state?

Mother: But I have seen him smile in all states of Samadhi.

Disciple: Of what complexion was he?

Mother: His complexion was like the colour of gold—like that of Harital (yellow orpiment). His complexion blended with the colour of the golden amulet which he wore on his arm. When I used to rub him with oil, I could clearly see a lustre coming out of his entire body. A youth with a very fair complexion once came to the Kali temple at Dakshineswar. The Master said to me, "Both of us (the man and the Master) will walk side by side in the Panchavati. You judge who is the fairer of the two." They started walking and I observed that the youth was slightly fairer than the Master. He was 19 or 20 years old.

When the Master would come out of his room in the temple, people used to stand in line and say to one another, "Ah, there he goes!" He was fairly stout. Mathur Babu gave him a low stool to sit on. It was a rather wide stool, but it was not quite big enough to hold him comfortably when he would squat on it to take his meals. People would look at him wonder-struck when he went with slow, steady steps to the Ganges to take his bath.

When he was at Kamarpukur, the men and women there looked at him with mouths agape whenever he chanced to come out of the house. One day as he went out for a walk in the direction of the canal known as 'Bhutir Khāl', the women who had gone there to fetch water looked at him agape and said, "There the Master goes!" Annoyed at this, Sri Ramakrishna said to Hriday, "Well, Hridu, please put a veil on my head at once."

I never saw the Master sad. He was joyous in the company of everyone, were he a boy of five or a man of ripe old age. I never saw him morose, my child. Ah, what happy days those were! At Kamarpukur he would get up early in the morning and tell me, "Today I shall eat this particular green, please cook it for me." With the other women of the family I would accordingly arrange for his meal. After a few days he said, "What has come over me? The moment I get up from sleep I say, 'What shall I eat? What shall I eat?' " Then he said to me, "I have no desire for any particular food. I shall eat whatever you will cook for me."

He used to go to Kamarpukur to get relief from the severe diarrhoea from which he was suffering at Dakshineswar. He used to say, "Goodness, my belly is filled only with filth. There is no end to it!" Suffering thus, he developed a kind of hatred for the body and thereafter he did not pay much heed to it.

Once, in Kamarpukur, the Master came across a big fish, which had come on the road from the nearby overflowing tank. He helped it back into the tank, saying, "Run, run for your life! If Hridu sees you, he will finish you off in no time." Returning home, he told Hriday, "O Hridu ! Today I saw a very big fish of yellow hue, that had come on the road. I helped it back into the tank." "O Uncle ! What have you done !", cried Hriday, "Alas ! A big fish like that would have made a delicious dish !"

Nowadays you see so many devotees everywhere. There is so much excitement and noise. But during the illness of the Master one of the devotees ran away in order to avoid giving twenty rupees! The expenses for the treatment of the Master during his illness were raised by subscription, and this devotee had been asked to contribute that sum. Now it is not at all difficult to serve the Master. For though food is offered to him, it is really eaten by the devotees. If you make the Master sit, he will sit. If you make him lie down, he will remain in that position. After all, he is only a picture!

The Master saw (in a vision) Balaram Babu with a turban on his head and his hands folded, standing by the image of Kali. Balaram always remained with folded hands before the Master. He never saluted the Master by touching his feet. The Master understood his thought and would say to him, "O Balaram, my foot is itching. Kindly massage it gently." Immediately Balaram would send for Naren or Rakhal or someone else among the boys who attended on the Master, and ask him to massage his feet!

Disciple: Once I asked Swami Brahmananda about Sri Ramakrishna's complexion. He said, "The Master's complexion was just like ours."

Mother: Yes, he looked like that when Rakhal and other disciples met him. At that time he had lost his former good health and complexion. For example, look at me and see my complexion and health. Did I look like this formerly? No, I was very pretty then. I was not stout, but later on I became so.

In Dakshineswar I lived very quietly and unobserved by people in general. The manager of the temple used to say, 'We have heard that she lives here, but we have never seen her.' At that time I would see the Master perhaps once in two months. I used to console my mind by saying, 'O mind, are you so fortunate that you can see him everyday?' I used to stand behind the screen round the verandah of the Nahabat, and hear the Master sing and see him dance in ecstasy through the holes in the screen. It was standing there long that brought on the rheumatism in my legs. He would tell me, 'A wild bird, if kept within a cage day and night, gets rheumatic. So you should have a walk at times in the neighbourhood.'

I would bathe at 4 a.m. As the day advanced, a little sunshine would come near the staircase, and I would dry my hair then. I had very long hair in those days. A small room, after all, in the Nahabat! And that too used to be full of things. Many things were even stored in stringed suspenders from the ceiling. But I never experienced any difficulty.

It was the time of worship. The Mother made herself ready to go to the shrine room. I came downstairs. After the worship was over, I went upstairs again to bring the Prasada for the devotees. As I took the leaves containing the sweets and fruits, suddenly my elbow touched the Holy Mother's feet. "Ah!" said the Mother, and saluted me with folded hands. "That's nothing," said I. But she was not satisfied with merely bowing down before me and said, "Come, my child, let me kiss you." She touched my chin with her hand and kissed the hand and so became pacified. Thus she used to respect her disciples as the manifestations of God, and at the same time show her affection to them as a mother does to her children.

UDBODHAN (PRAYER-HALL)

29th October, 1910

It was early in the morning. I was seated near the Mother's bed. She began to talk to me about the Master.

Mother: On the very day I reached Puri, I quickly finished the worship of the Master in the morning by placing his picture on a tin containing ghee. Then I went to visit the temple of Sri Jagannath after locking the room. When I returned, I saw the picture of the Master at the foot of the tin. The others too came and observed it. All felt that some thief might have entered the house in our absence. But all the things in the room remained undisturbed. At last I noticed that big red ants had gathered on the tin—it was a ghee tin, you see. Since they had approached the picture of the Master also, he had come down and settled himself below!

Disciple: Does the Master really live in the picture?

Mother: Of course, he does. The body and the shadow are the same.[1] And what is his picture but a shadow?

Disciple: Does he live in all the pictures?

Mother: Yes. If you pray to him constantly before his picture, then he manifests himself through that picture. The place where the picture is kept becomes a shrine. Suppose a man worships the Master there (*pointing to a plot of land north of the Udbodhan*), then the place is associated with his presence.

Disciple: Well, good and bad memories are associated with all places.

Mother: It is not exactly like that. The Master will pay special attention to such a place.

Disciple: Does the Master really partake of the food that you offer him?

Mother: Yes, he does.

Disciple: But we do not see any sign of it.

Mother: A light comes out of his eyes and licks all the articles of food. His ambrosial touch replenishes them again, so there is no decrease.

The Lord comes down from Vaikuntha (the heavenly abode of Sri Vishnu) to where the devotee calls him. On the night of the Kojagari Purnima, Lakshmi (the goddess of wealth) comes down to the earth from Vaikuntha. She visits and accepts the worship

[1]It is for this reason that one does not walk over the shadow of an elder. One day, while living at Jayrambati, I was returning home after my bath. The Mother was also coming back from the tank. I was walking by her side, and now and then I stepped over her shadow. The Mother asked me to walk on her other side. At first I did not know that I had been walking over her shadow.

in those places where she wants to bestow her special grace. My mother-in-law had seen at Kamarpukur a fair girl, about 14 or 15 years old, with ear-rings made of conch-shells, and with diamond bangles on the arm. The goddess Lakshmi Herself, who had come in the form of the girl, spoke to her under the Bakul tree (opposite the house of the Master). My mother-in-law asked, "Who are you, dear?" Sri Lakshmi replied, "Oh! I have specially come here!" My mother-in-law asked, "Have you seen my son (Ramkumar, the elder brother of Sri Ramakrishna)? He has gone to perform worship. It is already so late, and he has not returned yet." "Yes, he is on his way back," said Lakshmi, "From that place itself, I have now come to visit your house." "No, dear," said my mother-in-law, "there is nobody at home. Please do not come now." Hearing such repeated refusals to entertain her, the goddess disappeared, saying, "All right. Anyway, I will look after you all in a general way." So, you see, their circumstances never improved to a great extent. However, they could maintain themselves on coarse food and clothing.

My mother-in-law had seen the girl come from the direction of the house of the Lahas, where the corn used to be stored. On his return, when my brother-in-law heard of all this, he exclaimed, "O Mother, you did not understand! Today is Kojagari Purnima. Lakshmi Herself had come!" He could fortell things, and verified this incident by astrological calculations.

Why? Does the Master require any food? He doesn't. He eats the food-offering only for the gratification of the devotees. The sacred Prasada purifies the heart. The mind becomes impure, if one eats food without first offering it to God.[1]

Disciple: Does the Master really partake of the food-offering?

Mother: Yes, do I not notice whether he partakes of the food or not? The Master takes the seat before the plate and then partakes of the food.

[1] A devotee had once accepted from the Holy Mother the ochre robe of the monastic life. He suffered from illness for some years and had been to several places for change of air. Later he spent some time at his home instead of living at the monastery. One day he came to Jayrambati and returned the ochre robe to the Holy Mother. Referring to the incident, the Holy Mother said, "Alas! His mind has become impure on account of his eating the food of worldly-minded people."

Disciple: Do you then actually see it ?

Mother: Yes. In the case of some offerings, he actually eats and in other cases he merely looks at them. Take your own case. You don't like to eat all things at all times. Nor do you relish the food offered by anyone and everyone. It is like that. One's love of God depends entirely upon one's inner feeling. Love of God is the essential thing.

Disciple : How does one get love of God? Even if one's own son be brought up by someone else, he does not recognize his own mother as his mother.

Mother: Yes, that is true. The grace of God is the thing that is needed. One should be fit to deserve the grace of God.

Disciple: How can one speak of deserving grace, or not deserving it? Grace is the same for all.

Mother: One must pray sitting on the bank of the river. He will be taken across in proper time.

Disciple: Everything happens when the proper time comes. Then where does God's grace come in?

Mother: Must you not sit with the fishing rod in your hand, if you want to catch the fish?

Disciple: If God be our 'own', why then should one sit and wait?

Mother: That is true. It may happen even out of season. Don't you see nowadays how people get fruits like mango and jack out of season? How many mangoes grow nowadays in the month of Bhadra?

Disciple: Is it all, that He sends us away by giving us what we deserve? Or, can one get Him as one's very own? Is God my very 'own'?

Mother: Yes, God is one's very 'own'. It is the eternal relationship. He is everyone's 'own'. One realizes Him in proportion to the intensity of one's feeling for Him.

Disciple: Intense feeling is like a dream. A man dreams what he thinks.

Mother: Yes, it is a dream. The whole world is a dream; even this (the waking state) is a dream.

Disciple: No, this is not a dream, for then it would have disappeared in the twinkling of an eye. This state exists for many, many births.

Mother: Let it be so; still it is nothing but dream. What you dreamt last night does not exist now. (As a matter of fact, on the previous night the disciple had an amazing dream). A farmer who lost a son dreamt at night that he was a king and the father of eight sons. When the dream vanished, he said to his wife, "Shall I weep for my eight children or for this one?"

After arguing thus with the Mother, I said, "Mother, I don't really bother my head about what I just said to you. All that I want to know is whether there is anyone whom I may call my 'own'."

Mother: Yes, such a One exists.

Disciple: Surely?

Mother: Yes.

Disciple: If He be really our 'own', then why should we pray unto Him in order to see Him? One who is truly my 'own' would come to me even if I did not call on Him. Does God do things for us as our parents do?

Mother: Yes, that is true, my child. He Himself has become our father and mother. He Himself brings us up as our parents. It is He alone who looks after us. Otherwise where were you and where are you now? Your parents brought you up, but at last realized that you did not belong to them. Have you not seen a cuckoo brought up in the nest of a crow?

Disciple: Shall I realize God as really my 'own'?

Mother: Yes, surely you will realize Him. Whatever you yearn for, that you will get. Did not Swamiji (referring to Swami Vivekananda) realize Him? You too will realize Him as Swamiji did.

Disciple: Mother, please see that I am not overcome by fear or slackening of faith.

Mother: There is no such danger for you. For I myself have hooked the fish.

Disciple: That is good. We all shall enjoy it.

Mother: Yes, that is right. One makes the mould and many others make their images from it.

Disciple: Yes, we shall get everything if you only work for us. You cannot set us aside.

Mother: Yes, my child, you will have all if I do it for you.

UDBODHAN

26th November, 1910, 7 *a.m.*

The Mother had gone the day before to see Gupta Maharaj (Swami Sadananda) who was ill. Boshi and Tabu were nursing him with great care. The Mother praised them, saying—, "They are really holy. Blessed indeed are they! Whom else shall we call holy?"

"Yogin Chatterjee's (Swami Nityananda's) disciples too nursed him carefully. They were all from East Bengal. All young boys used to serve the Master at Kasipur. He used to keep them in good humour by saying all sorts of things. He used to say, 'How will they be able to endure so much hardship, if they do not get any joy?' He was very tactful. He didn't need much nursing. His diet too was very spare.

"One day he wanted to eat Amalaki (myrobalan). Durgacharan (Nag Mahashaya) came three days later with two or three very big ones. He had not eaten for three days. Taking the Amalaki in his hands, the Master was in tears. He said to Durgacharan, 'I thought that you had left for Dhaka or somewhere.' He then asked me to prepare a pungent dish for Durgacharan, as people from East Bengal like it pungent. When it was ready, the Master himself sat down to eat. Durgacharan had Prasada after the Master had tasted all the various preparations.

"The expenses at the Kasipur household were very high. Three separate menus had to be prepared: one for the Master, one for the youngsters like Naren, and one for the rest. Subscriptions were raised to meet the expenses. One of the devotees dropped away for fear of having to pay!

"The Master's disease was due to accepting the sins of others. He used to say, 'It is due to Girish's sins. He would not have been able to bear all this suffering.' The Master had the power to die at will. He could have easily given up the body in Samadhi. But he would say, 'It will be nice if I unite all these youngsters together in a close bond of love.' Until then, merely a 'how-do-you-do' relationship existed between them: 'Naren Babu, how are you?', 'Rakhal Babu, how do you do?', and so on. That is why, the Master did not give up the body early, in spite of so much suffering."

UDBODHAN

14th April, 1911

In the morning I carried to the shrine the flowers meant for the worship of Sri Ramakrishna. It was late, so the Mother said, "Please come with the flowers as soon as they are brought." The Mother used to perform the worship after making all the necessary arrangements for it herself. She was sitting on her cot, and beckoned me near her and enquired about a certain devotee.

Mother: Is he downstairs?

Disciple: Yes, Mother.

Mother: What does he do? Is he studying?

Disciple: May be. But probably he is not a regular student.

Mother: Won't he go to the Belur Math?

Disciple: No. He doesn't want to go there.

Mother: All of you should persuade him.

Disciple: I tried my best. You please tell him, Mother. May be then he will go and stay at the Math at least for some days.

Mother: I have also told him, but he would pay no heed. He doesn't want to go. He fears that others may tease him for going there. Sarat also spoke to me about that boy: "Shouldn't the boy have some regard for our advice, and the words of Maharajji (Swami Brahmananda)? Let him go and stay for at least two days at the Math in obedience to Maharajji's wish." That is right. The boy should go with Rakhal and stay for some days at Puri. How will the boy be able to wander about alone? Where will he get food?

Disciple: That is no problem. He will beg for food. But he should go to tne Math once, at least in obedience to the advice of Maharaj and the other elders.

Mother: That is right. The advice of the elders must be obeyed. The boy has no desire to work. How can the mind be kept well without any work? Is it possible to meditate for all the twenty-four hours of the day? So one has to take up some work. That keeps the mind in good shape. How is your work going on?

Disciple: It is going on all right.

Mother: You had written about going to Rameswaram. It is good, my child, that you did not go. The journey is indeed hazardous.

Disciple: Sarat Maharaj wanted to send me. But from where could the funds come? Had I gone, all the burden of bear-ing my expenses would have fallen on Sasi Maharaj.

Mother: Yes. He has already spent a thousand rupees on our pilgrimage.

UDBODHAN

15*th April*, 1911

The next day Mother was preparing betel-rolls in the room to the south of the shrine. It was nearly 11 a.m. When I went to her, she enquired about the boy who had come on the previous day, "Has he left?"

Disciple: Yes. He may stay for a day or two at the house of Dr. Kanjilal. Sarat Maharaj said, "If the boy has left with pride and egoism, then he will degenerate more and more as days pass. And if he has left out of shame, then if the Master wills, he may again turn over a new leaf."

Mother: What does it matter? He is after all a boy, not a girl. It is easy to break. How many can build? All can criticize and make fun of him; but how many can bring him on the right path? Man is prone to weakness.

Disciple: Sarat Maharaj said, "It is possible for only a noble-minded person to live alone, while one with an impure mind becomes all the more degenerated thereby."

Mother: Why should he fear? The Master will protect him. Are there not many monks who live all alone?

Disciple: Even Hriday Mukherjee lost the company of the Master in later days.

Mother: Is it possible for anyone to enjoy a good thing eternally?

Disciple: He, it seems, had also troubled the Master a lot, and used very offensive language with him.

Mother: When one has done so much dedicated service, what does it matter if he says a few unpleasant things? It is natural for one who really takes so much care, to say sometimes things like that.

Disciple: This boy too served you very much—and now see what has happened!

Mother: How is it possible to get along without any discipline? How else can one improve?

JAYRAMBATI

In the month of Aswin, on the day of the Mahasaptami, the first day of the worship of Mother Durga, two young devotees presented themselves before the Mother. On the Mahashtami day they offered lotus flowers at the feet of the Mother. One of them said, "Mother please, ordain me into the vows of Sannyasa." The other young boy too joined in the request. The Mother smiled a little and said, "All in due course, children. Why do you worry?" The devotee persisted, "Mother, you must give us Sannyasa. Give us the ochre cloth."

The Mother now spoke a little seriously: "What will you gain by putting on the ochre cloth? What is so special in it? Neither of you has entered married life; you are already Sannyasins. All the other things will follow in due course."

The devotee said, "Mother, I wish to throw away my sacred thread, cloth, and all, and remain absorbed in the contemplation of the Divine like Trailanga Swami." Mother said smilingly, "It will happen, child, when the right time comes." Now the devotee began speaking rather excitedly: "Mother, here it is—I am throwing away the cloth and the sacred-thread," and actually was about to do so, when the Mother said rather hurriedly, "Enough of it now. At proper time, these things will leave you by themselves."

Still his childish behaviour did not stop. He said, "Bless me Mother, with at least a drop of madness that had come upon the Master. Make me mad, Mother." And again, "Mother, will you not endow us with devotion? Won't you bestow on us the vision of the Master?" Mother said, "Everything will come to pass, my child, in due course." Both the boys went out of the room after prostrating themselves before the Mother.

At noon, all sat down for meals. The same young devotee again spoke, "How have you cooked this rice-pudding? It is not at all tasting well." The Mother smiled and said, "What can I do, child? Sufficient quantity of milk is not available here." Kedar's mother was nearby. She said, "Very good. You are all Mother's children. Bring plenty of things, then the Mother will be able to feed you to your heart's content." This did not even reach the devotee's ears. He went on, "Mother, today I could not eat my fill. I will come again and eat to my satisfaction. You must also allow me to meet you one day at the Udbodhan." The Mother agreed to this request.

In the forenoon a devotee had arrived from Shillong. Doubtful about the divine nature of the Mother, he had taken a vow that he would not visit her unless he had seen her in dream seven times. He had the requisite visions. Therefore he had gone to Jayrambati to pay his respects to her. In the afternoon, as he was about to take leave of her, he said, "Mother, I shall say good-bye now. Do I need anything else?"

Mother: Yes, surely. You must have your initiation.

Devotee: I may have it at Baghbazar in Calcutta.

Mother: Better finish that task, my child. Have your initiation today.

Devotee: But I have eaten the Prasada.

Mother : That doesn't matter.

After the initiation, the devotee departed.

The mental state of the eccentric devotee who had come in the morning took a turn for the worse after he returned home from Jayrambati. He became restless for the vision of the Master and felt piqued to think that though the Holy Mother could, by her mere will, make him get a vision of Sri Ramakrishna, she refused to do so. In a very angry state of mind he came back to Jayrambati and said to her, "Mother, won't you enable me to see the Master?" The Mother said tenderly, "Yes, you will see Him; dont't be so restless." He could not stand it any longer. He said in an angry voice, "You are only deceiving me. Here is the rosary you gave me. Take it back. I don't care for it any more." With these words he threw the rosary at her. "All right," said the Mother, "remain for ever the child of Sri Ramakrishna!" He left the place at once.

Afterwards the devotee went really mad. He began writing abusive letters to the Swamis of the Ramakrishna Mission and did not spare even the Holy Mother in this respect.

One day, referring to this devotee, I asked the Holy Mother, "Did he also return the Mantra? He threw away his rosary. Can anyone ever return the Mantra?"

Mother: Is it ever possible? The word of the Mantra is living. Can anyone, who has received it, give it back? Can he, once having felt attraction for the Guru, get rid of him? Some day in the future this man will come round and fall at the feet of those whom he now abuses.

Devotee: Why does such a thing come to pass ?

Mother: Such things do happen. One Guru may initiate many disciples, but can they all be of the same nature? Spiritual life manifests in a devotee according to his nature. He said to me, at Jayrambati, "Mother, make me mad." "Why?" said I, "why should you be mad, my child? Can anyone, without committing much sin, ever be mad?" He said, "My younger brother has seen the Master. Please let me also have a vision of Him." I said in reply, "Who can ever see him with the physical eyes? But one may do so by closing one's eyes. Can we not visualize a picture by closing the eyes? Your brother is a child. He may have visualized the Master with his eyes closed, but he thinks that he has seen him with his eyes open." I asked him to continue his spiritual life—to practise spiritual disciplines and pray to the Master—and told him that he also would have the vision. Man knows in his own mind how far he has advanced and how much knowledge and consciousness of God he has attained. He knows in his innermost soul how much of God he has realized. Besides, who has been able to see God with his physical eyes?

This devotee, after having been scolded at the Udbodhan Office, used to live on the bank of the Ganges. Sometimes he would sit on the door-step of the Udbodhan Office and would take his meal there. After some time, he was brought once to the Holy Mother with her permission. She tried to pacify him in various ways and said, "The Master used to say, 'At the time of death I shall have to stand by those who pray to me.' These are words from his own mouth. You are my child. What should you be afraid of? Why should you behave like a mad man? That will disgrace the Master. People will say that his devotee has become mad. Should you conduct yourself in a way that will discredit the name of the Master? Go home and live as others do. Eat and live like them. At the time of your death, he will reveal himself to you and take you to him. Can you tell me if anyone ever got a vision of him with physical eyes? It was only Naren (Swami Vivekananda) who saw him thus. That happened in America when he had intense yearning for him. Naren then used to feel that the Master was grasping his arm. That vision also lasted only for a few days. Now go home and live there happily. How miserable are the worldly people! The other day Ram's son passed away. You can at least sleep with an easy heart."

The devotee was much pacified by the Holy Mother's consolation and words of instruction. He took his meal at the Udbodhan Office and later returned to his native village. He gradually regained his normal state of mind.

JAYRAMBATI
26th May, 1911

The Holy Mother returned to Calcutta from her pilgrimage to Rameswaram and after a few days went back to Jayrambati. One evening, while seated on the porch of her old house, she asked me about a monastic devotee.

Mother: What did he say?

Disciple: He felt a yearning for you for three or four months.

Mother: How strange! A Sannyasin must sever all the bondage of Maya. A golden chain is as good a shackle as an iron one. A Sannyasin must not entangle himself in any form of Maya. Why should he constantly say, "Oh! Mother's love! Mother's love! I am deprived of it"? What ideas! I do not like men constantly hanging on me. At least he has the form of a man; I am not talking of God. And I have to move about with women. Ashu also used to come to me frequently to make sandal paste or on some other pretext. One day I warned him.

Disciple: Will the Sannyasins who profess the ideals of the Vedanta attain to Nirvana?

Mother: Surely. By gradually cutting off the bonds of Maya they will realize Nirvana and merge themselves in God. This body is , no doubt, the outcome of desires. The body cannot live unless there is a trace of desire. All comes to an end when a man gets rid of desires completely.

Children (*i.e.* devotees) come here, eat their meals, enjoy themselves and then go away. Why should I be attached to them? One day Hazra said to the Master: "Why do you constantly long for Narendra and other youngsters? They are quite happy by themselves, eating, drinking and playing. You had better fix your mind on God. Why should you be attached to them?" At these words, the Master took his mind away from the young disciples completely and merged it in the thought of God. Instantaneously he entered into Samadhi; his beard and hair stood straight on end like the Kadamba flower. Just imagine what kind of a man the Master was! ......His body became hard like a wooden statue. Ramlal, who was attending on him, said repeatedly, "Please be your former self again." At last the mind came down to the normal plane. It was only out of compassion for people that he kept his mind on the lower plane.

At the time of death, Yogen (Swami Yogananda) wanted Nirvana. Girish Babu said to him, " Look here, Yogen! Don't accept Nirvana. Don't think of the Master as pervading the entire universe, the sun and the moon forming his eyes. Think of the Master as he used to be to us, and thus thinking of Him, go to Him." Deities and angels, whoever they be, are born again on this earth. They do not eat or talk in their subtle bodies. Hence, they cannot stay in those planes for long.

Disciple: If they neither eat nor talk, then how do they spend their days?

Mother: Immersed in meditation they remain where they are, like wooden images, for ages! Like the images of the kings I saw at Rameswaram, standing there dressed in royal robes! When God needs them, he brings them down from their respective places. There are different heavenly planes, such as the Jana-loka, Satya-loka, and Dhruva-loka. The Master said that he had brought down Narendra (Swami Vivekananda) from the plane of the Seven Sages (*Saptarṣi*). His words are verily the words of the Veda. They can never be untrue.

Disciple: Must we also, then, live like images of wood or clay?

Mother: Oh, no! You will serve the Master. There are two classes of devotees. One class devotes itself to the service of God, as on this earth; and another group is immersed in meditation for ages, like the images.

Disciple: Well, Mother, the Master used to say that the Isvara-kotis can come back to the relative plane of consciousness even after the attainment of Nirvana; others cannot do so. What does that mean?

Mother: The Isvarakoti, even after the attainment of Nirvana, can gather back his mind from it and direct it to the ordinary plane of consciousness.

Disciple: How can the mind that has merged itself in God be brought back again to the world? How can one ever separate a jar of water from the water of the lake, if it has been poured into it?

Mother: Not all can do so. Only the Paramahamsa can. A Hamsa can separate the milk from a mixture of water and milk, and drink only the milk.

Disciple: Can all get rid of desires?

Mother: If they could, then this creation would have come to an end. The creation is going on because all cannot be free of desires. People with desires take their births again and again.

Disciple: Suppose a man gives up his body standing in the waters of the Ganges.

Mother: Freedom from birth is possible only when there is no trace of desire. Otherwise, nothing else is of any avail. If one does not get rid of desires, what will one gain, even if this be one's last birth in this world?

Disciple: Mother, infinite is this creation; who can tell what is happening in a remote plane? Who can say if any living beings inhabit any of those innumerable stars and planets?

Mother: It is possible only for God to be omniscient in this realm of Maya. Perhaps there is no living being in those planets and stars.

* * * *

One day in the rainy season of the same year, 1911, Swami Saradananda, Yogin-Ma, Golap-Ma and several other devotees went to Kamarpukur from Jayrambati. Yogin-Ma slipped on the road. Some parts of her body were injured and blood flowed. I returned to Jayrambati ahead of the party and told the Holy Mother about Yogin-Ma's accident. The Mother said sadly, "Golap said before they set out, 'Yogin is going with us; let us see how often she slips on the road.' Yogin fell down to vindicate Golap's words. After all, those were the words of a spiritual woman. She practises spiritual disciplines. Therefore her words must bear fruit. Hence a holy person must not say anything bad about anyone."

UDBODHAN

16th January, 1912

In the morning I was with the Holy Mother in her room. I said to her, "Mother, Sri Chaitanya one day blessed Narayani, saying, 'May you have devotion to Krishna!' The words had such a magic effect that the girl, only three or four years old, rolled on the ground uttering. 'Ah, Krishna! Ah, Krishna!' We have read a story about Narada. After he had realized God, one day he felt compassion for an ant. He said to himself, 'I have attained to perfection as the result of practising austerities through many human births, and this poor ant will have to wait so long, even before it is born as a man!' Tenderly he blessed the ant, saying,

'Be free!' Immediately the ant assumed such non-human forms as birds, beasts, and so forth, and gradually took the body of a man. It passed through many human births, enjoyed the experiences associated with them, and step by step, directed its attention to spiritual disciplines. It worshipped God and attained salvation. Narada saw in the twinkling of an eye all these events of innumerable births. Therefore one may get liberation instantaneously through the grace of a great soul."

Mother: That is true.

Disciple: But I have also heard that one cannot keep one's body long, if one accepts the burden of the sins of others. The body that might have been instrumental in getting salvation for many, withers away for the sake of one sinful person.

Mother: That's also true. Further, a great soul thus loses his power. The power of austerities and spiritual disciplines that might have been utilized for the liberation of many souls is spent for the sake of one person. The Master used to say, "I have all these physical ailments because I have taken upon myself the sins of Girish." But now Girish also is suffering.

Disciple : Mother, one day I had a dream. I saw that a man with shaggy hair came to you and insisted that you must do something for him at once. He had previously been initiated by you. But he himself would not practise any spiritual discipline. You said, "If I do something for him then I shall not live; my body will fall off immediately." With all the earnestness I could command, I forbade you to show any kindness to this man and said, "Why should you do anything for him? He will achieve his own salvation. Let him practise Sadhana." As he insisted again and again, you became disgusted with him, did something to him by touching his chest and neck, and said repeatedly, "If I do something for him, then I shall not live; my body will fall off immediately." Then my dream disappeared. Well, is it true that one's power becomes limited when one is born in a physical body?

Mother: Yes, that is so. Many a time, disgusted with the repeated requests of some persons, I think, "Well, this body will die some day. Let it fall off this moment. Let me give him salvation."

Disciple: Mother, does the vision of God mean the attainment of knowledge (Jnana) and spiritual consciousness (Chaitanya)? Or, does it signify something else?

Mother: What else can it mean except the attainment of these?

Does anybody mean to say that a man of realization grows two horns?

Disciple: Many of your devotees explain the vision of God differently. They believe that one sees God with physical eyes and talks to Him.

Mother: Yes, they say, "Please show us the Father." But he (Sri Ramakishna) is nobody's father. The three words—Guru, Master (Kartā) and Father (Bābā)—pricked him like thorns. How many sages practised austerities for ages and ages! Still they could not realize God. And now people will not practise disciplines or undergo austerities, but they must be shown God immediately! I can't do it. Can you tell me if he (Sri Ramakrishna) had shown God to anyone?

Disciple: Well, Mother, we hear that some seek but do not get, while others do not seek but get. What does this mean?

Mother: God has the nature of a child. Some beg, but He does not give them, while others do not want but He asks them to acccpt. Perhaps the latter had many meritorious acts to their credit in their past births. Therefore God's grace descends on them.

Disciple: Then is there discrimination even in the grace of God?

Mother: Yes, that's true. Everything depends upon Karma (one's past actions). The moment one's Karma comes to an end, one realizes God. That is one's last birth.

Disciple: I admit that the cessation of actions (*Karma-kṣaya*), spiritual disciplines and time are the factors in the attainment of spiritual knowledge and consciousness. But if God be our very 'own', then can't He reveal Himself to His devotees by His mere will?

Mother: That is right. But who has this faith that He is his 'own'? All practise these or those disciplines because they think it their duty to do so. But how many seek God?

Disciple: Once I said to you that the child does not recognize even its own mother, if it is deprived of her care and love.

Mother: Yes, you have spoken truly. How can one love another unless one sees him? You see, you have seen me. I am your Mother and you are my child.

UDBODHAN

1st February, 1912

It was about half past nine in the evening when I went to the Holy Mother. I had not seen her for the whole day.

Mother: Where have you been the whole day?

Disciple: I have been busy with accounts downstairs.

Mother: Yes, Prakash told me so. Can anyone who has renounced the world relish these things? Once there was a mistake in the accounts relating to the salary of the Master. I asked him to talk to the manager of the Temple about it. But he said, "What a shame! Shall I bother myself about accounts?" Once he said to me, "He who utters the Name of God never suffers from any misery. No need to speak about you!" These are his very words. Renunciation was his ornament.

UDBODHAN

8th February, 1912

A mat used to be spread on the northern side of the room adjacent to the shrine. The Mother used to sit there often in the mornings. Sometimes she would perform Japa there facing the east. Whenever we came to talk with the Mother, we too would sit there. Today also the Mother was sitting on the mat.

Disciple: Mother, how long did you stay at Dakshineswar?

Mother: For a long time. I came when I was sixteen.[1] Since then, I was always there. Occasionally, I would visit our village-home, as when I did to attend the wedding of Ramlal. I would go there every two or three years.

Disciple: Were you alone at any time?

Mother: Yes, on some occasions. My mother-in-law would be there at other times. Sometimes Golap, Gaurdasi and others would stay with me. We cooked, lived and ate all in that tiny room.

I used to cook for the Master. He had poor digestion. So he could not eat the food offerings from the Kali temple. I had to cook also for the devotees of the Master. Latu lived with

[1]Actually eighteen. Her first visit to Dakshineswar was in March 1872.

him. Having had a difference with Ram Datta, he had come away. The Master said to me, 'He is a nice boy; he will knead flour for you.' Cooking went on day and night. For instance Ram Datta would come, and would shout after getting out of the carriage, 'Today I shall have Chapatis (Indian bread) and gram Dāl (a kind of soup).' Then I would at once start cooking. I used to make Chapatis out of three or four seers of flour. When Rakhal lived there, I often made Khichuri for him. The Master one day asked me to cook nicely for Naren. I prepared some Mung (green gram) soup and Chapatis. When the meal was over, the Master asked Naren,' 'How did you enjoy the meal?' 'Very well,' he replied, 'but it tasted like sick diet.' At this the Master said to me, 'What sort of stuff have you cooked for him? You must prepare for him thick gram Dāl and heavy Chapatis.' Finally I prepared those things and Naren was very pleased. Suren Mitra gave ten rupees a month for the expenses of the devotees. Gopal Senior did the marketing. Dancing, devotional music, ecstasy and Samadhi went on day and night. I made little holes in the bamboomat screen, so that I could watch through it. As a result of standing there continually, I got this rheumatism at last.

There was an old woman who came often. She had led an impure life. Now in old age, she had become religious. I was alone. So whenever she came, I would talk to her. One day the Master saw this and said, "Why do you allow her here?" I said. "Now she speaks of only good things, talks only of God. What is wrong with it? One's mind cannot be coloured always by one's former condition." The Master said, "No, no, she is a fallen woman. Why talk with her? However changed she may be, it is better to keep away." He used to forbid me from even speaking with such people lest their evil influence may affect me. Such was the extreme care he took of me.

Once a man came to meet the Master at Kamarpukur. He had a bad character. No sooner had he left, than the Master said, "Throw away a basketful of soil from this place." When no one heeded his words, he himself dug out with a spade some soil from the spot where the man was seated. "Wherever such people sit," he said, "even the soil of that place becomes impure!"

Durgacharan of East Bengal would visit him. What great devotion he had for the Master! He brought Amalaki (myrobalan) at the time of the Master's illness. Since it was not the proper season he had brought it after a vigorous search for three full days, with no thought of food and sleep! Once I gave him Prasada on a leaf-plate (at the old Baghbazar residence on the banks of the Ganga). Such was his devotion, he ate it leaf and all! He was dark and thin, but his eyes were large and sparkling—eyes of a devotee, always moist with the tears of divine love!

In those days there were many such great devotees. Those who come nowadays simply keep on saying, "Give us the vision of the Master!" They do no spiritual practice, no Japa, no meditation; Lord knows, how many wicked things they have done in their past lives—*go-hatyā* (killing of a cow), *brahma-hatyā* (slaying of a Brahmana), *bhrūṇa-hatyā* (feticide)! First of all, the evil effects of these wicked acts have to be counteracted slowly and steadily. Suppose the moon is covered by the clouds. Only when the wind gradually takes the clouds away the moon becomes visible. Do the clouds vanish in the twinkling of an eye? Spiritual life also is like that. Karma is exhausted gradually. When one realizes God, He endows one with spiritual illumination within. One becomes aware of it oneself.

UDBODHAN

9th February, 1912

Girish Chandra Ghosh had given up his body on the previous night. Referring to him, I asked the Holy Mother, "Well, Mother, do those who give up their bodies in a state of unconsciousness attain to a higher spiritual state afterwards?"

Mother: The thought that is uppermost in mind before one loses consciousness determines the course of one's soul after death.

Disciple: Yes, that is true. A little after six o'clock in the evening Girish Babu exclaimed, "Jai Ramakrishna! Let us go," and then fell unconscious. Afterwards he never regained his consciousness. A few minutes before, he had been constantly saying, "Let us go, let us go!" "Hold me a little, my son!" and so forth. I said to him, "Why do you only say, 'Let us go, let us go![1] You had better repeat

[1]Girish Babu had the intense desire to be taken to the Ganges at the time of death. Therefore he made these remarks. His brother said, "Does my brother need the Ganges for the welfare of his soul?"

the name of Sri Ramakrishna, which will do you real good.' I said that a couple of times when Girish Babu replied, "Do I not know that?" I said to myself, "Oh, he is fully conscious within!"

Mother: He remained immersed in the thought that was in his mind when he became unconscious. They (referring to Sri Ramakrishna's disciples)all have come from him and will go back to him (i.e. the Master). They all have come from him—from his arms, feet, hair and so forth. They are his limbs, his parts.

UDBODHAN, *Mother's Room*

21*st February,* 1912

It was seven o'clock in the morning. The Holy Mother was seated on the floor near her couch. Swami Nirbhayananda, who had gone to Dwaraka[1] on pilgrimge, sent the Mother some Prasada from the shrine of Dattatreya[2] in the Girnar Hills. The Mother asked, "Who was Dattatreya?"

Disciple: He, like Jada Bharata[3] and others, was a great sage—an Isvarakoti.

Mother: Like some of the children of the Master?

Disciple: Well, how is it that some of the Isvarakotis among the Master's disciples are immersed in worldliness with their wives and children?

---

[1]Dwaraka is a great place of pilgrimage in Western India, Gujarat. It is reputed to be the place where the palace of Sri Krishna, the greatest of Divine incarnations, stood.

[2]A great sage of the Puranas, considered to be a Divine incarnation. Shrines dedicated to him are, however, very rare.

[3]'Jada' means 'inert', idiotic. He is called so for the following reason: On account of his attachment to his pet deer, he had to be born as a deer, as explained earlier. Afterwards he again attained the human birth. Though his spiritual evolution was arrested during these births, he had not lost the memory of his glorious attainments in his birth as King Bharata. So when he was again born as man, he was endowed with Divine knowledge at the very birth, but in order to avoid complications from attachments as he got into before, he shunned all associations by pretending to be dumb and senseless. So he was called Jada Bharata. Eventually he gave proof of his great spiritual attainments.

Mother: Yes, they are rotting there. Purna was forced to marry. His relatives threatened him, saying, "If you go to him (referring to Sri Ramakrishna), we will smash his carriage with stones and brick-bats when he comes to Calcutta."

Disciple: Well, they might have married. Nag Mahasay also married. But to have children and lead a worldly life!

Mother: Perhaps they had some such desires. Let me tell you one thing. There is great complexity in this creation. The Master does one thing through one man and another thing through another person. Oh, it is so inscrutable! But even a householder can be an Isvarakoti. What is the harm?

Radhu was ill. She had pain and fever. The Mother was worried about her and said, "She cannot get well when I am alive. Who will look after her when I am gone? Will she live then?"

Disciple: What a crowd of devotees the whole day! You could not get a moment's respite.

Mother: Day and night, I say to the Master, "Please lessen this rush. Let me have a little rest." But I hardly get it. It will be like this for the few more days I am in this body. The message of the Master has spread everywhere; therefore so many people come here. There was such a massive crowd at Bangalore! As soon as I got down from the train, there was an incessant shower of flowers all the way. The road became full of flowers. Such crowds used to visit the Master also during his last days. I try to persuade people so earnestly, saying, "Have initiation from your family preceptor (Kulaguru). They expect something from you. I do not expect anything." But they will not leave me. They weep and it moves my heart. Well, I am nearing the end; these few days I continue to live, will be spent in this manner.

Disciple: Oh, no, Mother! Why should you say that? You are well. You have no particular ailment. Why do you, then, want to leave this world? Never say that again.

During those few days the Mother appeared very sad and indifferent about things.

Golap-Ma was having an argument with someone downstairs. Hearing that, the Mother asked, "What is going on there?"

Disciple: Golap-Ma is scolding somebody.

Mother: It is not good to be so much talkative. One only invites misery for oneself by constantly dwelling on defects in everything. Golap has lost all sense of delicacy in her obsession about speaking the truth. I, for one, cannot bring myself to do that. An unpleasant truth should never be told.

On another occasion too Golap-Ma had told a very unpleasant truth to somebody. Mother had exclaimed, "What is this, Golap? How has your nature become like this?"

During the noontime a hot-headed man had come to the Holy Mother and created a row. Referring to this, she said, "The Master did not let anybody know of my existence. He protected me always with infinite care. Now the thing has gone to the other extreme; they are advertising me, as if by beat of drum in a market-place. M. is at the root of it all. People are beside themselves after reading the *Kathamrita* (or the *Gospel of Sri Ramakrishna*). Girish Babu enforced his demands on the Master and abused him; now people are doing the same thing with me.

"Why should they always bother me about initiation? There are my children (referring to the direct disciples of the Master) at the Belur Math. Have they no power? Everyone is being sent here! I went so far as to tell people that they would be incurring great sin if they give up their hereditary preceptor. But still they would not leave me alone."

Disciple: You initiate the devotee because you desire to do so.

Mother: No, I do so out of compassion. They won't leave me. They weep. I feel compassion for them. Out of kindness I give them initiation. Besides, what do I gain by it? When I initiate devotees, I have to accept their sins. Then I think, "Well, this body will die anyway; let them realize the Truth."

UDBODHAN

24th April, 1912

It was 1.30 p.m. I went to the Mother's room after noon-meals to bring betel-rolls. Referring to somebody, the Mother recited a verse. I asked her what it meant.

Mother: It means that a man cannot change his nature. Sri Chaitanyadeva said, "I adore him who is able to give up his past habits and worship the Lord."

Disciple: Once you had said at Jayrambati, "It would be well if one were able to change one's nature." On another occasion you had said, "There are some whose very appearance evokes feelings of love; and some there are who evoke just the contrary feelings."

Mother: You are right, my child. One's nature is what really counts. What else matters?

Disciple: Sarat Maharaj said about Golap-Ma, "If she gives even a tender-coconut, the entire household will know of it by her shoutings."

Mother: True, nowadays such indeed has become their habit. For minor things, they raise a hue and cry. Yogen (Yogin-Ma) was very calm and steady earlier. Now I find she has changed. Forbearance is a great virtue. No other quality is greater than this.

I had a severe headache. I went to the Mother's room in the afternoon and told her about it. She said, "It is probably due to the heat." She then mixed up some ghee and camphor, and making a paste of it, applied it on my forehead with a gentle massage. "Whenever the Master had headache, he would apply this medicine," she said.

I started feeling a little better after a few minutes of massage, and came downstairs. After some time, the headache really disappeared. I went and told the Mother, "The headache is no more there, Mother!"

One lady from Poland had come to India to study Vedanta. She had heard in Calcutta about the Mother, and had come to meet her. She spoke to the Mother for some time. Referring to the Bahai sect, she said that its teachings were similar to the teachings of Sri Ramakrishna—they too preached the harmony of all religions. From her talk it appeared that the lady herself belonged to the Bahai sect.

After she had left, I asked the Mother, "How did you find her?"

Mother: Very nice.

Disciple: These people have come from very far..... Now the news has spread like wild fire! Where is Poland, and where indeed is the Udbodhan Office! Mother, you are not even aware of it!

Mother: The Master had said once in a divine mood, "In course of time, I will be worshipped in every home. Innumerable indeed will be my devotees!" Nivedita once said, "Mother, we too are Hindus. As a result of our Karma, we were born in another country. But we too will become Hindus in true spirit!" This is their (of Nivedita and others) last birth.

UDBODHAN, *Prayer-Hall*, 7 *a.m.*

April, 1912

Sri Surendra Chakravarty had visited the Mother a few days back along with his wife. A few days later he came alone. Prostrating before the Mother, he said, "Mother, we alone have been deprived of the vision of the Master."

Mother: You will get it in due course. This is your last birth. Nivedita said, "Mother, we too are Hindus. But due to our Karma, we were born Christians." This birth is the last one for them too.

The Mother often said this birth being the last one about many people. So I decided to ask her about it that day.

Disciple: Mother, what is the meaning of the 'last birth'?' The Master spoke about the last birth of many people. You too often say it.

Mother: The last birth means that the person has not to come again and again (i.e. he does not have to take repeated births). This life marks an end of all that.

Disciple: But it is seen that many of these people are not free from desires—their family, wife and children. Unless the desires are given up, how can the repeated coming be ended?

Mother: Whatever the Master has said about anyone, *will* come to pass, come what may. His words cannot be falsified. Whether or not the person has desires in his present state, the Master had forseen that in the end, all the desires will leave such a person. He had divined this regarding some people.

Disciple: Does the last birth imply the attainment of Nirvana?

Mother: Of course, it does. In some cases, it is possible, that the mind will become absolutely bereft of all desires just before death.

Disciple: Mother, the Master has referred to many people as his very 'own'. What does it mean?

Mother: He used to say, "Some of them have come from this body, some from the hair, some from the hands and feet. They are my eternal companions." As, for instance, a king. Wherever he goes, all his companions follow him. If I go to Jayrambati, do not all my companions accompany me? Exactly like that, those who are one's 'own' are companions age after age.

The Master used to say, "Those belonging to the 'inner circle' are my companions in weal and woe." Pointing to the young boys who came to him, he would say, "They are happy in my happiness, miserable in my sorrow; in weal and woe they are always with me."

Whenever he comes, all the others follow. He had brought Naren from the *Saptarshi*. While meditating in the Kali temple at Dakshineswar, he saw in a vision Sambhu Mallick standing behind Mother Kali. He had even seen Balaram Babu in a vision. When he met him for the first time, he could immediately recognize, "Yes! I saw him like this—with a turban, and of fair complexion."

Once the Master said, "Why did they offer the food before the photograph (of the Master) instead of offering it to the Mother Kali?" We were a little uneasy that this smelt of a bad omen. The Master, however, comforted us, saying, "Don't worry. You will see, in due course, I will be worshipped in every home. I swear, it will come to pass!"[1]

The people nowadays are clever—they have taken his photograph! Take the case of Master Mahasaya. Is he an ordinary soul? He has noted down all the words of the Master. Which Avatara has been photographed, and whose words been recorded in this fashion?

Disciple: Master Mahasaya said about the *Kathamrita* (or *The Gospel of Sri Ramakrishna*) that the available material with him will make up ten or twelve volumes. Lord knows, when all of it will be published!

Mother: True. He too has become old now. Who knows, he may not live long enough to complete everything.

Disciple: Mother, didn't you tell me at Jayrambati, that the Master will come again among his white-skinned devotees?

Mother: No, I said that many white-skinned devotees will come to him. Don't you see, for instance, many Christians getting attracted towards the Master? He had said, he will stay for a hundred years in the hearts of the devotees, and then come again. I told him, "I do not want to come again!" Lakshmi too said that she wouldn't come again, even if she were chopped into shreds like tobacco leaves! The Master smiled and said, "How can you escape? Our roots are twined together like the *Kalmi* plant

[1]See p. 62.

(a kind of aquatic plant). A tug at one end will bring the whole lot up!"

But what do all these things matter? The Master used to say, "You have come to eat the mangoes. What is the use of counting the leaves and branches?"

Disciple: Mother, I feel it is purposeless to live unless we have a direct vision of God. Once I asked a Mussalman Fakir, "A man sits with an angling rod on the bank of a lake or a river in the expectation of catching fish. He never does so near a mud-puddle. Have you got a glimpse of that for which you have become a religious mendicant?"

Mother: What did he say?

Disciple: What could he say?

Mother (after a little reflection): You have said the right thing. That is true. What does it avail a man unless he gets some kind of realization? But one should continue to have faith in things spiritual.

Disciple: The other day Sarat Maharaj said as Swamiji (Swami Vivekananda) also had remarked earlier, "Suppose there is a lump of gold in the adjoining room and a thief sees it from this room. There is an intervening wall which prevents him from taking possession of this precious metal. Under that condition, can the man ever sleep? All the time he would be thinking of how he might get at that lump of gold! In the same way, if a man is firmly convinced that there is such an entity as God, can he ever indulge in worldly life?"

Mother: That is true, indeed.

Disciple: Whatever you may say, Mother, renunciation and dispassion are the chief things. Shall we ever acquire them?

Mother: Certainly, you will gain everything if you but take refuge in the Master. Renunciation alone was his splendour. We utter his name and eat and enjoy things because he renounced all. People think that his devotees also must be very great, as he was a man of such complete renunciation.

Ah me! One day he went to my room in the Nahabat. He had no spices in his small bag. He used to chew them now and then. I gave him some to chew there, and also handed over to him a few packed in paper to take to his room. He proceeded; but instead of going to his room, he went straight to the embankment of the

Ganges. He did not see the way, nor was he conscious of it. He was repeating, "Mother, shall I drown myself!" I became restless with agony. The river was full to the brim. I was then a young woman and would not go out of my room. I could not see anyone about. Whom could I send to him? At last I found a Brahmana belonging to the Kali temple coming in the direction of my room. Through him I called Hriday, who was then taking his meal. He left his plate, ran to the Master, caught hold of him, and brought him back to his room. A moment more, and he would have dropped into the Ganges!

Disciple: Why did he go towards the river?

Mother: Because I put a few spices in his hand, he could not find his way. A holy man must not lay things by. His renunciation was hundred per cent complete.

Once a Vaishnava Sadhu came to the Panchavati. At first he showed a great deal of renunciation. But alas! finally like a rat, he began to pull and gather various things—pots, cups, jars, grain, rice, pulses and so forth. The Master noticed it and said one day, "Poor thing! This time he is going to be ruined!" He was about to be entangled in the snare of Maya. The Master advised him strongly about renunciation and further asked him to leave the place. Then he went away.

A devotee came in to salute the Mother. After he had left, she said, "I was once deceived by showing Harish my affection. Therefore I do not nowadays express my feelings towards anyone."

UDBODHAN

1*st May*, 1912

In the forenoon I went upstairs to read letters to the Holy Mother.

Disciple: The daughter of a devotee has written from her father-in-law's place that she would like to come here to see you. She has sent you her salutations. She has further requested you to be careful so that her husband's relatives might not know about her writing to you.

Mother: Then do not write any reply to her. She wants me to conceal it from her relatives! I do not know such a game of hide and seek. At Jayrambati, Jogindra, the postman, used to write letters for me. Many complained, saying, "Does the postman see our letters?" They did not like my asking a man in humble position to write my letters for them. Why? There is no deceit in me. Anybody who likes may see my letters.

Another devotee inquired as to when the Holy Mother would return to Jayrambati. I asked her, "May I tell the devotee that you will return there in autumn at the time of the Jagaddhatri Puja?"

Mother: Oh, no, no! Can one be sure of it? As to where I shall be, that remains entirely in the hands of God. Today man is, and tomorrow he is not.

Disciple: O Mother, why should you talk like that? It is because you are alive that so many people are able to see you and get peace of mind.

Mother: Yes, that is true.

Disciple: Please do remain for our sake.

In a tender voice, choked with emotion, she said, "Alas! How fond they are of me! I am also very fond of them." Her eyes were moist with tears. The disciple was fanning her. She said to him in a a most compassionte voice, "My child, I bless you from my heart that you live long, attain devotion, and enjoy peace. Peace is the principal thing. One needs peace alone."

Disciple: Mother, one idea crops up in my mind constantly: Why do I not get the vision of the Master? As he is our very 'own', why does he not reveal himself to us? Can't he do so by his mere will?

Mother: That is true. Who can say why he does not reveal himself when you suffer from so many miseries and sorrows? Once Balaram's wife was ill. The Master said to me, "Go to Calcutta and visit her." "How can I go?" I said, "I don't see any carriage or other conveyance here." The Master replied in an excited voice: "What! Balaram's family is in such trouble and you hesitate to go! You will walk to Calcutta. Go on foot." At last a palanquin was brought and I set out from Dakshineswar. Twice I visited her during her illness. On another occasion I went on foot at night from Shyampukur. Where, indeed, will man be if God does not protect him in his trouble?

Disciple: I know sorrows and sufferings are inevitable so long as a man lives in the physical body. I do not ask the Master to remove the sufferings. But can't he console us by revealing himself to us in the midst of our troubles and sorrows?

Mother: You are right, my child! The only son of Ram

(*i.e.,* Balaram's grandson) died the other day. Ram's wife and mother came to me for peace of mind. They were relieved of their grief to some extent. I used to speak to the Master of such things and he would say, "I have millions of them. I shall cut my goat at the tail or through the back, and then kill it. It is my sweet will."

Disciple: Does he not see our suffering?

Mother: But he has so many like you. He used to tell me, "It is the ocean of consciousness and bliss. How many waves crop up and disappear! There is no end, no limit."

Disciple: A man in the street, whose spiritual consciousness has not been awakened at all, is quite happy. But those whose consciousness has been partially awakened and who want to realize God, suffer a great deal if they do not see Him. They alone know how much they suffer!

Mother: Ah! how true it is! Ordinary people are quite happy. They eat, drink and make merry. The devotees alone know no end of suffering.

Disciple: Don't you suffer at the suffering of the devotees?

Mother: Why should I? He who has created the world looks after all.

Disciple: Don't you want to come back to this earth in a human form for the sake of the devotees?

Mother: Oh! Such suffering in a human body! No more! No more! May I not be born again! At the time of his illness, the Master expressed the desire to eat Āmalaki. Durgacharan procured some after searching for them for three days without food and sleep. The Master asked him to take his meal and himself took some rice in order to turn the food into Prasada. I said to the Master, "You are taking rice quite well. Why, then, should your meal consist only of farina pudding? You should take rice rather than pudding." "No, no," said he, "I would rather take farina during these last days of my life." It was such unbearable suffering for him to eat even the farina! On some days, it would all spill out through his nose or throat!

Ah! I went to the temple of Siva at Tarakeswar, but that too proved fruitless. I lay before the Deity there for two days without food and drink, supplicating for some divine remedy for the Master's illness. On the second night, I was startled to hear a sound. It was as if some one was breaking a pile of earthen pots with one blow. I woke up and the idea flashed in my mind,

"Who is a husband in this world, and of whom? Who is related to whom here? For whom am I sacrificing my life?" At a stroke all earthly ties were cut asunder, and the mind filled with renunciation! I groped my way through the darkness, and sprinkled my face with the holy water in the basin behind the temple. I also drank a little of it. The throat had dried up due to the two days' fast. Then I felt refreshed. The next day I returned to Cossipore. As soon as the Master saw me, he asked in good humour, "Well, did you get anything?—nothing at all!"

The Master too saw in a dream an elephant going out to get a medicine. Just as the elephant began digging the earth for the medicine, Gopal came and woke him up. He asked me whether I had seen any such deam.

I saw Mother Kali with her neck bent to one side. I asked Her, "Mother, why do you stand like that?" She replied, "It is because of this (pointing to the Master's sore in the throat); I too have it."

The Master told me, "I am being subjected to all the sufferings that there can be; none of you need have it again. I have taken upon myself the miseries of the whole world." The Master's disease was due to taking upon himself the sins of Girish.

All our sufferings are on this earth. Is there anything elsewhere? People suffer from endless miseries on account of their egoism and at last they say, "Not I, not I; it is Thou, O God! It is Thou!"

Disciple: Will you keep us in your mind hereafter?

Mother: Perhaps not when I enjoy divine bliss after my passing away. My child, time alone is the principal thing. Who knows what will happen in course of time?

Disciple: True, Mother, everything, no doubt, happens under the dominance of time; but there is also a subduer of time.

Mother: Yes, that is true.

Disciple: Please keep yourself well; then everything will be all right.

It was eight o'clock. The Mother asked, "Is it eight o'clock? Perhaps it is. It is time for worship in the shrine room. Let me go now."

I went upstairs with her mail. One of her disciples had passed away at Banaras. The Mother heard the news and remarked, "All must die some day. Instead of dying in a pool or on the bank of a lake, he has died in Banaras!"

Her brothers had written to her asking for money and telling about their family quarrels. I said to her, "Please see that they get plenty of money. Please tell the Master about it. Let them enjoy the material life and come to satiety."

Mother: Will they ever be satiated? Nothing can satisfy them; no, not even if they have plenty. Are the worldly people ever satiated with enjoyments? They always spin out the tale of their woes. It is Kali (one of her brothers) who always wants money. Now Prasanna (another brother) imitates him. Varada (a third brother) never asks for money. He says, "Where will sister get money from?"

Disciple: What about that insane lady? Does she want money?

Mother: She won't accept it even when offered.

Disciple: Why were you born in that family?

Mother: Why not? My father and mother were very good people. My father was a great devotee of Rama. He had unswerving devotion to the ideal of a Brahmana's life. He could not accept gifts indiscriminately. He loved to smoke, and as he smoked—he was so simple and humble—he would address in a friendly way every passerby that crossed his door and say cordially, "Come in, brother. Have a smoke."

UDBODHAN

25th June, 1912

It was morning. The Mother was seated near the bedstead in the room adjacent to the shrine. We were engaged in conversation.

Disciple: Some say that it is not good for the Sadhus (of the Ramakrishna Order) to work in the Sevashramas (Homes of Service) and dispensaries or to be pre-occupied with selling books, accounting and so forth. Did the Master ever undertake such activities? Works of this kind are thrust upon the seekers who enter the Order with a yearning for the realization of God. If anyone must do some work, it must be worship in the shrine, meditation, Japa and devotional music. Activities other than these entangle one in desires and turn one away from God.

Mother: You must pay no heed to those who talk in that manner. What will you do day and night if you are not engaged in work? Can one practise meditation and Japa for twenty-four hours? You referred to the Master. His case was different. Mathur used to supply him with proper diet. You are able to get your food because you are doing some work. Otherwise you would have to roam from door to door begging for a morsel of food. Perhaps you would fall ill. Besides, where are people today to give alms to the Sadhus? Never pay any heed to such words. Things will go on as the Master directs. The Math will be run on these lines. Those who cannot adjust themselves will go away.

One day Mani Mullick visited a Sadhu and reported to the Master. "Well," said the Master, "how did you like him?" "Yes," said Mani, "I saw the Sadhu but—." The Master asked, "But—what?" "All want money," Mani Mullick replied. The Master said, "How much does a holy man want? Perhaps a pice for tobacco to smoke. That's all. You need your cups of ghee and milk, a mattress and such things; and the Sadhus want a pice for their smoke. Should they not have it?"

Disciple: Enjoyments come from desire alone. A man may live in a four-storeyed mansion; but he does not really enjoy anything if he has no desire for it. And a man may live under a tree but if he has desire, he gets all enjoyments from that alone. The Master used to say, "A person may have no relatives anywhere; but Mahamaya may cause him to keep a cat and thus make him worldly. Such is Her play!"

Mother: That's true. Everything is due to desire. What bondage is there for a man who has no desire? You see, I live with all these things, but I do not feel any attachment; no, not in the least!

Disciple: Indeed, you can have no desires. But how many insignificant desires crop up in our minds! How can we get rid of them?

Mother: In your case these are no real desires. They are nothing. They are mere fancies that appear and disappear in your mind. The more they come and go, the better for you.[1]

Disciple: Yesterday I wondered how I could fight with my mind unless God assured me of His protection. The moment one desire disappears another crops up.

---

[1]A Sannyasin devotee once asked the Holy Mother, "I have been practising religious disciplines. I do not relax my efforts in that direction. But it appears that the impurities of mind are not growing less." The Mother said, "You have rolled different threads on a reel—red, black and white. While unrolling you will

Mother: So long as the ego exists, desires also undoubtedly remain. But those desires will not injure you. The Master will be your protector. It will be a heinous sin on the part of the Master if he does not protect those who have taken shelter at his feet, who have taken refuge in him renouncing all, and who want to lead a good life. You must live in a spirit of self-surrender to him. Let him do good to you if he so desires, or let him drown you if that be his will. But you are to do only what is righteous, and that also according to the power he has given you.

Disciple: Have, I, O Mother, surrendered to him to that extent? Sometimes I feel that I can depend upon him to a small extent, and the next moment it disappears. What will be the way for us if he does not protect us? Sometimes I think that because you, O Mother, are alive, we can report our dangers and difficulties to you and gain peace by a look at your face. Who will protect us when you leave us? We shall feel safe if you give us assurance.

Mother: Don't be afraid, my child. You have nothing to fear. You will not lead a worldly life with wife and children. You will have none of these. Why should you fear? And in the meantime, before I depart, you will be able to build up a secure foundation for your spiritual life.

Disciple: What will Japa and austerities avail us if God does not cast His benign look upon us? We shall be protected, only if He protects us.

Mother: You have nothing to fear. The Master will certainly protect you. Don't worry.

UDBODHAN

7th July, 1912

Disciple: Mother, was it not arranged that you would visit Puri at the time of the Car Festival (*Ratha-yātrā*)?

Mother: Is it good to go there when there is such a rush of people? Perhaps there will be an epidemic of cholera then. Lakshmikanta, the priest, said, "All the rooms and houses have already been rented. There is no place now to stay in. Even the small

---

see them all exactly in the same way." There are two kinds of desires: one that stimulates enjoyment and the other that quickens dispassion. Though externally they appear the same, their effects are different.

rooms have been rented for ten rupees each. Please come during the winter."

Disciple: Whose image is worshipped there?

Mother: In a dream, I saw that it was really the image of Siva!

Disciple: Did you not see the image of Jagannath there?

Mother: No,—I saw only the image of Siva. The Lord Jagannath Siva was seated on the altar made of a lakh of Salagrams (an emblem of Vishnu). Is it without any reason that thousands of devotees visit the temple? There is also the image of goddess Vimala. A special offering is made to her on the Mahashtami night. Vimala Devi is another form of Sri Durga. So is it not natural that Siva too will be present there?

Disciple: Some are of the opinion that this was originally a Buddhist temple, and the image of Buddha was installed there. When the temple fell into the hands of the followers of Sankaracharya, the image was converted into the emblem of Siva, and still later, when the Vaishnavas got control, they converted it into the image of Sri Jagannath-Vishnu.

Mother: I do not know all this. But I saw the image of Siva!

Disciple: How many temples, how many images of gods and goddesses the Mussalmans have destroyed! They have cut off the noses of some of the images and the ears of others.

Mother: The image of Sri Govindaji of Vrindaban was taken to Jaipur in fear of these Muslim invaders. The priests became upset and insisted that the Deity be brought back. At last they heard a Divine Oracle: "The image has gone, not I! Prepare another image and I shall stay in it!"

Disciple: There is the temple of Somanath in Gujarat. The priests, in former times, used to bathe the Deity daily with water from Gangotri. Every day people used to carry water from the Himalayas in pots on their heads. Sultan Mohammed demolished the image and carried away the temple doors that were made of sandal wood. Why should that happen?

Mother: The wicked do not feel the Divine presence in the image. The Deity disappears, as it were, before them. He can do whatever He likes by His mere will. This also is a sport of God.

Disciple: Can the effect of Karma be made null and void? The Scriptures say that knowledge alone can destroy Karma. Still one must reap the result of Prarabdha Karma.

Mother: Karma alone is responsible for our misery and happiness. Even the Master had to suffer from the effect of Karma. Once his elder brother was drinking water while delirious. The Master snatched the glass out of his hand after he had drunk just a little. The brother became angry and said, "You have stopped me from drinking water. You will also suffer likewise. You will also feel such pain in your throat." The Master said, "Brother, I did not mean to injure you. You are ill. Water will harm you. That is why I have taken the glass away. Why have you, then, cursed me in this manner?" The brother said, weeping, "I do not know, brother. These words have come from my mouth. They cannot but bear fruit." At the time of his illness the Master told me, "I have got this ulcer in my throat because of that curse. None of you need suffer in future. I have taken all your sufferings." I said to him in reply, "How can an ordinary man possibly live if such a thing as this can happen to you?" The Master remarked, "My brother was a righteous man. His words must come true. Can the words of anyone and everyone be thus fulfilled?"

The result of Karma is inevitable. But by repeating the Name of God, you can lessen its intensity. If you were destined to have a wound as wide as a ploughshare, you will get a pin-prick at least. The effect of Karma can be counteracted to a great extent by Japa and austerities. This was the case with king Suratha. He had worshipped the Goddess by slaughtering a lakh of goats. Later on, these hundred thousand goats killed the king with one stroke of the sword; he did not have to be born a hundred thousand times. That was because he had worshipped the Divine Mother. Chanting God's holy Name lessens the intensity of Karmic effects.

Disciple: If that be so, then the law of Karma is supreme in this world. Then why should one believe in God? The Buddhists accept the law of Karma but not God.

Mother: Do you mean to say that there are no Deities like Kali, Krishna, Durga and the like?

Disciple: Is the effect of Karma destroyed by austerities and Japa?

Mother: Why not? It is good to do the right kind of work. One feels happy in doing good and one suffers by doing evil.

UDBODHAN (*Morning*)

Disciple: Mother, sometimes I see you reading the Ramayana. When did you learn to read?

Mother: Sometimes I used to accompany the other children to the village school. There I learnt a little. Later on Lakshmi and I used to read the Bengali Primer at Kamarpukur. My nephew Hriday snatched the book away from me. He said, "Women should not learn to read and write. Are you preparing yourself in this way to read novels and dramas later on?" But Lakshmi did not give up the book. She belonged to the family; therefore she held on to her book. I too secretly had a copy bought for one anna. Lakshmi used to attend the village school. On returning home she would teach me. But I really improved my capacity to read only long after, at Dakshineswar. The Master was staying then at Syampukur for treatment. I was all alone. A girl belonging to the family of Bhava Mukherji used to come to the temple garden to bathe in the Ganga. Now and then she would spend a long time with me. She used to give me lessons and afterwards examine me. And in return, I would give her a large quantity of greens, vegetables and other articles of food that were sent to me from the temple-garden.

Disciple: Mother, did the Master visit Jayrambati often or just once or twice?

Mother: He visited many times. Sometimes he even stayed there for ten or twelve days. Whenever he would visit Kamarpukur, he also visited Jayrambati, Sihar and other places. He once fed the village cowherd boys at Sihar.

Disciple: When was this? During the period of his Sadhana, or later on?

Mother: It was later on. During the period of Sadhana, he was filled, as it were, with a terrible divine madness. Had he visited his father-in-law's place then, all would have stamped him as insane.

When Siva visited his father-in-law's house, all began lamenting, "Oh! Dear Uma, great indeed has been your misfortune! You have at last fallen into the company of this hemp-addict!" Ah! In those days (after the mariage), the things they spoke about the Master!—"Alas! A mad son-in-law! What will happen now?" and so on.

Disciple: Yesterday Sri Manindra Gupta came. I had not met him earlier.

Mother: He did come once before. As a young boy, he used to visit the Master.

Disciple: The younger Naren too never comes here.

Mother: No, he doesn't. At Dakshineswar, he used to go to the Master. He was dark and slim, with face covered with pox marks. The Master had great affection for him.

Disciple: Paltu Babu came here only once. Tarak Babu (of Belgharia) comes occasionally.

Mother: Paltu too visits now and then. He gives me a rupee every month. He is very poor himself. If I am in Jayrambati, he sends the money there.

Paltu and Manindra visited the Master as kids merely ten or eleven years old! At Cossipore, on the day of the *Dol-Yātrā*, all were out celebrating the festival, sprinkling *ābir* (a kind of red perfumed powder) over one another with great joy. These two boys did not go. Both were fanning the Master, changing hands frequently. They were too young to manage it single-handed! They massaged the Master's feet. The Master was suffering from severe headache due to cough. So constant fanning was necessary.

The Master told them, "Go, go out and play with *ābir*. See, all are out enjoying!" Paltu said, "No, sir, we will not go. We will remain here. Is it possible for us to leave you here all by yourself?" No amount of persuasion made them go out to participate in the festive occasion. The Master wept as he said later, "These are indeed my Ramlala come to take care of me. So tender in age, yet the festivities outside could not make them leave me and go!" Saying this the Master's eyes were full of tears.

Disciple: Many devotees used to visit the Master. Where are they now? None of them comes to see you.

Mother: Oh, they are all leading happy lives!

Disciple: What? Happy!

Mother: You are right. How can a man be happy in this world with his wife and children? They have forgotten themselves in 'woman and gold'. Everything in the world results in suffering, after all.

Disciple: Besides, the mind has outgoing propensities.

Mother: Kali, the Mother of the universe, is the Mother of all. It is She alone who has begotten both good and evil. Everything has come out of Her womb. There are different kinds of perfect souls—perfect from very birth (*Svataḥ-siddha*), perfect through spiritual disciplines (*Sādhana-siddha*), perfect through the grace of the teacher (*kṛpā-siddha*), and made perfect all of a sudden (*haṭhāt-siddha*).

Disciple: What is the meaning of 'made perfect all of a sudden'?

Mother: It is like becoming wealthy suddenly by inheriting the riches of another.

Just then Nalini, the Mother's niece, entered the room after a bath in the Ganges. Finding the water-closet a little dirty, she had washed it with a few pots of water, and hence had taken bath in the Ganges for purification. The disciple and the Mother opined that she need have bathed under the tap alone.

Nalini: How is that enough? A water-closet!

Mother: I too had to purify myself for coming into contact with filth on several occasions. But I only chanted the Name of Govinda[1] a few times and felt pure. The mind is everything. It is in the mind alone that one feels pure and impure. A man, first of all, must make his own mind guilty and then alone he can see another man's guilt. Does anything ever happen to another if you enumerate his faults? It only injures you. This has been my attitude from my childhood. Hence I can't see anybody's faults. If a man does a trifle for me, I try to remember him even for that. To see the faults of others! One should never do it. I never do so. Forgiveness is Tapasya (austerity).

Disciple: Swamiji (Swami Vivekananda) used to say, "Suppose a thief entered the house and stole something. The idea of a thief would flash in your mind. But a baby has no such idea. Therefore it would not see anyone as a thief."

Mother: That's true, indeed. He who has a pure mind sees everything pure......

One could be born with a pure mind if one had performed many austerities and spiritual practices in a previous birth.

Disciple: Mother, my mind does not feel joy in doing Japa or spiritual practices.

Mother: (*smiling*) Why? Not a little even?

Disciple: Oh, I do a little rather half-heartedly. The next moment I think, "What is the use of mumbling? Let me rather try meditation."

Mother: Can you meditate?

Disciple: No, I cannot do even that. I understand everything but I cannot practise it at all and get peace. One may know the

[1] A name of God.

road to Dakshineswar very well, but can one walk all the way?

Lalit Babu entered the room and saluted the Mother. They became engaged in conversation, the disciple joining in it now and then.

Mother: The Master used to say, "The way is extremely difficult, like the sharp edge of a razor." (*After a little pause*) But he has kept you in His arms. He is looking after you.

Lalit: The Master will take us in his arms after death; is there anything great in that? If he would only do so while we are in this body!

Mother: He is holding you in his arms even in this body. He is above your head. Truly he is holding you.

Disciple: Does he really hold us? Are you telling the truth?

Mother: (*firmly*) Yes, really, truly.

The Mother finished the morning worship and distributed Prasada in Sal leaves to the devotees. Then she swept the room. As she took the dirt in her hand, a pin entered her little finger. The finger bled and the Mother suffered terribly from pain. As soon as the disciple heard about it he ran upstairs. Someone asked him to apply hot lime. That greatly relieved the pain. The Mother said affectionately, "My child, you are my own. Truly you all are my very own."

16*th August*, 1912 (*Evening*)

Mother: When I was thirteen, it was time for me to go to Kamarpukur and I went there. The Master was then at Dakshineswar. After a stay of a month or so at Kamarpukur, I returned to Jayrambati. Five or six months later, I again went to Kamarpukur and stayed for nearly six weeks. The Master was still at Dakshineswar, but his elder brother, my sister-in-law and others were then at Kamarpukur. When the Master came to Kamarpukur with the Bhairavi Brahmani (in the year 1867), he sent for me. I went to Kamarpukur, and this time stayed for nearly three months. The Brahmani went to see Jayrambati, Sihar and other places. One day she had a tiff with Hriday over a matter concerning the removal of the leaf-plate of Chinu (Srinivas) Sankhari.

Disciple: Was Chinu Sankhari alive then?

Mother: Yes. He was alive, but had become disabled due to old age.

Disciple: In some books one gets the impression that Chinu had died during the Master's boyhood itself.

Mother: He passed away much later. The Brahmani said, "Chinu is a devotee of the Lord. What harm is there in my cleaning the place where he has taken food?" Hriday was annoyed at this, and said, "What? Will you really do such a thing? Then we won't allow you to remain inside the house." The Brahmani was not the person to yield to threats. She replied, "What harm, if you don't? Manasa[1] will go to bed in Sitala's room[2]!" Hriday rejoined, "Well, let us see how Manasa will sleep in Sitala's room!"

All this raked up a great quarrel between the two. Hriday hurled something at her which struck her on the ears which started bleeding. The Brahmani began to weep. The Master said, "O Hridu! What have you done? She is a holy person, a devotee of God. Your quarrel may attract all the people around and a scandal may ensue !"

Then one day, the Brahmani saw the Master in an ecstatic mood and curiously enough, some sort of fear seized her. Looking up, she began saying, "Oh! Where shall I go? What shall I do? Shall I go to Puri or Vrindaban?" and so on. She disappeared some days later without anybody's knowledge. None could know where she had gone. She did not return.

Before her departure, one day the Brahmani made garlands of various flowers, smeared them with sandal-paste, and adorned the Master as Sri Gauranga. The Master entered into an ecstasy. She then sent for me. No sooner had I come, than the Master asked, "How does it look?" I somehow managed to say, "Fine", and came away after a hurried prostration. His state of divine inebriation had frightened me.

After this I returned to Jayrambati. The village people were saying all sorts of things about the Master—that he was insane, had gone fully mad, was wandering about naked, and so on. None could understand then the state of his mind. When all people talked thus, I told myself, 'Let me go and see him'. An opportunity soon came. Many women of the neighbourhood were going to Calcutta for the holy dip in the Ganga on an auspicious day which

[1]Manasa—goddess of snakes. The Brahmani thus compared herself to the angry snake.

[2]The temple in which Sitala, a goddess, was installed.

was near at hand.[1] I told a friend, "I shall go to Dakshineswar to see him," and she communicated everything to my father. I, of course, could not speak of this to my father, because of fear and bashfulness.

My father said, "Does she want to go? Very good." He too accompanied us.. On the way, I fell ill. I was lying unconscious owing to fever. Just then I saw a woman, jet black in complexion, sitting by my side, and stroking my head. She said, "I come from Dakshineswar." I said, "I too am going to Dakshineswar. But how are you related to us?" She replied, "I am your sister. Don't you worry! You will recover soon."

The very next day, the fever left me. My father got me a palanquin. We reached Dakshineswar at about 9 p.m. I went straight to the Master's room, while the others went to the Nahabat where my mother-in-law stayed. The Master said to me, "Ah! You have come!" And he asked someone to spread a mat on the floor. Then he added, "Alas! Would that my Mathur were alive now! By his death, my right hand, as it were, is broken!" Mathur had died a few months before. Akshay (the son of the Master's elder brother) had also passed away.

Disciple: Oh! Wasn't Mathur Babu there?

Mother: No. He had passed away about 7 or 8 months earlier. Had Mathur been alive, would I have been put up in that tiny inconvenient room (in the Nahabat)? He would have built a mansion for me!

After seeing the Master, I wanted to go to the Nahabat. But the Master said, "No, no. Stay here. It would be inconvenient for the doctor to see you there." I spent the night in his room. A woman companion slept beside me. Hriday gave us two or three baskets of puffed rice, for all had finished their supper when we arrived.

The next day, a doctor came and examined me. After a few days I became well, and went to stay in the Nahabat. My mother-in-law too was then staying there. Before that she had been living in a room in the bungalow used by the owners of the temple-garden. Akshay had breathed his last there. Therefore she had

---

[1]According to some, the occasion was *Dol Pūrṇimā* which fell on 25th March, 1872. According to others, it was *Ćaitra-saṅkrānti* which came a month later.

come away from that place, saying, "I shall not stay there any longer. I shall live in the Nahabat, and pass my days looking at the Ganga. I do not need the bungalow any more."

The Master performed the Shodasi Puja about a month and a half after my arrival at Dakshineswar (probably on the night of the Phalaharini Kali Puja, June, 1872). I had then commenced my sixteenth[1] year. At about nine at night, he sent for me. Hriday had made all the necessary arrangements for the worship. The Master asked me to be seated. I sat on the stool facing the jar of Ganga water which used to be kept at the north-western corner of the room. The Master sat near the western door and was facing eastward. All the doors were closed. The articles for worship were on my right.

Disciple: How did he worship?

Mother: I soon became semi-conscious due to spiritual fervour. Hence I do not know how exactly the worship proceeded.[2]

Disciple: What did you do when you became conscious?

Mother: I saluted the Master mentally and came away.

Disciple: It was the night of the (Phalaharini) Kali Puja. There must have been many people present. Did none come to know about the worship?

Mother: Did I not say that the doors were all closed? The Kali Temple was full of festivities that night. All were busy with that. And besides, what business had they with the Master? Nothing beyond seeing him and saluting him!

Disciple: Was anyone else present at the time of worship?

---

[1]Actually nineteenth.

[2]I heard later from Lakshmi-didi that the Mother had told her: "First he painted my feet with *āltā*(liquid lac-dye), and put vermilion on my forehead. Then he clad me in a new cloth. He also fed me with sweets and betel-roll." Lakshmi-didi asked her smilingly, "You are so shy, dear. How did he put the cloth on you?" The Mother replied, "I was in an altogther different state of semi-absorption then."

The Mother had related this incident to Jnanananda also. He too had asked her, "Mother, did you not feel any hesitation or shyness when the Master offered flowers at your feet and fed you with sweets with his own hands?" The Mother had told him, "No, I saw him, no doubt, doing all this, but I had no inclination to utter a word even."

Mother: A boy named Dinu, from Mukundapur, a distant nephew of the Master used to stay with him. The Master loved the boy very much. He had picked the flowers and the Bilva leaves for the worship. Hriday had made all the other arrangements. There was nobody except the Master when the actual worship began. At the close of it, Hriday came in.

Ram Babu has mentioned in his book[1] that the Shodasi Puja took place at Jayrambati. Ah me! People in that part of the country are so gossipy. As it is, they used to comment, "To whom have you given the girl in marriage? A crazy, insane man!" Now imagine what would have been the consequences of worshipping a woman there!

After the worship, I continued to stay at Dakshineswar for a year. Then I fell ill and returned to Jayrambati. At Dakshineswar, Sambhu Babu (Sambhunath Mallick) had arranged for my treatment by the physician Prasad Babu.

Disciple: Were you at Dakshineswar when the Master's mother passed away (27th February, 1875)?

Mother: No, I was ill at Jayrambati then. I had returned after suffering for a year at Dakshineswar. For treatment of the spleen trouble, I went to the Siva temple at Badanganj where it was singed.[2]

After I had visited Dakshineswar twice or thrice, Captain (Viswanath Upadhyay) gave Sal wood. Sambhu Babu constructed

---

[1]The biography of Sri Ramakrishna in Bengali, written by Sri Ramachandra Datta.

[2]Badanganj is about 4 miles off Jayrambati. This process of scorching was a painful remedy of those days. After ablution, the patient was made to lie on the ground and held down by three or four persons, so that he might not run away because of the unbearable pain. Then a person would take in hand a burning piece of jujube wood and rub it on a plantain leaf laid over the region of the spleen. The skin would get burnt, and the patient would shriek and scream.

When the Mother came for the treatment after ablutions, some persons came forward to hold her down. But she said, "Nobody need hold me; I shall myself lie down quietly." And in fact she went through that ordeal in silence. The people in those regions believed that this treatment cured malaria. It is said that the Master too had once submitted to this remedy.

a cottage for me near the place where now Ramlal stays. At night, a high tide in the Ganga carried away one of the logs. Hriday scolded me saying, "You are ill-starred!", and so on. The Captain, unmindful of the loss, sent another log.

I stayed in that cottage for some days. During the monsoon, once the Master came to this cottage. It rained so heavily that he was unable to return to his room that night. He finished his meal there and laid himself down for the night. He said to me jokingly, "This is as though I have come home, like any other priest of the Kali Temple going home at night!"

An aged woman from Banaras at last persuaded me to come to the room in the Nahabat. The Master was suffering then from a severe attack of dysentery. I began attending on him. I searched in vain for this woman when I visited Banaras.[1]

The next time my mother, Lakshmi, myself and some others went to Dakshineswar. I made a votive offering of my hair and nails at Tarakeswar for recovery from my last ailment. As (my brother) Prasanna was with us, we first went to his rented house in Calcutta. It was perhaps in the month of March (year 1881). Next day we all went to Dakshineswar. No sooner were we there than Hriday, for reasons best known to him, began saying, "Why have they come? What have they got to do here?" He was discourteous to them. My mother kept silent. Hriday hailed from the village Sihar, and my mother too was born and brought up there. So he utterly ignored my mother. She said, "Come, let us go back home. With whom shall I leave my daughter here?" For fear of Hriday, the Master kept mum all through. We all left that very day. Ramlal called a boat for crossing the river.

At the time of departure, I mentally prayed to the Mother Kali, "Mother, I shall come here again only if You deign to bring me back." Hriday had to leave the Kali Temple for worshipping

---

[1]Yogin-Ma once told me that due to shyness, the Mother had always remained veiled before the Master. It was this woman from Banaras who took the Mother one night to the Master's room, and in his presence removed her veil. The Master in an ecstatic mood went on discoursing on divine topics, which kept them spellbound. None of them was even aware that the whole night had elapsed, and it was dawn when he stopped!

the daughter of Trailokya (son of Mathurbabu) placing flowers at her feet (June, 1881).[1]

Ramlal became the permanent priest of the Kali Temple. That turned his head! He was elated with the thought, "How grand! I am now the priest of Mother Kali!", and began to neglect the Master. The Master would be lying down somewhere in an ecstatic mood, and his food would remain uneaten. It would finally become stale and dry up. There was no one else at the Kali Temple to look after him, so the Master suffered much. He began to send word for me through people coming to those parts, to rejoin him at Dakshineswar.

Through Lakshman Pyne of Kamarpukur, he sent the message, "I am suffering here. After becoming a priest, Ramlal has joined the group of other priests of the Temple. He does not now look after me much. You must come. Take a litter or a palanquin. I shall bear the cost—be it ten rupees or twenty." Hearing this earnest call, at last I came to Dakshineswar(in February or March, 1882). I was coming after a lapse of a year.

Disciple: Where was the Master when Rani Rasmani passed away?

Mother: He was at Dakshineswar then. I heard from him, as also from some others, that at the time of Rasmani's death, suddenly the lamps in the Kali Temple at the Kalighat got blown out, and the Mother revealed Herself to Rasmani. All her relatives too passed away at the Kalighat residence, with the exception of Mathur Babu, who breathed his last at Janbazar.

BELUR MATH

16*th October,* 1912, (*Wednesday*)

It was the time of the Durga Puja. That day was the day of Bodhan.[2] The Mother was expected at the Math in the evening.

---

[1] It is usual to adore little Brahmana girls as symbols of the Divine Mother. Trailokya, a non-brahmana, feared that the worship of his daughter by a Brahmana would spell ruin; so he dismissed Hriday immediately from his position as the priest of the Kali temple, with the warning that he should never again enter the precincts of the Temple.

[2] The ceremonial awakening of Goddess Durga on the sixth lunar day, on the eve of Her autumnal worship. The actual worship takes place on the three succeeding days, and the image is immersed on the tenth lunar day.

Evening was advancing and yet there was no sign of her coming. At this delay, Baburam Maharaj (Swami Premananda) became restless. At the gate he saw that the plantain trees and sacred pitchers had not been arranged as yet, and he said, "These things have not been done as yet; how can the Mother come?"

No sooner was the Bodhan ceremony concluded, than the Mother's carriage reached Belur Math. When the carriage stopped, Golap-Ma carefully helped the Mother out of it. The Mother then looked around with beaming eyes and said, "Everything is arranged spick and span. It is as though we ourselves have come attired like the goddess Durga!"

The Mother and the women devotees were accommodated in a bungalow north of the Math premises. The Mother stayed in the southern room of that bungalow. On the day of the Mahashtami, more than three hundred devotees bowed down before the Mother, one by one. She was sitting on her cot facing west. Three or four persons were initiated by her that day.

In the evening, during the course of a conversation, the topic of Girish Babu's sister came up. She had all of a sudden passed away on the night of the Bodhan. The Mother said, "Human being—today he is, tomorrow he is not. No one will accompany a person after his death. Only his actions—good and bad—follow him, even after death."

A boy had received from the Master the sacred Mantra in a dream. He had approached the Mother for guidance. Referring to him, the Mother said, "The Master took that **Brahmin boy on** his lap and gave him the Mantra."

Disciple: Did you give him a Mantra again?

Mother: No. I told him, "You are favoured by the grace of the Lord Himself. You will attain everything by the repetition of that Mantra." I did not even ask him what the Mantra was. I merely explained to him the technique of repetition.

On the day of the Vijaya Dasami, when the image was being taken away on a boat for immersion in the Ganga, Dr. Kanjilal had danced, gesticulated, and made faces at the image like a child. That had sent all roaring with laughter. One Brahmacharin, who held puritanical views, was much annoyed at those gestures and postures. The Mother was watching the whole scene from her residence and enjoying it. Later I told the Mother about the critical reaction of the Brahmacharin. She said, "No, no! It is perfectly all right. The Goddess has to be entertained in every way through music, fun and frolic."

The Mother returned to the Udbodhan on the next day, and after staying for a few days there, she left for Banaras.

BANARAS

5th November 1912 (*Tuesday*)

The Mother arrived at the Ramakrishna Advaita Ashrama at Banaras around 1 p.m. After sometime she went to the new residence of Kiran Babu which was very near the Ashrama. The wide verandah of the house pleased the Mother and she remarked, "We are indeed fortunate. A narrow place makes the mind narrow, while a commodious place expands it."

The Mother stayed on the first floor with Golap-Ma, Master Mahasaya's wife and some women devotees. Swami Prajnananda and all of us stayed below.

The very next day, the Mother went in a palanquin to the shrines of Viswanath and Annapurna. On the day following Kali Puja (November 9), she visited the Ramakrishna Mission Home of Service, also known as the Sevashrama. Swami Brahmananda, Swami Turiyananda, Charu Babu (Swami Shubhananda), Dr. Kanjilal and others were present. Kedar Baba (Swami Achalananda) accompanied her palanquin and showed her round the wards of the hospital

When she had seen every department, she sat down and expressed to Kedar Baba her delight at all the buildings and gardens she had seen, and the good management she had noticed. She further added, "The Master himself is present here, and the Mother Lakshmi is here in all Her splendour!"

She was curious to know how the institution had taken shape and with whom the idea had first originated. Kedar Baba referred to the zealous efforts and perseverance of Charu Babu and others. Swami Brahmananda told her about the efforts, enthusiasm and the hard work of Kedar Baba for this institution. The Mother was much pleased. She remarked, "The place is so beautiful; I feel like staying on in Banaras."

Soon after she had reached her residence, a devotee came to the Sevashrama with a ten-rupee note and handing it over to the

Head, said, "Kindly accept these ten rupees as the Mother's donation to the Sevashrama."[1]

On December 14th, the Mother visited the shrines of various gods and goddesses of Banaras. After her visit to the Temple of Vaidyanath and Tilabhandeswar, she said that the Siva image there was *Svayambhu*[2]. A little after dusk, she visited the Kedarnath Temple, and attended the evening Service there, after having a look at the holy Ganga. About Kedarnath, she said, "This Kedar and the Kedar in the Himalayas are identical,—they are connected. If you see this, it is as good as seeing that. The Deity here is a living Presence!"

One day the Mother visited Sarnath. When she saw some foreigners observing with evident astonishment the Buddhist ruins there, she said, "These are the very people who built these things in their previous birth. Now they have come again, and are amazed at their own doings!"

At the time of returning, Swami Brahmananda sent the Holy Mother in his own carriage. The Mother could not be persuaded at first. She said, "No, no. Rakhal and others came in that one, and they will ride back in it. I have no difficulty in travelling in this one." But she complied at last. No sooner was her carriage out of sight, than the horse of the carriage in which the Swami was travelling, ran amuck and landed in a road-side ditch along with the carriage. The Swami was seriously injured.

On hearing of this incident, the Mother said, "The accident was really in store for me, but Rakhal quietly diverted it upon himself. Otherwise with so many young ones (Radhu, Bhudev and others) in my carriage, who knows what would have happened to them?"

The Mother visited two holy men this time at Banaras—one of them was a follower of Guru Nanak, and the other was Chameli Puri. When Golap-Ma inquired of Chameli Puri, "Who arranges for your food?", the grand old monk replied with great faith and earnestness, "It is the Mother Durga alone who does. Who else would?" This reply pleased the Mother immensely.

---

[1] That note is still treasured at the Sevashrama as an invaluable asset and the blessing of the Holy Mother.

[2] Those that are not man-made, but found in natural surroundings, springing from the earth.

Returning home in the evening, she said to us, "Ah! The old man's face comes to my mind—it is just like a child's!" The next day she sent him some oranges, sweets and a blanket. When on a subsequent day I asked her if she would visit some more holy men, she said, "What more holy men have I to see? I have seen that holy man. Which other holy man is here?"

One day some local women-folk came to visit the Mother. They found her very busy with Radhu, Bhudev and other children, and asking Golap-Ma to mend her torn cloth. One of them could not help blurting out, "Mother, I see you terribly entangled in Maya!" The Mother replied in an undertone, "What to do, dear, for I myself am Maya!"[1]

Another day there came three or four women to meet her. The Mother was then seated on one side of the verandah, while Golap-Ma and others sat on the other. Seeing Golap-Ma, who appeared older and possessed an imposing personality, one of the visitors mistook her for the Holy Mother and saluted her. As she was about to say something, Golap-Ma saw the mistake and said, "There sits the Holy Mother." Seeing the simple appearance of the Holy Mother, she thought that the "Mother" (actually Golap-Ma) was just making fun. But when Golap-Ma repeated what she had said, the woman went towards the Holy Mother to salute her. The Mother too smilingly said, "No, no. She indeed is the Holy Mother!"

The woman was now in a fix! Golap-Ma and the Mother, both were pointing to each other saying—"There! She is the Holy Mother!" We were watching all this fun. Finally, the woman adjudged Golap-Ma to be the 'real' Holy Mother, and again advanced towards her. Now Golap-Ma rebuked her, saying, "Have you no sense of judgement at all? Don't you notice the difference between a human face and a divine face? Does any human being appear like that?"

The Mother indeed possessed something unique in her simple and gracious appearance which truly made one feel her uncommon nature.

[1] Maya may mean delusion, as also the Universal Divine Mother who is its source. The latter is often called Mahamaya, the Great Maya.

BANARAS, *Kiran Babu's House, Morning.*

Disciple: All the pilgrims touch the image of Visvanatha (Siva). Therefore it is bathed in the evening. Afterwards the priests worship the Deity and give the food-offering.

Mother: The priests allow people to touch the image out of greed for money. Why should they do so? It is enough to see the image from a distance. Otherwise people of immoral character would touch the image.

There are some people whose very touch creates a burning sensation in the body. It is so painful. Therefore I wash my hands and feet after they touch me. Fortunately the rush of people here is less than in Calcutta.

Disciple: One can see you here only after obtaining the permission of the senior Swamis. This arrangement has been made in order to lessen the rush.

Mother: Who cares to hold court, as it were, at different places?

Her lunatic sister-in-law tormented her even in Banaras. Referring to this she said: "Perhaps I worshipped Siva with Bilva leaves having thorns. Therefore I have this thorn in my life in the shape of this sister-in-law."

Disciple: How is that? What's the harm in offering thorny Bilva leaves to Siva unknowingly?

Mother: No, no. It is extremely difficult to worship Siva. It harms a person even if he makes a mistake unconsciously. But the fact is that those who are having their last birth suffer from the effects of past Karma in this one.[1]

I do not remember having committed any sin since my very birth. I touched the Master at the age of five. I might not have understood him at that time, but he undoubtedly touched me. Why should I suffer so much? By touching him others are being freed from Maya; why should I alone have so much entanglement? Day and night, my mind wants to soar high. I force it down out of compassion for people. And yet I am so tormented!

---

[1]A Sannyasin disciple had once asked her, "Mother, why do we suffer so much due to various ailments?" The Mother had replied, "This is your last birth. So you are exhausting the fruits of all your Karmas of previous lives."

Disciple: Let them do whatever they like. Please bear with us all. A person cannot be angry so long as he is conscious of himself.

Mother: Right you are, my child. There is no other virtue higher than forbearance. This is a body of flesh and blood. Sometimes I may say something in a fit of anger.

Then the Mother added, saying to herself, "He who warns in time is a true friend. What's the use of saying 'Ah!', when the right time has passed?"

11*th December,* 1912

The Holy Mother, while in Banaras, used to listen to the reading of the *Kasī Khaṇḍa.*[1] One evening, after the reading of the book, she was engaged in conversation with the disciple.

Disciple: Do all that die in Banaras gain liberation?

Mother: The Scriptures say, "Yes."

Disciple: What is your direct experience? The Master saw that Siva Himself whispers the holy Mantra (*Tāraka-Brahma*) into the ears of the dead.

Mother: I don't know about it, my child; I have not seen anything of this kind.

Disciple: I cannot believe unless I hear something from you on this point.

Mother: Well, I shall tell the Master. "R—does not want to believe. Please show me something about it."

I referred to the destruction of temples in many places in India during the Mussalman rule and said, "There was so much oppression. What did God do to prevent it?"

Mother: God has infinite patience. People worship Siva by pouring water in jugs over His head day and night. Does it affect Him in the least? Or they worship Him, covering the image with dry clothes. Does it trouble Him at all? God's patience knows no limit.

The following morning the Holy Mother said to Khagen Maharaj, "Yesterday night I lay awake on my bed when I suddenly saw the image of Narayana of the Seth's temple of Brindavan standing by my side. The garland of flowers round the neck of the Deity hung up to the feet. The Master stood with folded

---

[1] A canto of the *Skanda Purāṇa* (a Hindu religious scripture), relating specially to Banaras.

hands in front of the image. I thought, 'How could the Master come here? 'I said, 'R—does not want to believe.' The Master said, 'He must. This is all true.' He meant that one dying in Banaras does gain liberation. That Narayana image told me two things. One was: 'Can one ever get the knowledge of Reality unless one knows the truth about God?' The other thing I do not recall."

Khagen Maharaj: Why did the Master stand with folded hands before the image of Narayana?

Mother: That was his characteristic attitude. He was humble before all.

I called on the Mother in the morning and asked her, referring to the conversation of the previous day: "Please tell me if one dying in Banaras gains liberation. What have you seen?"

Mother: The Scriptures say so. Besides, so many people come here with this faith. What else can happen to him who has taken refuge in the Lord?

Disciple: It is, of course, true that he who has taken refuge in God will be liberated. But take the case of those who have not surrendered themselves to God, who are not His devotees, or who belong to other faiths,—will they also get liberation by dying at Banaras?

Mother: Yes, they too. Banaras is permeated with the spirit of God. All living beings of this place, even the moths and insects, are filled with divine consciousness. Any being that dies here—be it a devotee, an atheist, one belonging to another religion, or even an insect or moth—will surely be liberated.

Disciple: Are you speaking the truth?

Mother: Yes, it is true, indeed. Otherwise how can you explain the glory of the holy place?

Nearby there were some sweets that had been offered to the Lord. A fly, buzzing about, sat on my arm. Pointing to it, I said, "Even this fly?"

Mother: Yes, even that fly. All living beings of this place are filled with the spirit of God. Bhudev wanted to take home two young pigeons that had been caught in the niche over the staircase. I said to him. "No, no; you must not take them away. They are inhabitants of Banaras." The women coming from East Bengal live in the Bangalitola. Have they no love for their homes and properties, friends and relatives? But they all have settled down here in order to breathe their last in Banaras. They have such wisdom. They are without attachment.

Disciple: You see, how spiritual are the people of East Bengal!

Mother: Yes, that's true. People of our district are devoid of spiritual wisdom. Take the case of the father-in-law of Radhu. His family owns a house in Banaras. Still the members of the family are frightened at the very mention of Banaras. They fancy that they will not die if they cling to their native village. Death, however, moves with us as our shadow.

Disciple: Are you really speaking the truth when you say that one dying here gains liberation?

Mother: (*sharply*) I cannot swear before you thrice. Swearing once is bad enough. Swearing three times! And that, too, in Banaras!

Disciple: (*smiling*) Please see that I do not die in Banaras! In that case where shall I be and where will you be? We shall not see each other!

Mother: (*smiling*) How stupid! He says that he does not want to die in Banaras!

Disciple: Mother, seeing is believing. One believes in a statement when it can be corroborated by direct perception.

Mother: What else shall you do if you do not believe in the words of high-souled men? Is there any other way except the one trodden by sages and seers and other holy men?

Disciple: None, indeed! What else can I do but listen to the seers who have had direct perception? That is why I have put the question to you. I shall let you go only when you have given me a direct reply!

Mother: Does it matter in the least to God whether you believe or not? Even the sage Suka Deva was to Him like a big ant at the most. Infinite is He. How much can you understand of Him? Our Master was a man of direct perception. He saw everything; he knew everything. His words are the words of the Veda. What will you do if you do not believe in his words?

Disciple: The Scriptures differ. Some Scriptures say 'this' and others 'that'. Which shall we accept? That is why I am bothering you.

Mother: That's true, indeed. The almanac makes a forecast of rain. But you do not get a drop by squeezing its pages. Besides, the Scriptures are filled with many useless things also. One cannot observe to the letter the injunctions of the Scriptures. The Master used to say, "The Bhakti hedged round by the Scriptural injunctions hardly justifies the name."

While staying at Kamarpukur after my return from Brindavan, I took off my bracelets for fear of public criticism. In fact, people were already talking about it. I also wished to go for bath in the Ganga, for which I have always had a special devotion. But the river is far away from Kamarpukur.

Now one day I saw, to my great surprise, that the Master was coming towards the house from the direction of Bhuti's canal. He was followed by Naren, Baburam, Rakhal and many other devotees. Further I saw that from his feet sprang a stream of water which flowed in front of him in waves. I said to myself, 'I see he is everything. The Ganges has sprung from his lotus feet!' Quickly I plucked flowers from the side of the Raghuvir temple and offered handfuls of them into the stream. The Master than said to me, "Don't take off the bracelets. Do you know the Vaishnava Tantras?" I said "What are they? I do not know anything about them." Thereupon he said, "Gaurimani (Gauri-Ma) will come here this afternoon. She will tell you about them." That very afternoon Gaurdasi arrived, and I learned from her that to a woman her husband is Chinmaya (Pure Spirit).[1]

In this Kali Yuga one attains to God if one simply sticks to truth. The Master used to say, "He who speaks nothing but truth is resting on the lap of God!" During the Master's illness at Dakshineswar, I used to boil and condense milk for him and take to him two pounds of milk saying that it was one. I would not tell him the correct quantity. One day he came to know about it and said, "What is this? Stick to truth. You see, I have bowel complaints on account of my taking a large quantity of milk." Surprisingly enough, that very day he suffered from disorder of the bowels. He had all powers, but it is not so with us.

Disciple: My asking you all these questions or talking in this

[1]Later when Yogin-Ma visited Kamarpukur, the Mother while describing this incident to her, added, "The Master then stood at the foot of yonder peepul tree. I saw at last the Master disappearing in the body of Naren. Take the dust of this place and bow down!" When this news travelled from mouth to mouth and reached Swami Vivekananda, he said that it would have been better for him not to have heard of the entry of the Master into his body.

manner is not really meant for me. I do not worry about myself, I have a different feeling about it. What I want to know is this: I address you as my mother. Are you really my mother?

Mother: Who else am I? Yes, I am your own mother.

Disciple: You may say so. But I do not clearly see this. Naturally and spontaneously I know the mother who gave birth to my body as my own mother. But can I think of you likewise?

Mother: Alas, it is true indeed!

A few moments later, she added, "My child, He alone is our father and mother. He alone has become our father and mother."

16th December, 1912

I raised the topic of "visions", and asked the Mother, "People have various "visions". Are they subjective or can they be actually seen by one's physical eyes?"

Mother: They are all subjective. But I had seen one actually with these physical eyes. It was at Kamarpukur. A girl like Radhu (about 11 or 12 years old), wearing ochre clothes, with a string of Rudraksha beads around her neck, her hair all rough and dry, would accompany me wherever I went.

Then I performed the *Pañcatapā*[1] at Nilambar Babu's rented house at Belur. Yogin (Yogin-Ma) too did it. After this the girl disappeared, and I saw her no more.

Disciple: What is the need of Tapasya (austerity)?

Mother: It is very necessary. Look at Yogin. How much does she fast even now? She practises intense austerities. Golap is an adept in Japa. One day Naren's mother came to visit me. Naren said to her, "Perhaps you had practised austerities. Therefore you got Vivekananda as your son. Repeat them and then you may get another."

The Master practised all kinds of disciplines. He used to say, "I have made the mould; now you may cast the image."

Disciple: What is the meaning of casting the image?

Bhudev: It means to meditate on the Master and mould yourself after him.

---

[1] *Pañcatapā* means 'austerity of the five fires'. The aspirant lights four fires, each seven feet apart in a square formation. Sitting in their midst, with the burning sun above as the 'fifth fire', the aspirant practises prayer and meditation.

Mother: Yes, he has understood it. To cast the image means to meditate and contemplate on the Master, to think of the various incidents of his life. By meditating on him, one gets all the spiritual moods. He used to say, "One who remembers me never suffers from want of food or from other physical privations."

Maku: Did he himself say this?

Mother: Yes, these are the very words from his mouth. By remembering him one gets rid of all sufferings. Don't you see that all his devotees are happy? Elsewhere you will not find devotees like those of the Master. Here, in Banaras, I see so many holy men; but can you point out one who is like his devotees?

Disciple: There is a reason for that, Mother. About him we feel as if the market has only just come to a close. All the signs of the market are there. People are still moving about. The devotees and the intimate disciples of the Master are still alive. We feel that the Master, as it were, is very near us. He has not gone away to any great distance. We shall get the response if we but call on him.

Mother: Yes, many people do get it.

Disciple: Krishna, Rama and others seem to belong to a bygone age. They do not seem near enough to respond to our prayer.

Mother: Yes, that is true.

Referring to the Cossipore Garden, I said, "It is a sacred place and now a European gentleman lives there."

Mother: At the Cossipore Garden the Master spent the last days of his life. The place is associated with so much meditation, Samadhi and the practice of austerities. It is the place where the Master entered into Mahasamadhi. It is a place permeated with intense spiritual vibration. One realizes God-consciousness by meditating there. The place may be acquired if the Master commands its owner through dream to hand it over to the Belur Math.

One day at Cossipore, Niranjan (Swami Niranjanananda) and others planned to drink the juice of a date palm. To my astonishment, I saw the Master too going behind them. When I asked him about this the next day, he said, "Oh! It is all your imagination! Your brain must have been heated by too much cooking!"[1].

[1] A more detailed version of this incident was related by the Mother to the mother of Nirad Maharaj:—The Master was then completely bed-ridden at Cossipore. Swamiji and other

Vijay Goswami had a vision of the Master at Dacca. He even felt the touch of the Master's body!

After the passing away of the Master, Naren and other youngsters said, "Let us continue to stay here (at the Cossipore Garden-house) at least for some days more, to help the Mother get over the shock. If necessary, we will feed her by begging food." But Ramchandra Datta and other older devotees were not willing. They said, "You need not go about begging to feed her," and the house was given up.

I can stay at that place (Udbodhan, Calcutta) only so long as Sarat is there. After him, I do not see anyone who can shoulder my burden. Yogen (Swami Yogananda) was there. And there is Krishnalal too, — calm and quiet— a disciple of Yogen. Sarat can look after me very well. Sarat is my 'burden-bearer'.

Disciple : Can't Maharaj (Swami Brahmananda) do so ?

Mother: No. Rakhal is not of that temperament. He can't face troubles physically. He can do so intellectually or through someone. He is of a totally different make-up.

Disciple: What about Baburam Maharaj (Swami Premananda)?

---

intimate devotees were serving him to the best of their ability. One evening they planned to drink juice by tapping a date palm which was in one corner of the Cossipore garden. The Master was told nothing of this plan. In the evening, all of them proceeded towards the tree. The Mother was staying then in the same building. She suddenly noticed the Master darting down like an arrow. Startled at this, she wondered, "Is it possible? How can one, who has to be helped even to change sides on his bed, rush down like that?" And yet, she had seen it happen actually before her eyes! She went to the Master's room and found his bed empty. In a bewildered state of mind, she searched for him everywhere. Not finding him, she returned to her room in extreme confusion and apprehension in her mind. A little later, she saw him again returning to his room as swiftly as he had left it. Later when the Mother asked him about this, he said, "Oh! Did you notice it?" He then continued, "They are all youngsters. They were proceeding merrily to drink the juice of the date palm in the garden. I saw a black cobra at the foot of the tree there which was so ferocious that it would have bitten them all. The boys did not know it. So I went by a different route and drove it away after warning, 'Never come here again'. The Mother was dumbfounded on hearing this. The Master had asked her not to divulge this to anyone then.

Mother: No, not even he.

Disciple: How then is he managing the Belur Math?

Mother: That may be. But taking the responsibilities of women! He can at the most make enquiries from a distance.

Then the Mother talked about the disciples of the Master, whereupon the disciple asked her, "Please tell me who these disciples of the Master are. We cannot recognize them."

Mother: What do I know? But it is true that those who had been born with the Master in his previous incarnations have accompanied him this time also.

Disciple: I do not have any such desire as to see a four-handed Deity and the like. I am quite satisfied with what we have.

Mother: That is also the case with me. What shall we gain by these supernatural visions? For us the Master exists—and he is everything.

UDBODHAN

11*th February*, 1913

Disciple: Mother, Swamiji has initiated so many people with the Mantra and you also have initiated so many. They come and go away, and are not remembered.

Mother: So many people come. Can all be remembered? When the fire burns, do not the moths come? It is like that.

Disciple: They take the Mantra. But what do they get? We find the man remains as he was.

Mother: Power passes through the Mantra—the Guru's goes to the disciple and the disciple's comes to the Guru. That is why the Guru at the time of initiation takes on himself the sins of the disciple and suffers so much from physical maladies. It is extremely difficult to be a Guru, for he has to take the responsibilities for the disciple's sins. If the disciple commits a sin,that affects the Guru too. On the other hand, the Guru is benefited if the disciple is good. Some disciples make quick progress, and some do it slowly. It depends on the tendencies of the mind acquired by one's past deeds. That is why Rakhal (Swami Brahmananda) hesitates about giving initiation. He said to me, "Mother, as soon as I initiate a disciple, I fall ill. The very idea of giving initiation makes me feel feverish."

One Swami sent a boy to the Holy Mother for initiation. She

heard all details from him and said, "You have your own hereditary Vaishnava Gurus. Take initiation from them." Whatever may be the reason, the mother did not initiate him.

After supper I went to bring a betel roll. The Holy Mother was tying the mosquito curtains for the children in the next room. I heard her speaking to the mad aunt, "Don't take me for an ordinary mortal. You abuse me so recklessly. I do not take it to heart, considering it only as so much noise. If I take notice of it, who will save you? It is to your advantage that I am alive. Your daughter is yours only. I am here only until she grows up. Otherwise what is attachment for me? I can cut it off this moment. When I pass away one day like camphor, you will never get a trace of me."

Mad aunt: When did I scold you? I just said a few words. The trouble is when you give, you give without reserve.

She was of the opinion that the Holy Mother should keep all her money for Radhu.

Mother: Mine is a child-like nature. Do I keep meticulous accounts? I give to whoever asks.

Returning from Banaras, the Holy Mother stayed a few days at Calcutta and then left for Jayrambati. On 25th February she reached Koalpara. She was given the room next to the shrine. I brought out a banian seed and said, "See, Mother, this seed is smaller than the seed of red spinach. And yet from this comes such a huge tree! What a wonder!" She replied, "Why not? Just see, how small is the *Bīja* (mystic syllable) of the Lord's Name. Yet from that, springs forth in due time spiritual consciousness, devotion, love and what not!"

We came to Jayrambati and sat for meal at night. Someone said, "Mother, did you notice how inconsiderate these people (the Mother's brothers) are? They knew of your coming. Yet, they did not send anyone to receive you at the river-crossing." Thereupon the Mother said to the eldest brother (Prasanna): "Why did you not send a man to help me cross the river? My children (referring to the disciples) accompanied me. You did not go yourself, nor did you send a man."

The brother replied, "I did not do so for fear of Kali (the next brother.) He might complain that I was trying to win you over to my side. Do I not know what you are and what these devotees are? I know everything, but I am helpless. Please bless me that I may have you as my sister in my future births also. I do not want anything else."

Mother; Do you think that I shall be born again in your family? I have had enough of it this time. Sri Rama once prayed, "Never may I be born again in the womb of Kausalya!" And to be born in your family again! Our father was a devotee of Rama and always helped others; our mother too had such a kind heart. That is why I was born in this family.

One day Uncle Prasanna came to the Mother and said, "Sister, I hear that you appeared to someone in a dream and initiated him. You also told him that he would be liberated. You have brought us up from our childhood, and shall we remain just as we are?"

In reply, the Mother said, "The Master's will shall prevail. And look here, Sri Krishna was so intimate with the shepherd boys. He played with them, laughed and wandered with them, and shared their food; but did they know who he really was?"

One day some of the devotees were about to clean the place where they had just finished their meals. The Mother prevented them saying, "No, no. Please don't do all that. You are all precious jewels of the Lord." When the devotees insisted on going ahead with it, the Mother said, "There is a person appointed for that work. The maid will do it."

JAYRAMBATI

14th March, 1913

Dr. Lalit of Shyambazar and Probodh Babu arrived. At about four o'clock in the afternoon they came to the Holy Mother and saluted her. The following conversation took place:

Lalit Babu: Mother, what rules and regulations should one observe regarding food?

Mother: One should not eat the food given at funeral obsequies (*Srāddha* ceremony). It does harm to devotional life. Sri Ramakrishna used to forbid it. Besides, first offer to God whatever you eat. One must not eat unoffered food. As your food is, so will be your blood. From pure food you get pure blood, pure mind and strength. Pure mind begets ecstatic love (*Prema Bhakti*)

Lalit Babu: Mother, we are householders. What shall we do at the *Srāddha* ceremony of our relatives?

Mother: Supervise the ceremony and give help to your relatives so that they may not be offended; but try somehow to avoid taking meals on that day. If you cannot do that, then on the day of the *Srāddha* ceremony eat what is offered to Vishnu or other gods. The devotees can partake of the food of the *Srāddha* ceremony if it is offered to God.

Lalit Babu: Many a time there remains an excess of unused food-stuff procured for the *Srāddha* ceremony. Can one cook and eat that?

Mother: Yes, you can. That will not injure you, my child. A householder cannot help it.

Prabodh Babu: Mother, the Master loved renunciation, but how little we practise it!

Mother: Yes, you will acquire it slowly. You make some progress in this life, a little more in the next and so on. It is the body alone that changes, the Atman always remains the same. Renunciation of 'lust' and 'gold'!

The Master used to say, "I can change Kamarpukur into gold, if I so desire, by requesting Mathur Babu to do so; but what good will that do? It is all transitory." Regarding some devotees, the Master used to say that it was their last birth. He would remark, referring to some devotee, "You see, he has no desire whatsoever for anything. This is his last birth."

The devotees prostrated themselves before the Mother and took leave of her.

Speaking about the objection of certain people that some of Sri Ramakrishna's Sannyasin disciples, being Sudras, are not entitled for Sannyasa, according to orthodox rules, the Mother said, "The disciples of Sri Ramakrishna are Jnanis and therefore Sannyasins. A Jnani can be a Sannyasin. Take the case of Gaurdasi. A woman cannot be initiated into Sannyasa, but is Gaurdasi a woman? She is more than a man! How many men are there like her? See what she has achieved—built a school, acquired horses, a carriage, and so forth. The Master used to say, 'If a woman embraces Sannyasa, she is certainly not a woman; she is really a man.' He further used to say to Gaurdasi, 'I am pouring water, you will make the clay.' "

JAYRAMBATI

28th March, 1913

It was morning. I entered the inner apartment of the Holy

Mother's house and found her cutting the Kalmi green. Seeing her cutting something else also along with it, I said, "What is this that you are cutting up with the Kalmi green?" "This is grass," the Mother said, "this is also a kind of green. The complexion of Krishna was like this grass."

I was seated for the mid-day meal. Radhu's mother arranged a leaf-plate and a cup of water in the verandah of her house for another guest, perhaps one of her relatives. A cat drank a little water out of the cup, so Radhu's mother changed the water. The cat again drank some of the water, and again she changed it. A third time the cat drank, whereupon Radhu's mother chased it and screamed, "You rogue, you burnt-faced cat, I will kill you!" It was the hot season. The Holy Mother was there. She said, "No, no, you must not prevent a thirsty animal from drinking. Besides the cat has already touched the water." At this Radhu's mother shouted in anger, "You don't have to become compassionate towards the cat. You have shown enough compassion towards man! Why not reserve your kindness for man?"

The Mother said in a serious voice, " He is unfortunate, indeed, who does not gain my compassion. I do not know anyone, not even an insect, for whom I do not feel compassion."

I was seated for the evening meal. The Mother herself had cooked a curry, potatoes and other vegetables. She gave some of them to me and said, "Eat and tell me how you like it."

Disciple: This is patient's diet—cool and bland. Who cooked it?

Mother: I myself.

Disciple: You yourself?

Mother: Yes.

Disciple: Well, it could be done better. It is not exactly to the taste of people of our part of the country.

Mother : You had better taste a little of the liquid portion.

Nalini: O aunt, you never put any red chilly in your curry. Can anybody relish it ?

Mother: *(to Nalini)* Don't listen to him. When you eat it, you will find it tastes good.

Disciple: For some days past I have been asking about the curries you prepare and I have tasted some of them, but they all taste alike.

Mother: Very well, one day I shall cook as they do in your part of the country. You must show me how to cook. I am sure you add a lot of chillies. Don't you?

Disciple: Not so much. But a curry need not necessarily taste bad because it is less pungent.

Mother: (*to Nalini*) Bring some gram tomorrow. I shall make some soup. I used to cook very well; now I am out of practice. At Kamarpukur, Lakshmi's mother and I used to cook. She could cook very well. One day the Master and Hriday sat for their meals. Referring to a preparation made by Lakshmi's mother, the Master said, "O Hridu, the one who has cooked this may be compared to the physician Ramdas." And tasting the curry prepared by me, he said, "Ah, whoever has cooked this is Srinath Sen." Now Ramdas was a renowned physician while Srinath Sen was only a quack! At this Hriday said, 'What you say is true. But you can get your quack physician at all times to render you all kinds of service, even to massage your feet. You have only to send for her and she comes. But physician Ramdas takes a big fee for his visit, and you cannot get him at all hours. Moreover, people at first consult a quack. He is your friend at all times." The Master said, "That's true, that's true. She is always available."

JAYRAMBATI

8th May, 1913

Radhu was indisposed, being laid up with pain and fever. Her eccentric mother began to scold the Holy Mother, saying, "You are about to kill my daughter with medicines." As she kept on scolding, she lost all control over her tongue. Uncle Varada was called in. He chased Radhu's mother out of the house. The Holy Mother, too, could bear it no longer. She spoke some sharp words to Radhu's mother.

Addressing us the Mother said, "I was married to one who never addressed me as *tui*. One day at Dakshineswar, I carried the Master's food to his room. As I was leaving the room, the Master thought that it was his niece Lakshmi, and called out, 'Close the door behind you (*tui*).' I said, 'Yes, I am closing it.' Recognizing my voice he was embarrassed and said, 'Ah, it's you! I thought it was Lakshmi. Please don't mind.' That unintentional disrespect upset him so much, that the next morning he came to the Nahabat saying, 'Look here, my dear. The whole of last night I couldn't sleep, worrying how indeed I spoke so rudely to you!' And look at this Radhu's mother! How she abuses me day and night! I do not know what sin I committed to deserve all this. Perhaps I worshipped Siva with a thorny Bilva leaf. That thorn has now become this thorn—this Radhu's mother."

JAYRAMBATI

12th May, 1913

Referring to Radhu's illness, the Mother said, "My mind now does not dwell upon Radhu even in the slightest degree. I am sick of her illness. I force my mind upon her. I pray to the Master, saying 'O Lord, please divert my mind a little to Radhu. Otherwise who will look after her?' I have never seen such illness. Perhaps in her former birth she died of an illness for which she had not performed any penance. I have in mind to do these two things— one, to invoke the help of a *Caṇḍa* (a fierce spirit) through adequate rites, and the other, to undertake the *Cāndrāyana* vow.

"Whenever the Master experienced Mahabhava, he used to experience excruciating burning sensation in his chest. You must have read all about it in the books. My brother-in-law then brought him to the village-home. He called in a few exorcists, and with their help a *Caṇḍa* was invoked. He addressed the Master by his childhood name and said, 'O so-and-so (Gadai), your state of Mahabhava is due to the grace of God. It is not a disease. Do not eat too much betel-nut. It increases lust.' If a man dies for a particular illness without doing the necessary penance, he gets the same illness in his next birth[1]; but this rule does not apply to a holy man."

Kedar's mother: The monk dies repeating the Name of God and therefore he attains to God.

Mother: Yes, that's true. The other day a young man died at

---

[1]The idea is that an illness is brought about by one's evil Karma. In the case of the last illness, it may be that one dies before the Karma is fully exhausted, and in that case, one may have to suffer for that residuary Karma in the next birth, the suffering taking the shape of the same old disease. Hence one should perform penance, charity, worship, etc. as atonement for one's sinful Karma during one's last illness, and thus one gets over the effects of that Karma.

Koalpara. Will he be reborn? No. That was his last birth.

At the time of his illness at Cossipore, the Master once remarked, "I am ill. The officers of the Kali temple may criticize me for not performing any penance." Then to Ramlal he said, "Take these ten rupees and go to Dakshineswar. Offer the money to Mother Kali and distribute it among the Brahmanas and others."

A Sadhu is not entitled to perform any ritual. Therefore the Master asked Ramlal to offer the money to his Chosen Deity and later on distribute it among the Brahmanas and others. In ancient times the hermits and Rishis used to live in the forest. Could they perform penances like the *Cāndrāyaṇa*? They used to offer only fruits and roots to their Chosen Ideal and later on distribute them among the needy. That was enough for them.

Radhu's Mother: My aunt died of a certain illness. Do you mean to say she has been born again with that illness?

Mother: Do you think that your aunt has not been reborn? Certainly she has again taken birth and inherited that illness as well. Many a time a man born in a particular family takes birth and dies again and again in the same family as a result of his Karma.

JAYRAMBATI *(Mother's old House)*

8th June, 1913

Surendranath Bhaumick and Dr. Durgapada Ghosh had been staying at the house of the Holy Mother. They were to leave that afternoon. In the morning, after their bath, they came to the Mother and saluted her. She blessed them by placing her hand on their heads and asked them to take their seats. After the exchange of a word or two, Surendra said to the Holy Mother, "Mother, while worshipping the Master I find one difficulty. Suppose a devotee has a general belief that his Ishta Devata and the Master are one and the same. He worships the Goddess through the image of the Master. Afterwards he surrenders the fruits of the Japa to the image of the Master, uttering the words, *tvat prasādāt maheśvari*—'O Great-Goddess, through Thy grace,' and so forth. This creates a confusion in my mind."

The Mother said with a smile, "Don't worry, my child. Our Master alone is *Maheśvara* (Supreme God) and *Maheśvari* (Supreme Goddess) as well. He alone is the embodiment of all Deities. He alone is the embodiment of all mystic syllables.

One can worship through him all Gods and Goddesses. You can address him as *Maheśvara* as well as *Maheśvari*.

Surendra: Mother, I cannot concentrate my mind in meditation at all.

Mother: It does not matter much. It will be enough if you look at the picture of the Master. The Master was ill at Cossipore. The young disciples used to attend on him by turn. Gopal also was there. One day instead of serving the Master, he went for meditation. He meditated for a long time. When Girish Babu heard of it, he remarked, "The one upon whom he is meditating with closed eyes is suffering on a sick-bed, and fancy, he is meditating upon him!" Gopal was sent for. The Master asked him to stroke his legs. He said to him, "Do you think I am asking you to stroke my legs because they are aching? Oh, no! In your previous births you did many virtuous acts; therefore I am accepting your service." Look at the picture of the Master and that will be enough.

Surendra: Mother, I do not succeed in regularly counting the beads three times a day.

Mother: Even if you don't, try to remember the Master always and perform your Japa whenever you can; at least you can salute him mentally, can't you?

Durgapada : Mother, I do not quite understand what rules one should observe regarding one's food.

Mother: The Master was very particular about one thing in regard to food. He used to forbid all the devotees from eating the food of the *Srāddha* ceremony. He used to say it affected one's devotion. Apart from this you may eat what you like, but remember the Master when you do so.

Durgapada: Mother, while performing my duties in the hospital, many a time I feel thirsty. I feel compelled to drink water, without consideration for place and persons. As a matter of fact, I do so. What do you say to that, Mother?

Mother: What else can you do? You do it in connection with the discharge of your duty. Remember the Master while you drink the water. As you do this while on duty, it will not injure you. Is it ever possible for those who are called upon to perform various odd duties to observe all religious injunctions regarding food?[1]

Surendra: You see, Mother, we householders live in families with many relations. Sometimes it happens that while the food is being cooked, some members of the family partake of it; later on that food is brought to me. I hesitate to offer that food to God.

Mother: That is inevitable in the case of householders. We also have to face similar situations. Take an instance: there may be a sick person in the family. Part of the food may be kept aside for him. But when food is placed on the plate, remember the Master, think that he himself has given this food, and eat it. Then it will not have any injurious effect on the growth of devotion.

Surendra: Mother, how can I describe to you my mental condition? You are the inner guide. You understand everything. I have been undergoing all possible sufferings for the last few years. But for your blessings I would perhaps have been dead by this time.

Mother: Yes, my child, you do not have to tell me of the sufferings in the life of the world. There is no limit to it. In your case it is inevitable. Look at me, my child. What sort of life I am leading by the will of the Master! How much I am suffering on account of this girl (Radhu)!

Surendra: Yes, Mother, your condition gives us consolation and hope. You yourself know the sufferings of the world; therefore we can expect your compassion.

---

[1]This part of the conversation is to be understood in the light of the injunctions of the Hindu Scriptures on the purity of the food consumed by spiritual aspirants. In so far as the vital energies of the body are renovated by the food consumed and in so far as the vital energies condition the functioning of the mind, the food taken in has an effect on the state of one's mind. Food is contaminated or made impure not only by hygienic causes, but also by its quality and contacts. Certain food-stuffs are condemned because they are obtained by injuring other creatures or from experience found to lead to mental excitement. The motive and character of the giver, as also of the person preparing it, are said to make food impure. In later times these ethical and spiritual injunctions became petrified into rigid caste rules in the matter of interdining. The Holy Mother does not seem to favour these caste rules very much, but accepts the validity of the original spiritual principles behind them. The *Srāddha* food is condemned, because the sins of the dead are supposed to contaminate it.

Mother: Don't be afraid, my child. The Master is ever-present. He alone will protect you, both here and hereafter.

Surendra: Mother, we are living so far away. Are dreams real?

Mother: Yes, they are. Dreams regarding the Master are real, but he forbade his disciples to narrate, even to him, dreams regarding himself.

Surendra: Mother, we do not know what the Master was like. We have not seen him. So for us you are the Master and everything else.

Mother: Don't fear, my child. The Master will look after you. He will watch over you here and hereafter. He will protect you always.

After the meal the two devotees took leave. Uncle Varada accompanied them. He was going to Calcutta. The Mother walked part of the way with them and looked on until they were out of sight.

Surendra was the head-master of a school at Ballaratanganj. Some butchers of that place used to flay cows alive. One day the rogues did so in front of the school. Surendra, the other teachers and the students—Hindus and Mussalmans alike—made a strong protest. The butchers were beaten. This created some trouble. Surendra was threatened by the butchers. At this time two or three students of the school were preparing to leave for Jayrambati for taking initiation. Surendra sent a letter to the Holy Mother through them. The boys also narrated the incident to her. She was extremely shocked and said, "If you do not protest against such action, who will do so?" According to her instruction a letter was written to Surendra giving him assurance and encouragement. Further, he was asked to see that a repetition of such cruel action did not take place. Later on the Mother again wrote to Surendra, saying, "If God really exists, then He shall certainly redress the grievance." Some time later a law-suit was filed, and as a result butchery of that heinous kind was stopped.

JAYRAMBATI

11th June, 1913

It was noon. Along with another, I was taking food on the verandah of the Mother's room.

Mother: Radhu says that this time in the month of Asvin,

there will be fierce fighting (*mārāmāri*). It is written so in the almanac.

Disciple: It is not 'fighting'; but a devastating epidemic (*mahāmāri*) is anticipated.

In the course of conversation, the Mother said: "Satya Yuga has begun since the birth of the Master. Many luminaries have accompanied him. Naren was the chief among the Seven Sages (*saptarṣi.*) Arjuna came as Yogen. How many such great souls can there be? Sour mangoes can be had without number. But *fajli* (a certain variety) mangoes—can one get so many? Countless ordinary people take birth and die. But only these jewels among men come along with the Incarnation for the sake of His mission.

Disciple: Swamiji also said that with the advent of the Master the Satya Yuga has begun.

Mother: That is so.

JAYRAMBATI
12th June, 1913

At noon the Holy Mother was feeding Radhu. She said while coaxing her to eat, "When the Master was ill, Ganga Prasad Sen of Kumartuly was consulted. The physician prescribed some medicine and forbade him to drink water. The Master began to ask one and all, 'Well, will I be able to live without water?' He asked this question of everyone, even of a five year old child. All replied, 'Yes, sir, of course you can'. 'Can I?' he asked me. 'Of course,' I replied. He then said, 'You should wipe the water from even washed pomegranate seeds. See if you can do it.' In reply I said to him, 'Well, everything will be done by the grace of Mother Kali. We shall try our utmost.' The Master made up his mind at last. He stopped drinking water and took the medicine. Every day I used to give him three to four seers of milk to drink—later I increased it to even five to six seers. The man who milked the temple cows used to give me milk in large quantities. He would say to me, 'If I give all this milk to the temple, the priests will take it home after worship and give it away to anyone and everyone. But if I leave the milk here, the Master will have it.' He used to give me up to five or six seers of milk. He was a good man, full of devotion. I gave him Rasagolla, Sandesh—all kinds of sweets and other things that lay at hand. The devotees used to bring plenty of these. I would boil the milk down to a seer and a half. The Master would ask me, 'How much milk is there?' I would say, 'How much, indeed? May be 4 or 5 quarters of a seer!' He would remark, 'Perhaps more. I see such thick layer of cream!'

"One day Golap was there. He asked her, 'How much milk is there?' And she told the truth. 'Ah! So much milk!' he exclaimed, 'that is why I get indigestion. Call her, call her!' I came in, and he told me of what Golap had said about the milk. I pacified him telling, 'Oh! Golap does not know the measurement. How can she know how much the pot contains?'

"Another day he asked Golap about the milk and she said in reply, 'One full bowl from here and another from the Kali temple.' At this the Master got nervous again. He sent for me, and began to ask about the exact capacity of the bowl. I replied, 'I do not know all those calculations. You will drink milk. Why all these enquiries about measurement? Who cares for all those calculations?' He was not satisfied. He said, 'Can I digest all this milk? I shall get indigestion.' Really, that day he did get indigestion. He did not take anything that night, except a little sago water.

"Golap said to me afterwards, 'Well, Mother, you should have told me about it before. How could I know? His whole evening meal is spoiled!' In reply I said to her, 'There is no harm in telling a lie for feeding someone. In this way I coax him to eat.' Anyway he picked up his health and was almost cured of his illness."

Disciple: I see that mind alone is everything.

Mother: Exactly. It is mind alone. Indeed, when he was not told, he could consume quite a lot.

At night Vibhuti and I were taking food. I said to Vibhuti, "Would it not be good to get Radhu an amulet for hysteria, from a dependable person?"

Mother: Yes. The priests at the temple of Dharma[1] known by the name 'Swarupa-Narayana', give medicines. I have a mind to try it for Radhu. Now I wish to try some supernatural remedies for her. My mother had once recovered from her illness

[1] Literally, virtue or right norm, deified in Buddhism. The worship of Dharma in these regions began probably during the transitional period in the history of Bengal when Buddhism was being re-absorbed into Hinduism together with its deities of whom Dharma, under various names, was one.

as a result of a consecrated flower from the temple of Swarupa-Narayana Dharma. Since then I have begun to have faith in these things.

Vibhuti: Oh, the priests of Dharma? The Buddhists were distributing medicines, weren't they? The deity Dharma is actually the Lord Buddha.

Mother: We also have a Dharma temple. There it is.

Disciple: I know Dharma is represented by the image of Buddha in all places.

Mother: Here it is known as (Sundara) Narayana, and is of the form of a tortoise.

Vibhuti: The image is like a seat, isn't it, with four heels at the bottom?

Mother: Yes, but slightly raised in the middle.

Vibhuti: That is not a tortoise. It is the seat of Buddha. The state of Buddha is beyond existence and non-existence. There can be no image of His and so they just make a seat for Him.

Mother: That may be. The boys worship our Dharma. There is no set ritual. They give whatever they like. Perhaps one or two red flowers. Whatever is prepared is given. He takes no notice of any faults. He is happy with whatever is given.

Disciple: People often get supernatural remedies for their illnesses. It seems this is not in her (Radhu's) lot.

Mother: When I was ill, my whole body was swollen and the eyes and nose were running incessantly. Umesh (Holy Mother's brother) said, "Sister, Simhavahini is present here. Will you make a vow of fasting before Her?" He persuaded me and almost carried me there. That night of full moon was a dark night for me. I couldn't see anything. Due to incessant watering, my eyes were almost blind. I went and prostrated in front of the Devi. In addition I had diarrhoea. One woman whom I called god-mother lived nearby. She used to grunt loudly now and then, so that I might not be frightened in the dark silent night. I was lying there alone. Just a little later She (Simhavahini) came to my mother, in the form of a blacksmith girl of about Radhu's age, and said, "Go and bring her back. She is so ill and can she be left lying about? Bring her this moment. Use this medicine and she will be all right." Here She advised me, "Crush the gourd flowers with salt and apply that juice drop by drop in the eyes. You will get well." I took that medicine. The juice of gourd flowers was applied to the eyes drop by drop.

And immediately there was such a burning sensation that it cleansed the eyes of all dirt. My eyes got well that very day. The swelling in the body also went down, and I felt very light. Soon I got well. When people asked me about it, I used to reply, "Mother gave me medicine." From then on, the fame of Mother Simhavahini spread. I got the medicine and the world also was blessed. Earlier none knew much of this Mother Deity. My uncle made a vow of fasting before Her. But black ants bit him, and so he could not carry out his vow. She said to my mother in a dream, "Now I am sleeping. Why has he taken the vow now? He is a Brahmana, doesn't he know this? Go, and bring him back." My mother rejoined, "You have said so much, you could have as well given the medicine!"

My mother saw Her once. On one occasion during the village Kali Puja day, Naba Mukherjee, out of rivalry, refused to receive our rice. My mother had made ready rice and other things for the Puja. When he refused to take them from our home, my mother wept all through the night. She thought: "I have made rice for Kali and he has not taken it. Who will eat this rice now? Can anyone eat Kali's rice?" And then in the night she saw Jagaddhatri, red in colour and sitting cross-legged near the door. Then there was only one room, Varada's, in our house. When the Master came, he also would stay in that room. Jagaddhatri raised my mother, patted her and said, "Why are you weeping? I shall take Kali's rice. Why do you worry?" My mother asked, 'Who are you?' Jagaddhatri replied, "I am the mother of the universe. I will receive your worship in the form of Jagaddhatri."

Next day my mother said to me, "Look, Sarada, who is that Deity, red in colour and sitting cross-legged? I shall do Jagaddhatri's Puja." She brought about thirteen maunds of paddy from Viswas. It was raining non-stop. My mother said "Oh Mother, how can I worship you, I cannot even dry the paddy!" In the end by Jagaddhatri's grace there was sunshine. The Mother's image had to be dried by fire and painted. Prasanna informed the Master at Dakshineswar of the Puja. He heard and said, "Mother will come. Very good. But weren't you in straitened circumstances, my dear?" Prasanna said "You also will come. I have come to take you." He said "You go and perform the worship. It will be very beneficial for you all." Thus Jagaddhatri Puja was performed. The whole village was invited. Every expense was met out of that rice. At the time of farewell to Jagaddhatri, my mother whispered in her ear "Mother Jagai, come again next year. All through the year I shall be making things ready for you." Next year my mother told me, "Look, you give something. My Jagai's worship will be celebrated." I replied, "Oh, such a trouble I cannot bear. You have performed it once, why bother again?" That night I saw in a dream that three of them arrived—Jagaddhatri and Her two companions, Jaya and Vijaya. I remember it distinctly. They said to me, "Shall we go away then?" "Who are you all?" I asked. One of them said, "I am Jagaddhatri." In reply I said, "No, why should you go? Stay here. I did not ask you to go away."

Since that time I have been going home as far as possible every year at the time of the Jagaddhatri Puja. I used to help in polishing the utensils and to look after other things. Formerly there were not many people in the family. I would go home to cleanse the pots and pans. Later Yogen (Swami Yogananda) got a set of wooden utensils. He said to me, "Mother, you do not have to scour pots and pans any more." He also secured a piece of land to provide for the expenses of the Puja. Ah! My mother was like goddess Lakshmi. Always she used to keep everything well arranged and spick and span. She would say, "Mine is a family of devotees and gods. Perhaps one day my Sarada (Swami Trigunatitananda) will come, Yogen (Swami Yogananda) may come. All this is necessary." Whatever good rice she got, she would process it and keep ready. She would say "As long as I am here, Brahma also is here, Vishnu is here, Jagadamba, Siva and everybody is here. When I go, they also will accompany me. Is it possible for you to take so much trouble? Mine is a family of gods and devotees."

I had a little diarrhoea. Hearing of that the Mother said, "He is disposed to diarrhoea. He had it in Banaras also." I replied "Before going to Banaras, I suffered from it in Calcutta also. This disease is in our family itself. My father and many others died of diarrhoea."

Vibhuti: What of that? What does it matter if one's father died of some particular ailment?

Mother: Yes. What does it matter? Giving examples is not good. One has to suffer for that. Who dies when! Who is father, who is mother! God is everything.

JAYRAMBATI
14*th July*, 1913

Mukunda and I were seated in the porch of the Mother's house for our midday meal. The Mother was seated in the porch of the adjoining house. Nalini arrived dressed in wet clothes. She had taken her bath, because a crow had 'urinated' on her!

Mother: I am an old woman now, but I have never heard of crows urinating! Your mind is impure. Can the mind lose its purity without great sins? The sister of Krishna Bose had such mania for cleanliness. While bathing in the Ganges she would ask people whether the top of her head was under water. That is an obsession. As a result the mind never feels pure. An impure mind does not easily become pure. The more you emphasize your obsession, the more obsessed you become. It is true of all things.

Disciple: I have seen Mahapurushji (Swami Shivananda) fondle dogs and then go to the shrine room to worship the Master. Perhaps someone would pour a little water in his hand and he would sprinkle a few drops over his face. At that time Ganga water was used for everything.

Mother: It is quite different with them. How pure is their mind! It is the mind of the Saint. They are gods, indeed, who live on the banks of the Ganga. Can anyone but gods live on the banks of the Ganga? Sins committed daily are expiated by ablution in the Ganga.

Nalini: Golap-Ma one day cleaned the toilets in the Udbodhan Office and then dressed fruits for offering in the shrine after merely changing her cloth. I said to her, "What is this, Golap-Didi? Go and bathe in the Ganga." Golap-Ma said to me, "Why don't you do it, if you so desire?"

Mother: How pure is Golap's mind! How high-souled she is! Therefore she does not discriminate so much between pure and impure things. She does not at all bother about rules regarding external purity. This is her last birth. In order to acquire a mind like that you need to be born again in a different body.

Pure air blows for eight miles on both the banks of the Ganga. This air is the embodiment of Narayana. The mind is rendered pure as the result of many austerities. God who is purity itself cannot be attained without spiritual practices.

What else does a man obtain by the realization of God? Does he grow two horns? No, his mind becomes pure, and through such a pure mind one attains knowledge and spiritual awakening.

Disciple: There are devotees who surrender themselves to God fully and do not practise austerities. How do they attain to this state?

Mother: That they surrender themselves to God, that they live placing implicit trust in Him, is their spiritual discipline. Ah! Naren said, "Let me have millions of births, what do I fear?" It is true. Does a man of knowledge ever fear rebirth? He does not commit any sin. It is the ignorant person who is always seized with fear. He alone gets entangled and becomes polluted by sin. For millions of births he suffers from endless miseries, he undergoes infinite pains, and at last he craves for God.

Disciple: Yes, through experience he gets his lessons and then attains knowledge.

Mother: Yes, the calf makes the sound of 'Hāmbā, Hāmbā.' It makes the same sound even after drums and other instruments are made from its hide and entrails. At last it goes into the hand of a carder, and then comes the sound 'Tuhu, Tuhu.'[1]

JAYRAMBATI

18th September, 1913

In the course of a letter to a devotee the Mother wrote: "There is no happiness whatever in human birth. The world is verily filled with misery. Happiness here is only a name. He

---

[1] The reference is to a parable often related by Sri Ramakrishna: "The cow cries, 'Hāmbā!', which means' I'. That is why it suffers so much. It is yoked to the plough and made to work in rain and sun. Then it may be killed by the butcher. From its hide shoes are made, and also drums, which are mercilessly beaten. Still it does not escape suffering. At last strings are made out of its entrails for the bow used in carding cotton. Then it no longer says, 'Hāmbā! Hāmbā!', 'I! I!', but 'Tuhu! Tuhu!', 'Thou! Thou!' Only then are its troubles over."

—*The Gospel of Sri Ramakrishna* (Madras: Sri Ramakrishna Math, 1980), vol. I, p. 105.

on whom the grace of the Master has fallen, alone knows him to be God Himself. And remember, that is the only happiness."

A Sannyasin disciple had gone to Rishikesh, visiting the Holy Mother at Jayrambati on the way. After a few days he wrote to the Mother, saying, "Mother, once you remarked that I would get the vision of the Master in course of time, but that has not happened as yet." Hearing the contents of the letter the Mother said to the disciple, "Write to him: 'Sri Ramakrishna has not gone to Rishikesh for your sake or simply because your are there.' He has become a Sannyasin. What else is he to do but call upon God? He will reveal Himself to the devotee when it is His sweet will."

UDBODHAN

A young man, placed in very poor circumstances, had come twice or thrice for initiation, but could not, unfortunately, succeed owing to the Holy Mother's illness. So he wrote, "Please do not refuse me any more. It is with great difficulty that I go over there. I want to know whether the next time I come, I shall get initiation or not." In reply the Holy Mother said to a disciple, "A person, whoever he may be, must go back, if I am not well. Even if I am well, I cannot invite people for initiation. People get facilities and opportunities according to their past Karma. A person comes here several times, but does not get the opportunity to see me, either because I am ill or for some other reason. It is his bad luck. What can I do? You may say that it means a great deal of expense for him, and everybody does not have money. But a Guru may turn away a person seeking to be a disciple, time after time. He who is really eager for the blessing of the Guru, however, will come to him even by begging. The truth is this: He who is really anxious to cross the ocean of the world, will somehow break his bonds. No one can entangle him. Financial difficulties, awaiting a reply, the fear of going back with unfulfilled desire—these are mere excuses."

A woman wrote to the Mother, "Mother, I am young in years. My father-in-law and mother-in-law do not allow me to go to you. How can I go against their will? It is my desire to receive your blessing." The Mother asked the disciple to write to her, "Child, you need not come here. Call on the Lord who pervades the entire universe. He will shower His blessings upon you."

UDBODHAN (*Prayer Hall*)

30*th September*, 1918

It was morning. The Holy Mother was dressing fruits for the worship. The disciple was reading to her a letter written by a devotee. He had written in such a strain that it seemed as if he were piqued with God. The Mother dictated the reply: "The Master used to say, 'Sages like Suka and Vyasa were at best big ants.' God has this infinite creation. If you do not pray to God, what does it matter to Him? There are many people who do not even think of God. If you do not call on Him, it is your misfortune. Such is the Divine Maya that He has thus made people forget Him. He feels, 'They are quite all right, let them be.' "

Disciple: Mother, it is not that people do not want to see God, Otherwise why should such a question arise in their mind at all? The thing is that they feel greatly hurt that God, whom they like to feel as their very 'own', moves away from them. Buddha, Chaitanya, Jesus Christ and others like them did so much for their devotees in order to insure their welfare.

Mother: That was also the attitude of our Master. It is not possible for me always to recollect all the devotees. I say to the Master, "O Lord, please bless all, wherever they may be. I cannot remember everyone." And see, it is He who is doing everything. Otherwise why should so many people come?

Disciple: That is true, indeed. It is rather easy for men to believe Kali, Durga and other Deities to be God, but is it easy to accept a man as God?

Mother: That depends upon His Grace.

A day later a devotee arrived. The disciple said to the Mother, "Mother, it is this devotee who wrote to you that letter." The Mother said, "Is it so? I see he is a good boy." Then she said to the devotee, "You see, it is the nature of water to flow downwards, but the sun's rays lift it up towards the sky; likewise it is the very nature of the mind to go to lower things, to objects of enjoyment, but the grace of God can make the mind go towards higher objects."

It was about half past ten in the morning. A householder devotee arrived and saluted the Mother. "Mother," said he, "why do I not see the Master?" The Mother said, " Continue to pray without losing heart. Everything will happen in time. For how many cycles did the Munis and Rishis of old practise austerities to realize God, and do you believe you will attain to Him in a flash? If not in this life, you will attain to Him in the next. If not in the next, it will be after that. Is it so easy to realize God? But this time the Master has shown an easy path; therefore it will be posisible for all to realize God."

After the devotee left, the Mother said, "He is so deeply engrossed in worldliness. He is the father of scores of children and still he says, 'Why do I not see the Master?' Many women used to come to the Master. They would say to him, 'Why can't we concentrate our mind upon God? Why can't we steady our mind?' and things like that. Sri Ramakrishna used to tell them, 'You still smell of the lying-in room. First get rid of that smell. Why are you so worried about God-realization now? Everything will happen in course of time. In this life we have met. In the next we shall again meet and then you will attain to your goal.' It is easy to see a person as long as he lives in the body. I am now living here, so one can see me by merely coming here. How few have the good fortune to see the Master now with physical eyes! Vijay Goswami had seen the Master at Dacca. He felt his body. At that the Master said, 'That my soul goes out is not good; perhaps this body will not last for many more days.'

"Can you tell me who has seen God? He made Naren attain to God-realization. Suka, Vyasa and Siva are like big ants at the most; they had glimpses of Him. One may see a vision in dream, but to see God in a physical form is a matter of rare good fortune.

(*Excitedly*) "Why can't one meditate if one has a pure mind? Why should one not be able to see God? When a pure soul performs Japa, he feels as if the holy Name bubbles up spontaneously from within himself. He does not make an effort to repeat the Name. One should practise Japa and meditation at regular times, giving up idleness. While living at Dakshineswar I used to get up at 3 o'clock in the morning and practise Japa and meditation. One day I felt a little indisposed and left the bed rather late. The next day I woke up still late through laziness. Gradually I found that I did not feel inclined to get up early at all. Then I said to myself, 'Ah, at last I have fallen a victim to laziness.' Thereupon I began to force myself to get up early. Gradually I got back my former habit. In such matters one should keep up the practice with unyielding resolution.

"Austerities, worship, pilgrimage, the earning of money—

one should do all these in the days of youth. You see, even I had visited so many places at Banaras and Vrindaban on foot in my early years, but now I need a palanquin to go even a few feet. I lean upon others. In old age the body deteriorates. It does not possess any strength. The mind loses its vigour. Is it possible to do anything at that time? It is quite right that the young Sannyasins of our Math have been directing their mind to God from an early age. This is the right time for them to do so. (*To the disciple*) My child, austerities or worship, practise all these things right now. Will these things be possible later on? Whatever you want to achieve, achieve now; this is the right time."

Disciple: Lucky indeed are those who receive your blessings now. Those who come later on cannot have this rare opportunity.

Mother: What do you mean? Do you mean to say they will not succeed? God exists always everywhere. The Master is always present. They will succeed through his grace. Are not people of other countries making spiritual progress?

Disciple: The mind feels longing when it knows that it is loved, but do you really love us?

Mother: Do I not love you? I love even those who do a little for me, and you are doing so much. Whenever I touch anything at home, I remember you. I often think of those of you who are with me, and as for those who live far away, I say to the Master, "O Lord, please look after them. I cannot always remember them."

UDBODHAN (*Prayer Hall*)

The Mother was seated on her bedstead. The disciple was reading to her the letters of her devotees. Krishnalal Maharaj was also there. The letters contained such statements as "The mind cannot be concentrated," etc. The Holy Mother listened to these and said in a rather animated voice, "The mind will be steadied if one repeats the Name of God fifteen or twenty thousand times a day. It is truly so. O Krishnalal, I myself have experienced it. Let them practise it first: if they fail, let them complain. One should practise Japa with some devotion, but this is not done. They will not do anything, they will only complain, saying, 'Why do I not succeed?' "

A devotee entered the room and asked the Mother about meditation and Japa. She said, "Repeating the Name of God a fixed number of times, telling the rosary or counting on fingers, is calculated to direct the mind to God. The natural tendency of the mind is to run this way and that way. Through these means it is attracted to God. While repeating the Name of God, if one sees His form and becomes absorbed in Him, one's Japa stops. One gets everything when one succeeds in meditation.

"The mind is by nature restless. Therefore at the outset, to make the mind steady, one may practise meditation by regulating the breathing a little. That helps to steady the mind. But one must not overdo it. That heats the brain. You may talk of the vision of God or of meditation, but remember, the mind is everything. One gets everything when the mind becomes steady.

"It is quite natural that man forgets God. Therefore whenever the need arises, God Himself incarnates on earth and shows the path by Himself practising Sadhana. This time He has also shown the example of renunciation."

THE GOSPEL OF SRI SARADA DEVI
THE HOLY MOTHER

SECTION II

Translated by

Swami Prabhananda

1

(RECORDED BY YOGIN-MA)*

SOME days after I had been introduced to Sri Ramakrishna, I paid a visit to Dakshineswar. Learning that, being in a hurry, I had not taken my meal, the Master said, "Ah! you haven't taken your food. Go to the Nahabat and take rice and curry." There at the Nahabat I saw the Holy Mother for the first time. Rama's mother[1] and others had been there once or twice before. At the Nahabat they told the Mother that I had not taken my meal. The Mother promptly served me rice, curry, *luchi,* and whatever else she had in stock. Even at this, my first meeting with the Holy Mother, I became quite intimate with her. The next time I went to Dakshineswar I found that the Mother was going on a trip to Kamarpukur that very day to attend Ramalal-Dada's marriage. I felt very sad at the thought that I would not see her for many days. The Mother came to salute the Master before leaving on the journey. The Master came to the northern verandah when the Mother took the dust of his feet. The Master said, "Move cautiously. See that you don't leave behind any of your belongings in the boat or railway compartment." I had had the desire to see them together, and that day my desire was fulfilled. The Mother left by boat. As long as it could be seen, I stood gazing at the boat. As soon as the boat was out of sight, I went to the spot in the Nahabat where the Mother used to meditate, and wept bitterly. I sat for meditation facing south on the western verandah. While passing by the Nahabat the Master heard me sobbing and sent for me. When I went to his room, he said, "Have you been deeply grieved at her departure?" Then to console me, as it were, he began to recount

---

*Yogindra Mohini Biswas, a disciple of the Great Master, and a life-long companion of the Holy Mother.

[1]Wife of Balaram Bose.

the spiritual disciplines he had practised at Dakshineswar. He concluded, saying, "Don't divulge these to anyone." I, a mere housewife, was shy, but on that day I sat quite close to the Master and talked with him. The Mother returned to Dakshineswar after about a year and a half. The Master had written to her, "I am having difficulties regarding my food." On her return the Master said to her, "That girl with big, beautiful eyes loves you dearly. The day you left she wept bitterly, sitting in the Nahabat." The Mother said, "Yes, her name is Yogin."

Whenever I went to Dakshineswar, the Mother used to tell me all that had happened. She sought my advice. I used to braid her hair. She liked so much the way I braided it that she would not undo it at the time of bathing, even after three or four days. She used to say, "No, Yogin braided my hair; I shall unbraid it on the day she comes next." I used to visit the Master every seven or eight days. I would take Bilva leaves from Dakshineswar for worshipping Siva at home. I used to worship Siva with those leaves even when they got dried up. One day the Mother asked, "Yogin, do you worship using dried Bilva leaves?"

Yogin-Ma: Yes, Mother, but how did you know?

Mother: During my meditation this morning I saw you worshipping with dried Bilva leaves.

One day the Mother was preparing rolls of betel leaf in the Nahabat and I was sitting by her side. I noticed that she prepared some rolls with cardamom and a few others with simply betel and lime. I asked, "Why didn't you add cardamom to these? For whom are these meant and for whom are those?" The Mother replied, "Yogin, these (specially spiced betel rolls) are meant for the devotees; by taking good care of them I have to make them my own. And these (the ones without cardamom) are for the Master; he is already my own."

The Mother had a good musical voice. One night she and Lakshmi-Didi were singing in a low tone. It was very resonant and reached the ear of the Master. The next day he said, "Yesterday you were singing. That's good, very good."

During her stay at Dakshineswar, the Mother couldn't find even a little time for rest. For the devotees who came, she had to make Chapatis out of three to three and a half seers of coarse flour. How many rolls of betel leaves she had to prepare! Then she would boil down the milk meant for the Master; for he was fond of cream. Then soup had to be prepared for him. He used to take his food at the Nahabat as long as his mother lived. After her death, however, he used to dine in his living room. On the days male disciples were not present, the Mother would rub the Master's body with oil before his bath. The Master asked Golap-Didi one day to bring his meals to his room. From that day Golap-Didi carried the Master's meals everyday. Thus the Mother was deprived of her only opportunity of seeing the Master daily. Golap-Didi used to spend long hours in the evening with the Master, and some days she didn't return to the Nahabat even by ten o'clock. The Mother had to keep an eye on Golap-Didi's food on the verandah of the Nahabat and was, therefore, experiencing inconvenience. One day the Master heard her saying, "Let this food be eaten by a dog or a cat. I can't look after it any more." The next day the Master said to Golap-Didi, "You spend a long time here. That inconveniences her; for she has to keep watch over your food." "No," Golap-Didi said, "The Mother loves me very much and calls me by my first name, as if I were her own daughter." Though Golap-Didi could not understand that the Mother was hurt because she was being prevented from coming to the Master, the latter could understand it.

One day Golap-Didi said to her, "Mother, Manmohan's mother says, 'The Master is a man of such great renunciation and yet, the Holy Mother wears ear-rings and other ornaments. Does it look well?'"

The next morning when I visited Dakshineswar, I noticed that the Mother had only a pair of gold bracelets on her wrists and had taken off all other ornaments. Surprised at this, I asked, "Mother, what's this?" The Mother replied, "Golap said......"

After much persuasion I succeeded in making her put on the ear-rings and one or two other ordinary ornaments. But she never again put on all the ornaments she had taken off, because just after this the Master fell ill.

When the Mother first came to Dakshineswar she didn't understand much about household problems, and she didn't experience trances either. Though she devotedly practised meditation and Japa every day, we didn't hear of her going into Samadhi. Rather, she even became very frightened and worried at the sight of the Master's Samadhi. For, I heard from her lips that during her first visit to Dakshineswar, the Master had asked her to stay with him at night. In those days the Master and the Mother slept in the same room. The Master used to occupy the larger bed and the Mother the small cot. The Mother would say, "The Master used to pass through spiritual trances and so I couldn't sleep. Out of fright I used to keep almost inert, wondering all the time when the night would end. One day he showed no signs of coming back to the normal state. Then I became much worried and sent for Hriday through Kali's mother (the maid-servant). Hriday came and repeated aloud the name of the Lord; this made him regain his consciousness. The next day, the Master taught me the particular Mantra I would have to utter at each kind of spiritual trance into which he entered."

A few days after I had become acquainted with the Mother, she said to me, "Please tell him that I would like to experience a little of spiritual ecstasy. I don't find him alone to speak about this matter myself."

I thought it was quite all right that, since the request was from the Mother, I should convey it to the Master. The next morning when I went to his room the Master was seated alone on his bed. After saluting him I informed him of the Mother's request. He listened without replying and became grave. When he was in such a serious mood, no one dared utter a word. So I left the room after sitting there quietly for a while. Returning to the Nahabat, I found the Mother seated for her daily worship. I opened the door a little and peeped in and found her laughing. Now she was laughing, and now weeping. Tears were streaming from her eyes. After a while she gradually became still. I knew she was in Samadhi. So I closed the door and came away. After a long while I again went to her room. She asked me, "Are you just returning from the Master's room?" I said, "How is it, Mother, that you say you never experience high spiritual moods?" An abashed Mother began to smile.

After that incident I began to spend occasionally the nights with her at Dakshineswar. Althought I wanted to sleep on a separate bed, she would never allow me. She would drag me to her side. One night somebody began to play on the flute. At the sound of the flute, the Mother entered into a high spiritual mood, and she laughed every now and then. With hesitation I sat on a corner of the bed for a long time. I thought that I, being a worldly person, should not touch her at that moment. After a long while the Mother came back to the normal state.

One day, on the roof of Balaram Bose's house, the Mother passed into Samadhi while she was meditating. After she regained external consciousness, she said, "I found that I had travelled to a far-away country. There everybody showed me great tenderness. My appearance became exceedingly beautiful. The Master, who was present, affectionately made me sit by his side. I can't describe the joy I felt at that time. When I regained a little body-consciousness, I noticed my body lying nearby. Then I began to wonder, 'How can I enter into that hideous corpse?' I didn't feel the least inclined to get into it once again. After a long while I persuaded myself to enter into it, and I regained my body-consciousness."

One evening, on the roof of Nilambar Babu's house, the Mother, Golap-Didi, and I were meditating side by side. When my meditation was over, I noticed that the Mother was still absorbed in meditation—motionless, in Samadhi. When after a long while she regained partial consciousness, she began to say, "Oh, Yogin, where are my hands, where are my feet?" So we began to press her hands and feet, saying, "Here are your feet, here are your hands." But in spite of this, it took the Mother a long time to regain consciousness of her body.

One morning in Kalababu's grove in Vrindaban, the Mother was meditating, when she became absorbed in Samadhi. All attempts to bring her mind down to the physical plane proved futile. I repeated the Lord's name in her ears for a long time, but it produced no effect. At last Swami Yogananda came and repeated Sri Ramakrishna's name, which brought her mind down to the semi-conscious plane. Then, just as the Master used to do on similar occasions, she said, "I will eat something." Some sweets, water, and betel were placed before her, and she partook of a little of each, as the Master used to do towards the end of such periods of ecstasy. Even in taking the betel, she cut off its end in the manner of the Master. We were surprised to find that her manners, her way of taking food, and her general behaviour exactly resembled those of the Master. When she finally came down to the plane of physical consciousness, the Mother told us that the spirit of the Master had entered into her at that time. Swami Yogananda put to her some questions while she was in that mood, and she replied very much like the Master.

A few days after the passing away of the Master, the householder devotees like Ram Dutta settled off the rent of the Cossipore Garden House and decided to give it up. The Mother was therefore taken to the residence of Balaram Babu. Soon after, the Mother went on a pilgrimage in the company of Yogen Maharaj, Kali Maharaj, Latu Maharaj, Lakshmi-Didi, and a few others. The party stopped at Varanasi, where they spent eight to ten days. Finally arriving at Vrindaban, the Mother resided at Kalababu's grove for about a year. I had come to Vrindaban a few weeks before the demise of the Master. On meeting me at Vrindaban she clasped me to her bosom, crying in grief, "Oh, Yogin!", and began to weep bitterly. After the death of the Master, this was my first meeting with her. At the beginning of her stay in Vrindaban, the Mother used to weep often. One day the Master appeared before her and said, "Well, why are you crying so much? Here I am. Where have I gone? It is just like going from one room to another."

One day in Vrindaban the Mother saw a dead body being carried to the cremation ground, decked with flowers and to the accompaniment of devotional songs. On seeing the procession she said, "Look, how blessed this person is to die in holy Vrindaban! I also came here to die. Strangely enough I haven't had the trace of even a fever. And yet how old I am! I have seen such elderly persons as my father and my husband's elder brother!" At this we laughed and said, "Indeed, you saw your father! Who does not see one's father?" In those days the Mother indulged in such childish talk. In Vrindaban, at first the Mother wept bitterly for the Master, but later the Master kept her always immersed in bliss. The Mother then moved about like a carefree girl. She used to go round the temples daily. One day in the temple of Radharamana it appeared to her as if Navagopal Babu's wife was standing by the side of the image of Radharamana and fanning it. On returning home, the Mother said to me, "Yogin, Navagopal's wife is very pure. I saw her like this."

One day at Vrindaban the Master appeared before Mother and said, "Initiate Yogen with this Mantra." On the first day the Mother thought it was a freak of her mind. On the second day the vision was repeated, but she paid no heed to it. On the third day when she had the vision again, she said to the Master, "I don't even speak to him. How can I initiate him?" The Master said, "Ask daughter-Yogin to be with you at the time of initiation."

The Mother asked Swami Yogananda, through me, if he had received initiation already. He replied, "No, Mother, the Master did not give me any Ishta Mantra. I repeat a holy Name of my own choice." On hearing this, one day the Mother initiated him. The Mother was worshipping before a picture of the Master and the urn containing his relics. She sent for Swami Yogananda and asked him to sit by her side. While performing worship, she went into ecstasy and in that state gave him the initiation. She uttered the Mantra so loudly that I could hear it in the next room.

From Vrindaban we accompanied the Mother to Hardwar. Swami Yogananda was in the party. While travelling in the train, he contracted high fever. When I was feeding him with pomegranate juice, it appeared to the Mother as if I were feeding the Master. Swami Yogananda, in his delirious condition, saw a hideous-looking figure which said to him, "I would have taught you a lesson, but what can I do ? Paramahamsadeva (Sri Ramakrishna) has ordered me to leave this place right now. I am unable to stay here even for a moment." Pointing to a woman wearing a red bordered sari, the figure further said, "Feed this woman with some Rasagollas." Curiously enough, soon after this vision, Swami Yogananda was relieved of his fever. Subsequently we went to Jaipur from Hardwar. There we saw the image of Govinda and visited the various temples. While going round, Swami Yogananda suddenly noticed an image by the side of a temple and cried out, "I was asked to offer Rasagollas to this deity." And in front, we found a shop selling Rasagollas. We purchased eight annas (fifty paise) worth of Rasagollas and offered them to the deity. On enquiry we learnt that it was an image of Sitala.

From there, the Mother returned to Calcutta, and after a few days' stay at Balaram Babu's house, she left for Kamarpukur. After about a year at Kamarpukur, the Mother went to stay at Nilambar Babu's house at Belur, rented for her by the devotees. There in 1888 she stayed for about six months. She left the rented house in Kartik (October-November) and spent a few days at Balaram Babu's house at Calcutta. Shortly afterward she went on a pilgrimage to Puri. From Calcutta she travelled to Chandbali, where she boarded the Cuttack Canal steamer, and from Cuttack she went to Puri in a bullock cart. Sarat (Swami Saradananda), Rakhal Maharaj (Swami Brahmananda), Swami Yogananda, and others accompanied the Mother to Puri. She was accommodated in a house called 'Kshetrabasi', which belonged to Balaram Babu's family. There she stayed from Agrahayana (November-December) to Falgun (February-March). The Mother lived in a room with a porch in the front. Since the Master had not visited the temple of Jagannath, the Mother one day took his photograph to the temple concealed under her wrapper and uncovered it before the image of Jagannath.

After visiting the temple of Jagannath, the Mother remarked, "I saw Jagannath to be like a lion among men seated on his precious altar, and I was attending on him as his handmaiden." On her return to Calcutta from Puri, the Mother stayed at the house of Master Mahasaya (Mahendranath Gupta) for three to four weeks and then went to Antpur (birthplace of Swami Premananda) together with Baburam (Swami Premananda), Naren (Swami Vivekananda), Master Mahasaya, Sannyal (Vaikunthanath Sannyal), and a few others. After about a week's stay there she travelled by bullock cart to Kamarpukur via Tarakeswar in the company of Master Mahasaya and some others, and there she lived for about a year. Then she went to Calcutta before the Dol-festival and stayed with Master Mahasaya's family at Combulitola for about a month. Thereafter she lived in Balaram Babu's house during the latter's last illness and continued there till his death. Next she lived in a rented house at Ghusuri near the cremation ground of Belur from Jaistha (May-June) to Bhadra (August-September) of 1890. As she had an attack of blood dysentery there, she was removed to a rented house at Baranagar belonging to Sourindramohan Tagore for her medical treatment. Following a short stay there, the Mother moved to Balaram Babu's house, from where she returned to Jayrambati after the Durga Puja.

The Mother again came to Nilambar Babu's rented house at Belur in Ashadha (June-July, 1893). Then she spent the month of Falgun at Kailwar (Bihar), and from there she visited Varanasi and Vrindaban a second time, together with her mother and brothers. Coming back to Calcutta, she lived with Master Mahasaya at his Colootola residence for about a month and then returned to her native village. The next time when she came to Calcutta, the Mother lived for five or six months in a house attached to a godown on the bank of the Ganga at Baghbazar. It was at this house that Nag Mahasaya (Durgacharan Nag) saw the Mother. Then she again went to her native village and lived there for a year and a half. On coming back to Calcutta she stayed in a house in front of Girish Babu's. In this house Nivedita lived with the Mother for three weeks. Her next residence was at 16, Bosepara Lane, close to Girish Babu's house. It was here that Nivedita first organized her school. Next, the Mother lived in a house in front of Ramakrishna Lane on Baghbazar Street. Sarat too stayed there. From there the Mother moved back to her native place.

Again she came back to Calcutta on the occasion of Durga Puja at Girish Babu's house and stayed at Balaram Babu's house. At that time she was very much reduced owing to an attack of malaria. Then, following still another stay in her native village, she came to live in the new 'Udbodhan' house soon after it was constructed. She next visited Kothar (in Orissa), Madras, Bangalore, Rameswar, and other places, and then returned to the 'Udbodhan' house. Two days later the Mother went to her native village where she gave away Radhu in marriage. This time she returned from Jayrambati to Calcutta after about a year, and from there she went to Varanasi in Kartik (October-November) 1912. After staying there for about three weeks she returned to Calcutta.

In her younger days Mother had to cook often. Whenever her mother was unable to cook for some reason or other, she had to do the cooking herself. The Mother said, "I used to cook and my father would lift the rice-pot from the fire." Later the Mother spent much of her time in attending to her relations and devotees.

2

(RECORDED BY SMT. KSHIRODBALA ROY)

The day I came from our suburban home to Calcutta to see the Holy Mother for the first time, I was feeling unwell. I went to Baghbazar in a carriage. On the way I felt giddiness and nausea. I somehow arrived at the Mother's house at Baghbazar and, climbing the staircase, saw the Mother at the door of the long room adjoining the staircase. She was on her way to take her bath. She was standing with one of her hands on the door frame as if waiting for me. As soon as her eyes fell on me, she smilingly said, " Where do you come from, child? Why have you come?" I replied, "I have come to see the Holy Mother." At once she said, "I am the Mother, my child. The Master (his picture) is in the other room. Salute the Master and take your seat there. I shall be coming after my bath." Saying this, the Mother left the place.

I went to the door of the shrine room and saluted the Master from there, and then sat down. I had carried some sweets to offer to the Master. Nalini-Didi came and, sprinkling a little Ganges water on the packet of sweets, took the packet from my hand and kept it in the room. In the meantime the Mother hurriedly finished her bath and returned. I noticed that the worship of the Master and the offerings of fruits and sweets to him were already over and everything was still lying in the shrine room. As I was feeling giddy, I was afraid that if the Mother gave me Prasada to take, I might vomit. When she asked me, "Have you brought something for the Master?" I pointed to the packet of sweets I had brought, saying, "Yes, it has been kept there." The Mother held the packet containing the sweets before the Master's face and said, "O Lord, please eat."

Then she gave me Prasada consisting of some fruits on a brass dish and a little sherbet in a glass, and said, "Take this Prasada; it will not cause any vomiting." Taking a little Ganges water from a water-pot, she sprinkled it on my head and said, "I shall wait for you in the other room. Come there after taking the Prasada." Strangely enough, immediately after eating it I began to feel all right. Then I went to the room where the Mother was seated. To me it appeared as if she were the Universal Mother seated on an *asana* like a queen. Golap-Ma, Gauri-Ma and Yogin-Ma were seated around her. Though I felt the Mother to be one of my very 'own', the presence of others sitting there made me somewhat hesitant. I became worried whether I would be able to tell the Mother my innermost thoughts. I said to her, "I could not see you during the last eight years in spite of my utmost efforts. Even after coming as far as Calcutta I could not see you; I had to go back." On hearing this, Gauri-Ma remarked, "Can anybody see the Mother before the time is ripe?" I said, "I feel that the time has come now, Mother; now I have seen you. Kindly accept me. I have come here with the desire of receiving initiation from you. I have heard that one cannot have initiation before the time is ripe. Again, I hear that you send back some persons on the plea that they do not belong to this place. But if you refuse me, I shall not be able to live any longer."

Staring at me intently, the Mother said, "No, you will have initiation." Then she asked, "Daughter, what do you take on *ekadasi*?" I replied, " Formerly I used to eat sago, but learning that it is adulterated with various other things, I don't take it now." As soon as she heard this, the Mother said, "No, no, I say you should take sago; it will keep your body cool." Then with deep sorrow in her voice the Mother said, "Child, you have been practising much austerity. I say, don't do it any further. Your body has almost turned into a piece of wood. How will you perform spiritual practices if your health is spoiled, my child?"

She asked whether I used oil. I said, "I haven't used it ever since I was widowed." On hearing this she said, "The use of oil keeps the head cool. Therefore use oil." I said, "As I have not used it for a long time, I have begun to hate to touch it. I shall not be able to use oil, Mother." Golap-Ma said, "Though she is a mere child, she has spoiled her health by fasting and practising other austerities." Gauri-Ma said, "Dear, why have you cut off your hair?" I said, "Widows in our part of the country do not grow their hair." She replied, "Without hair one's eyesight deteriorates. Since you have dedicated your body to Sri Krishna, how does your hair belong to you. dear?" Yogin-Ma now said, "This body is the temple of God. It is wise to keep it fine." But the Mother said. "You have done well. Keeping one's hair gives rise to a feeling of fashionableness to some extent ; for one has to take care of it. So what you have done is right. You have overcome the craze for luxuriant locks, and you have also come here. You have now achieved that for which you lived so austerely. Now, I say, don't indulge in such austerities any longer. You will have initiation tomorrow. Come here at eight o'clock in the morning. It will be nice to take a holy dip in the Ganges and to see Mother Kali on the day of initiation."

I reflected that in seeing the Holy Mother I had already seen the Mother Kali, and that I had become pure by touching her holy feet. Then I saluted her and left for home.

My husband's younger brother Satishchandra Roy, a disciple of the Holy Mother, had accompanied me to the Mother's house. On reaching my home I requested him to come from his residence again the next morning to escort me to the Mother's house. After my return from Baghbazar I was feeling giddy once again. Nevertheless, I prepared myself for going to the Mother's the next morning. But Satish did not turn up at the appointed hour. I became very dejected indeed. At noon Satish came and explained, "The Holy Mother sent me word last night, saying, 'My daughter will not have initiation tomorrow; for she is not keeping well. Bring her the day after tomorrow before ten in the morning.'" So this was the reason for his coming late. I was astonished to think of the Holy Mother's divine foresight.

The next morning I was feeling all right. Satish came at the appointed hour to escort me. Following the Mother's instructions I arrived at her house with some fruits, sweets, flowers, Bilva leaves and a Sari with a narrow red border. The Mother's appearance, it seemed to me, was wonderful. Wearing a yellow-coloured Sari, the Mother was standing at the door assuming, as it were, the form of my Ishta As her eyes fell on me, she said, "You are already late by five minutes. Hurry up, come to the shrine." She herself spread an *asana* in front of the picture of the Master and cleaned it with her hand. I thought, "How can I sit on the *asana* spread by her?" Instantly the Mother pushed the *asana* with her right foot, saying, " Are you satisfied now? Goodness! The girl is fastidious." While coming from home I had tied two rupees in coins in the loose end of my Sari to pay the coachman with, but I had forgotten about it at that moment. As I was about to take my seat, the Mother said, "Child, you have come to take shelter in the Master who had renounced 'woman and gold'. There are two rupees tied in the loose end of your Sari. Take them out." Immediately I removed the coins, kept them on the floor near the wall and took my seat on the *asana*.

It struck me that this Mother was not the same person I had seen the other day. At this thought I lost consciousness. Then and there the Mother caught hold of my hand and made me sit upright on the *asana*. Placing her hand on my head she uttered thrice in a sweet voice the assuring words, "Don't be afraid." She added, "Have no fear; now you have been reborn. I am assuming the fruits of all the deeds of your past lives. Now you are pure; you are free of sin." Then I regained my normal state and the Mother gave me initiation.

I asked her, "Is there any Mantra prescribed for giving up the fruits of Japa?" The Mother said, "Don't say 'Giving up the fruits of Japa'; say 'offering the fruits of Japa.'" She placed in my hand a little Prasada of sweets and said, "After initiation one should not stay with one's Guru for long. So go home today, and come tomorrow and take your noon-meal here." I returned home after saluting her. The next day I went to the Mother's house at noon and had Prasada. After the meal was finished I came and sat near her. She asked me, "Do you know how to read and write? Read a small portion of the Gita daily and also *Kathamrita* of the Master and *Sri Sri Ramakrishna Punthi*. Many other books about the Master have also been published. Read them."

I said, "Mother, you certainly know that I cannot give my mind to domestic affairs at all and with what difficulty I live among worldly people. I pray to you, please don't keep me in the midst of worldly people." The Mother said, "Child, what is worldly life to you? For you worldly life is as good as living under a tree. But is life in the world separate from God? He is everywhere. Besides, you are a woman; where will you go, dear? Be content with wherever and in whatever situation He places you. The goal is to call upon Him and to attain to Him. If you call upon Him, He will lead you by the hand. You will have no fear if you can depend on Him. Another point — it is not wise that a Guru and his disciple live together, for while living together a disciple observes the life and activities of his Guru and very often takes his Guru to be a mere human being. This causes harm to the disciple. It would be very good if the disciple could live in a place close to his Guru's residence and spend some time daily in visiting his Guru, enjoying his company and receiving his instructions. However, unless there is some occasional contact between the two, the Guru may not remember his disciple always. You should come here daily."

At these words of the Mother I could clearly perceive the direction the remaining portion of my life was to take. The thought that I was destined for worldly life and not for a life of renunciation made me weep bitterly. Seeing me thus weep, the Mother very anxiously tried to console me. She said, "Child, I have spent my entire life in domestic situations. You are quite young. It is more dangerous to visit here and there for the sake of religion. I say, wherever and in whatever condition you may live, the dirt of the world will cause no harm to you. The Master is there; you need not be afraid, you need not worry."

After this, I saluted the Mother and returned home. From that time I used to go to the Mother almost daily, usually in the afternoon, and return before dusk. She had given me the necessary instructions for my spiritual practices. And she had also advised me to get any doubt or question resolved by her. But the very sight of the Mother used to fill my heart with joy. I felt that I had achieved everything, that everything had been accomplished, and that I had nothing else to ask for. To me, the Mother was no other than the Universal Mother in all Her glory and my Chosen Deity who was present before me as Guru. What else could I expect to receive? This thought gave me unbounded joy. Never did I ask the Mother any questions. I was content with whatever she said on her own. One day I said to her, "Mother, you are the In-dweller, you know everything. Still, I emphatically say that I very much detest and fear the ways of worldly people. I have no family, house or wealth, and I shall never ask you for any of these things. You are aware of my heart's desire. Please grant me that, and keep me away from worldly people." Saying this, I wept bitterly. In reply the Mother consoled me with simple words just as a mother comforts her small child. And I forgot my worries and floated on an ocean of joy .

At times the Mother would say, "The Master used to say,

'Don't jump into the ocean of Maya, for you may be eaten up by sharks and crocodiles.' But why should you worry? You have the Master with you."

The Holy Mother lived a life very much hidden from public view, and she made me do the same. I saw women devotees mostly; I hardly saw the monks of the Belur Math. But even by seeing the Mother alone I felt that I had seen all that was worth seeing in the universe. Now I think that she had accepted me only because I had such an attitude. The Mother used to say only this much : Be content in all circumstances and take His name.

One day Sudhira-Didi brought some girls of the Sister Nivedita Girls' School to the Mother. One of them said to her, "Mother, why do you not please allow Kshirode-Didi to stay with us? She can stay there and coach the girl-students." But I never had, even absent-mindedly, talked with them about my board and lodging. Therefore, I was irked a little and thought, 'Why should they speak like this?' The Mother replied, "All persons are not born for the same purpose. You will learn and teach girls in turn—this is your purpose. But Kshirode is not meant for this. No doubt teaching is a noble profession, but it is not meant for all." After the girls had left, the Mother remarked, " Is it an easy task to teach girls?"

Once I went to my native place and while returning I brought a pair of conch bangles for Radharani. But when I tried to put them on her wrists, I found that they were too small. Radhu couldn't wear them at all, and she broke into tears. It brought tears to my eyes too. I thought : With so much hope I brought them, but Radhu can't wear them. Nalini-Didi, Sarala-Didi, Radhu and I were discussing the matter quietly, when the Mother, who was then in the shrine room, called Radhu and said, "All of you come here." When we went to her, she asked, "What's the matter?' Radhu said, weeping, "This sister has brought for me such a beautiful pair of conch bangles, but I am unable to wear them ; they are too small." Instantly the Mother said, "What do you say! My daughter has brought the conch bangles, and they do not fit you! You should have come to me first. Come, let me see why they don't fit." Saying this, the Mother put them on Radhu's wrists in five minutes. This made us all surprised. Radhu, her eyes still brimming with tears, now broke into a smile. The Mother said to her, "Now you have a beautiful pair of conch bangles. Go and make Pranam to the Master, to me and also to my daughter." As she uttered this, I felt my heart palpitating. I thought, "Mother has never asked me about the locality of my home, my caste or my relatives." I said, " Mother, I belong to the Kayastha caste. Why should Radhu make Pranam to me?" The Mother bit her tongue and said, "Don't say this. Don't I know whether you are a Brahmana or a Kayastha woman ? You have stayed here so long — are you a Kayastha still?" Saying this, she told Radhu, "Go and salute your elder sister." Immediately Radhu made Pranam to Sri Ramakrishna, to the Holy Mother and then to me. I returned her salutation. The Mother laughed heartily and said, "So, you returned the salute?" But the situation made me feel uncomfortable and so I remained speechless.

One day Radhu, Nalini-Didi and the others anxiously got hold of me. I was to tell them where my home was, what my caste was, and also about my near and dear ones. But I was reluctant to disclose any such thing. That day the Mother called them and said, "Why are you teasing my daughter so much? Come here to me; I shall tell you everything." All of them rushed to the Mother. I too followed them. I thought : "The Mother never asked me about these personal details. Today I shall hear what she says." They all began to tell the Mother, "Kshirode Didi has been here so long but she has never disclosed her native place, her caste or who her relations are. Today we requested her so endearingly but she won't disclose anything." The Mother said, "I can tell you everything. She was born in the land where oranges are grown. Her father-in-law lives in another district and he is a very close relation of Chandrakanta. She has no one, not even her mother But she has a brother." Saying this, the Mother asked me, "Have I said correctly, my daughter?" As she mentioned the name of my mother, I heaved a deep sigh. The Mother being the In-dweller, she could grap the innermost thoughts and feelings of others. She understood that my sigh was a sign of grief. Immediately she said, "Ah! When I mentioned your mother, you were overcome with sorrow, weren't you? But even if she had been alive, what could she do for you? She would have been a helpless spectator of your miseries. Do you still feel bereft of your mother even after having a mother like me?" On hearing these words, I began to shed tears of joy. The Mother asked Nalini-Didi and the others, "What more do you want to know?"

They said, "What's her caste?" The Mother replied, "I shall not disclose this—they are devotees, they belong to one caste." The Mother's words made me beside myself with joy; I couldn't utter anything.

On a Kalipuja day I went to see the Holy Mother in the evening. The Mother's house was very crowded on that day. On my way I bought five *champak* flowers for fifty paise. With much difficulty I could offer those flowers at the holy feet of the Mother. She said, "Today there is a big crowd. You need not stay here. See Sudhira and then go to Gourdasi's place and talk with her before you return home." I was quite surprised at these words of the Mother. Never before had I received such instructions from her. I asked, "Should I go in a carriage or should I go on foot? Should anyone accompany me or should I go alone?" The Mother said, "Walk the distance and go alone. Will you remain a minor for ever? Now go, and come again later."

Then taking the Mother's name I went out at once without any further consideration. Inquiring of passers-by, I reached easily the school, of which Sudhira-Didi was the headmistress. She was quite surprised to see me and asked, "How could you come here in the dark? Why have you come?" I replied, "I don't know the purpose of my visit. I have come because the Mother asked me." On hearing this, Sudhira-Didi called the resident girls of her school, saying, "Stop your studies and come here. Kshirode-Didi has come from Mother's place. Come and see her."

All the girls came and surrounded me. But I wanted to leave and so I said, "As the Mother has directed, I must leave for the Saradeswari Ashrama just now." Sudhira-Didi asked, "Should you go alone?" I replied, "The Mother's direction was that I should go alone."

I set out. As soon as I started walking, a gentleman came out from a room to the rear of the girls' boarding house and followed me. That an unfamiliar man was accompanying me made my heart palpitate. Gauri-Ma was of such a strict nature that she was likely to scold me on seeing an unknown man with me. But I didn't speak with him. On arriving at the gate of the Saradeswari Ashrama I said to the gateman, "Call Ma-ji. [1] Tell her that a

---

[1] Gauri-Ma was respectfully called Ma-ji.

woman from the Mother's house at Baghbazar has come to see her."

A little later Gauri-Ma came down with a ghee lamp in one hand and an incense pot containing burning resin in another. As I went to salute her, she said, "Can I accept your Pranam today?" She stubbornly refused to accept my Pranam. I was amazed at Gauri-Ma's waving of light in front of my face, as if she was performing an Arati. Soon after, the said gentleman moved forward to salute Gauri-Ma. Instantly her appearance changed. She asked, "Where do you come from? Where do you live? Why have you come here?" Pointing at me, he said, "She had gone to Sudhira Basu's and had mentioned that she was coming to this place. I thought that since I had never met you, I would be able to see you if I accompanied her. That's why I have come."

"What's your name?" asked Gauri-Ma. On disclosing his identity, I recognized him, for I had heard his name. Gauri-Ma said, "I have heard of you. You belong to Sylhet (now in Bangladesh). Since Gauri-Ma does not live in purdah, you could have met her anywhere. If you want to see monks, go to the Belur Math. What is there in seeing a nun?" The gentleman said, "If I come here on Sunday, I can talk with you, I hope." Gauri-Ma replied, "No, no, my daughters are staying here. I can't meet you here." Hearing this, the gentleman saluted Gauri-Ma and left.

Then Gauri-Ma turned towards me and said, "What do you think of the Holy Mother? She is none other than the Empress of Kailash. None should think of her as a human being. The Mother is the Guru of the world, the Mother of the Universe. Since you have accepted her as your Guru, what is there to worry about?" Then Gauri-Ma talked about the Holy Mother and Sri Ramakrishna for about two hours. I remained standing at the door-step just as when I had come. She too was standing while talking. All of a sudden she caught hold of me and said, "Let's go; we shall worship the Mother." I said, "I didn't have any instruction to go to Baghbazar today once again. Besides, it has become rather late, how shall I return home afterwards?" She said, "Come, I shall tell the Mother." So I went with Gauri-Ma. She also took two young girls, one of them carrying flowers and Bilva leaves and another carrying fruits and sweets. She herself was carrying a Kamandalu (water pot with a handle). People in the street looked at us amazed. As we arrived at the door of the Mother's house, I heard Mother say, "Now Gaurdasi has come making a spectacle in the street!" After going there I realized that Gauri-Ma was the last one to worship the Mother that day; all others had finished their worship. Gauri-Ma worshipped the Mother for a long time as one does in the Kali Puja. The worship was worth seeing indeed. Afterwards everyone present partook of Prasada. Gauri-Ma said to the Mother, "I have brought Kshirode here again. She told me that this wasn't your instruction. But I said to her that I would mention it to you." The Mother replied approvingly, "You have done very well." I spent the night at the Mother's house. I shall never forget in this life the joy I experienced on that night.

A year prior to my becoming a widow, I had one day cut and dressed a number of papayas and prepared a curry with them. The juice of the papayas caused an itching sensation on my fingers which became very much swollen, and the skin of my fingers cracked within a few hours. This created such a bad sore on my hand that various kinds of medical treatment failed to cure it. I suffered from it for twelve years. I had to use a spoon for taking my food. At times the condition would subside. But when it became aggravated, the contact of my hands with water made the sore septic. Though I had been in close association with the Holy Mother for the last one year, I had never shown my hands to her. I had decided never to say anything to her about this impermanent physical body of mine. And I had kept this chronic disease a secret from her lest it should somehow infect her too. I avoided visiting her when the disease became aggravated. One day, however, I went to see her when the sore was rather bad. On reaching her place I avoided making Pranam to her lest she should notice the sore while I touched her feet. But this thought made me quite restless. Just then I saw that a widow took the dust of Mother's feet, wrapping her hand with the loose end of her Sari. This gladdened my heart. And so I too took the dust of her feet, wrapping my hand with the end of my Sari. No sooner did I salute her than the Mother asked in surprise, "Daughter, why did you take the dust of my feet wrapping your hand with your cloth? Is there anything wrong with your hand?"

I was now in a fix, and my heart began to quiver. I thought, "Mother could have questioned the other woman. But instead of asking her, she has asked me, 'Why did you take the dust of my feet in this way?'" So I replied, "I have a disease on my hand." She then said, "Let me see." On seeing my hand, she lamented so deeply that I was astounded. She said, "Ah! Dear, you are here so long and your hand is in such a condition! Though I am your mother, I wasn't aware of it. I feel so sorry, my dear." Then she asked me how long I was suffering and how I had contracted the disease. I had to disclose everything now.

Then the Mother said, "Dear, I am in such a state that I remain absorbed within myself. So I failed to observe you. You perform Puja with this hand; that's why the disease is lingering. Well, come with me. The flowers and leaves offered to the Master and the Charanamrita (holy water of worship) will be removed and thrown into the Ganges. Come quickly." I followed her to the other room. She said, "Look, the Kamandalu contains the Charanamrita as well as flowers and leaves. Dip your hand up to the wrist into it."

I did accordingly. Then she added, "Your hand will be free from the disease. But avoid handling fish, meat, onion and garlic as far as practicable. You cannot completely keep away from them. When you handle them, there may appear some eruptions on your hand. Perform the Master's worship daily. As soon as you notice some eruptions, apply the Master's Charanamrita on them. It will cure you. Had you trimmed your finger nails on the day you cut the papayas?" I replied, "I don't remember." She said, "You must have pared your nails and then come into contact with the papaya juice. These two together are responsible for your trouble."

In the afternoon the Mother said to the other women, "None of you, including your husbands and children, should cut your nails with the nail-cutters of barbers; for it may lead to many bad infectious diseases. My daugher here has contracted such a disease on her hand. But by the will of the Master it will not linger." On that occasion, the Mother spoke of the various dangers involved in eating together with others from the same plate, in lying on the same bed with another, and in using somebody else's cloth and bath-towel. She also told us how a person's good or bad physical condition is transferred to the body of another.

Strange enough, I had never told the Mother how I passed my days, and that I was compelled to cook fish and meat also.

But she said, "You will not be able to avoid them. Whenever you handle meat and fish, you will have eruptions on your hand, but as soon as the Master's Charanamrita is applied, you will get cured." It was a matter of pleasant surprise that the day on which I dipped my hand in the Charanamrita—from the very next day I got permanently cured. Whenever I touched fish, meat or such other food, I got eruptions on my hand, but they disappeared in an hour's time after applying Charanamrita on them. When I had become cured of this disease, I said to her, "Mother, I haven't come to you to get my bodily ailments cured. You can't get rid of me as easily as this!" The Mother laughed and said, "Child, your body is also my body. I suffer if you do not keep good health."

It was my resolve that I would never ask verbally or even mentally for any physical comfort or monetary or other material gain. I was afraid that the Mother might appease me by bestowing those things. Whenever I complained that I could not get any result from my worship, the Mother used to say, "I am your Guru; I know whether you are making progress or not. How can you understand it? You'll achieve everything, you'll achieve everything. Most obstacles in worship are not external; they are internal. They will gradually fall off one after another by taking the Master's name and by meditation. Do your duty. Don't pay attention to whether the blemishes of the mind are persisting or not." She also used to say, "The branch of a cocoanut tree drops off by itself at the proper time, but one has to exert much to tear off the branch before the proper time arrives. Likewise, everything will come about at the proper time." Then I asked her as to why I could not become absorbed in Japa and meditation. She said, "You are doing all that is necessary; everything is going all right. My child, it is a great good fortune for you to have come here a widow at a tender age. You won't have to do much. All that you have to do is to pay obeisance to God at the end of the day. If a man firmly takes hold of one idea, he doesn't have to perform any other discipline. You will achieve everything spontaneously."

I was married when I was ten, and became a widow at fifteen. Taking refuge at the holy feet of the Mother, I had said to her, "Mother, I am surrendering myself at your holy feet. Kindly protect me." The Mother had assured me, saying, "There is nothing to fear. The Master will lead you by the hand." Not a single word which came from her lips proved to be untrue. Now I am nearing sixty. The Mother's holy hand has touched my head, and my head and hands have touched her holy feet—thus I have become blessed. Holding to her words, "There is nothing to fear. The Master will lead you by the hand," I have lived this long life, without ever being haunted by the desire for enjoyment. I have experienced only bliss, nothing but bliss. Except on the day the Mother gave me initiation, she never instructed me as to what I should do. She used to say that the Master would do everything. We may not understand this, but her words are true. Even if one does not call on the Master and the Mother all the time, they protect their children from dangers and misfortunes. I have firmly realized that without their grace none can conquer worldly attachment by simply displaying bravado.

The Mother had said,"One should not go to see a deity empty-handed." Therefore I used to carry something or other when I went to see her daily. One day she said, "You have no money; why do you bring these things every day, my child? It will be enough if you bring a myrobalan. I eat through the mouths of all of you, dear! Your eating is as good as my taking food. How much I have eaten since coming to the circle of the Master!"

My second brother, who was seriously ill, came to Calcutta for medical treatment. He was to be operated upon by Dr. Sarbadhikari. All the members of our family had come to Calcutta. I had come to understand that the surgeon was not sure of the survival of a patient after this kind of surgical operation. I took my brother to see the Mother. It was a Sunday. The male devotees used to make Pranam to her in the afternoon. While on the way, my brother purchased a garland of flowers to offer at the Mother's feet. It had escaped my notice. On reaching there, I began to brood that my brother would salute the Mother along with a crowd of people and I would not be able to stay nearby. Would the Mother notice him at all? While Pranams were being made, I remained within the room. When the Pranam-making was completed, the Mother called Radhu and the rest of us. She removed a large quantity of flowers and garlands which had been offered at her feet. Taking out a garland of tuberoses from among them, she presented it to Radhu, saying, "My daughter's brother has given it to me." Then she said to me, "I have noticed your brother." I was surrprised, for my brother had not come there earlier. I began to wonder whether my brother had brought that garland of tuberoses. Among the many garlands I could see only one of that kind.

I said to her, "Mother, it is because of him that I wish to keep myself away from worldly life. I wept bitterly in your presence only with the prayer of shunning their company. If he dies, I shall have to bear the burden of his family. Mother, because I am in the midst of worldly people, I am not likely to survive, even though I have taken refuge at your feet. Now what will happen to me? Please tell me what I am to do."

The Mother replied, "Even if your brother survives this operation, he will die one day, will he not? And if he survives, what good will he bring to you? So why should you worry so much?" I thought, then perhaps my brother's life would not be spared this time. But that very moment the Mother said, "Don't be afraid; the Master is there. Keep a photo of the Master in the operation theatre where your brother will be operated on. He will protect him."

After hearing her say this, I returned home and disclosed it to all the family members. Then all began to say, "No more fear. He has touched the living Goddess Kali. There's no reason to fear." My brother came round by the grace of the Holy Mother and returned to his native place. When my uncle and elder brother, who had seen the Holy Mother, were told that in seeing the Mother they had actually seen Mother Kali Herself, they accepted the idea and began to express the view that they had seen and touched the feet of Mother Kali who was worshipped by Sri Ramakrishna himself, and that they would not have to go elsewhere for their spiritual welfare. I was the first among our family members to go to the Mother. Now, by her grace, almost everyone in our family has taken refuge at the holy feet of Sri Ramakrishna.

One afternoon I was at the Mother's house when a widow with a rosary of basil beads around her neck and wearing a cloth printed with the names of God, arrived to see the Mother. Before her arrival, the Mother had assumed a solemn attitude. When the widow advanced to salute her, the Mother said, "Don't touch my feet; salute me by touching the floor." But she ignored these words and saluted the Mother touching her feet. The widow was amazed to see the photo of Sri Ramakrishna and other things, and said to me, "Do you see? How beautiful it is!" "What do you show her?" the Mother asked. "Know that she worships him whose photo you are pointing to." Next, pointing at me, the widow asked the Mother, "Is she your daughter?" The Mother replied, "Yes, my child." The widow asked next, "How many children have you?" The Mother said, "Beings all over the universe are my children." Then the woman asked, "How many children you have given birth to?" The Mother replied. "My husband was a man of renunciation." Unable to understand its import, the woman pestered the Mother further with questions. I, too, was about to lose patience. The Mother said to me, "You explain these matters to her, I can't do it any further." Then I went on, "You know nothing about the Mother, I see. Why then, have you come to see her? Those who come to the Mother do not simply see and salute her. There is much to know about the Mother. There are so many books about her. You can know all about her from many devotees too. Had you known a little about her, you would not have dared to ask her so many questions. You had better tell me what you have got to say. Please don't disturb the Mother." Still the woman continued, "My daughter visits this place. She brought big radishes here the other day." The Mother said, "Many persons present a lot of things. Can I take a note of all of them? I don't know your daughter." Thereafter the widow left and the Mother said to me, "Bring a little water and wash my feet. Fan me a little." I obeyed her.

One of my cousins was suffering from lachrymal fistula, and to get it operated by an eye-surgeon, he along with his parents and many other members of our family had come to Calcutta. I took him to the Mother before his operation. Earlier I had told the Mother about it. Approaching the Mother I saluted her and pointing to the boy, said, "Mother, this boy's eye is to be operated on." The Mother said, "Let me see his eye." Taking a look at his eye, the Mother observed, "Now-a-days, my child, we see various kinds of diseases and also physicians specializing in them. Formerly people did not suffer from so many ailments; nor did they know of so many kinds of medical treatment. Take, for example, the case of Radhu. She had so many ailments and had to pass through various kinds of treatment. Besides, I made promise of offerings to various deities for her cure, and yet she does not keep well. The Master alone knows what is in his mind." On hearing her, I laughed a little and reflected within myself: "How ignorant we are about the Mother! From her words it would appear that Radhu is her all. Thus she keeps her real nature hidden." None could understand her from her movements. Only he could recognize her to whom the Mother had revealed herself. Regarding the boy, the Mother did not say anything after seeing his eyes. We left after saluting her. Anyway the eye operation was successful.

Later, my aunt, before her return to her native place, came to visit the Mother one morning along with her children. Sitting with her legs stretched, the Mother was then cutting fruits for offering to the Master. They went straight to the Mother and saluted her. The Mother said to my aunt, "Are they all your children?" My aunt replied, "Yes, Mother, they are mine." The Mother said, "Very well. Oh, how devoted they are! All of them have prostrated themselves! My daughter knows everything about this place; still she has brought them here at this inconvenient time. It is now time for worship of the Deity. I have no time now to talk with you even for a while." My aunt said, "She (Kshirode) objected to our coming here at this time. But as we have no other time, we have come to you now. Mother, we want to take Kshirode along with us to our native place for some days. I seek your approval." The Mother said, "What harm is there in taking her to your native place? But it will be nice if you bear her travelling expenses when sending her back." "We shall certainly do so," said my aunt. She, along with others, then got into their carriage.

One girl, known to me, had never seen the Mother. Her husband did not like such visits. But one day after her husband had left for his office, she pressed me to take her to the Mother and bring her back before her husband's return. I said, "The Mother takes rest at this hour of the day. You cannot see her now." She said, "Let's go, no matter what happens." As soon as I entered the Mother's house along with her, I saw Golap-Ma having her meal. I went to her with the idea that we would see Mother after she awoke. On seeing me, Golap-Ma burst out, "How queer are your ways! Why have you brought her at this time of the day? Aren't you aware that this is the time when the Mother takes rest?" I said, "Why are you scolding me? Am I so foolish as to go to the Mother, before she wakes up from sleep?" After a while I heard Mother calling me, saying, "Come here, daughter." Approaching near, I saw her standing by the side of her bed. She asked, "Who is this girl, dear? Did Golap scold you because you have come at this hour? Well, it is the Master's kingdom! No rules and regulations are valid here. Here the door is open to all. Whenever one gets the opportunity one may call on me. Don't take the scolding seriously, my child." We paid obeisance to the Mother and left. I told Golap-Ma, "Have you noticed with what a longing heart people come to see the Mother. Why only the Mother, people want to see you, too. But the door-keepers of the Mother's house as you are, you want to push them out. Mother does not belong to one or two persons, she is the Mother of all." Laughing, Golap-Ma said, "Well, you have won." The affection Golap-Ma, Gauri-Ma, Lakshmi-Didi, etc., had for us is indescribable.

Lady doctor Pramoda Dutta of Calcutta, a relation of mine, hailed from the same place as myself. Her husband, too, was a doctor. They were Brahmos. One day Dr. Pramoda Dutta expressed her desire to see the Holy Mother. She very much pleaded with me to escort her to the Mother's house. So, one day we were ready for the visit. Instead of wearing her professional robe, she put on a Sari with red border. She did not even wear shoes. She sprinkled a little Ganges water on her head before she started for the Mother's house.

Going to the first floor in the Mother's house, one could see in the room adjoining the stairs, a photo of the Holy Mother in meditation posture. As her eyes fell on this picture, Pramoda Devi inquired, "Whose photo is this?" I said, "It is the Mother's." She gazed at it for long and remarked, "She's Radha herself." I felt inclined to laugh, for being a Brahmo how could she utter this! On the first floor she met the Mother and saluted her. After a while the Mother asked Sarala-Didi. "Bring that boy and get him examined by her." Now I do not remember whose child it was. As the Mother uttered these words, Pramoda Devi quietly asked me, "How could she guess that I was a doctor?" The child was brought before her. At 4 p.m. sweets were offered to the Deity and the Mother distributed the Prasada to all except Pramoda Devi. I could not but feel embarrassed at this. Now, Pramoda Devi was repeatedly telling me, "She gave Prasada to all, but why not to me?" I said to her, "Why don't you ask the Mother?" I did not dare to give her the Prasada that was in my hand. Later Pramoda Devi said to the Mother, "Mother, you distributed Prasada among all; but why didn't you let me have a little of it?" The

Mother said, "You are a Brahmo, dear. How can I give you Prasada unless you ask for it?" Pramoda Devi said, "Give me a little Prasada." The Mother too had kept apart one Rasagolla, and she now gave it to Pramoda Devi. The latter tied the Prasada at the loose end of her Sari, saluted the Mother, and returned home. She said to her husband, "Look, the place where I had gone today is a heavenly abode. The person I saw and whose feet I touched there is verily Radha. I have brought a little Prasada for you. I shall give you only if you accept it respectfully." Dr. Dutta said, "What does it matter to the Universal Mother if an insignificant person like me does not eat Her Prasada?" Saying this, he took the Prasada in his palm, touched it by his head, and ate. Pramoda Devi, too, described to him her experience in detail, and said repeatedly, "Today I visited Vrindaban and saw the holy feet of Radharani. I have been blessed."

When my aunt and others left for their native place, I did not accompany them. Back at the native place, my uncle wrote me a letter, saying, "I feel very sorry that you have not come. It fills my heart with great joy when I think that you have dedicated yourself to the feet of the Divine Mother. If you ever happen to come to your native place, do so after surrendering at the feet of the Mother your mind which is at the root of all troubles. Only then will you be free from all worry." I read out the letter to the Mother. On hearing its contents the Mother said, "Is the mind the cause of troubles only? Even when you try to attain to Brahman, you shall have to carry with you the mind, too. When you attain to It, none of them will be there. At the present stage the assistance of the mind is very necessary. It is the pure mind which shows man the path." I wrote to my uncle these words of the Mother. On this occasion the Holy Mother said this also, "As you turn the direction of the wicked mind, that mind itself will be able to grasp the Chosen Deity. However, you have nothing to worry. The Master is holding you by the hand. In every circumstance he is always with you." I deeply felt many a time in my life the immense strength behind those words of the Mother.

One afternoon there came some women, one of whom asked the Mother, "Mother, many people say that Gauranga Mahaprabhu is not an Incarnation of God. Is it true?" The Mother said, "People may say so, for it is not easy to comprehend a human being as an Incarnation of God. In brief, if everybody could comprehend him as an Incarnation of God, he would not have had to preach divine love at the cost of being beaten up." While saying this, tears rolled down her cheeks. Soon after,she added, "Can everybody recognize an Incarnation? One or two persons only can recognize him. How much suffering do they undergo for the liberation of human beings! Even when the Master used to vomit blood, he never stopped speaking. He was all the while worried about the well-being of people."

There is a statement of Gauranga Mahaprabhu, "Come, repeat the name of Hari, and you shall have delicious soup of Magur fish and the embrace of a young woman." The Mother explained the context of this statement, also what people took it for, and its real purport. At length she said, "What do you need an Incarnation for? To anyone, his own Guru is far superior to even an Incarnation of God. Try to understand this and keep steady."

The Mother used to keep a close watch over the conduct of women who lived with her at Baghbazar. She used to express her annoyance even if a metal pot or a bowl fell from somebody's hand. None of them was permitted to talk without some plausible reason. One day Radharani, with her tinkling anklets on, was going down the steps hurriedly. On hearing the jingling of the anklets, the Mother stared hard upward in such a manner that I became apprehensive. As soon as Radharani appeared, the Mother said, "Radhi, are you not ashamed? My Sannyasin children are staying downstairs, and you are running along the stairs with anklets on. Tell me, what they will think of you. Take off the anklets right now. Men and women who are here have not assembled for fun. Everyone of them is doing spiritual practice. Do you know the consequences, if their practices are disturbed?" As the Mother said these words, Radhu took off the anklets and threw them towards the Mother. Fearless though she was, we all became frightened. Another day Radhu after her bath was combing her hair and making some design by pressing her hair with a towel. Seeing this, the Mother said, "What are you doing? You think you look very beautiful by such means. Far from it; all this seems ugly to me. I never braided my hair myself. Gaurdasi used to come from time to time and braid my hair. Then again, I could not retain the braid for long and undid it soon. These days I find you behaving otherwise." Golap-Ma, who was nearby, said, "Mother, you are *muktakesi*,[1] indeed! Therefore what will you do but keep your hair unbraided?"

One day the wife of a Munsiff (a judicial officer) came to the Mother. The women present there were discussing the World War. The Munsiff's wife asked the Mother, "Everybody says that the war is going to extend over here. If so, what will happen to us, Mother?" The Mother replied, "These are but rumours. Why should the war spread up to this place? The warfare is not as intense there even as it should have been. Why should it then extend over here?" Many others present spoke variously on this subject. The Mother sat quietly, seemingly disinterested.

Famine was raging throughout the country. The Ramakrishna Mission was rendering much relief to the famine-stricken people. One day the Mother narrated the famine conditions very vividly. She spoke of the distress of people at various places, the amount of money the Mission was spending to redress their sufferings and the way the monastic members of the Order were working. It seemed to me that she was feeling in her heart of hearts all the sufferings of the world.

Off and on I used to call upon Lakshmi-Didi at Dakshineswar. She often spoke to me in confidence, "Tell the Mother that I do not like to stay here. The nieces who attend upon me here don't like any devotee to come to me. But I cannot stay at a place where there are no devotees. Tell the Mother that I shall go to Vrindavan and that I shall take you along with me." I told Mother everything. The Mother said, "See, daughter, Lakshmi goes mad at the sight of devotees. That's why those two girls (nieces of Lakshmi-Didi) feel annoyed at the coming of devotees there. They should not be blamed, dear. Tell Lakshmi, I shall go to her one day. Besides, you should not go to any place in her company. If she comes across a devotee on her way, she would stay there for a week. Someone has to be always with her to guard her. She wants to stay in Vrindavan. People are so pestered with monkeys there. Will she be able to stay there?" I passed on to Lakshmi-Didi everything the Mother had said. I further added, "You are now in such a mental state that if you are to be sent anywhere, some special arrangements are to be made for you.

---

[1]One of the names of Goddess Kali. It literally means a woman with locks flowing.

I hear you too have the same experience as the Master." No sooner did I utter this, than Lakshmi-Didi began to rebuke me, saying, "Does it happen to a human being what happened to the Master? I am the victim of a disease; that's why I cannot move out from here." These days Lakshmi-Didi behaved like a child.

One day a woman vendor came to sell blankets. Nalini-Didi was trying to settle the price of a blanket. The vendor demanded one rupee and twenty-five paise, but Nalini-didi was trying to settle it at one rupee. The Mother heard their talk from a distance. She called Nalini-Didi and said, "What are you haggling with her for?" Nalini-Didi said, "I want to pay one rupee for a blanket but she is asking for a quarter of a rupee more." Being a little displeased at this, the Mother said, "How is it that you are haggling with her so long just to save one quarter of a rupee? Fie upon you! She moves from door to door, carrying blankets on her head, for earning some money. And you have detained her for saving a few coins. Moreover, what do you want a blanket for? You have everything, still you want to purchase one more blanket." Then pointing at me, the Mother said, "It would rather be nice if you could give one blanket to my daughter. She doesn't use anything except a blanket. But she possesses only one blanket. She passes the winter days with this. Still, she does not ask anyone for another piece of blanket. She has perhaps never used more than two Saris at a time throughout her life. In spite of this she is quite happy. You don't see the bright side of others." I was simply stupefied. I wondered how the Mother was posted with so much information about me, although I never mentioned to her anything about my blanket or Sari. How many times she made me understand that she was truly our Mother! Discarding her physical body the Mother is now bestowing her blessings much more. Whoever calls upon her, the Indwelling Mother approaches him and settles all his problems. Formerly one had to make various arrangements to see her. Now, sitting at a place if someone sincerely applies one's heart, one can find the Mother. When her disciples are in trouble, she comes on her own and protects them. I have heard many such anecdotes.

Once I came from my native place to Calcutta on the Saptami-Puja day (the first day of Durga puja). I was keeping rather poor health and was running a temperature. Intending to worship Mother with the temperature on, I went to her carrying some select flowers. A few days ago Revered Swami Premananda Maharaj had passed away. That year Durga Puja was suspended at the Belur Math. Durga Puja was, however, being held at the monastery at Varanasi. I approached the Mother and worshipped her. As her eyes fell on me, she lamented, saying, "Ah, you look very much pulled down, my child!" She then mourned for Premananda Maharaj, too. She continued, "You should leave for Varanasi this very night. Some Sannyasins and Brahmacharins of this place are going to Varanasi. Your health is very much run down. Stay at Varanasi for about a month." I said, "What's the use of going there? I love to stay here." The Mother said, "What do you say? Varanasi is the abode of Lord Visvanath." I said, "This is the abode of Annapurna." The Mother laughed and said, "Nevertheless, you will come round, if you stay there for some days."

I had brought with me some pickle of tamarind from my native place for presenting to the Mother. Seeing a big crowd at the Mother's house, I wondered where I should place it and whether it could be of any use to the Mother. The Mother, the Indwelling Spirit of my being, called Golap-Ma and said, "Keep this pickle with care. I shall take it later. Give my daughter some fruits for her consumption during her journey." I received them. We left for Varanasi.

Varanasi was in the grip of a virulent kind of influenza at the time. As soon as the monks there saw me, they said to me, "Now the attack of influenza is so devastating here that you, instead of regaining your health, are very likely to contract influenza and suffer." I kept quiet thinking, come what may, I shall stay here; for I have come on the advice of the Mother. Nalini-Didi and a few others, who had accompanied me, left Varanasi just after the Puja, but I continued to stay there. I stayed in the Rana Mahal. Some days later I contracted influenza. Then the monks helped me much by sending a physician for me and providing medicines. One day I saw the Mother appear before me in a dream. She said, "There's nothing to fear. I am here. I shall take care of you." Next day my illness took a turn for the better, and I came round in a few days' time. As soon as I had completed one month in Varanasi, I returned to Calcutta. On seeing me, the Mother said smilingly, "It's a relief to me, dear. I sent you to Varanasi for your good, but the illness you contracted there was about to harm you."

3

(RECORDED BY SWAMI SANTANANDA)

I asked the Holy Mother, "How shall I lead a spiritual life, Mother?" She said, "Spend your days as you are doing now. Pray to Him earnestly and remember Him always."

Disciple: Mother, the fact that even great men become degraded frightens me terribly.

Mother: When a person has enjoyable things all around him, their influence naturally affects him. My son, don't look at a woman, even if it be only a figure made of wood. Avoid the company of women.

Disciple: Men can't do anything on their own. It is He who is making them do all that they do.

Mother: True it is that He is causing men to do everything. But do they have that understanding? Being filled with egotism, they think they are the doers of everything and that they don't have to depend upon God. Those who rely on Him are protected by Him from all dangers.

Then, pointing to a monk, the Mother continued: "The Master used to say, 'Monk, beware!' A monk has always to be on the alert. He should be cautious all the time. A monk's path is very slippery. In walking along a slippery path, one has to move cautiously at every moment. Is it easy to become a monk? A monk must not even glance at a woman. While walking he should keep his eyes fixed on his toes. The ochre cloth of a monk protects him as does the collar on a dog. No one hurts such a dog, for they know it has a master.

"A man's mind runs after bad things. If he wants to act virtuously, the mind fails to co-operate. In earlier days I used to leave my bed daily at three o'clock in the morning to meditate. One day I felt unwell and out of laziness dispensed with the meditation. Because of this my meditation was stopped for a few days. Therefore, if one wants to achieve something noble, he must be sincerely arduous and seized with a firm resolve. When I used to stay in the Nahabat, on moonlit nights I would look at the reflection of the moon in the still waters of the Ganges and, weeping, pray to God, 'There are stains even on the moon, but let my mind be absolutely stainless.' During my stay there the Master forbade even Ramlal to see me, although he was a nephew. Now-a-days I talk with all and come out in the presence of others.

"You are a Calcutta boy. Had you so desired, you could have married and led a householder's life. Since you have renounced everything, why should you give your mind to it again? Should one again take in the spittle that has been once spat out?"

Disciple: Mother, is it good to practise *asanas, pranayama,*[1] and other exercises?

Mother: Asanas and *pranayama* endow one with occult powers and these lead a man astray.

Disciple: Is it good for a monk to go to places of pilgrimage?

Mother: If one's mind is at rest in a particular place, then what need is there to go to places of pilgrimage?

Disciple: Mother, I don't have time even for meditation. Kindly make my Kundalini awaken.

Mother: It will certainly awaken. A little Japa and meditation will awaken it. Does it wake up on its own? Do Japa and meditation. The practice of meditation will lead your mind to such one-pointedness that you won't like to give up meditation. But when you do not achieve such concentration of mind, don't force yourself to meditation. On such occasions finish your spiritual practice by simply saluting the Lord. The day on which you have the right mood, you will have meditation spontaneously.

UDBODHAN

19 *June* 1912

Disciple: Mother, why is it that my mind does not become steady? When I try to think of God, I find it drawn to various worldly objects.

Mother: It is harmful if the mind is drawn to worldly objects like money and members of one's family. Nonetheless, the mind naturally dwells on one's daily activities. If you don't succeed in meditation, practise Japa. Japa leads to perfection. One attains perfection through Japa. If a meditative mood sets in, well and good. If not, don't force your mind to meditate.

---

[1] *asanas* and *pranayama:* exercises for gaining mastery over the vital energies, through the control of body and breath.

26 *Agrahayana* (*November-December*) 1912:

Disciple: For practising spiritual disciplines in Varanasi, should one live in the monastery or in some lonely place?

Mother: If you practise spiritual disciplines for some time in a solitary place like Hrishikesh, you will find that your mind has gained in strength, and then you can live in any place or in the company of anyone without being in the least affected by it. A sapling must be protected by a fence all around, but when it grows big not even cows and goats can injure it. Spiritual practice in a solitary place is essential. When worldly thoughts crop up in your mind, and they possess it, then you should go away from the company of others and pray to Him with tears in your eyes. He will remove all the dross of your mind, and will also give you understanding.

Disciple: I don't have enough strength for doing spiritual disciplines. I have surrendered myself to your holy feet: please do as you will.

With folded palms the Mother began praying to the Master, "May the Master protect you in your vows of Sannyasa. He is looking after you: what should you be afraid of? If the mind is kept engaged in some work, it doesn't indulge in silly thoughts. But if you sit idle, the mind is likely to indulge in various kinds of thoughts."

VARANASI

17 *Pous* (*January-February*) 1912:

Disciple: How and where should I perform spiritual disciplines?

Mother: Varanasi is the place for you. Spiritual discipline means holding the mind steadfast at His holy feet all the time and immersing the mind in thoughts of Him. Repeat His Name.

Disciple: What can repetition of His Name achieve, if it is not attended with earnestness?

Mother: Regardless of whether you get into water willingly or are pushed, your clothes will be soaked. Practise meditation regularly, for your mind is still unripe. After prolonged practice of meditation, your mind will become steady. And you should constantly discriminate between the real and the unreal. Know the worldly objects to which the mind is drawn to be unreal and surrender your mind to God. A man was angling in a pond all by himself when a bridegroom's procession with its music passed by. But his eyes remained fixed on the float.

Disciple: What is the aim of life?

Mother: The aim of life is to realise God and remain immersed in the contemplation of His holy feet always. You monks belong to the Master. He is watching over your earthly life as well as your life to come. What worry do you have? Can anyone think of God all the time? Spend some time relaxing and some time absorbed in thoughts of Him.

VARANASI
18 *Pous, Thursday*

Mother: A monk must be free from anger and hatred, he must tolerate everything. The Master used to tell Hriday, "You will bear with my words and I shall bear with yours—then only we can satisfactorily pull on. Otherwise, the cashier of the temple estate may have to be called for settling our disputes."

VARANASI
23 *Pous, Tuesday,* 9.30 *A.M.*

Mother: The Master used to tell me, "Take short walks, otherwise you won't be able to maintain your health." In those days I lived in the Nahabat. I used to bathe in the Ganges at 4 o'clock in the morning and would then enter the Nahabat, not to come out of it again during the daytime. One day the Master said to me, "Today a Bhairavi will come. Dye a cloth and keep it ready: I have to give it to her." The Bhairavi[1] arrived that day when the worship of Mother Kali was over. The Master began to chat with her on various topics. She was a little hot-headed. She used to boss over me always. She would tell me at times, "You must keep Panthabhat[2] for me; otherwise I shall pierce you with my trident!" Hearing this,I would get frightened. But the Master would reassure me,saying, "You needn't fear. She is a true Bhairavi. That's why she is somewhat hot-headed." Sometimes she brought such a large quantity of alms that it would last for seven or eight days even. At this the cashier of the Temple estate would say, "Mother,

---

[1]A nun of the Tantric school

[2]Boiled rice soaked in cold water.

why do you go out and beg your food? You can get it here."

The Bhairavi would reply, "You are my Kalanemi[1] uncle, Can I rely on you?"

The Mother continued, "During the years of his spiritual practices,theMaster would shrink through fear at the sight of various objects of temptation; he would shun all these allurements. One day in the Panchavati grove he suddenly saw a boy approaching him. This started him thinking, 'What is this?' Then the Divine Mother explained to him that a shepherd boy of Braja would join him as his spiritual son. When Rakhal came, the Master said, 'My dear shepherd boy has come. Tell me, what's your name?' 'Rakhal,' he replied. The Master remarked, 'Yes, yes, that's right.' This was exactly in keeping with what he saw at the Panchavati grove.

"Hazra[2] told the Master, 'Why do you think so much about Narendra, Rakhal and the othes? Why don't you immerse your mind in thoughts of God all the time?' The Master said, 'All right, I'll keep my mind immersed in God.' Saying this,he went into Samadhi, and his hair stood on end. He continued in that state for about an hour. Then Ramlal began to utter the names of various gods and goddesses. After he had done this for a long time, the Master regained his bodily consciousness. When his Samadhi had passed, he remarked to Ramlal, 'Did you notice the mental state into which I enter whenever my mind dwells on God? That's why I keep my mind at a lower level by thinking of Narendra and the others.' Ramlal said, 'No, please continue to stay in your own mood.'"

Disciple: I'm practising a few breathing exercises. Should I continue them?

Mother: You may practise them a little. But it's not safe to do them for very long, for it may throw you off your balance. What need is there of breathing exercises if your mind becomes concentrated on its own?

Disciple: Unless the Kundalini is aroused, nothing worthwhile can be achieved.

Mother: Certainly it will awake. Repetition of His name will

---

[1]King Ravana's maternal uncle in the *Ramayana* who, though a close relation, was inimical to Ravana.

[2]Pratap Chandra Hazra.

lead to the goal. Even when your mind does not become concentrated you can repeat the holy Name thousands of times. One hears the *anahata-dhvani*[1] prior to the rousing of the Kundalini. But this is not possible without the grace of the Divine Mother.

The Mother continued, "In the early hours of the morning I was musing that I would not be able to see Lord Visvanath. It is a tiny emblem of Siva covered all over with vilva leaves and water to such an extent that one can hardly see it. As I was thinking this way, all of a sudden appeared the jet-black stone emblem of Siva—Visvanath Himself! I saw Nati's mother[2] run her fingers over the head of Siva. Then I too quickly came and put my hand on Siva's head."

Disciple: Mother, I don't like the stone emblem of Siva anymore.

Mother: How is that, my son? How many great sinners come to Varanasi and get emancipation by touching Lord Visvanath! He is accepting the sins of all with perfect composure. When people come here on weekends and salute me, I feel a burning sensation in my feet. Only after I wash my feet can I be at peace again.

Disciple: If the Lord is the Father and Mother of all, why does He induce people to commit sins?

Mother: True it is that He has become all living beings, but everybody reaps the fruit of his actions according to his past impressions and deeds. No doubt the sun is one, but its shining varies according to the place and the objects it illumines.

1 *January* 1917:

I said to the Mother, "Mother, kindly bless me so that I may have good meditation and get immersed in His holy thoughts."

The Mother blessed me by touching my head with her hand and said, "Also you should always discriminate between the Real and the unreal."

Disciple: You see, Mother, sitting quietly I am able to discriminate, but when the real test comes in the field of action I am simply carried away. Mother, please give me strength so that I can keep steady at such times.

[1]The mystical, primordial sound of the universe, the symbol of which is OM.

[2]Nikunja Devi, the wife of 'M' (Mahendranath Gupta).

Mother: My son, the Master will protect you. May you attain knowledge and illumination.

Then she said to another monk, "You are all monks; it is very harmful for you to keep connection with householders. It is bad even to be in the vicinity of worldly people."

KOALPARA
27*th May* 1919

Disciple: Mother, so many days have passed! What have I achieved?

Mother: Pulling you free from worldly tribulations the Lord has placed you at His holy feet. Is this not a rare fortune? Yogen (Swami Yogananda) used to say, "Whether I perform spiritual practices or not, I am free from worldly botherations." Don't you see how much I suffer from Maya owing to Radhu?

Disciple: I want to practise Sadhana in a solitary garden for some days.

Mother: This is the time for such practices. One must do them at a young age. And you shall do so, of course. But be careful about your food. Because of too much austerity, Yogen suffered terribly until at last he died prematurely.

KOALPARA
29th *May* 1919

Disciple: ...... Babu doesn't visit the Math any more. Nor does he call on you here. Why is he acting like this?

Mother: True, he didn't see me when I was in Calcutta.

Disciple: He is an old devotee; how did this change come over him?

Mother: All this is the outcome of his past deeds. The actions of many births had accumulated. At long last he has been forced to yield to their effect. But all these accumulated waves of past actions will pass off. He will be liberated in one birth.

Disciple: If everything happens in accordance with His will, then why does He not cut away the bondage of Karma?

Mother: If it is His will, He can certainly cut it all away. But don't you see that even the Master had to suffer from the consequences of his past deeds. Once his elder brother Ramkumar, while in delirium, was drinking water, when the Master took away the glass from him. Annoyed at this, Ramkumar cursed him, saying, 'As you have prevented me from drinking water, so you too will not be able to eat or drink anything in your last days.' The Master said, 'Brother, I took away the glass of water from you for your own good, and you have cursed me for that!' Then Ramkumar wept saying, 'Brother, I don't know why I uttered such words.' See, even the Master had to reap the fruit of his past deeds. He couldn't take any food during his last illness. This devotee too has changed owing to his deeds in many past lives. Don't you see what happened to A....? It's really difficult to understand why and how such things happen.

KOALPARA

4th *June* 1919

Disciple: Mother, shall I keep count while I do Japa ?

Mother: If you count while you do Japa, your attention will be drawn to the counting. Do Japa without counting.

Disciple: Why doesn't my mind get absorbed while doing Japa?

Mother: You will succeed through practice. Don't give up your practice of Japa, even if your mind doesn't become steady. Do your spiritual practice ardently. Repeating His name will make your mind steadfast like the flame of a lamp protected from wind. Wind makes a flame unsteady. Similarly, desires prevent the mind from becoming concentrated. Besides, if the Mantra is not pronounced correctly, it takes more time for one to achieve any result. A woman had '*Rukmiṇi nāthāya*' as her Mantra. She used to utter 'Ruku', 'Ruku', and on account of this her progress was retarded. But through the Lord's grace she later got her Mantra corrected.

KOALPARA

12th *June* 1919

Disciple: I have been practising Asanas for some days to keep my body fit. It helps in digesting food and in maintaining continence.

Mother: If you practise them too much, your mind may become attached to the body, but if you give them up, you stand the risk of falling sick. Keeping this in mind, act accordingly.

Disciple: I practise them for only five to ten minutes in order to have good digestion.

Mother: Then go ahead. I was trying to impress upon you that a man's body becomes unwell when physical exercise is given up. I bless you, my boy. May you be illumined.

4

(RECORDED BY SWAMI SANTANANDA)

Pointing to the flag hoisted on the top of the temple of Veni-madhava at Varanasi, the Mother observed, "You see me so incapacitated now, but when I visited Varansi after the demise of the Master, I climbed to the top of the temple of Veni-madhava to fasten the flag. I also climbed the Chandi Hill at Hardwar and the Savitri Hill at Pushkara."

In those days a certain monk of the Ramakrishna Order had been practising hard auserities at the Manikarnika Ghat at Varanasi. When I was leaving for Calcutta he told me, "Please ask the Mother when God will bestow His grace upon me." When I conveyed this to the Mother, she became grave and said, "Write to him that there is no such rule that God's grace will fall on him simply because he is practising austerities. In olden times the ascetics practised austerities for thousands of years with their feet up and heads down, and with fires burning under them. Even then, only some of them received God's grace; others did not receive it at all. It entirely depends on His will."

At the Udbodhan house one day a young man expressed to the Holy Mother his desire to become a monk. Smiling a little, the Mother pointed to a monk standing nearby and said, "If everybody becomes a monk, who will look after them? Who will supply provisions for them?" The young man married subsequently.

Once it was proposed that I should travel to Varanasi in the company of a distinguished householder devotee of Sri Ramakrishna. He had agreed to pay my fare. On hearing of this, the Holy Mother said to me, "You are a monk. Won't you be able to procure your passage money yourself? These are houeholders; why should you travel with them? As you will all be travelling by the same compartment in the train, they might tell you, 'Do this, do that.' Being a monk why should you take such orders from them?"

On another occasion it was decided that I should be transferred from Calcutta to Varanasi, but I could not make up my mind on this. So I asked the Mother for guidance. She said, "Look, people at Calcutta right from the morning rush about engaged in their job or business or something else, whereas people at Varanasi keep themselves busy from early morning in bathing in the Ganges, seeing Lord Visvanath, practising Japa and meditation, and so on." I replied, "But here I am engaged in your service." The Mother said, "Yes, this too is a point that should be taken into consideration so long as this body lasts."

One day, in the course of a conversation, the Mother said, "Is the Master's hair a trifle? After his passing away, when I went to Prayag (Allahabad), I carried some of his hair to offer at the confluence of the Ganges and Jamuna. Standing in still water I was holding the hair in my hand and was thinking of immersing it in the water, when suddenly a wave rose and swept away the hair from my hand. The water, already sacred, took the hair from my hand in order to increase its sanctity."

One day I asked the Mother, "Mother, there are some who have different Gurus for their Mantra and their Sannyasa. Now, whom should they meditate upon as their Guru?" The Mother replied, "The giver of the Mantra is the real Guru, for by the repetition of this Mantra one obtains dispassion, renunciation, and Sannyasa."

5

(RECORDED BY SURENDRANATH SIRCAR)

During the Christmas holidays of 1910, I saw the Holy Mother for the first time at Kothar. Sri Hemanta Mitra and Sri Birendra Majumdar, two devotees from Shillong, had come with me. Sri Ramakrishna Bose, Swami Dhirananda, Swami Achalananda, Swami Atmananda, and Sri Haraprasanna Mazumdar, a devotee of Nag Mahasaya, were staying at Kothar at that time.

It was about 1 p.m. when we reached the place. We had brought with us some fruits, oranges, honey, etc. for the Holy Mother. Ramakrishna Babu carried them to her. After our bath we were called for our noon meal. In the meantime we heard some of the monks whispering, "As they have come from such a long distance, they must be permitted to meet the Mother, but they should not be allowed to talk much." Biren Babu, who overheard it, passed on the message to me. I told him, "Mother willing, it will be done. What is there to worry about?" When my companions proceeded for their meals, I told Ramakrishna Babu, "I shall not take any food before I pay my respects to the Holy Mother." Ramakrishna Babu carried this message to the Mother, and he soon returned conveying her permission. On entering the inner courtyard, we saw the Holy Mother sitting in the verandah. She waited for us, covering her body with a wrapper, and her face by the end of her Sari. As I approached the Mother, Golap-Ma said, "He is a mere boy, Mother. The boy has come to pay his respects to you." At these words, she lifted up the cloth from her face. We could clearly see the face of the Holy Mother. Since that occasion the Mother never kept her face covered in my presence. I prostrated flat on the ground and uttered, "I take refuge in Thee." Touching my head, the Mother blessed me, saying, "May you have devotion."

Disciple: Mother, it is my desire to spend a few days here. But in a rich man's house like this, it is rather difficult to meet you.

Mother: I shall send for you. Now go and take your food, and have some rest.

After the noon meal we rested. In the afternoon the Revered Golap-Ma brought me a cup of pudding which had been offered to the Mother and said, "The Mother has given you this consecrated pudding." A little later someone came and announced, "The Mother is calling you." I saw her for the second time. My salutations over, I said, "Mother, I want to speak a few personal things to you, but I hesitate to do so in the presence of others." "All right," said the Mother. "Please leave this place for a while," she said to the person who had called me. The person went away.

Earlier I had seen Sri Ramakrishna as well as the Holy Mother in my dreams. Now I disclosed this to the Mother. On hearing it she said, "What you have seen is true." Mother asked me concerning the other two devotees, "Well, what do they want?"

Disciple: Mother, if you are pleased, they want spiritual initiation from you.

Mother: Well, you all see me tomorrow morning after your bath.

Disciple: Mother, your holy feet were worshipped by Sri Ramakrishna himself. We, too, wish to worship them by offering flowers.

Mother: All right, your wish will be fulfilled.

Disciple: Where shall I find flowers?

Mother: The attendants here will procure them for you.

We saluted the Mother and returned to the parlour.

The Holy Mother had asked me, "What do *they* want?", but she did not even mention my case. After returning from the Mother, I felt worried over this omission . At last I pacified myself thinking that whatever the Mother wills, would come to pass. I did not say anything.

The next day after our bath we kept ourselves in readiness with flowers and other materials necessary for spiritual initiation. The Mother said to us, "Come inside one by one." I was the first to enter. It appeared that the Mother had finished her morning worship. As I entered she said, "You will repeat the Mantra that the Master has given you. I, too, shall give you something." With these remarks, she gave me the great Mantra.

Later we worshipped the holy feet of the Mother. She accepted the offerings standing. I said, "Mother, I do not know the rituals." The Mother replied, "Offer the flowers without any Mantra. That will do." I offered the flowers at her feet uttering '*Jai Ma*' (Hail Mother). There was one stramonium flower amongst them.

Pointing to it, she said, 'Don't offer this one, for this is used for the worship of Lord Siva."

I presented her with a rupee and a Sari that I had brought for her. At this the Mother said, "You are in financial difficulties already. Why do you give money?" Strange enough, although there was no talk about the wants in my household, the Mother seemed to know everything about it. I said, "It belongs to you, and it is only being presented to you. If a small fraction of what we earn is used for your service, we shall consider ourselves fortunate." At this the Mother observed, "Ah! What a devotion, my dear!" I said, "Mother, devotees call you Kali, Adyasakti, Bhagavati, etc. In the Gita it is mentioned that the saints Asita, Devala, Vyasa, and others called Sri Krishna as Narayana Himself. Sri Krishna himself told this to Arjuna. By mentioning it himself in the Gita, the idea has been still more emphasized. I believe everything that I have heard about you. Still, if you will please speak of it yourself, my doubts will be dispelled. I want to hear from you directly whether these things are true." "Yes, true they are," said the Mother. After this I never asked the Mother any question relating to her real nature.

I said, "Mother, I want this much—I want to see my Chosen Ideal, touch Him, talk with Him as vividly as I now see you and talk with you. Kindly bless me."

Mother: Well, your wish will be fulfilled.

The next day when I saluted the Holy Mother before taking leave of her, I saw her smiling face and her very graceful appearance. Golap-Ma strongly suggested to me, "Why not visit Puri before going back home.?"..I replied, "What more would I see ? The holy feet of the Mother are a million times more holy to me. I need nothing more." When the Mother heard this, she intervened, "Well, leave it. You need not go there."

I saw the Holy Mother for the second time at the Udbodhan house in May 1912. This time the wife of Rajendra Mukhopadhyaya and my wife received spiritual initiation from her. On this occasion I could not have any significant talk with the Mother on account of Radhu's illness. My mother , grandmother, and two sons, who had accompanied me, were blessed by seeing the Mother and touching her feet.

I saw the Mother next at Jayrambati in 1913. It was three or four days before the marriage of Bhudev, the Mother's nephew.

Arriving at the Koalpara Monastery, I heard that one devotee, Dwarakanath Mazumdar, had passed away at Koalpara on his return journey after meeting the Holy Mother. Swami Keshavananda observed, "Mother has prohibited all from going to Jayrambati now. There is a spell of drought there. None should go there before the rains set in." Naturally I became a little worried. I had already covered such a long distance; but then how could I disregard the Holy Mother's instruction and proceed to her place? I took rest after the noon meal. Strangely enough, by the grace of the Mother there came a good shower of rain. The next morning I went to Jayrambati and paid my respects to the Holy Mother. After exchange of a few preliminaries, the Mother said, "My son, we had a nice shower of rain yeasterday. It is rather cool today." Referring to the devotee who had recently died, the Mother said, "He died the death of a holy man. I can see him, as it were, even now. But I feel sorry for his bereaved old father." With these words the Mother started weeping.

At that time, Brahmachari Devendranath arrived at Jayrambati, from Varanasi. He used to say that he could know the details of his past life. He had told me four or five years earlier that I was his spiritual preceptor in my previous birth. But I knew nothing about it. I used to laugh away these talks as a mad man's prattle. As soon as both of us presented ourselves before the Mother, she herself said, "Earlier you two were at the same place, and now you have come together once again." Hearing this, Devendra whispered to me, "Look, now do you see that all I told you was true?" I replied, "It may be, but I know nothing of it."

After leaving the Mother, Devendra pleaded with me, "I have come to receive initiation into Sannyasa from the Mother, but my desire won't be fulfilled unless you make a formal request to her. It is owing to the Master's will that I am here now. The Master has brought you too here, because my prayer will not be granted without your consent. At Varanasi I saw Sri Ramakrishna and the Holy Mother in a vision and talked with them." I replied, "I am not going to tell her anything on my own initiative. Let me see what happens." Devendra said, "I say, it won't do."

We had been staying at Jayrambati for seven or eight days. In the meantime Devendra was found to have become quite restless, which struck me as something unusual. However, one morning I saw the Holy Mother all alone and said. "Mother, can I say something?" Smilingly the Mother replied, "Well, please come a little later when I prepare the vegetables."

After a while the Mother began dressing vegetables. As soon as I went up to her, she said, "You can now tell me what you wanted to say."

I said, "Mother, you are quite aware that the Master appeared before Devendra in a vision. You too blessed him similarly. Now he wishes to take the vow of Sannyasa. He is not going to continue in the worldly life. Then why not please grant him his prayer?" When the Mother heard this, she said smilingly, "If he takes the vow of Sannyasa, will it cause any suffering to others?" I replied, "His parents are already dead. He has one elder brother who has embraced Brahmoism, but he is an earning man. I don't think his Sannyasa will cause suffering to any one." Then the Mother said, "All right, his prayer will be fulfilled. Get a new cloth dyed ochre from the Koalpara monastery. He will be given Sannyasa tomorrow itself." I disclosed everything to Devendra, who was extremely delighted. All the preparations were made. The next morning the Holy Mother performed the worship in front of the picture of Sri Ramakrishna and handed over to Devendra the new ochre cloth and loin cloth. She asked Devendra to see her after changing into the new clothes. I was then sitting near the Holy Mother brooding over my situation. Just then the Mother, as if understanding my feelings, said tenderly, "Son, will you take the sugar syrup offered to the Master?" "Yes, Mother, give me," I replied.

The Mother herself drank a little of it and lovingly handed over the glass of syrup to me. In drinking the syrup which the Mother also had taken, I considered myself blessed. I thought, "Compared to this good fortune, what is there in Sannyasa? This is not even within the reach of gods!" My heart was filled with a wondrous feeling.

When Devendra entered the room with ochre clothes on and saluted the Holy Mother, she said to me, "Do you see? He is a new man, as it were. He is no more that old self of his."

Uncle Kali, the Mother's second brother, who was also Bhudev's father, began to persuade me to accompany the party in connection with the marriage of his son Bhudev, but I wanted to stay with the Mother. Mother appreciated my attitude and intervened, saying, "No, he need not go. Let him stay here."

Brahmin cooks were busy cooking for the marriage feast. Devendra and I were watching them from a distance. Observing us, the Mother said, "You make fun of them because they do not wear the sacred thread. But who can equal them in cooking?"

As part of the marriage festivities, one of a group of athletes broke into pieces a stone placed on his chest. While he was pounding the stone to pieces, the Mother was constantly praying, "Master, protect him." When the performance was over, the Mother asked me, "My son, do they know some Mantra (esoteric incantation)?" I replied, "No, Mother, there is no such thing behind this display of strength. He has gradually mastered this feat by practice. I once heard a story. An American cowboy used to carry a calf in his arms every day to a far off grazing field. The calf gradually grew into an ox. Still he could carry the ox and used to surprise others by his great strength. All this is the outcome of practice." The Mother observed, "Well, do you see how effective is the power of practice? In the same way, man achieves the highest goal through the practice of Japa. Japa leads to success. Yes, Japa leads to success!"

In the biography of Nag Mahasaya it is mentioned that once the Holy Mother herself fed Nag Mahasaya with some food after herself tasting a bit of it, thus converting it into her Prasada. Overwhelmed by this benevolent gesture of the Mother, Nag Mahasaya said, "Mother is kinder than Father, Mother is kinder than Father!" When I read this portion of the biography, it struck me, "Will the Mother ever feed me in that fashion? But I shall never express this desire to the Mother. Let it happen only if she chooses to do so." Strange enough, one day she fed me with consecrated food in that very way!

At that time a monk, who did not belong to the Ramakrishna Order, but was known to the Holy Mother, came to Jayrambati. One morning I was taking food. The new Swami too was sitting there a little away from me. The Mother said to me, "My son, do you think accepting ochre robes is as simple as that?" Then pointing to the monk, the Mother said, "Just see what he has done." To me she said further, "What's the necessity of the ochre robe? You will have everything even without it."

I had brought a pair of Saris for the Holy Mother. As I

presented them to her, I said, "I hear that you distribute presented clothes to others, Mother. But I shall be greatly delighted if you will kindly use these clothes yourself." When the Mother heard this, she said nothing, but smiled a little. When I went to see her the next day, she said, "Look, my son, I have put on the cloth you had brought."

On my humble supplication the Holy Mother gave me one of her old Saris. While handing it over to me, she said, "It is quite unclean. Please wash it." I said: "No, Mother, I want to preserve it exactly in the condition in which you have presented it to me. I don't want to send it to a laundry." "Well, as you please," replied the Mother.

One day, Devendra and I presented ourselves before the Mother while she was taking her food. The Mother asked, "Would you like to have Prasada?" Both of us extended our hands to receive it. After she had partaken of a small quantity of the food, the Mother gave a good amount of it to each of us. Lest it should fall from our hands, she pressed it placing it on our palms. The Mother belonged to an orthodox Brahmin family and I to a Kayastha. With an utter disregard of the caste rules she touched my hand and began taking her food. Indeed, she looked upon us as her own children.

Whenever I went to see the Holy Mother, I brought fruits or some other articles I could procure. I had heard that the Mother could not offer to Sri Ramakrishna things brought by anybody and everybody, and so I sometimes felt an apprehension whether the Mother would accept our presents because of our not being very pure souls. But I used to feel reassured on the Mother telling, "My son, I presented to the Master the article you had brought. It was quite good, very sweet. I too have partaken of it."

One day I asked her, "Mother, does not the practice of repeating God's name gradually reduce the accumulated effects of a man's past actions?" "Everyone must experience the consequence of his past actions," the Mother replied. "Nevertheless, the remembrance of God's name helps one this much—instead of losing a leg one may suffer merely from a thorn entering one's foot."

I said, "Mother, I can hardly perform spiritual practices, and I don't think I shall ever be able to." The Mother assured me saying, "What else will you do? Do what you are doing now. Remember that the Master is behind everyone of you. I, too, am behind you."

One day the Mother observed that Radhu was feeling restless owing to illness. She said to me, "O my son, please see what's the trouble with Radhu." I did not know how to feel the pulse. However, to satisfy the Mother I felt Radhu's pulse and said, "There is nothing serious. She is somewhat weak. Please give her some milk to drink." The Mother, who was of a childlike nature, immediately began feeding Radhu with milk. After a while Radhu's mother came and seated herself close to Radhu. This made the latter excited; she did not like the idea that her mother should stay nearby. Pushing her a little with her hand, Radhu said, "Please move away." The Holy Mother's hand accidentally touched the feet of Radhu's mother. Being already very much perturbed, she cried out, "Why have you touched my feet? What will become of me now?" The Mother had a hearty laugh at the behaviour of Radhu's mother. Rashbehari-Da, who was standing nearby, said, "Mother, you see how this madcap of a woman speaks ill of you always and even tries to hurt you? But now she seems to be frightened because your hand has touched her feet!"

The Mother said, "In spite of his knowing that Rama was but Narayana, the infinite Brahman, and that Sita was the primordial energy, the Mother of the universe, Ravana nevertheless created so much trouble. Does not the mad woman know who I am? She knows everything; yet she creates all this fun."

Referring to the rheumatic pain in her leg, I told her, "Mother, I hear that your accepting the sins of others is responsible for this illness of yours. I have one earnest prayer to you—kindly do not suffer on my account. Kindly allow me to undergo sufferings for my past deeds." The Mother replied, "How is that possible? Let all be happy, and I shall suffer for them." Ah! What an unfathomable manifestation of compassion I saw in her!

Prior to leaving Jayrambati, as I prostrated before the Mother, she placed her hand on my head and mentally repeated the name of the Lord. Then she said affectionately, "Ah! They feel like staying with me. But what can they do? They have so much of household work to look after!" Expressing her solicitude like the mother of a man bound for a far off country, the Mother walked with me some distance from her house and stood gazing with her eyes full of tears.

Once I stayed in Calcutta for three weeks. I went to the Holy Mother's house at Baghbazar. After making obeisance at her feet, I said, "Mother, I shall be in Calcutta for a few days. A rule has been introduced here permitting people to see you only twice a week. If you kindly permit me, I shall come to see you now and then." The Mother replied, "Certainly. Come whenever you can and inform me."

During this period, one day I approached her, and said, "Mother, I do not find peace of mind. My mind remains agitated all the time. I am not free from desires." On hearing this, the Mother looked intently at me for a long time but did not utter a word. Her look of distress brought me remorse. I wondered why I should have told her these things. Taking the dust of her feet, I bade her farewell and went to Master Mahasaya's residence in Guruprasad Chowdhury Lane. I saluted him and said, "You massaged the Master's feet many a time. Kindly stroke my head a little; for I feel greatly agitated." Master Mahasaya replied, "What's this? You are the Mother's son; she loves you dearly. Why should you seek consolation from me? Didn't the Mother cast her benign glance upon you?" "Oh yes, she looked at me for a while," I replied. Thereupon Master Mahasaya said : "What more do you need? 'If Shyama casts her glance on a man, he swims in Eternal Bliss.'" He emphatically repeated this saying three times. Now I realized the significance of the Mother's looking at me for a while. I became quiet. It now appeared to me that the Mother had sent me to Master Mahasaya just to enable me to understand the meaning of her gracious glance.

Early one morning I went to see the Holy Mother. My wife and one of my daughters accompanied me. I told her, "Mother, my wife and daughter cannot see you often. Permit them to stay with you for the whole day. I shall come in the afternoon to take them home." The Mother agreed. My wife had not put on her forehead the vermilion mark of married women. One of the lady devotees then asked her, "Well, why do you not have a vermilion mark on your forehead?" When the Mother heard this, she said, "What does it matter, if she has not? She has such a noble husband. What if she hasn't worn the mark?" Saying so, the Mother herself put a vermilion mark on my wife's forehead.

My wife was thinking, "If the Mother permits, I shall massage her feet." Strangely enough, the Mother called her after a while and said, "Daughter, please rub some oil on my head and body." While my wife was combing the Mother's hair after putting oil on it, the thought came to her, "Mother permitting, I shall take these hair-strands home." The Mother smiled, and on her own took out the hair-strands from the comb and presented them to my wife saying, "Take these."

A woman devotee asked the Mother, "Who is this daughter?" The Mother replied, "She is the wife of Suren who lives in Ranchi. Suren has great faith in the Master."

That day the Mother took my wife to the Ganges when she went for her bath. The Brahmacharins had mixed up the Sari and towel we had brought for Mother with a few other clothes. But the Mother picked up our Sari and towel when she went for her bath. After the holy bath in the Ganga, the Mother paid one paise to the 'priest at the ghat',[1] saying, "Put a sandal paste mark on the forehead of this daughter."

While taking her meal the Mother gave my wife Prasada from her own plate. After the meal, she asked my wife to massage her feet. My young daughter, who was lying on a piece of blanket, soiled it. My wife was about to wash it when the Mother took it from her and washed it herself. My wife asked, "Well, Mother, why should you wash it?" The Mother replied, "Why should I not, dear? Is not the child my own?"

In the afternoon I went to the Udbodhan Office and found that Upen Babu was the only visitor there. I learned that all the others had gone to attend the celebrations at the Vivekananda Society. I went upstairs straight to the Mother and saluted her. She said, "Look, there is no male attendant here today. Devotees will be coming to see me. Today you will serve as the usher and also distribute Prasada to the devotees." A little later I showed some devotees into the Mother's drawing-room, and after they saluted her, gave them Prasada. Gradually the devotees thinned out, and finally all left.

Mother: Today you have served as a member of this household; you showed the devotees in and gave them Prasada.

---

[1]A Brahmin priest who attends to the orthodox rituals after a holy bath.

Disciple: Why! Don't I belong to your household?

Mother: Yes, that's right. You are my own son.

Saying this, the Mother continued, speaking to my wife, "Yes, dear, all are my children, no doubt. But some of them are specially related. He bears a special relationship with me. Don't you see how he frequents this place? He is close to me."

Then the Mother gave us Prasada and betel leaf. Touching my chin endearingly, she said, "You need have no fear hereafter. Feel quite at ease. This is your last birth."

Disciple: Certainly, your grace makes everything easy.

My wife brought for the Mother an *āsana*[1] which she herself had made. It pleased her very much. Showing it to everyone, she said, "Ah! Look at it. What a beautiful *āsana* my daughter has made." Even a trifling thing from a devotee used to gladden her so much!

Another time I proceeded for Jayrambati in the company of four devotees. We left the monastery at Koalpara early enough to arrive at the house of the Holy Mother before sunset. But we were delayed. Though we had with us a local porter, and though I too was familiar with the place, we took a wrong road when we were close to the Mother's house. We found it difficult to ascertain the road leading to our destination. The local porter too got confused and could not help us. Dusk passed into night and the surroundings were scarcely visible. My companions got bewildered. Finding no other alternative, I spread a blanket in a bamboo grove and sat down. I was overcome with the thought, "Mother, how is it that we alone should search for you, and you yourself should do nothing whatsoever?" Soon after, we noticed Rashbehari-Dada,[2] and Hemendra[3] coming, with a lantern in hand. We were amazed at their appearance at such an odd hour. They explained, "We had no plan to come by this road. But luckily we just happened to take this route!"

When we met the Mother and saluted her, she asked, "Well, sons, you have wandered a lot, haven't you?"

Disciple: Yes, Mother, we took a wrong road.

---

[1]A small carpet on which one person can sit.

[2]Swami Arupananda, an attendant of the Holy Mother.

[3]Brahmachari Hemendra was another attendant.

At that time the Mother's new house was being constructed and the two Brahmacharins just mentioned were terribly busy with the work. Two devotees from Sylhet had come. Of the two, one was a devotee of Swami Dayananda of Arunachal. The latter had declared this disciple of his to be an incarnation of Prahlada. I escorted them to the Mother. After they saluted her, I said, "Mother, in Arunachal there is a monk by the name of Dayananda. He proclaims himself to be an incarnation of God. This gentleman is a disciple of his. Dayananda says he is Prahlada." The Mother laughed and said, "An Incarnation indeed!"

The Mother gave those two devotees spiritual initiation this time. Referring to the monk, I told the Mother that he was giving spiritual initiation to many persons. The Mother said, "They belong more or less to the class of commerical monks. Still, even they bring some good to people. Men normally do not do any spiritual practice. But following the advice of these monks, they will at least do some practice. If one is sincere he will finally come here. Don't you see how the holy name of Tarak Brahma[1] is spreading? Those who have worth in them cannot help but come under its influence."

The Mother initiated all the four companions of mine. One of them was rather young. When his initiation was over, the Mother told him, "Repeat the Mantra one hundred and eight times." But this did not satisfy him. He wanted to chant the holy name one hundred million times a day. Smiling a little, the Mother observed, "Now you are thinking like this. But because of your multifarous duties you can't do that much. Well, it would be fine if you can do more."

One day I procured some lotuses for worshipping the Mother. She said, "Go and offer some to Simhavahini and keep the rest here." One devotee said, "I want to worship you with all the flowers I have brought." To him the Mother replied: "Well, it may be done! But don't you see these old feet of mine? Why would you worship them?"

A number of devotees were near about when I told her, "Mother Sri Ramakrishna used to say, 'Pure devotion is the essence of all.' You kindly bless me so that I can have that kind of devotion." The Mother kept quiet. The people present gradually left

[1]The Supreme Lord.

the place. Then the Mother quietly said, "Is it possible for anybody and everybody to have that? But you will have it."

The Mother told Radhu, "Radhu, he is your elder brother. Salute him." I wonderd, "How's that! I belong to a Kayastha[1] family. Won't it cause me harm if she, a Brahmana girl, salutes me?" At last both of us saluted each other.

One day I had a great desire to take *pānthābhāt*[2] and asked the Mother for it. She said, "Wait for a while. I'll fry hot chillies and pulse-cake in oil. People in your part of the country are very fond of chillies." The Mother mimicked the tune of a traditional gramaphone record, saying, 'I shan't give you even one less than thirty-two chillies.'[3] Saying this, she began to laugh heartily.

Another day at Jayrambati, the Mother said, "I have to face much hardship, you see,all through the day. Devotees come every minute, one batch following another. There is no end to this. This body of mine is almost at the breaking point. Praying to the Master I have somehow fixed my mind on Radhu and thus kept it on the worldly plane." It struck me that this was parallel to Sri Ramakrishna's keeping his lofty mind on the worldly plane by clinging to such desires as "I shall drink water" or "I shall smoke." Was not the Mother bearing so much trouble for the good of the many?

While taking leave of the Mother, I said, "Mother, you have millions of children like me, but I have not another Mother like you." On hearing this, the Mother with tears in her eyes endearingly fondled me, touching my chin with her hand.[4]

Once I went to Jayrambati to request the Mother to go to Ranchi for a change of climate after her illness. It was the month of Chaitra (March-April). When she heard this proposal, the Mother remarked, "One should not go out in the month of Chaitra. Even Sarat (Swami Saradananda) came here to escort me to Calcutta and stayed here a long time awaiting my convenience. Calcutta should therefore have my preference."

---

[1]Originally a class of warriors. It is the second in the hierarchy of the Hindu caste system.

[2]Boiled rice kept in water overnight—a common dish in rural Bengal.

[3]The people of East Bengal are fond of hot chillies and the people of West Bengal make fun of it.

[4]The way Indian mothers show affection for their grown-up children.

About that time one of the sisters of Swami Keshavananda died. Referring to this, I observed, "Mother, it is a pity that Swami Keshavananda's mother should suffer a bereavement in her old age." The Mother replied, "Bereavement will not upset her peace of mind." On my return journey I met the old lady at Koalpara and found that she had no trace of grief at all. She was all smiles as usual. I wondered, "Even a great sage like Vasishtha experienced bereavement. But here I find the contrary."

Once I called upon the Mother at the Udbodhan house in the company of Sri Rajendra Mukhopadhyaya. When we saluted the Mother, she prayed to Sri Ramakrishna with folded palms, "Master, kindly fulfil all their desires." Thereupon I asked, "How's that Mother? We shall be ruined if all our desires are fulfilled. How many bad desires are there in the heart!"

The Mother laughed and said, "You need not be afraid of that. The Master will grant only those desires which you really need and which will bring you good. Continue to practise what you are doing now. Why fear? We are with you."

Very early one morning a calf was pitifully crying in the outer courtyard of the Mother's house at Jayrambati. The calf was kept separated from its mother for the purpose of milking the cow. On hearing its cry the Mother rushed out, saying, "I am coming, child, I am coming. I shall release you just now." Coming to the courtyard, she freed the calf. I was wonderstruck on seeing this revelation of the compassion of the Divine Mother towards all beings. Alas! Only such an anguished cry can bring about the release of the soul.

I do not have the language to give expression to the Holy Mother's boundless affection, infinite compassion and limitless kindness. We are all blessed by seeing her lotus feet, touching them, and receiving her grace. Our families have been made holy and our mothers have been blessed. Hundreds of devotees have been turned into gold by this touchstone.

6

(RECORDED BY BRAHMACHARI ASHOKAKRISHNA)

One morning during her last illness I went to see the Holy Mother. There was no one else in her room at the time. She was staying in the southernmost room. During daytime the Mother's bed used to be spread on the floor of that room. She had been keeping better health for the last few days.

It was the first week of the month of Chaitra (third week of March). As soon as I made salutations to the Mother, she began to enquire about the other members of my family. Seeing her very lean and thin, I said, "Mother, your health has very much deteriorated. I have never seen you so weak before."

The Mother said, "Yes, my son, the body has become quite emaciated. It seems that whatever the Master had wanted to get done through this body has already been accomplished. Now my mind is constantly directed towards him. Nothing else brings happiness to the mind. Look, how dearly I loved Radhu, how much care I took in looking after her. But now all this is changed. Now when Radhu approaches me, I feel uneasy. I feel, why should she try to drag my mind down? For the sake of his work, the Master kept my mind tied down to the world through these aids. Otherwise, would it have been possible for me to continue in this world after he passed away?"

Disciple: Mother, such words from you are very painful to us. If you leave us, what will happen to us? We don't practise austerities. We have hardly any renunciation. If you don't maintain your body for our sake, how shall we get the strength to survive in this realm of Mahamaya? Whenever any weakness would assail my mind, I used to tell you everything and find a way out every time. But where shall we go now? We shall all be helpless.

Mother: What! Why should you be helpless? Does not the Master guide you through good and bad? Why should you be so worried? I have deposited you at his holy feet. You will have to move about within that circle; you can't go beyond it. He is always protecting you.

Disciple: Even though I remember the mercifulness of the Master, I fail to understand it all the time. Though I often have faith in it, I am haunted by doubts at times. But I can see you directly. I tell you everything, and you instruct me on how to follow the best course for my own good. This has instilled in me the conviction that I am under your protection.

Mother: Always remember that the Master is the only protector. If you forget this, you will have trouble. Do you know why I enquired about your family so much? I first heard from Ganen that you had lost your father. So I asked him about the close relations of your mother, whether she has means to maintain herself and whether she can manage her affairs without you. When I heard that she can pull on even without you, I felt relieved and thought, "Well, the boy has taken a good resolve, and now by the grace of the Master he will not face any serious trouble."

She continued "Everyone should serve his mother, particularly those of you who have come together here to serve all people. Had your father not left behind some wealth, I would have asked you to earn money with which to serve your mother. It is by the will of the Master that you are not burdened by any such trouble. It will be enough if you can make some arrangement, so that the family property is not squandered while under the management of a woman. As for yourself, you are in a very advantageous position. Men can hardly earn money through honest means, and even this contaminates their mind very much. That's why I advise you to settle these monetary affairs as early as possible. Money is such a thing that one develops an attachment for it, if one is associated with it for long! You may think that you have no attachment for it, that since you have renounced it once for all you will not get attached to it, that you will be able to be free from it whenever you wish. Oh, no! Never harbour such an idea in your mind. Money will find its way somehow to grip you unawares by the neck, as it were. I am telling this particularly to you who belong to Calcutta—you are free with money, aren't you? Settle your family affairs as early as possible and leave Calcutta. And if you can take your mother to some place of pilgrimage, both of you will be able to call upon God, forgetting the mother-and-son relationship. It will be nice if you can arrange it now while your mother is mourning. She is already aged. Try to explain your intention to her. Discuss this with her.

"You will play the true role of a son only if you can help her acquire the means for her higher evolution in the hereafter. Don't forget that you have grown up by sucking the milk of her breasts. Remember with what difficulty she tended you. To serve her is your highest religion. It would be different, of course, if she stands in the way of your progress towards God. Please bring your mother here once. I want to see what she is like. If I find her helpful to you, I shall give her some advice. But beware, don't engage yourself in worldly affairs under the cover of serving your mother. The real issue is to provide board and lodging for her because she is a widow. Is a big amount of money necessary for this? Try your utmost to quickly settle these affairs, even if there be some monetary loss. The Master could not touch money at all. Since you have renounced everything to realize the Master's ideal, always remember his words. Money is at the root of all evil in this world. At your tender age, your mind will easily feel tempted if you possess some money. Beware!"

Disciple: I thought of bringing my mother to you one day. But considering the present condition of your health, I don't dare to bring her here.

Mother: No, no, bring her one day. Many people are coming. The condition of this body will deteriorate day by day. Bring her once very soon. I don't feel too bad in the mornings. Can you not bring her in the morning one day? Don't be too late in the day, otherwise the attendant may not permit her to see me.

Disciple: Mother, your words are very painful to me. Your repeated mention of your health suggests that you don't desire to keep your body any more.

Mother: The continuation of this body is not under my control; it all depends on His will. Why are you all so impatient? How long do you really stay near me? You stay at the Math (Belur Math) sometimes, or somewhere else at other times. How many of you find an opportunity to speak to me or stay near me? You don't even care to inform me of your whereabouts.

Disciple: Yes, it is true that there is hardly any scope for our staying with you, but we know in our heart of hearts that you are here. Whenever any weakness assails us, we rush to you, and we are relieved.

Mother: Suppose the Master lets this body of mine perish—do you think I can be free even then so long as a single person of whom I have taken charge remains in bondage? I shall have to be with them all. I have taken the responsibility for their well-being.

Giving initiation is no joke. One has to bear on one's shoulders such a big burden, you see! How much I have to worry over them. Just see, when your father expired, I felt very sad. I thought, the Master has again put this young man to the test. I worried as to how you would manage in this situation. That was why I talked with you so long. Do you really understand everything? If you could, the burden of my worries would have diminished. The Master is sporting with different people in different ways. And now, you see, I have to bear the brunt of it all! Surely, I cannot leave those whom I have accepted as my own.

Disciple: Mother, I become frightened whenever I wonder what will happen to us when you are gone. Whom shall we approach in your place?

Mother: My son Rakhal (Swami Brahmananda) and others are there. Are they any the less worthy? You dearly love Rakhal also. You can seek his help. Besides, what else have you got to ask? To question too much is not good. It is difficult to properly assimilate even one thought. Now why should you trouble your mind by harbouring ten thoughts? Dive deep with the noble idea that you have received. Repeat the holy Name, meditate upon it, keep good company, and subdue the ego by all means. Do you see the child-like nature of Rakhal, as if he is still a young boy? Don't you see Sarat (Swami Saradananda), who does so much work, bearing all tribulations silently? Being a monk, he has no need for all these troubles. These monks can fix their minds on God all the time if they so wish. They bring their minds down only for your welfare. Keep them before you as an ideal and serve them. And make it a point to remember always whose child you are, who has granted refuge to you. Whenever any evil thought haunts you, tell your mind: 'Being her child, can I stoop so low as to indulge in any such activity?' You will find that you gain strength and peace of mind.

7

(RECORDED BY PRABODH BABU AND MANINDRA)

I first saw the Holy Mother in 1907. It was during the rainy season of 1908 that I saw her for the second time. This time I arrived at Jayrambati at about 11.30 a.m. After I saluted her, the Mother asked, "Are you a pupil of Master Mahasay?"

Disciple: No, Mother, but I visit him frequently.

Mother: How is he? Have you seen him recently?

Disciple: He is keeping fine. I met him only eight days back.

While I was taking my noon meal, I asked the Mother, "Will you be going to Calcutta now?"

Mother: I wish to visit Calcutta during the Durga Puja holidays. Then whatever the Divine Mother wills. . . . Do you get paddy from your landed property?

Disciple: Yes, Mother.

Mother: Good. We don't get good quality paddy in this part of the country. Do you grow *Kalai* pulse?

Disciple: Yes, Mother.

Mother: That's fine.

While I was taking my night meal, the Holy Mother asked, "Do you stay at home now?"

Disciple: Yes, Mother, I am living at home now. I am in grave danger. I had a serious illness, and it has been followed by my marriage.

Mother: How old is the bride?

Disciple: She is about thirteen.

Mother: What has happened is for good, certainly. What can you do?

Disciple: Master Mahasaya asked me not to marry.

Mother: Ah! He himself has suffered much. That's why he says, "None of you should marry."

Disciple: Worldly life is a great impediment. Engrossed in worldly life, one loses one's manliness.

Mother: Surely. There is only one cry—money, money, money.

Disciple: It is very painful.

Mother: The Master has householder devotees too. Why do you worry?

In spite of these words I was still worried. After a while the Mother said, "My brothers too are married."

Disciple: Did they marry with your consent?

Mother: What is to be done? The Master used to say, "The worms seen in excreta thrive well there, but if kept in a pot of rice, they will simply die." These days nieces do not serve their uncles as sincerely as we used to do.

Disciple: Things are changing gradually.

Mother: That's true. Don't you see? Formerly I couldn't kill even an ant, but these days I sometimes beat a cat! The Master used to say, "*Tuhu, Tuhu*"—"Thou, Thou!" He meant that only after terrible sufferings does a man resort finally to "Thou, Thou (Lord, Lord)." Selfishness—well, it persists as long as a person is self-assertive, but not when that is overcome. Why entertain any fear? All conditions can turn favourable by the will of the Master. Perhaps your wife has some good deeds to her credit. The Master used to say, "*Avidyā* is more powerful than *vidyā*." That is why *avidyā māyā*[1] has kept the world enchanted.

It was Sunday, 20 April, 1919. The Holy Mother was staying at Jagadamba Ashrama at Koalpara in the district of Bankura. At about ten in the morning Manindra, Satu, Narayana Iyengar and others had come to salute the Holy Mother. The Mother had been staying here for more than a month. The male devotees were staying and taking their meals at the Koalpara monastery.

The son of the Holy Mother's niece Maku was seriously ill at Jayrambati ; he was suffering from Diphtheria. The child was under the treatment of Vaikuntha Maharaj (Swami Mahadevananda). The Mother was terribly worried as to what might happen to the child. This topic came up for discussion as soon as the devotees took their seats after saluting the Mother. Narayana Iyengar said, " Mother, the child will be cured through your blessings." The Mother folded her palms and pointing to

---

[1] *Avidyā māyā* or the 'Maya of ignorance' which entangles man in worldliness. *Vidyā māyā* leads one to liberation. These are the two aspects of *māyā* or ignorance obscuring the vision of God.

the picture of the Master inside the room said, " He is superintending everything."

Satu : He (Narayana Iyengar) has done a lot for Maku's child. He sent a messenger to Calcutta to bring injections for Diphtheria as well as other things.

Mother : Yes, he is a noble soul. He has spent money to send Kalo to Calcutta. Who would have done all this, had he not been here ?

Narayana Iyengar: I am the machine and the Master is the engineer. He is driving me like a machine.

Mother: The Master used to say, "He who possesses food and money may distribute them to the poor. He who does not have, should give himself to repeating the name of the Lord."

Narayana Iyengar : Is it necessary to wash oneself before doing Japam?

Mother: Yes, washing is necessary when Japa is practised at home. But it will be sufficient just to repeat the holy Name during journeys or walks.

Narayana Iyengar: Only the repetition of the holy Name? Not even the repetition of the Mantra?

Mother: Yes, you should certainly repeat the Mantra also. However, calling upon God with one's mind steadfast is equivalent to a million repetitions of the Mantra. What is the good in doing Japa for a whole day if there is no concentration of mind? Collectedness of one's mind is essential, then only His grace descends.

Narayana Iyengar: Whatever I am doing, is it sufficient or do I need to do something more?

Mother: Continue to practise what you are doing. You are already a recipient of His grace.

Narayana Iyengar: One can have a vision of God if one earnestly calls upon Him for two or three days at a stretch. I am calling upon Him for so long. Why do I not have His vision?

Mother: Yes, you will have it. The utterances of Lord Siva and the words of the Master—they cannot be untrue. The Master told Surendra Mitra, "He who has wealth should distribute it, and he who has not, should do Japa."

Drawing the attention of all present, the Mother said further, "If you can't do even that, then take refuge in the Master. Remember this much: 'I have someone to look after me. There is certainly a Mother or Father.'"

Narayana Iyengar: Since you are telling this, we cannot but accept it and have faith in it.

Radhu had given birth to a child. Since the birth of the baby, Radhu was lying ill. It was time to feed Radhu. The Mother got up and said, "Now I shall go to feed Radhu." The devotees finished prostrating at the Holy Mother's feet. Narayana Iyengar saluted the Holy Mother touching her feet. The Mother blessed him by touching his head.

When Manindra bowed at her feet, the Mother said, "What a strong faith your mother has! When asked to visit Varanasi, she remarked, 'This is my Varanasi, I shall not go anywhere else.'" Manindra's mother, who used to live with the Holy Mother, had died more than a year earlier. She had served the Holy Mother very devotedly. The Mother had told her, "None except Kedar's mother and you could stay here for long."

As dusk approached, news reached that the condition of Maku's son had become precarious. This made the Holy Mother very anxious. She told Brahmachari Varada, "Keep the palanquin ready. If the boy survives the night, I shall go to see him tomorrow morning. But how shall we get news of the child early tomorrow morning?"

Manindra: Satu and I shall bring the news early tomorrow morning.

After a while Vaikuntha Maharaj returned from Jayrambati. On hearing this, the Mother started and asked, "Is not the child alive?" Finding all silent, the Mother asked once again, "When did he pass away?"

Vaikuntha Maharaj: At half past five.

Mother: Can I see him if I go there now?

Vaikuntha Maharaj: No, Mother, the dead body has been removed.

Mother began to cry profusely. If she stopped crying for a while, she would begin again all the more. When Swami Kesavananda tried to pacify her, she cried out, "O Kedar, I cannot forget the child."

Once when the boy and his mother Maku were about to start for Jayrambati, he collected a few wild roses and placed them at the Mother's feet, saying, "Look, Auntie! How beautiful they look!" Then the boy bowed down and took the dust of the Mother's feet. Afterwards he picked up the flowers, put them into his pocket, and left for Jayrambati. Sarat Maharaj(Swami Saradananda) dearly loved the boy. During his illness, the boy called out, "Red Uncle! Red Uncle!" referring to the Swami's saffron cloth. Now, the Mother observed, "May be, some devotee had been reborn as he. But this must have been his last birth. Otherwise, how could you explain the kind of intelligence the boy showed or the way he used to perform his Puja at the age of three? I brought him up and hence the loss is so terrible to me." The weeping and wailing continued until late in the night. At the dead of night the Mother asked the women if they had taken their night meal. When she heard that they had not taken any food, because she had not taken, she took a little milk and two *luchis*. The next day during the evening hours Manindra and Prabhakar went to see the Mother. She was very gloomy on account of the premature death of Maku's child. Now the conversation turned to that topic.

Mother: The child once asked me, "Who created red flowers?" I replied, "The Master has made them." He then asked, "Why?" I told him, "Because he wanted to wear them." The death of the child will cause deep sorrow to Sarat. Sarat used to place the child on his lap without caring about the pain in his leg. Once while seated on Sarat's lap, the boy asked him, "Where is your Mother?" Pointing to Maku, Sarat said, "Here is my mother." Then the boy said, "No, your mother has gone to the school building." About that time, the Holy Mother lived along with the ailing Radhu in the boarding house of Nivedita's school; for Radhu could not stand the noise of the Udbodhan House.

Manindra: The Master too suffered terribly on the death of Akshay.

Mother: The Master said, "The pang in my heart was like the wringing of a towel." One of my nephews named Dinu used to worship in the Vishnu temple. Hriday used to worship in the Kali temple. Dinu would entertain the Master by singing "Yasoda used to rock you by calling you Nilamani"[1] and such other songs. Then, Akshay had an attack of cholera.

Manindra: Were you then living at Dakshineswar?

Mother: Yes, I was staying in the Nahabat. The dust of the Master's feet, the dust of my own feet, and the water with which

---

[1]Part of a song in adoration of Gopala or the baby Krishna.

the image of Mother Kali had been bathed were offered to Akshay but to no avail. He didn't survive. The Master suffered much anguish.

"My youngest brother passed the Entrance Examination creditably. Afterwards he was studying medical science and was doing fairly well. When he went to see Naren, the latter asked, 'Well, does the Mother have such a person as her brother? Almost all of them are priests, earning a living through that profession.' He further said to him, 'You will have to operate on abscesses in the stomach.' Naren said to Yogen (Swami Yogananda), 'You will have to meet his (the Mother's brother's) educational expenses.' However, Yogen died. Rakhal (Swami Brahmananda) bought books worth forty rupees for my brother. Rakhal and Sarat used to play cards with him. But that brother of mine passed away early.

"The world is a fetter of Maya . . . (*In a pitiful voice*) Ah! Maku had a child who was so helpless that he couldn't even turn from one side to another by himself. Just imagine! How painful it was!

"In bringing up this girl Radhu, I have had to endure so much pain. Well, one cannot escape it. When Radhu was born to Surabala (*Chota Bau*) my mother said, 'Chota-Bau's mother wants to take her (Surabala) home. Why not let her do so?' Then at the time of my morning worship in Calcutta I had a vision which appeared to me in the way a drop-scene appears at a theatrical performance (*making a gesture with both her hands*). I saw the mother of Radhu in distress at her village home. I saw Radhu lying in the courtyard and picking up from a mass of straw and dust strewn all around, a few grains of puffed rice given to her by her mother and eating them. Radhu's mother had her arms wound with red and blue threads, just as a mad woman could have. The other children of the family, I noticed, were taking puffed rice and other things along with sweets. Seeing this I almost started gasping. I felt choked like a person forcibly kept under water. Then I realized that Radhu's condition would be like what I saw if I left her in the hands of her mother."

The Holy Mother dearly loved her youngest brother Abhay. She had brought her brothers up. On his death bed Abhay had said, "Sister, I am leaving behind everything. Please look after them." Radhu was then in her mother's womb. After her confinement, Radhu's mother came to Calcutta along with the Holy Mother. Subsequently she turned insane and was sent to Jayrambati. Radhu had to endure so much of tribulations there. One morning when the Holy Mother was performing her worship in her rented house in Baghbazar, she had that vision of Radhu. Remembering the last words of Abhay, she returned to Jayrambati in a few days' time. The Mother used to say, "Through this girl I have been caught in the snares of Maya." At some other time the Holy Mother was lying seriously ill at Koalpara. One day all on a sudden Radhu left for Jayrambati with the idea of visiting her father-in-law's house. Before leaving, she said to the Mother, "You have so many devotees to look after you but who have I except my husband?" Referring to this incident, the Mother said, "The way Radhu threw away the bondage of my attachment yesterday and went to her husband's home worried me. I said to myself that perhaps the Master does not want me to live any longer." The Mother further said, "My constant doting on Radhu uttering 'Radhi, Radhi' is nothing but a form of Maya with which I am bound."

The twilight of dusk was advancing towards the darkness of night. Manindra and Prabhakar were getting ready to take leave of the Mother. They wanted to reach Arambagh that very night. The Mother said: "You take some food and go."

Prabhakar: We have come here after taking our food.

Mother: Won't you please take at least some little refreshment? Dear, please bring some sweets for them.

She later told us, "You should take food and some rest before you leave."

Manindra: Yes, Mother.

Mother: Have you hired a cart?

Manindra: Yes.

When we saluted her while taking leave, she blessed us saying, "May your mind be inclined towards God."

Manindra: May our bond of Maya break asunder.

On hearing this, the Mother cast an approving glance.

23*rd April*, 1919.

When the devotees went to prostrate at the feet of the Holy Mother, Narayana Iyengar told her, "Mother, your mind is now disturbed because of the premature death of Maku's son. I am therefore thinking of leaving this place soon."

Mother: Joy and sorrow, where will they go? They are our

companions. Why should you worry about it? Stay here. You may leave this place on the 4th or 5th of Jaistha (May).

Monday, 12 *Jaistha* (*May-June*)

Swami Santananda and Swami Harananda had come from Varanasi. Manindra, too, had come again. In the morning Swami Santananda and Manindra went to salute the Holy Mother. The devotees were put up in the Koalpara monastery and the Mother was staying in the Jagadamba Ashrama.

Santananda: How is your health, Mother?

Mother: I am keeping all right.

One young man, released from internment,[1] had come there the previous day. Anticipating trouble from the police, the devotees tried to send him away then and there. When the Mother was asked about it, she said, "Keep him here for the day. He will go away tomorrow." Swami Kesavananda, instead of keeping the young man in the monastery, placed him somewhere else; for the village policeman used to visit the monastery every evening and record the names and addresses of new arrivals. The next day the Mother enquired about the young man. "Where is that young man? Has he already left?" she asked.

Manindra: He hasn't left. He will go after his noon meal.

Mother (*to Swami Santananda*): Where did he spend the night?

Santananda: I don't know, Mother. He didn't tell me.

Mother: Do you have rain in Varanasi also, when the monsoon sets in here?

Santananda: No, Mother. There the rainy season begins in the month of Sravan (July-August). But in some years storms take place in the month of Vaisakh (March-April) and destroy the mango and other crops. The old women who go to Varanasi with the desire of dying there suffer terribly. Sometimes the remittance from home is stopped. Besides, they have to live in damp dark rooms on the ground floor.

Mother: Yes, I myself saw the extent of their suffering when I stayed in the house of Bansi Dutta at Varanasi. I saw them taking a small quantity of rice procured by begging and soaked in water. They didn't cook.

---

[1]In connection with the Freedom Movement.

Santananda: Many old women live long, although they go there to die early.

Mother: They earn remission of their sins by seeing and touching Lord Visvanath, and thereby they live long. In Vrindavan, people take consecrated food and sprinkle holy water from a conch[1] on their body; so they live long.

Mother then turned the conversation to the topic of Radhu. She said, "I wish Radhu would overcome her physical weakness now and get up. Her bedroom still serves as her bathroom. I don't know what the Master will do—how long he will keep me like this!" Then she began telling Swami Santananda about Maku's son. "Nothing else overwhelms a man like mourning. Sarat too suffered much on account of Maku's son. Kalo was sent to Calcutta to bring medicine for him. These people here advised him not to meet Sarat. I intervened, saying, 'How can it be that he will go to Calcutta and not meet Sarat?' "

Manindra: Yes, Sarat Maharaj wrote, "Let Kalo come straight to me."

Mother was dressing vegetables. Pointing to the *chelo* (a local vegetable) Swami Santananda observed, "This vegetable is not found in Calcutta."

Mother: It can be prepared as a curry fried in a little oil and also as a sauce. It is a good vegetable, as it is cooling to the system. (*Turning to Manindra*) Is it available in Jehanabad?

Manindra: Yes, Mother.

Swami Santananda raised the topic of the people's suffering. He said, "I hear that six million people have died of influenza. Paddy and rice are costly—people are suffering much."

Mother: Yes, my son. People don't have enough to eat. Those who have children suffer all the more. In fact, this is only the beginning of their suffering. It will end only if there is an abundant paddy crop after a good rain. I heard that some European officer had come to Calcutta. He wanted to ban the movement of paddy and rice from one place to another. He has left, I am told.

Manindra: That attempt is still being made.

Swami Santananda: The suffering of the people is on the increase. Is this the outcome of men's Karma, Mother?

[1] Water contained in a conch is offered to the Deity at the time of the evening service.

Mother: How can this be the Karma of so many people? It seems something is wrong.

Swami Santananda: World War I is over. Why then are goods not sold at a cheaper price?

Mother: How is it that people are saying the War has begun once again?

Swami Santananda: They mean in Kabul. So much of suffering, fighting, and killing! Will this usher in a new age, Mother?

Mother (*smiling*): How can I say? How can I know what will happen by His will? The sin of a king brings ruin to his kingdom. Malice, deceit, killing of holy men—these are all sins. These lead to the suffering of the people and cause providential disturbances like war, earthquake, and famine. War ceases as soon as all the parties calm down a little.....

"Ah, how nice was Queen Victoria, the Empress of India! How happily and comfortably people lived then! Now, even a boy of five realizes the pang of suffering; for he complains of having no clothes to wear. Well, how much rice has already been distributed by Sarat?"

Manindra: I can't say exactly how much rice has been distributed. But rice worth thirty-four rupees is distributed every week among the distressed.

Mother: How much rice does every person receive?

Manindra: Everybody receives one quarter of a seer (equivalent to 0.930 kilogram).

Mother: How much does a family get?

Manindra: Six, seven or eight seers according to the size of the family.

Mother: How many people have received the dole?

Manindra: I don't know exactly. But the Muslim women constitute the largest number.

Mother: Yes, the Mohammedans are poorer here. Well where else is Sarat distributing relief?

Manindra: At Bankura, Indpur, and Manbhum. Relief is being given wherever there is famine.

Mother: Are my sons working there?

Swami Santananda: Yes, they are going from the Math.

Manindra: Indpur is the place where Satu was expected to go.

Mother: Satu's sister has been married to a man of Shihar.

Manindra: Yes, Mother. As Satu did not go to the marriage festival, his parents ......

Mother: Yes, they are sorry. That is natural. But how can a monk participate in a marriage ceremony? He will go there at some other time. It will be nice if Prabhakar's son turns out to be good. The Master used to say, "Everything in the world is jugglery. Though a jugglery, it is unfortunate that men are not aware of it."

In the afternoon of the 16th of Ashada (June-July) Manindra, Prabhakar, and Prabodh Babu of Shyambazar (Fului Shyambazar) came to see the Mother. As soon as Prabhakar saluted her, she asked, "Is your son all right? I heard that he was ill."

Prabhakar : He is all right.

Mother: When did you arrive here? Have you taken your lunch?

Prabhakar: Yes.

Manindra and Prabodh Babu wanted to get their daughters admitted into the Nivedita School. Prabodh Babu raised the topic, asking for the Mother's approval.

Mother: That's right. Write to Sarat.

Prabodh Babu : We have written to him already.

A woman devotee: Will they be able to stay there? They are too young.

Mother: Certainly they will. Girls of six or seven from East Bengal live there. They don't like to leave their hostel even when their parents come.

Prabodh Babu: I went to see the conditions in my native village today. The sufferings of the people are terrible. Men and women don't have even clothes to wear—they couldn't present themselves before us. Thatching can hardly be found on their house-tops.

Mother: Have you (i.e. the Panchayat Board of which he was the President) distributed rice to those people?

Prabodh Babu: It was distributed yesterday.

Mother: Do you distribute clothes?

Prabodh Babu: We distribute clothes selectively. Mother, I hear that you had seen in a dream a woman standing with a pitcher and a broomstick.

Mother: Yes, I saw a woman standing with a pitcher and a broomstick in her hands. I asked her, "Who are you?" She said, "I shall sweep off everything." Then I asked, "What will happen next?" She replied, "I shall sprinkle the contents of this pitcher of nectar." It seems that this vision is coming true. I heard from my mother that when famine sets in, it continues for three consecutive years. Has it continued for two years now?

Manindra: War has been going on for a long time.

Mother: There has been war for the last four or five years. That's something different. Has the famine continued for two years? If so, it may last for one year more.

The Mother then asked, "What's the price of paddy?" She was told the price in terms of the local rate.

Mother: Is it so costly? And everything else—cloth, oil, and all such things—must also be expensive. Those who have these things are also likely to be worried. This time "I shall eat your skin, and you will eat mine."[1] One has to gracefully accept the sorrows and miseries that God is bestowing. Whatever He wills, comes to pass.

Prabodh Babu: Mother, since even you have to suffer so much, what hope is there for others?

Mother: It's as if I have been put in a cage. I can't move about; there is no way for me to escape.

Prabodh Babu : Problems have again cropped up regarding the plot of land owned by the Master's family at Kamarpukur.[2]

Mother: Who is creating the problems? Is it Mahim Babu?

Prabodh Babu : No, Fakir Babu and Hem Babu.

Mother: What's the point in these trifles? Will the shifting of the boundary fence solve the problem?

Prabodh Babu : I have already fixed posts at the four corners of the plot. The area goes up to the road. Mahim Babu is rather pleased with the arrangement. We would have done better to fix the boundary posts a little further ahead. Then in the event of their raising objections, these could be moved back gradually. When one has to deal with such a businessman, one has to apply the same kind of intelligence.

On hearing this strange solution to the problem, the Mother laughed heartily.

Prabodh Babu: I have written to Sarat Maharaj. We shall do whatever he advises.

---

[1] The Mother was quoting a village proverb.

[2] To erect a temple on the birth-spot of Sri Ramakrishna, his ancestral home had been purchased. This refers to some litigation problems regarding the plot of land.

Mother: Formely a day-labourer used to earn four paise a day. I still remember when people used to write letters on large pieces of paper and send them to Calcutta by messengers who walked the whole distance. There was no postal arrangement.

Prabodh Babu: Now the postal system has made things convenient, Mother.

Mother: That's true. I am only narrating some details about the olden days. One could get a large quantity of oil for one rupee. Now a handful of paddy sells for one rupee. People are disposing of their stock of paddy, for it fetches them a good amount of money. Even the small quantity of paddy that is left cannot be stored for very long; for they have to use it for their own consumption. They have to appease their hunger. Prasanna sold paddy worth four to five hundred rupees. A portion of his remaining stock was pilfered. Raj Ghosh too has sold out his large stock of paddy. He received a letter saying, "There will be a robbery in your house unless you pay a certain amount." He produced the letter before the police. Perhaps some local ruffian played this trick.

When Manindra and Prabodh Babu went to salute the Holy Mother, Prabodh Babu asked her, "Mother, should anyone leave the worldly life forcibly?"

Mother (smiling): Some persons are actually doing so, my dear.

Prabodh Babu: One perhaps runs into difficulty if one renounces the world whimsically without obtaining the grace of Mahamaya.

Mother: Such a person returns to the world.

* * *

Manindra : Swamiji (Swami Vivekananda) also suffered terribly. But he was able to overcome his suffering and his physique could withstand the tribulations.

Mother: No, he too had to suffer much from urinary trouble (diabetes). He had a burning sensation all over his body. In spite of his bad health, he 'spilt his blood' in hard work.

Manindra : Did he actually lose blood?

Mother: No, he didn't. But he worked so hard that he almost bled.

Prabodh Babu : I have heard that once at Darjeeling, Swamiji put his arm around the neck of Hari Maharaj and shed tears, saying, "Brother, are you all to concern yourselves just with religious practices? See, I alone am working myself to death."

Mother: Yes, my son, he shed his blood for the sake of others. It is Naren who on his return from abroad did all this. That is how these young men have come to find a shelter. Four of them are now preaching in foreign lands?

Prabodh Babu : Yes, Swami Abhedananda, Swami Prakashananda, Swami Paramananda, and Swami Bodhananda.

Mother: What's the Sannyasa name of Kali?

Manindra : Swami Abhedananda.

Mother: Vasanta (Swami Paramananda) writes letters to people here and sends them money. He delivers lectures there.... Yogen (Swami Yogananda) practised much austerity. At places of pilgrimage he used to store dried crumbs of bread. He took a small quantity of this daily along with water held in his cupped palms. As a result of this he had some serious stomach trouble. It resulted in his premature death....Is there happiness in the world? There is and again, there isn't. The world is like a tree of poison. Poison permeates the whole of worldly life. But those who have plunged into worldly life—what else can they do now? Even if they understand the implications of worldly life, they can't act otherwise.

After saluting the Holy Mother the devotees returned to the Koalpara monastery. Manindra and Prabodh Babu went to the Holy Mother again in the afternoon.

Prabodh Babu : Sarat Maharaj has replied to my letter. Should I read it out?

Mother: Yes, read it.

Prabodh Babu read it out. Among other things he had written, "What can be done even if I agree? As regards keeping Prabodh Babu's daughter Bina here, (i.e. at the Nivedita Girls' school) the Master's will is otherwise."

Mother: Well, why has Sarat written in this way? He has closed the topic entirely. It must be that Sudhira did not agree. Sudhira told me, "Mother, I can't pull on any more. I am suffering very heavily." What an amount of trouble she takes for the girls. When she fails to meet the expenditure of the girls, she earns forty or fifty rupees per month by giving music lessons to the girls of well-to-do families. She has taught the girls of her school sewing, dress-making, and other skills. The institution earned three hundred rupees the other year and utilized it for the girls' travelling expenses during the Puja vacation. Sudhira is the sister of Debabrata

(Swami Prajnananda). Keeping himself in the background, he taught his sister how to purchase a ticket in a railway station, how to board a train without anybody's help, and so on....In the Nivedita School there are two unmarried girls from Madras between twenty and twenty-two years old. Ah! how nicely they have learnt to do various kinds of jobs. And then, just think of our girls! Here in this wretched part of the country, people insist on a girl getting married as soon as, or even before, she is eight years old. Ah! Radhu would not have been in such a miserable plight had she not been married!

8

(RECORDED BY AN ANONYMOUS LADY DEVOTEE)

It was the fifteenth day of Poush, 1320, of the Bengali calendar (A.D. 1914). I had been feeling a great desire to meet the Holy Mother, but I had had no opportunity of calling on her. Who would escort me to her place? I had finally resigned myself to the thought that I would see her only if she made circumstances favourable, when Kamala and Bimala came and said, "Sister, our mother is calling you." At these words it occured to me that this might lead to the fulfilment of my desire. Someone whispered into my ear, as it were, "Oh, dear! Mother is calling you."

I hurriedly got ready and arrived at the house of Bimala at about 7 o'clock in the morning. I found that Lalit and his mother were having a chat. On seeing me Lalit's mother said, "So, here is Binu. See, my darling, how crazy she is! She got the news and came here right away." Lalit asked, "Do you wish to visit the Holy Mother, Sister? If so, I can escort you to her today." "That would be a wonderful favour!" I replied. I could hardly believe the good news that I was really going to see the Holy Mother. So I told Lalit, "Brother, please tell me, are you really going? If you are, then please hire a hackney carriage." I then asked him, "Have you yourself seen the Mother?" With great joy Lalit replied, "I went to see the Mother only once. Ah what can I say of her kindness and deep affection towards us? The Mother asked us to call on her again."

Lalit now went out to hire a carriage. Before going he said, "I am going to bring a carriage. All of you please get ready." Shortly afterwards, Lalit's mother, Lalit's sisters, and I left for the Mother's place. Panchu too accompanied us.

Parul said to me, "Sister, are you sure that the Mother is now staying at the Udbodhan house?" I was startled; for, I really did not know whether the Mother was in Calcutta. I began to worry and to pray mentally to the Master, "O Lord! Please don't disappoint me." Our carriage arrived at the Udbodhan Office at 10 o'clock. As soon as it stopped, I hurriedly got out and went inside without greeting the Swamis who were working in the room on one side. The world seemed to me to be rather empty and meaningless. I didn't know what I would do if I were to hear that the Mother was not there. I was very anxious. I asked everybody I came across, "Is the Mother here?" But the Swamis did not give any reply. Instead they quietly went away with their heads lowered. In the meantime, Lalit had alighted from the carriage and gone straight upstairs. I was following in his footsteps, when he returned to announce, "The Mother is here." I was relieved of the cloud of anxiety which had been hanging over my mind. Now I went slowly to meet the Holy Mother. Leaving the front room on the right side, I proceeded along the balcony on the left. I found a woman standing with her face half veiled. As I noticed two or three devotees making salutations to her, I knew her to be no other than the Holy Mother. It was only to see her that I had rushed all the way from my home. I really don't remember what I did in those moments. On seeing me, the male devotees left the place. I rushed towards the Mother, caught hold of her feet and sat down on the floor. The Mother asked, "Where do you come from? Why have you come here?" I replied, "Mother, I really don't know why I have come. Mother, I am here because you have brought me."

By this time Lalit's mother and the others had entered the room. Standing there for a while, one of them asked, "Is she the Holy Mother?" I nodded. Everybody present made salutations to her. Then the Mother went into the shrine of Sri Ramakrishna. We followed her and made obeisance to the Master. The Mother sat on the wooden cot in front of the altar and said, "Sit down, dear, sit down." We all sat at her feet. Lalit's mother was a housewife. The Mother began to converse with her like an ordinary worldly woman.

Lalit's mother: Mother, kindly tell us a few things about Sri Ramakrishna. We are householders. Kindly give us some instructions.

Mother: I know nothing except what I directly heard from the Master. Well, my darling, read the *Kathamrita* (The Gospel of Sri Ramakrishna) and you will find all the necessary instructions there.

After paying the carriage fare, Lalit came straight to the Mother. He prostrated himself, placing his head on her feet, and began shedding tears profusely and praying pitifully, "Be gracious, O Mother, Thou embodiment of mercy! Mother, you are here to save the world. Kindly give me shelter. I shall not leave your feet. You must grant me refuge." He went on imploring like this. The Mother was all along standing like a statue. After a while, she said, "Please don't be so impatient. Get up, child."

Lalit was a boy of fifteen or sixteen. His latent spiritual nature was beginning to unfold. He was dark-complexioned and well-built. He was full of devotion to God, and his behaviour often exhibited it. Again he began shedding tears, saying, "Kindly grant me refuge at your holy feet, Mother. Kindly say, 'Yes'. Graciously say that you have accepted me, otherwise I shall not get up."

At this moment his feet touched an earthen pot containing clarified butter. He immediately shrank in self-condemnation and said, "What a sin have I committed! Someone gave the Mother this clarified butter with great reverence and now my wretched feet have touched it. Alas! What have I done?" In this way he was lamenting when one fair-complexioned old lady who was busy working in the shrine said, "Well, son, you need not fret. What if your feet have touched that pot? Your feet are not something outside of the universe. The two legs of men are parts of creation. The legs are a part and parcel of the human body." We glanced at her. The calmness on her face and her simple and meaningful words deeply impressed us. Lalit was pacified to some extent, and regaining his composure, he saluted the Holy Mother, saying, "Mother, kindly bless me." "The Master will bless you"—saying this the Mother placed her hand on Lalit's head. Pacified, he went downstairs.

About this time a middle-aged man appeared at the door of the Mother's room. He was holding the hand of a young woman about sixteen or seventeen years old. He said, "Mother, she is my daughter. Her baby died this morning, and she is grief-stricken. I have brought her here hoping that you will be able to console her." These words made us all apprehensive.

Mother: Come here, darling.

The young woman entered the room and sat close to the Holy Mother. As she extended her hand to touch Mother's feet in respectful salutation, the Mother moved away a little and said, "Well, should she touch me? She is now in a period of mourning." These words of the Holy Mother made the woman's face all the more pale. Feeling embarrassed, she quietly moved a little away.

As the Holy Mother looked at her face, her heart was filled with compassion. She said, "Ah, my poor girl! You have suffered much, so you have come to me for solace. And who knows how much I have hurt your feelings? Well, what does it matter if you are observing a period of mourning? Come, my dear, touch my feet." With these kind words the Mother came closer to the young woman. With her eyes full of tears the girl reverently placed her head on the Mother's feet. And the Mother blessed her by placing her hand on the girl's head. Sitting close to the girl, the Mother began to comfort her, saying, "What shall I tell you, darling? I hardly know anything. Keep a photo of the Master with you and know for certain that he is very near you. Pour out your heart's grief by shedding tears before him. Cry and pray earnestly: 'Oh Master! Please draw me towards you. Please grant me peace.' By repeatedly doing this you will find peace of mind. Have faith in the Master and turn to him in prayer whenever you feel distraught." The Mother looked towards us and said, "Ah! She has received this shock only today. Is it possible for her to regain her peace of mind in a day?" The girl's father was all the while standing in front of the door. Now he and his daughter saluted the Holy Mother, silently offering her their mental anguish, and calmly returned home.

Then finding everything quiet in the room, I said, "Mother, I have a question to ask. If you kindly permit, I shall place it before you." Finding me hesitant, that same middle-aged lady (later I knew her to be the Revered Golap-Ma) said, "Tell her, darling. You can tell the Mother frankly your innermost thoughts. Why should you be shy before her?"

Then I said, "Mother, I only wanted to say that I saw you and the Master in a dream. You seemed to be giving me spiritual initiation, but it was not finished. Ever since that dream I have felt a strong urge to take refuge at your holy feet." Mother graciously replied, "Well, I shall give you spiritual initiation today itself. But do you have the consent of your husband?"

Disciple: I asked my husband concerning it. He said, "I have no objection, but I am not going to take initiation now. You can have it."

Mother: Where does your husband live?

Disciple: In Raipur.

Mother showed me the bathroom and said, "Go and wash your hands and feet."

Disciple: Mother, I have not taken my bath yet.

Mother: That's all right. You need not take a bath.

After washing my hands and feet in the bathroom, I went to the shrine-room and found that the Mother had already spread two *asanas* there. Two canoe-shaped copper vessels containing Ganges water had been arranged for worship. The Mother was sitting on one *asana* facing the picture of the Master. She asked me to take my seat on the *asana* placed on her left. Taking water from the bigger canoe-shaped vessel, she performed the ritual called Achamana and made me also do the same. Next she asked me, "Which Deity are you devoted to?" On hearing my reply, she gave me spiritual initiation and then showed me the procedure for repeating the Mantra. That very moment a current of bliss swept over me. A gush of joy welled up within my heart and overwhelmed me. I was aware of practically nothing, but the Mother guided me in completing the initiation. When it was over, the Mother said, "Now give me the offering due to the Guru."

Disciple: Mother, I don't know anything. Please tell me what to do. I have not brought any money.

Mother got up and brought two handfuls of flowers, oranges, plums, etc. and handed them to me. Then she told me to pray: "I am offering to you whatever good or bad deeds I have done in my past or present life, knowingly or unknowingly." I repeated this, and the Mother graciously accepted them all. Mother! Oh, the compassion you have shown me, a good-for-nothing, unworthy person—a compassion that seeks no return! My whole being was consumed by it. Ah, what an experience! What things I saw! What words I heard! I surrendered myself, my being, my whole being, to the lotus feet of the Mother and became blessed.

After saluting the Mother I came out on to the verandah and stood like one possessed, holding the railing for about an hour. I was brought back to normalcy by the cry of a girl and subsequently by the voice of the Mother, and then I went back into the room. When the Mother saw me, she said, "Take your seat, dear, take your seat." When I had sat down, she said, "She is my niece, Radharani. Ever since her mother lost her mental balance, I have been taking care of the girl." The Mother was holding her, but she was vigorously trying to free herself and flee. In various ways the Mother tried to persuade her to be quiet. The Mother braided her hair, dressed her, fed her with her own hand, and said so many affectionate words to her! I was surprised to see this sort of typical worldly behaviour on the part of the Holy Mother. About this time, I was called for taking a bath in the Ganges and so I got up and left. On my return I found the Mother offering food to the Master. Coming out of the shrine, the Mother entered the room where the food offering was made to the Master. Then she shut the door of the room and came back to where we were. After that the Swamis took their noon meal. Golap-Ma served them. When the meal was over, the Swamis left the room.

The plate containing the food which had been offered to the Master was brought into the middle room. *Asanas* were placed for the womenfolk and for Panchu, the five year old boy who had accompanied me, to sit on. The Holy Mother and all of us took our meal together. I had a desire to take food consecrated by the Holy Mother and so I was quietly waiting. Everyone except me began to eat. Twice or thrice the Mother requested me to eat, saying, "Please take your food." Then Golap-Ma came up to me and enquired, "What's the matter with you?" I said, "Kindly give me a little food consecrated by Holy Mother." The Mother mixed her rice, ate a little of it, and placed a portion on my plate. Ah! What can I say? What a nectar I partook on that day! The cook had prepared *arahar* (the pigeon-pea) pulse, curried cauliflower, and a dish of *chalta* (Dillenia speciosa). Golap-Ma had prepared curried fish. All the preparations were very tasty. "I must have more of this curry. I must!" cried Panchu, and began to make a fuss. My whispered rebukes had no effect on him. At that moment Golap-Ma again appeared and asked, "What has happened? Why is this boy behaving like this?"

I said, "I did not want him to accompany me, Mother. I was trying to come here unobtrusively. But when the carriage had gone some distance, Panchu, who was playing on the street, came running and jumped in. And now he is making a fuss, saying, 'I shall take more of the cauliflower curry.'" When they heard this, Golap-Ma, and the others began to laugh. Golap-Ma said, "You wanted to avoid him, but how could you hope to succeed? It was on account of his good past-deeds that he was able to meet the Holy Mother. What a great good fortune it is! It will do him good." The Mother supported the viewpoint of Golap-Ma by saying, "Yes, that's right."

After the noon meal I waited upon the Holy Mother during the entire day. I was supposed to leave for Raipur, as Parul and Kamala had insisted that I should go. But it was a far-off place, and so lest I should miss seeing the Holy Mother in the near future, I didn't go.

The Mother sat in the sun on the roof to dry her wet hair and began talking about her parental home. She said, "I brought up Radhu, who is a mentally imbalanced girl. She wouldn't take food unless she is fed by others. Besides, I am not keeping good health; I suffer from rheumatism. For treatment I went to Varanasi and Vrindaban, but it was of no avail."

After we had talked about various matters the Mother said, "You are so young, a mere child. How is it that you felt an inclination for spiritual initiation?"

Disciple: Mother, I really don't know. I don't enjoy worldly life. In my heart I really want to shun worldly life. In fact, I was feeling great restlessness. At long last I have found peace of mind today. Besides, this world is something impermanent. It is really only for a few days. Everything around me seems unreal. So how can I give my mind to it?

About this time a lady of the same age as the Holy Mother came in and sat down. As I was sitting very close to the Mother, the latter's shadow fell on my person. Noticing this, the lady rebuked me, saying, "What sort of a girl are you that you are sitting on the shadow of the Holy Mother? You will incur sin. Please sit a little away." I sat very close to the Mother, for I had taken her to be my very own. Now, feeling embarrassed, I moved away a little. The lady then asked the Mother, "Who is this girl?"

Mother: The girl has received initiation today. She is very devoted.

At these words of the Mother I felt embarrassed, and so I went to the next room where Parul and the others were gossiping. Just then Lalit came and said, "Come on, Sister. The carriage is ready. It is nearing sunset." So I went to the Holy Mother to take leave of her. The Mother said: "When will you come here next, dear?"

Disciple: I shall come to you whenever you graciously remember me. I am not able to do so by my own effort. Mother, kindly bless me. Kindly remember me, O Mother.

Mother: Please come again, dear.

I looked at her with a sorrowful heart. She gave me two betel-leaf rolls. I prostrated myself at her feet and returned with my physical body, leaving behind with the Mother my real self. With tears in her eyes the Mother stood on the top of the staircase. I was full of joy within and without. I was hearing the voice of the Mother, as it were, even when I was travelling in the carriage.

The Mother kept her word; for, two years later, on my return from Raipur, I was able to see her again during her last illness.

9

(RECORDED BY SMT. SAILABALA CHOWDHURY)

On the morning of Sunday, 2nd Shravan 1311 B.S. (July, 1904) the Revered Gauri-Ma, her Durga[1], and I were travelling in a hackney-carriage to the most respected Holy Mother's rented house at Baghbazar. This was the first time I was going to pay my homage at her holy feet. On the way I expressed to Gauri-Ma with much feeling and many tears my hope that the visit might bring good to me. Arriving at the Holy Mother's house, Gauri-Ma went ahead of us to the first floor and we followed. Going upstairs, I noticed that Gauri-Ma was conversing with the Mother in a low voice. I don't know what passed between them but I heard the Holy Mother saying to her, "You brought Suren's wife here the other day, and now you have brought this daughter today—this seems to be your regular work." On hearing this, Gauri-Ma said, assertively, "Oh, you will certainly give her initiation, won't you? What else is the purpose of your existence?"

At this, the Mother quietly said, "Then come, darling, the time is auspicious now." The Mother ushered Durga into the shrine and shut the door. Gauri-Ma and I waited on the verandah.

The initiation was soon over, and Durga came out of the room. Then I went into the shrine room and the door was closed. The Mother was already inside. Gauri-Ma and Durga stood outside on the verandah. The Mother made me sit on the *asana* meant for the worshipper and then had me worship the Master. Before she gave me initiation, the Mother asked, "Does your family have a Guru?" I said, "Yes."

Mother: Do you intend to take initiation from him also?

Disciple: No.

From inside the room the Mother asked Gauri-Ma, "Gaurdasi, the Mantra of which deity shall I give her?" Then according to Gauri-Ma's suggestion, the Mother gave me initiation. I was accustomed to doing Japa. But when the Mother asked me to do Japa, my body and mind were in such a condition then that I

---

[1]Durga was a girl adopted by Gauri-Ma. She later became a nun.

was unable to comply. While making me repeat the Holy Name, the Mother herself held my hand and kept count on my fingers. Then the door of the shrine was opened. Gauri-Ma entered and told me to offer flowers at the Mother's feet. I obeyed.

When we had arrived at her house, the Mother was getting ready to go to the Ganges for her bath. But now our visit had prevented her from going. We took our noon meal and spent the whole day there.

That day the Mother was searching for a misplaced key. Noticing a key lying close to the cot, I told her, "Here is a key." I didn't know that the Mother was looking for that very key. I did not dare touch it. The Mother picked it up with great joy and blessed me.

I didn't feel like leaving the Mother. When I was saluting her at the time of taking leave, she said, "Come again, dear. Write to me now and then."

On the Janmashtami day of Bhadra (August-September), my third sister and I had gone to Kankurgachhi Yogodyan to attend the festival there.[1] We noticed that special arrangements were being made there for the reception of the Holy Mother. A place close to the temple had been enclosed for her to take rest in. I was feeling great joy to think that the Mother would come here and I would see her. Truly, the Mother's arrival created great excitement. The Mother along with Lakshmi-Didi walked along the long pathway on which a new cloth had been stretched. The conch was blown to mark the auspicious visit. Many among those assembled became anxious to see the Holy Mother. We also proceeded to meet her when we noticed her approaching solemnly, with her face partly veiled with her cloth. Seeing me, she said, "So you have come, my child!" As there had gathered a big crowd around her, I could not say anything in reply, and so I simply nodded. My Sej-Didi[2] was much grieved at the demise of her son. She said to me, "I have never met the Holy Mother. Please ask her

---

[1]A part of the sacred remains of Sri Ramakrishna were interred at Ramachandra Dutta's garden house at Kankurgachhi on the Janmashtami day (23rd August, 1886). Since then, that day is celebrated ceremonially every year.

[2]It literally means the third elder sister. Here it means the writer's third sister-in-law.

to bless me." But in the midst of the large crowd, I was not getting an opportunity to speak. As soon as I found her a little free, I said, "Mother, this is the wife of my husband's brother." No sooner had I spoken than the Mother said affectionately, "I know everything, my child." I couldn't tell her anything else.

One day my Sej-Didi and I went to see the Holy Mother. After saluting her we went to the shrine room to pay our homage to the Master. On our return the Mother said, "Take your seat." And so we sat down. After chatting for some time, in the course of conversation, I told the Mother, "Mother, you are Mahamaya; you have nicely deluded us by bestowing parents, husbands, and children on us." The Mother immediately replied, "Don't speak like this—that I have kept others deluded! The sufferings of people bound in the world pain me very much. But what can I do, my child? They don't seek liberation."

Another day, along with my Sej-Didi I went to see the Mother. After some talk, the Sej-Didi asked her, "Mother, where is God?" The Mother replied, "Dear, where else is God except very close to His devotees? If worldly people even visit the place used by holy men, the very atmosphere of the place can remove the dross of their mind."

One day Sej-Didi, Na-Didi, Mani, and I had gone to see the Mother. When Sej-Didi requested the Mother to give Na-Didi and Mani initiation, she kept quiet. After a while Sej-Didi raised the topic of initiation again. Mother said somewhat gravely, "They have their family Guru. It will be best to take initiation from him." A little later Sej-Didi left the room. I remained seated. Then Mother said, "Is the giving of initiation a trifling matter? One has to assume the entire responsibility for the disciple's sins."

I asked the Mother one day, "You have instructed me how to perform Japa of the name of the Master; but how shall I do Japa of your name?" The Mother replied, "You can do it with the name 'Radha' or any other name that suits you. If you cannot choose any such name, then repeat simply 'Ma'."

One day after our noon meal Sej-Didi and I went to see the Holy Mother. On arriving we found the doors of her room closed and learned that she was taking rest. After some time the door was opened and we went in and saluted the Mother and sat down. The Mother asked, "When did you arrive, my children?" We replied, "We came a while ago. As you were taking rest, we waited outside your room." After some talk I said, "Mother , people are blessed with various visions, but I have not had any." The Mother said, "These experiences belong to a lower realm." These words raised high hopes in me. It struck me that I would have something higher than these visions. Then I said, "Mother, shall I not attain anything?" She replied, "Of course you will, my child."

One day I asked the Mother about worshipping the Master. She replied, "You are involved in worldly life. You would not be able to manage the formalities of worship."

Whenever the Holy Mother was asked to give some instructions, she would say, "Call upon the Master. He will do everything for you. Uncle Moon is the uncle of all."

One day my mother and I were on our way to visit the Holy Mother. As we were proceeding we came across Sudhira-Didi who was returning after visiting the Holy Mother. When we raised the topic of Sudhira-Didi before the Mother, the latter remarked, "What a fine girl she is! She isn't married. How she stands on her own and moves about in a carriage alone!"

Another day my mother and I went to the Mother's house. After saluting her I said, "We have been trying to come here for a long while but were delayed on account of the carriage." The Mother said, "You come here to see the Deity. Why should you waste money by engaging a carriage? Come on foot."

One noon my mother and I had gone to see the Holy Mother. Golap-Ma became annoyed at our visit at such an inconvenient hour and said, "It is not really visiting Mother, it is only vexing her. Now the cooking is over. If you had intended to come at such an odd time, you should have informed us in the morning. Now, how can the others take their food without sharing it with you?" Golap-Ma said to the Holy Mother, "You are a fine person indeed! You entertain anybody who approaches you and calls you 'Mother.'" The Mother said in reply, "What can I do, Golap ? If someone comes here and calls me 'Mother', I can't neglect him."

Whenever I used to go along with my mother to see the Holy Mother, we would be late in reaching there; for my mother could go only after attending to her household duties. On the way to the Mother's house, I would be afraid lest we should come across Golap-Ma, who was likely to scold us for coming late. One day the Holy Mother told her, "What else can they do? They can come only after attending to all their duties." When we were about to take leave of the Holy Mother after saluting her, she said, "Why do you go without taking your meal?" We replied, "Our meal is ready at home. We shall leave now." The Mother wanted very much to have us for lunch. At last she remarked, "All right, my children, come again; Golap gets annoyed." The Mother gave us a little quantity of consecrated food in a cocoanut shell which we carried home.

One day my mother and I took flowers, Bilva leaves and basil leaves to the Mother's house with a view to offering them at her feet. At the very sight of us Golap-Ma was vexed, and so we stood quiet. After a while I told the Mother, "Mother, we have brought these flowers to offer at your feet." The Mother said, "Yes, you may offer them." I said, "Mother, where shall I get a little water?" The Mother said, "It is there. Take it." I sprinkled a little water on her feet and was about to offer the flowers and other articles, when she said, "Don't offer the basil or Bilva leaves. Offer the flowers only." After offering the flowers at her feet, I saluted her and asked, "What shall I do with these flowers?" The Mother replied, "Take them home."

I sent to the Holy Mother through a devotee a rosary which I had previously used when repeating the name of Lord Hari[1] and also a new rosary of Rudraksha beads. The Mother performed Japa using the new rosary, but as regards the old one she objected, saying, "This is an old rosary." Nevertheless, as a devotee requested her, she performed Japa using that rosary also. When I saw the Mother next, I asked her, "What Mantra shall I use with the Rudraksha beads?" The Mother repeated it to me. When I asked her, "Should I utter this Mantra also while using the rosary meant for repeating the name of Lord Hari?", she replied, "That rosary is only for remembering Lord Hari." It usually takes much time to count the beads of a rosary meant for repeating the name of Lord Hari but it would take a shorter time to count with the Rudraksha beads. And so I again asked the Mother what I should do with the old rosary. The Mother guessed my intention and said, "All right, use the string of Rudraksha beads. Then you can do the Japa quickly."

One night in a dream Sej-Didi had received instructions to present the Mother with a red-bordered Sari. So she purchased

---

[1]A name of Lord Vishnu.

one and went to the Mother's house along with me. After saluting the Mother, Sej-Didi told her about her dream, and placed the Sari at her feet. The Mother smilingly took the Sari in her hand and wrapped it round herself. After a short while she removed it and said, "How can I wear it, my child? People would say, 'The wife of the Paramahamsa (Sri Ramakrishna) is using a red-bordered Sari.' But since you have brought it I shall use it for taking my bath." Learning that the Mother would soon leave for Orissa, we came away that day.

When the Mother returned to Calcutta, Sej-Didi and I went to Baghbazar to see her holy person. The Mother talked much about Puri. Thereafter Sej-Didi enquired if the Mother had used the Sari. The Mother replied, "Yes, my child, I used it. But after a few days of use, I gave it to someone."

On another occasion, Sej-Didi and I went to see the Holy Mother. After conversing on various topics, we asked her, "What will happen to us?" The Mother replied, "Call on the Master." Sej-Didi said, "But we haven't seen the Master; we know only you." Then the Mother said, "Do you want me to drown myself like the Guru of the story? Once a disciple, uttering '*Jai Guru*' with great faith, crossed a river. Observing this, the Guru mused, 'So my name has so much power!' Then uttering 'I, I', the Guru went into the water—and was drowned!"

—

10

(RECORDED BY AN ANONYMOUS DEVOTEE)

The Holy Mother was living in Kothar, Orissa. My second brother, who was staying at Sashi Niketan in Puri, wrote to one of his friends in our native village, "The Holy Mother is now living in Kothar. You can go there to pay your respects." Till that time I had only a vague idea regarding the Holy Mother and Sri Ramakrishna. I had not read any book on them, nor did I know anything in particular about them. None the less I had felt a yearning to see her ever since I had heard about her. After being continuously seized for a few days by such an urge, I left for Kothar. It was almost past midday when I reached the place. But strange to say, my yearning had by now waned, and it was not so strong. The devotees were invited for their midday meal, and I accompanied them. The meal over, we seated ourselves in the parlour along with Revered Krishnalal Maharaj and Kedar Baba (Swami Achalananda), when Ram Babu, the only son of the late Balaram Bose, came and told Krishnalal Maharaj, "The Mother has sent for the boy who has come from Cuttack. He should go to salute her now." Krishnalal Maharaj replied, "I have asked him to see the Holy Mother in the afternoon." Ram Babu said, "No, that won't do; the Mother is waiting for him. Only after the boy meets her will she go for her meal." I accompanied Ram Babu and bowed down to the Mother. I had no talk with her then. The next day I came back home.

On my return home, I experienced a similar yearning once again, and so I went to Kothar. After a few days' stay there I went to the Holy Mother one morning and said, "Mother, I shall leave for home tomorrow morning." The Mother replied, "Well, stay here tomorrow and leave for home the next day." I came out of the room. After a while a monk came to tell me, "The Holy Mother is going to favour you. Keep yourself ready for it after your bath tomorrow morning." I wondered what the favour might be. I could make nothing of it and kept silent. Early next morning I made myself ready after my morning bath, when Radhu-Didi announced, "Who is Vaikuntha Babu ? The Mother has sent for him."

I said, "My name is Vaikuntha. Am I to go to the Mother?" She nodded and I followed her to meet the Holy Mother. On seeing me,the Mother said, "Come, come inside the room." She asked, "Will you take Mantra?" I replied, "If you are pleased, kindly give me. I know nothing about it." The Mother said, "Well, be seated here." Then she asked, "The Mantra of which deity would you like to have?" I replied, "I know nothing about these things." Thereupon the Mother said, "Well this Mantra will suit you."

The Mother initiated me with the Mantra that very day. It was the seventh lunar day of Magh of 1317 (January-February 1911). One day while on a visit I asked her, "Mother, can I have another spiritual guide for my lessons on Yoga?" In reply she said, "You may have guides for learning various other things, but should have no other person for spiritual guidance."

Ram Babu woke me up at about midnight prior to the morning I was to leave Kothar. He handed over a packet of sweets to me and said, "Vaikuntha, the Mother presents you with these sweets. Carry them with you. The Mother advised you not to take food from any wayside shop."

* * *

Another time I went alone to see the Holy Mother. She had then come from Jayrambati to Kamarpukur for a few days. This was my first visit to Kamarpukur. The revered Ramlal-Dada and Lakshmi-Didi were staying there too. On the first day Ramlal-Dada and I were seated on the verandah for dinner. The Mother herself was serving us food. While serving, she told me several times, "Vaikuntha, take everything, don't leave anything on the leaf." Everytime she served, she gave me more and more food. Ramlal-Dada too pressed,me saying, "Eat more; don't be shy." By that time I had already eaten so much that I was unable to take anything more. But I hesitated to say so. Now on hearing **Ramlal-Dada's words,** the Mother intervened saying, "Look here, he is a whimsical boy. He has taken enough. Please do not insist on his taking more." She said to me, "Vaikuntha, remove the leaf-plate and glass from here. One should not leave them behind in his Master's[1] house."

---

[1]Here the Mother is referring to Sri Ramakrishna. Although she was herself the Guru of the devotees, she normally did not

On the second day, as I went to salute her, she asked, "When will you be returning home?" I replied, "Mother, I have not seen Belur Math yet. I want to visit the Belur Math and then go home from there." The Mother said, "You need not go to the Math now. You leave for home today." I said, "Mother, I have come here from so distant a place. I do not intend to go back home without visiting the Belur Math."

The Mother, now firmly, said, "No, you go home. You must not disobey your Guru." After this I made no further protests. But I thought that I would contrive to visit the Math after leaving this place, thinking that the Mother would not come to know of it. About this time, two devotees, a man and a woman, had come from Allahabad. The Mother gave them spirial initiation that very day. The Mother sent for me and said, "You please go along with them." However, I was told that my accompanying them would cause them inconvenience, and so I dropped the idea. The Mother had come to the main entrance to see them off. A little earlier I had put my money bag in a niche in the parlour. Noticing it, the Mother had kept it in the living room. Subsequently she enquired of me through Lakshmi-Didi, "Where has Vaikuntha kept his money bag?" I looked for the bag in the parlour but could not find it. Lakshmi-Didi reported everything to the Mother. The Mother called me and said, "How can you afford to be so careless ? He who does not have even this much alertness, how will he look after his household? Your money bag is with me. Well, why did you not go with that party?" When I explained, she was evidently displeased with them. I assured the Mother, saying, "Why are you so anxious on that account? I shall fix up a person to accompany me and leave tomorrow." On hearing this, the Mother moved towards her room.

That afternoon she called me into the inner courtyard. She said, "Read out these letters; let me hear what news they are bringing." I read them out. I still remember the contents of

---

allow them to remove the leavings after their meal. She used to do it herself or get it done by servants or attendants. Though a spiritual Master, she was above all the Mother. Lest the wind should blow away the used dining leaves, the devotees would sometimes remove them themselves.

one of them. The letter was from Baghbazar, Calcutta. It said that the ailing Sashi Maharaj wanted to see the Holy Mother once and that he promised to follow the course of treatment that the Mother might suggest for him. On hearing the contents of the letter, the Mother remarked, "What more can I say about medical treatment? Sarat, Rakhal, and Baburam are there. Let them consult among themselves and take the best available decision. If I decide to go to that house, the patient will have to be removed from there.[1] Will that be good for him? Should such an acutely suffering patient be shifted? No, I shall not go. If something adverse happens to Sashi, shall I be able to stay there? You please write him a letter explaining why I do not intend to go now."

The next day after the noon meal I went inside the house to take leave of the Holy Mother. I found her sitting on the verandah and preparing betel leaves. She asked me, " Have you made salutations at the temple of Raghuvira ?" I said, "No, Mother."

Mother: Whoever visits this holy place should make some contribution there. Offer some money when you make obeisance to Raghuvira. If you do not have money, take some from me.

Disciple: No, Mother, I have money.

I went to the temple of Raghuvira to make my obeisance. On my return as I saluted the Holy Mother, she suddenly exclaimed, "Vaikuntha, take my name." But the very next moment, she added, "Call on the Master. Calling on the Master will alone serve everything." Lakshmi-Didi who was standing nearby intervened, saying, "Mother, what is this? This is quite improper. What will your children do if you confuse them in this way?"

Mother: Well, what have I done?

Lakshmi-Didi: Mother, you said a moment earlier ' Call on me ', and now you are saying ' Call on the Master '.

Mother: Everything is achieved when one calls on the Master.

Lakshmi-Didi came forward and said, "Mother, it is not proper for you to bewilder your children." Then she emphatically added, "Look, Vaikuntha, today for the first time I have heard the Mother saying, 'Call on me.' You must not miss this point. Who else is the Mother? You call on the Mother alone. Very fortunate

---

[1]Swami Ramakrishnananda was suffering from tuberculosis. As Mother used to move with a number of devotees and family members, the party needed spacious accommodation.

are you to be given the advice by the Mother herself. You call on none but the Mother." Turning towards the Mother, she said, "Well, Mother, this is explained, I believe." The Mother, through her silence, lent her support indirectly to the words of Lakshmi-Didi.

When I was taking leave of her, the Mother said once again, "Go straight home from here. It would not be wise for you to go to the Math or elsewhere now. Go home and look after your parents. Now you should serve your father." Then she gave me four betel leaves and bade me farewell. I gave up my previous plan, following the Mother's instruction, and returned home via Koalpara. When I had left home for Jayrambati, I had seen my father hale and hearty. Now on coming back home I found him seriously ill; and, in fact, my father passed away six or seven days after my arrival.

On a later occasion, while going to Kamarpukur, I brought with me a letter addressed to the Mother, from one of my fellow disciples. When I was about to hand over the letter to the Mother, she asked me to read it out. It contained these two questions: (1) "I am going to take up such and such an employment. Will I get entangled in Maya if I join there?" On hearing this, the Mother remarked, "Why should he get entangled in Maya if he simply takes service?" (2) To the question as to whether marriage will bring him good, the Mother did not give any definite reply. On the other hand, the Mother asked me, "My son, are you married?"

Disciple : No, Mother, I have not married.

Mother: Very well, do not marry. Marriage invites many complications.

Once during my stay at Kamarpukur I asked the Mother: "What is the harm in taking fish and meat ?"

The Mother replied, "This is the land of fish ; you can take fish."

It was during one of these days that I once requested her to give me a print of her feet. The Mother replied, "This cannot be done here now. Everybody here does not look upon me in the way you do. Some members of Laha Babu's family frequently visit this place. If I give you my footprint, the red paint will linger on my feet and I shall have to hide myself from them."

Another time I had gone to Jayrambati in the company of a few fellow disciples from my native district. On arriving there it occured to me several times, "I have come from such a distant place. I have not achieved anything worth mentioning till now. I would consider myself blessed if I could serve the Holy Mother."

One day my fellow disciples went to Kamarpukur while I stayed back. In the afternoon I went to see the Mother. She was sitting on the porch of the new house in front of the kitchen store. When the Mother saw me, she said, "My child, bring the pitcher of wheat flour from the store." I did as directed. She took out some quantity of flour, mixed it with water, and asked me to knead the dough. I finished the work and shortly after came back to the parlour. I went to her again in the evening when she was resting on the portico in front of her living room. There I sat quietly for sometime. After a while the Mother said, "Vaikuntha, my son, please stroke my legs a little." While I was doing so, the Mother said, "Why have my sons not returned from Kamarpukur yet? Have they taken the wrong road?" Saying this, she became quite anxious and sent for Brahmachari Jnan. When Jnan came, she said, "Jnan, see why they are so late in returning from Kamarpukur." Brahmachari Jnan walked quite some distance to trace their whereabouts and finally met them. They had indeed taken a wrong path! Had Brahmachari Jnan not gone to look for them, they would have taken much longer to reach Jayrambati.

At night we slept on the portico of the Mother's main house. In the early hours, at about 4 o' clock, we woke up. One of us said, "Ah, if only we could see Mother at this auspicious juncture of night and day!" and then began singing, "O gracious Mother, get up and open the door," etc. As soon as the song was over, we were surprised to see the Mother opening the door and standing in front of it. At this sudden and unexpected appearance of the Mother we were extremely happy. All of us saluted her in turn. Then she quietly went inside and locked the door.

On another occasion, during the worship of Vasanti[1], a few of us went to Jayrambati. Finding white lotuses in a pond on our way, we collected some of them. As we were preparing ourselves to offer those white lotuses at the feet of the Holy Mother, she sent word, saying, " White flowers cannot be used for the worship of

---

[1]Goddess Durga is worshipped as Vasanti, the goddess of Spring, in January every year.

the Goddess." On hearing this we procured some red lotuses and joyously offered them at her feet.

One day I heard her say to someone in the course of a conversation, "Don't tease me much, for if I admonish you, losing my temper, no one can give you protection."

On that occasion I asked her, "Mother, the Government is putting young men behind bars these days. What do you think will be its outcome?" "Yes, this is very improper," the Mother replied. "However, a solution will soon be found. You will not have to wait for long. Certainly it will bring good ultimately."

One day I told her, "Mother, kindly do something for me." To this she replied, "There are Sarat, Rakhal, and others. Why do you worry?" Then I said, "Mother, I greatly desire to live in the Math for some days." But Mother did not give her consent. She said, "You need not go to the Math now. Live in your own home."

This time the Holy Mother kindly initiated Kshirode Mukhopadhyaya of our native village. I learnt from Kshirode Babu that the Mother said at the time of his spiritual initiation: "All your sins committed in this life as well as in earlier ones are gone."

One day I made obeisance to the Holy Mother at her residence in Baghbazar, Calcutta. I was standing by her side, when she asked, "Have you saluted Master Mahasaya?' "No, Mother, I said, "I do not know him."

She then advised me: "Go downstairs. You will find him there. He is a noble soul. Please go and salute him." She deputed Golap-Ma to escort me and introduce me to Master Mahasaya. I went below, bowed to him, and came back upstairs. Just then two persons were going downstairs after saluting the Holy Mother, who was sitting on her cot in the shrine room. I heard her whisper, "The indiscriminate touch of people has caused me stinging pain!"

Once I had a quarrel with my brother regarding some worldly matters. I wanted to inform the Holy Mother of my intention of staying somewhere other than my own house, and I also wanted her permission to do so. After my salutation I was standing nearby. Addressing Golap-Ma, the Mother said, "O Golap, have you heard that Vaikuntha has come here to complain about his brother's slapping him on the cheek? Do not householders sometimes kick up a row? But then why should one go too far?" Now turning to me, she said, "Go home, my son. It is quite common to have occasional hitches in family life."

A fellow disciple of mine, who had forgotten his *gāyatri*[1] Mantra, asked me to teach it to him. I wrote to the Mother in a letter, "Should one disclose a Mantra to someone else?" The Mother was then on a pilgrimage to the South and was staying in Madras. She wrote in reply, "A Mantra should not be disclosed to anyone. You can, however, tell it to a fellow disciple. There is no harm in that."

One day, being depressed, I went to see the Holy Mother at the Udbodhan house in Baghbazar. I bowed to her and said, "Mother, I am here to tell you something."

Mother: What's that? Come on, tell me.

Disciple: When will you bestow your grace on this unfortunate child of yours?

Mother: Child, remember the Master. He will certainly bless you. Keep only holy company and do your spiritual practices. Everything will be achieved if the Master is remembered.

Disciple: I have tried, Mother, but nothing has happened. As I have not seen the Master, how can I remember him? I have received your blessings. Now that you are saying thus, you yourself kindly tell the Master about this unfortunate child of yours.

Mother: How can you achieve the goal without practising Japa and meditation? One must practise these disciplines.

Disciple: I don't feel like doing Japa, etc. any more; for nothing whatsoever is of any avail. Desire, anger, delusion—these still hold sway over my mind exactly as they did before. The impurities of my mind have not decreased yet.

Mother: Child, the repetition of the name of God will gradually remove impurities. How can you expect results without such disciplines? Don't be foolish and neglect them. Whenever you find time, repeat the holy name of God. And pray to the Master.

Disciple: No, Mother, I do not have that capacity. Whenever I try to repeat the name, I find my mind agitated. Either you make my mind concentrated on God so that no evil thought assails me, or you take back the holy name! I do not want to be a cause

[1]*Gāyatri* is a sacred Mantra of the Vedas that has become the holiest common prayer of the Hindus.

of suffering to you; for I have heard that a spiritual preceptor suffers if his disciples do not repeat the sacred name.

Mother: Well, what is this? My worries about you have made me restless. The Master has blessed you already.

These words brought tears to the Mother's eyes. With great feeling she said, "Well, you will not have to repeat the Mantra any more." This implied that she herself would do whatever was necessary on my behalf. But I failed to grasp the import of her words, and fear and apprehension gripped me. Thinking that my connections with the Mother were going to be snapped, I passionately said, "Mother, are you snatching away everything that I possessed? What shall I do now? Well, Mother, am I now doomed to annihilation?"

On hearing these words she said emphatically, "What! You being my child, can you be doomed? Those who have come here, those who are my children, have already achieved liberation. Even God can do no harm to my children!"

Disciple: Well, Mother, what should I do now?

Mother: Take refuge in me and keep quiet. And always remember that there is behind all of you one who in time will lead you to the abode of eternity.

Disciple: Mother, so long as I am here, I feel happy. No worldly thought disturbs me. But as soon as I return home various bad thoughts haunt me. I again get mixed up with unholy companions and commit evil deeds. However hard I try, I cannot get rid of bad thoughts.

Mother: All this is owing to the impressions gathered in your previous births. Can anyone forcibly get rid of them in a trice? Live in holy company. Try to be pure. And everything will be achieved gradually. Pray to the Master. I am with you. Know that you have already achieved liberation in this very birth. Why do you fear? In time he will do everything for you.

11

(RECORDED BY SRISCHANDRA GHATAK)

It was the Bengali month of Jaistha (May-June) of 1910. A party of us started from Shillong with the object of paying our respects to the Holy Mother at Jayrambati. All of us had seen the Mother's photo taken in her earlier days. While on the way, one of us saw the Holy Mother in a dream, just as she looked at the time. Later, on seeing her at Jayrambati, the striking resemblance of the dream image to the Mother herself brought us unbounded joy and wonder. One of us had already received spiritual initiation from a certain monk. On being told of this, the Holy Mother remarked, "The Mantra was given by a monk—you will be illumined." Except for him, the rest of us received the great Mantra from the Holy Mother this time. Soon after the initiation, we asked for her permission to visit Kamarpukur. She said, "How is that possible? Today, my children, I should feed you sumptuously."

We have read in the Gita, "What is action and what is inaction? Even the wise are puzzled over this question. Therefore, I shall tell you what action is. When you know that, you will be free from all impurity. You must learn what kind of work is to be done, what kind is to be avoided, and how one could reach a state of calm detachment in work. The real nature of action is hard to understand." So I wondered what else I would have to do for gaining emancipation from the worldly ties, after I had received the Mother's grace. I asked her. "Mother, what else have I to do?" She replied, "You have nothing more to do."

Disciple: Shall I have to do nothing else?

Mother: Nothing, dear.

Disciple: Nothing else, really?

Mother: No, nothing else.

Thus assured by the very same reply three times, I was convinced that she, who had bestowed her grace on me, had also taken upon herself the responsibility of releasing me from the cycle of birth and death.

I had studied the palm of Aunt Bhanu and said to her, "Auntie, you will live for another twenty-five years." Aunt Bhanu went to the Mother and said, "Mother, your son knows palmistry." The

Mother immediately called me. When I went to her, she said, "Dear, can you read the lines on my palm? Please tell me if I shall be cured of the gout in my legs?" I was struck dumb by her question, for I knew nothing of palmistry. I had simply made an intelligent guess in Aunt Bhanu's case. I had heard that the Holy Mother's acceptance of the sins of her disciples was responsible for the pain in her legs. I therefore said, "Since we are responsible for this suffering, can you really be free from this as long as we are with you?"

On hearing this, the Mother was deeply pained. Sinking to the floor, she murmured, "O Mother, what does he say?"

Seeing her so perplexed, I said, "Well, Mother, do you really want to be free from this suffering?"

Mother: Yes, of course.

Disciple: Then you will be cured.

Now, this made her glad. A little later the Mother remarked, "Do you see what kind of devotion he has! He feels that everything depends on my will."

I went to bid the Mother farewell on the day I was to leave for home. I told her, "Mother, I cannot correctly keep count while I tell my beads. When my fingers move, my lips do not; and when my fingers and lips move, my mind fails to get fixed." Mother replied, "In future see that your tongue and fingers do not move. Perform Japa mentally."

While taking leave, I saluted her and said, "Mother, I am going now." Immediately the Mother interjected, saying, "Dear, please say 'I am coming'; you should not say 'I am going.'" I corrected myself, and the Mother glanced at me with satisfaction.

Following the Durga Puja of 1912, the Holy Mother stayed for some time at Banaras. We too went to Banaras at the time of the Mother's birthday in the month of December. On her birthday we saluted her at Lakshminivas in the morning. We worshipped her with garlands of flowers. The Mother gave each of us a garland which had been offered to her by devotees. I partook also of sweets offered to the Holy Mother, and then went to the Advaita Ashrama where Homa was being performed after the worship. All those present were offering oblations. We too moved forward to offer our oblations, when some of those present protested, saying, "You have already taken food. Don't offer any oblation." As a result, everyone except me offered oblations. Just before this the Holy Mother had come to the Advaita Ashrama, and had noticed all that took place. Addressing the women devotees, the Mother said, "What they have received is my Prasada only. When did they take their food? They should offer oblations, of course." All this I heard from the women devotees later.

* * *

On the eighth day of the fortnight in the month of Magha (January, 1913), I brought my wife and widowed sister to the Holy Mother in expectation of her benign grace. The Mother was kind enough to grant both of them spiritual initiation. My wife said to the Holy Mother, "Mother, I feel like performing Siva Puja." The Mother replied, "You are too young; you will not be able to do it correctly. Later, at the proper time, you will learn how to worship Siva. Now you should rather devote time to the service of your elders at home." The Mother praised my sister, saying, "Her mind is quite pure." We had taken with us some mangoes. Mangoes were quite costly in those days. When the Mother saw the heap of mangoes, she observed, "Why have you purchased mangoes at such a high price? Besides, these mangoes are not ready for eating yet—they taste sour."

* * *

During the Janmashtami holidays of 1913, a number of us, fellow disciples, went to Jayrambati. It was already dusk when we reached the Math at Koalpara. As our holiday was short, we did not halt at the Math for the night, but proceeded towards Jayrambati. On the way we were caught in a heavy shower of rain. The night too was pitch-dark. The village paths were muddy and inundated at places. We braved all these hardships and finally reached Jayrambati. But as the night was quite advanced, the Holy Mother was not informed of our arrival. The next morning we saluted the Mother and told her of our ordeals. On hearing about them she said, "Oh dear, the Master must have protected you. How many snakes you must have trampled upon while traversing the muddy road in the dark! I am much pained to hear of your toils. It is not good to go about recklessly."

We said, "Mother, we were pining to see you, and the period of our leave is short. That's why we were in a hurry."

Mother: It is natural for you to have such yearning, but it causes me anxiety.

Srimati Sudhira, the former Superintendent of the Nivedita Girls' School, was then staying at Jayrambati. At noon that day the Mother sent for me and said, "Look, Sudhira will travel along with you up to Vishnupur. Please move cautiously. The bullock cart carrying her should be placed in between those of your party. You are all my own, my children."

Disciple: Certainly we shall escort her. And we shall strictly follow your instruction.

While we were taking our night meal, the Mother sat nearby and began to chat. Someone raised the topic of initiation of a boy who was about seven years old. The Mother said, "How can he have initiation? He is still quite young. He has perhaps not even learned how to bathe or wash himself! The boy is a devotee; let him live long. Let him be a servant of the Lord's devotees."

As the conversation proceeded, I asked her, "Mother, we take food from anybody and everybody—will this be spiritually harmful to us?"

Mother: The Master emphatically objected to one's partaking of food of the *śrāddha* ceremony[1]; for it affects the devotion of the person. Although in all such ceremonies Narayana, the Lord of Yajna is worshipped, he prohibited the taking of the food offered at a *śrāddha* ceremony.

Disciple: Then what should we do in the case of *śrāddha* ceremonies of our near relations?

Mother: Well, how can you avoid it in the case of your near relations? You can't.

The next day I went to see her at about 2 p.m. The Mother was seated on the floor in an absent-minded mood. A few days earlier a devastating flood from the Damodar river had caused havoc. I told her all that I had learnt from newspapers and hearsay. She listened patiently and then said in a voice full of pathos, "My son, do good to the world." Hearing these words from her lips, I mentally prayed to her to grant me the opportunity of serving the Lord manifested as the universe. As I saluted her before coming out of the house, I heard her murmur, "Only money! money! money!" Hearing these words, I got alarmed. I presumed that Mother was perhaps commenting on my excessive attachment to money.

---

[1]The annual death anniversary rites in the name of ancestors.

Immediately she looked at me and observed, "No, child, money too is a necessity. Look here, Kali[1] runs after money only."

On 24th December, 1915, I went with my family to see the Mother at the Udbodhan house. My wife was carrying in her hand some sweets. Revered Golap-Ma was putting them aside with the idea of offering them to the Master some other day, when the Mother objected, saying, "Well, don't do that. Please offer now to the Master whatever my daughter-in-law has brought. This will bring good to her." The next morning my wife went to see the Mother. On returning home in the evening she told me, "Today the Mother showered her grace so abundantly on me that its memory will give me joy forever. At about nine or ten in the morning the Mother had puffed rice and fried peas purchased for three Paise. Placing them on her apron and taking her seat on the floor, she began to leisurely partake of the snack. She now and then offered me a handful, saying, "Dear, take it please." Compared to various delicacies I had previously taken, the joy in eating this puffed rice was something unique. At noon the Holy Mother asked me to massage her feet. She also asked me to air her bedding in the sun. She thereby greatly favoured me by accepting my humble services. Besides, I had the following conversation with her.

Disciple: Mother, can I offer cooked food to the Master?

Mother: Yes, you can offer cooked food. The Master was fond of *Sukta* (a quasi-bitter preparation).

Disciple: Can I offer him preparations of fish?

Mother: Yes, you can. While offering them, you have to utter the prescribed Mantras.

Then the Mother asked, "Does my son (thereby meaning the lady's husband) take fish?"

Disciple: Yes, he does.

Mother: Yes, he should take as much as he likes.

In the course of conversation I remarked, "Mother, poverty is stalking the whole country as an offshoot of the World War. How much the people are suffering! Food and clothings have become very costly!"

Mother: In spite of these sufferings, people do not become sensible.

Disciple: Mother, will this War bring us good?

---

[1]Kali or Kalikumar was the third brother of the Holy Mother.

Mother: When the Lord descends, such thing happens. How many more will come to pass. . . .

When I went to take leave of her in the afternoon, the Mother recalled our trip to Jayrambati on the rainy night of Janmashtami, and rebuked me, saying, "To go about without any thought of possible risks is no good."

Disciple: I shall never do so again.

The Mother apparently understood me as saying that I intended not to go to Jayrambati henceforth. So she immediately rejoined. "Certainly you should come here, my son; but even a thorn in your foot affects me as an arrow in the chest!" Glancing at my wife, she said, "Daughter, you keep a watch on him; he should not move about in that way."

* * *

During the Puja vacation of 1917 I went with Jatin, one of my fellow disciples, to the Udbodhan house to pay our respects to the Holy Mother. We had taken two Saris for her. We placed the Saris at her holy feet and bowed down. She blessed us, saying, "Dear, you are not well off; why do you present cloths in this way?" Both of us felt a little hurt and said, "Mother, your well-to-do disciples present you with costly cloths. Now, your not-so-well-off disciples have brought these coarse ones. Kindly accept them and fulfil their hearts' desire."

Gladdened at heart, the Holy Mother now said, "My child, this is silk to me, this is my everything! These mean so much to me!" With these words, she endearingly took the two Saris in her hands. At that time the Mother was suffering from acute tooth ache. Referring to it she said, "My son, the Master used to say, 'He who never had a tooth ache cannot appreciate its intensity.' "

In the year 1917, I wrote to her a letter praying for her blessings for the successful accomplishment of Sri Ramakrishna's birthday celebrations at Ranchi. The Mother replied, "It is difficult to express in writing how delighted I was to receive your letter. You are all the children of the Master. In all such noble endeavours he himself will stand by you. Why do you worry on that account?"

In the month of Jaistha, 1919, I asked the Mother at Jayrambati "Mother, does the Master listen to the prayers mentally offered to him? And should we direct our prayers to him instead of telling you?"

In reply the Mother said in an agitated voice, "If the Master truly exists he definitely listens to all prayers."

While bowing down at her feet at the time of leaving Jayrambati, I told her, " Mother, if I do not find a bullock cart in the daytime, I shall walk on foot from Kotulpur to Vishnupur."

Mother: My son, why should you tax your body so much? Why should you exhaust yourself in this way ? You will certainly find a cart.

The Mother's prophecy proved true. I got a cart. This was my last meeting with the Mother in a physical sense.

12

(RECORDED BY SWAMI RITANANDA)

On that day the Mother was very busy with the Jagaddhatri[1] Puja at her village home in Jayrambati. Now and then she would say, "How will the Mother's worship be performed?" Today she was performing the daily worship of the Master very early. A large quantity of fruits, sweets, etc., was offered. At the time of offering them, she said to the Master, "Look, the Divine Mother's worship will be held today. Please take your food quickly, for I shall have to go to the place of worship." Then she uttered something inaudible. It seemed to me as if she was talking with a living person. When the Puja was over, she went to the place where Jagaddhatri was being worshipped and sat through the entire Puja, all the time looking intently at the image with adoring eyes.

One day I did the marketing at Koalpara. Then I collected flowers for the Mother to use in worshipping the Master, and went to Jayrambati. When I arrived there the Mother said, "I was thinking you would come just now and I would then go for bathing." She took the articles and then gave me puffed rice to eat. Then wearing a bathing cloth, the Mother began to rub her body with oil, all the while speaking about us, the inmates of the Koalpara monastery. All on a sudden she said, "I am your mother. Why should you feel embarrassed?" Then she finished her bath and went to perform the worship of the Master.

One day I thought I would ask the Mother how I should do my spiritual practices. In the afternoon she was doing Japa with her rosary while sitting on the verandah. But when I approached her, I forgot all that I wanted to ask. I didn't feel like asking her any question. Simply saying, "Mother, kindly take my responsibility," I broke into tears. Then the Mother comforted me, saying, "Don't weep. I have already taken up your responsibility long ago. And the Master too has taken up your responsibility long ago. Why do you worry?"

---

[1] An aspect of the Divine Mother. In this form She is represented as riding a lion while subduing a demon in the form of an elephant.

One day I dreamt that the Mother was telling me, "Take the vow of Brahmacharya." When I narrated it to revered Hari Maharaj (Swami Turiyananda), he said, "Go and tell this to the Mother." Some days later I told about this to the Mother at Koalpara. On hearing me, she smiled and said, "All right, come to see me with a new cloth tomorrow when I perform the worship. Let the visit be private." The next day I went to the Mother and found that she had finished the worship and was sitting on the verandah rubbing her teeth with *gul*.[1] No sooner had she seen me than she lolled out her tongue and said, "See, the worship is finished; I simply forgot. Nevertheless, I am coming after washing my mouth. Go and be seated in the shrine room." Entering the shrine room, the Mother said, "Shut the door. They (women members of the family) are there." Then she told me, "Take off your shirt." Taking water from the copper Puja vessel, the Mother sprinkled it over my body. Then with her hand she touched my navel, chest, and head, and uttered something mysterious. Taking the new cloth, she said, "Just see, the Master is here. Say : 'I am giving Thee my entire responsibility today.'" Next she gave me the cloth, saying, "Today I have given Sannyasa to your very soul." So elated had I become at that time that I even forgot to salute the Mother. This mood of mine persisted for a few days.

The Mother was living at Koalpara along with Radhu. Radhu, who was almost insane, was expecting a baby. The Mother was all the time worried as to how Radhu would come out safe through this ordeal, and with this end in view she was vowing offerings to various Deities and anxiously praying to them.

During these days the Mother told me once, "Look, it seems that the *Hanuman-charit* can predict the good or bad future of a person. Well, why don't you find out if it can forecast the fate of Radhu." I procured a copy of the book, and glancing through it, found a chequered table. One has to put his finger on any of the squares. Mother placed her finger on one square, and I read out the results for the same. It said that Radhu has a good future. Very happy at this, the Mother said, "Then Radhu will certainly be all right. Since it is his (Hanuman's) word, she will definitely come round."

---

[1] Remains of tobacco-cake after it has been smoked.

At one time the head of the Koalpara monastery had some difference of opinion with his colleagues. The Mother was then staying at Jayrambati. We often purchased provisions for her in Koalpara and carried them to Jayrambati. The Mother used to ask me in detail about the members of the monastery. She was well posted about everything that happened there. One day when her niece asked me about this disagreement, the Mother said to her, "Why are you inquisitive about it ?" After she left, the Mother said, "You see, you have to adjust yourself to all conditions. The Master used to say *sha, sha, sha*[1]—exercise patience in every thing. The Master is looking after everything."

Later when the Mother was staying at Koalpara, the Head of the monastery told her, "Mother, the monastic workers do not want to stay here. Please tell them that they will not get protection in any other monastery and that everyone of them will have to perform his own work. They want to go elsewhere. If you order them, they won't go anywhere else." No sooner did Mother hear this than she said with some annoyance, "How dare you ask me to speak to them that way? Do you mean to say I should tell them that they won't get shelter anywhere else? They are my children and they have taken shelter in the Master. Wherever they go, the Master will look after them. And you want me to say that they will not find shelter at any other place! I can never utter this." The Mother was then speaking in a loud voice. Everyone became frightened. At once the Head of the monastery fell at her feet and said, weeping, "Mother, please forgive me and protect me." The Mother immediately became quite calm.

One day a devotee from East Bengal came to receive initiation from the Holy Mother, who was staying at Koalpara. When the Mother was informed of this, she said, "No, he won't have initiation." On hearing this the devotee became despondent. The next day without telling anyone, he sat in the sun, outside the house where the Mother was staying, and began weeping. Learning of this situation the Mother said, "Why is he crying in this way? Ask him to go away." I went towards him to convey the Mother's command but seeing his

[1] Three consonants (ś, ṣ, s) of the Bengali alphabet, having similar sounds. In this context they stand for the Bengali word *sahya*, 'forbearance'. Thus the expression means 'forbear, forbear, forbear'.

pitiable condition, I could not speak out. In the meantime I noticed that the Mother had partly opened the main door and glanced at the devotee. As I entered the house, the Mother said to me, "Tell him he will have initiation tomorrow. " On hearing this, the devotee began to weep even more bitterly. He had his initiation the next day.

One educated devotee, Krishnaprasanna by name, stayed at the Koalpara monastery for some days. One day the Mother told us, "Look, in course of time many devotees will come from abroad. You should learn English from Krishnaprasanna." Accordingly we began to take lessons. But it was discontinued some days later when Krishnaprasanna left.

A certain woman devotee had with her a footprint of the Holy Mother, which was found missing one day. It led to a quarrel among the women. The Mother, who was staying at Koalpara then, laughed at this and said, "Why do you make so much fuss over this? I am here. Take as many footprints as you like!" Afterwards she brought some pieces of cloth and liquid lac-dye and gave a good number of her footprints. This settled the quarrel too!

One day at the residence of uncle Prasanna, the Mother said in the course of a conversation, "Before Radhu was born, she used to move about in front of me in the form of a shadow. Pointing to it, the Master said, 'Take her as a support to live.' Do you see how much attached I am to Radhu? How nicely Gourdasi has brought up her adopted daughter, and I have created a monkey!"

At the Koalpara monastery in those days, we used to take parboiled rice. Scarcity of money prevented us from getting enough vegetables. Such poor food resulted in the deterioration of the health of all the members of the monastery. Learning of this, the Mother said, "Why don't you eat fish? What's the good of spoiling your health by not eating fish ? I am telling you, there is no harm in it. Take fish." Afterwards the Mother repeatedly told this to the Head of the monastery and persuaded him to introduce fish in the diet of the monastery.

One day at Jayrambati a certain Swami approached the Mother with a paper, a pen and an inkpot, and said,"Mother,we are getting very little milk from our only cow; it is not sufficient to meet our needs. So I am thinking of buying another cow. If you kindly permit, I shall write to some devotees for money" The

Mother replied, "Very well, write. You are taking me for an instrument; aren't you? You think that if you write to devotees, money will be forthcoming, don't you?"

After he left, the Mother smilingly said, "See, what desire he cherishes! Once when Baburam was suffering from stomach trouble, I gave him sugar-candy syrup to drink. The Master noticed it and said one day, "What did you give Baburam to drink?" I replied, "Sugar-candy syrup." On hearing this he remarked, "They will have to be (all-renouncing) monks. What ill-habits are you helping them to form?" "

One day I asked the Mother, "How shall I perform spiritual practices?" She replied, "You will attain everything by calling upon the Master." As I was not satisfied with this, I asked her once again. Annoyed, the Mother said emphatically, "I don't know anything else. You will get whatever you ask him for."

A certain devotee had gone to the Mother for initiation. She asked him, "What is the Mantra of your family?" The devotee replied, " I don't know." The Mother remained quiet for a while, and then saying, "This is the Mantra of your family", she initiated him. Subsequent enquiry revealed that the Mother was correct.

One day at Koalpara a mentally deranged man began to play the lunatic in front of the Mother's house. Seeing his eccentric behaviour, the Mother remarked, "Just see, it is but a congregation of mad persons! As we have come, all crazy people are assembling here. Look, Radhu is insane, her mother is insane — such persons constitute my family." Saying this, she kept silent for a while. Then she uttered a verse, "The goddess Chandi will come to my home; I shall listen to the holy *Chandi*; there will assemble many *dandi sannyasins*,[1] Yogis and holy men with matted hair."

---

[1] *Sannyasins* who always carry a staff with them.

13

(RECORDED BY SMT. SUSHEELA MAZUMDAR)

From Bhowanipur, I went in the company of my husband and son to the Udbodhan House to pay our respects to the Holy Mother. I saw the Mother standing in front of the doorsill of the middle room on the first floor and talking with someone. As I saluted her, she asked, "Where do you come from, my daughter?" She behaved as if we had been acquainted with her for a long time. I replied, "Our home is in Dacca." Before this conversation could end, Golap-Ma summoned the Mother, saying that Ram Babu and Nitai Babu had come to see her. In the meantime, Kapil Maharaj told me, "Please wait a little. Balaram Babu's son and nephew have come. After they have finished talking with the Mother, you can speak to her." Nitai Babu came and stood in front of the Mother. After talking with him, the Mother gave me two Rasagollas and went to the adjoining shrine room to meet Ram Babu.

I remained waiting with two Rasagollas in my hand. After the Mother had spoken with Ram Babu, she called me to the shrine room and asked, "Why have you not eaten them? It is consecrated food. Please take them." At that moment a certain woman devotee entered and remarked, "The Mother fed those present with all the sweets. Now what shall we eat?" Abashed as I was at her remarks—for those two Rasagollas were still in my hand—I said, "You please take these two Rasagollas." She replied, "No, daughter, I didn't mean you; why should I take yours?" Then the Mother said to her, "O! Please don't say such things. It will hurt the devotees. As there are many persons, the Prasada was not sufficient, even though only two sweets were given to each. Ah, they have come from a very remote corner of the country with much difficulty." Then, as the Mother repeatedly requested me, I ate the sweets. The Mother herself brought water for me. Later she said, "The syrup from the sweets has made the floor dirty. Please wipe it with a wet cloth and wash your hands." After I had completed this task, the Mother sat down on the cot and began to enquire about me. Just as I was saying, "I have one son," Ni —— came there to salute the Mother. I said, "Mother, he is my son." Ni —— left after making Pranam to the Mother. Then she asked, "Have you not yet arranged for his marriage?"

Disciple: No, he hasn't married.

Mother: He is your only son. Why haven't you got him married?

Disciple: He doesn't want to marry.

Mother: Ah, these days this has become a fashion with young men! Why, can't a married man lead a virtuous life? It is through the mind that one achieves everything. Didn't the Master marry me? Has your son received initiation?

Disciple: Yes, he has been blessed by you.

Mother: Yes! Why should he not marry then? All right, I shall tell him. Perhaps he doesn't want to face hardship. He who holds on to the Lord, even when afflicted by sufferings, will certainly attain to Him. But tell me, what is your wish?

Disciple: Mother, I don't know what will be good for him. You know what is good and bad for him. Therefore it will be as you say. I don't have any other opinion.

Mother: You see, only those who belong to a high spiritual category can become monks and liberate themselves from all kinds of fetters. Some, again, are born just to enjoy the world. I say, it is good to finish in entirety enjoyments and sufferings. But it was different in the case of the companions of the Master.

Disciple: Mother, he is but your child. His good and bad depend on you entirely. Do whatever you wish to do.

Mother: I say, let him marry. Let all his enjoyments and sufferings pass off completely. Otherwise, it is difficult to foretell what kind of experience will come to him. Know it for certain, however, that since the Master has caught hold of him, he will never fall. You wait quietly with a placid mind. I have initiated him with a Mantra given by the Master. Can ill fortune ever befall him?

Then she said, "Would you take Prasada here?" As I replied in the affirmative, the Mother went out to tell the store-keeper and returned.

Mother: From whom have you taken initiation? Who told you about the Master?

Disciple: When we went to meet Nag Mahasaya at Deobhog, we heard from him the glories of Sri Ramakrishna. Observing Nag Mahasaya's lofty mental condition, I always felt a strong desire to see Sri Ramakrishna and you. I was not fortunate enough to see Sri Ramakrishna, but through your grace I have seen your holy feet and thereby my desire to see Sri Ramakrishna also has been fulfilled. I have not had initiation directly yet.

Mother: Have you received it in a dream?

Disciple: Yes, Mother. I saw you in a dream and received initiation from you.

Mother: Well, do you remember the Mantra? You had better tell me.

No sooner did I utter the Bija than the Mother said, "Yes, you belong to this category. You are fortunate, indeed!"

Disciple: Mother, will you not tell me anything more?

Mother: No, perform Japa with this Bija. Know for certain that this will bring you good. With whom have you come?

Disciple: I have come with my husband.

Mother: Where does he stay? What does he do?

Disciple: He is the manager of Ram Babu's estate.

Mother: Oh dear! You are the manager's wife? Why didn't you disclose this earlier? O Radhu, O Maku, come and salute the manager's wife.

Quite amazed at the Mother's action, I said, "Mother, what are you saying? I am a Kayastha. They being members of a Brahmana family, how can they salute me?" But the Mother said, " Don't speak like this. You are a devotee. Devotees are casteless. They will reap good if they salute you." As soon as Radhu and Maku came, I caught hold of their feet. Then the Mother said to them, "Stop, stop, she won't allow you. They are devotees, therefore they see the Lord in all beings. Well, what have you heard at Deobhog from Durga (Nag Mahasaya alias Durgacharan Nag)? How did you happen to visit him and become acquainted with him?"

Disciple: Once my husband went there to see the saint Nag Mahasaya. On that occasion he won the heart of my husband by his unselfish affection and told him repeatedly about Sri Ramakrishna. He very kindly visited our house in order to see me. Being charmed by his attitude and love, we have been visiting him for a long time. And he has graciously made us his own and told us of the greatness of you and Sri Ramakrishna. As a result, we feel drawn towards you and the Master in our heart of hearts. He would only say, "I am nothing; Sri Ramakrishna is my everything. If you desire good, take refuge in him heart and soul. There is no way out besides this. As luck would have it, I saw the holy feet of the Master and became blessed. I have seen Swamiji—Lord Siva Himself—and I have also seen the Divine Mother incarnate and received Her blessings. What more shall I tell you? With your whole body, mind, and soul take shelter at the holy feet of the Mother and the Master, and it will bring you good."

Mother: Ah, what shall I tell about him? He looked upon me as the Divine Mother Herself. When he came to see me for the first time I was observing the fast enjoined on the eleventh day of the lunar fortnight (Ekadasi). In those days no male devotee was allowed in my presence. Devotees used to salute me by touching the staircase with their heads. One maid servant used to announce the name of the visitor, saying, 'So and so (the person's name) is saluting you, Mother,' and I would send my blessings. On that day the maid said, 'Mother, who is this Nag Mahasaya? He is saluting you, but by striking his head so hard against the staircase that his head is likely to bleed. Maharaj (Swami Yogananda) is standing behind him trying to persuade him to stop, but he doesn't say a word. He seems to be unconscious. Is he a madman, Mother?' I said, 'Oh dear! Tell Yogen to send him here.' Holding him, Yogen himself brought him to me. I saw that his forehead was swollen, tears were rolling down his cheeks and his steps were unsteady. Blinded by tears, he couldn't see me. I made him sit. He was uttering only 'Mother! Mother!' as if insane, but otherwise he was quiet, calm and composed. I wiped away his tears. I had just sat down to eat my meal of *luchi*, sweets and fruit when he appeared. I partook of a little of the food and then tried to feed him with the Prasada. But he couldn't eat—he couldn't swallow the food; for he had no outward consciousness. He simply sat touching my feet and repeating 'Mother, Mother'. My women companions began to say, 'Mother your meal is spoiled. Let us tell Maharaj (Swami Yogananda) to remove him from here.' I said, 'Wait. Let him compose himself a little.' As I stroked his head and body and repeated the Master's name for sometime, he regained external consciousness. Then I began to take my meal and also to feed him. When he had finished taking food, he was taken dowstairs. Before he left, he only said, 'Not I, but Thou! Not I, but Thou!' I told those who were near about, 'Look, how wise he is.' He would do anything for me.

"Once he came wearing a dirty tattered cloth and carrying on his head a basket containing select mangoes from his own trees. He had in mind the desire to feed me while sitting by my side. But he wouldn't express this. He began to walk around with the basket on his head like a destitute. Yogen sent word, 'Tell Mother that Nag Mahasaya has brought mangoes. He doesn't speak a word and won't give the basket to anybody.' I said, 'Send him here.' When he was sent in, he came with the basket on his head. One Brahmacharin took the basket off his head. I had not yet finished my daily worship of the Master. After saluting me, he became unconscious, as on the previous occasion. He was repeating the name of the Master and saying 'Mother, Mother'. Tears were streaming down from his eyes. The mangoes were of a very good quality—some of them had been marked with spots of lime. Some were cut and offered to the Master. Daughter Yogin brought Prasada for me on a plate made of Sal leaves. I ate a little and told Golap, 'Give him a leaf-plate.' When the leaf-plate was brought I placed on it some pieces of mango from my plate and said, 'Please eat.' But who would eat? He had no body consciousness, and his hands were as if paralyzed. I took hold of his hand and tried to persuade him to eat, but he couldn't. Instead, he took a piece of mango and began to rub it on his head. I sent word downstairs and they had him brought down. By repeatedly making Pranam by touching the floor with his head, his forehead had got swollen. He didn't take his meal. I heard that after sometime he regained normal consciousness and left."

After a while leaf-plates were arranged. Mother said, "Come, you will have Prasada." As I followed the Mother into the dining room, she said, "Come, sit facing me in the opposite row." The Mother mixed her rice with butter, ate three morsels of it and said to me, "Take this Prasada, take it on your palm." When I stretched out my right hand, the Mother said, "Does anyone receive Prasada this way? Spread both your palms to receive it." I spread both my palms and the Mother placed the entire quantity of rice in them, pressing it with her hand. Then she said, "Touch your head with it and then eat." Being surprised, I said, "Mother, I am a Kayastha; you touched me while taking your meal. How can you take food now?" The Mother said, "You are all my children; what caste discrimination can there be between you and me? You are but my children. Now take the Prasada."

Then shyly I began to eat. Very cheerfully the Mother began to take her meal. She now and then asked what I wanted.

Mother: Well, dear, is there no place of pilgrimage in your part of the country (Dacca, Bangladesh)?

Disciple: No, Mother, I don't know of any holy place worth the name. But people take a holy dip on a certain day. It is called the Brahmaputra bath.

Mother: Yes, I have heard of it. All right, you take me there this time. I shall see your native place and make a pilgrimage too.

Disciple : Mother, will East Bengal (now Bangladesh) have this good fortune?

Mother: Why not? There are many devotees of the Master there. Naren went there, Sarat went there, and many others also. Why should I not go to a place where people adore the Master?

The Prasada contained pulse soup, two varieties of mixed curry and a sour soup. Now the Mother said, "Serve them fish."

Disciple: No, Mother, I am satisfied with the Prasada itself; I won't take fish.

Mother: How is that, dear? You are a woman whose husband is living, and you won't take fish![1] Why haven't you painted your soles with lac-dye?

Disciple: In our part of the country painting of the soles with lac-dye is not in vogue. Conch-bangles on the hand and mark of vermillion on the forehead indicate that a woman's husband is living.

Mother: It may be, but in this part of the country women wear conch-bangles and vermillion as a fancy. Here iron wristlets and lac-dye are the signs of a woman whose husband is alive.

The Mother was served with milk, a mango and a sweet. She mixed them, ate a little and said, "I am leaving the remaining portion for your son." When the meal was over, I was about to remove the leaf-plate when Lakshmi-Didi hurriedly came and caught hold of it. I was not willing to part with the plate, but neither would Lakshmi-Didi leave it. At last the Mother stood up and said, "Allow Lakshmi to carry it. Among them you are

[1] According to the Hindu tradition in Bengal a widow is prohibited from taking fish or meat, but women in the married state are allowed to take them.

the oldest; since they are here, why should you carry it?" Thus I was compelled to leave the plate. Then I accompanied the Mother to the washing place. The Mother filled a pot with water from the bucket and gave it to me, saying, "Wash your mouth and hands." I felt very awkward. I said, "Mother, I can't obey you." The Mother said, "Why not? It will bring you good if you do what I say. Come, hurry up and wash; there are others waiting behind you. Well, touch the water-pot with your forehead." Having no other course left open, I obeyed her command. After this, as I was moving away, the Mother said, "What's this ? Why did you not wash your feet?" I said, "I shall wash them later." The Mother said, "No, no, come. I shall pour the water." Then I went up behind the Mother and said, "Mother, I can't do this." The Mother replied, "What's the matter? First sprinkle some water on your head. If you listen to my words, it will be for your good." And so with no other course open, I did as she told me, and at her directive I followed her to her room.

Entering the room, the Mother stood as if taken aback, and after a moment cried out, "O——, what have you done? What will my son take?" I noticed that a certain woman devotee was saying to herself, "Everything will be eaten by her children, and we shall die of starvation!" and was merrily eating the Prasada the Mother had kept for Ni——. Seeing this, I laughed heartily. Lakshmi-Didi and the other woman present also finally began to laugh too. I could hardly control my laughter, but the Mother appeared very concerned and stood there quietly. Then the Mother sent some one to enquire whether the cook had closed the kitchen, and if not what food had been left behind. Learning that there were some rice, pulse and curry, the Mother said, "Well, ask the cook to bring a small quantity of each of them." When the cook brought them on a plate, the Mother mixed them together, ate a little from it and left the remaining portion covered, saying, "This is for my son." Standing behind her, I was wondering how the Mother could eat rice twice. I was also musing how I could offer a small personal service to the Mother. I had used water given by her for cleaning my mouth and washing my feet, but I could give no service to her. I was walking behind the Mother. When she had entered the shrine room she said to me, "My towel is hanging on the panel of the door; please bring it and wipe my feet." Hearing this, I was overwhelmed with joy. I brought the towel, and then the Mother said, "Well, let me sit on the cot. Please wipe the soles of my feet nicely." While I wiped her feet, I touched them with my head several times. Smiling a little, the Mother said, "All right, stop now."

Lakshmi-Didi brought a betel leaf and said, smiling, "Fortunate you are; the Mother showed a favour on you unasked for. Now take a betel roll." But blinded by tears, I couldn't see it. The Mother took the betel roll and gave it to me, saying, "Now spread that mat on the floor and cover it with that carpet, and place those three pillows." When the bed was prepared, the Mother lay down. Sitting close to her I began to massage her feet, when she said, "Now lie down by my side." Seeing my hesitation, the Mother said, "Lie down placing your head on my pillow." I said, "No, Mother, when I fall asleep my feet may touch your body, so I wont't lie down." The Mother replied, "How is that, dear? I'm telling you, lie down." I was in a fix. I had to follow her order. The Mother said, "I found much joy in meeting you, just as a mother feels joy at the home-coming of her daughter from her father-in-law's house after a long time. Well, when will you return home?" I said, "I shall leave this evening. Mother, kindly remember me, your beggar daughter." Saying this, I began to weep. The Mother said, "Oh, dear, dear! Why do you speak thus? You are my princess. I myself have initiated you. You have nothing to feel sad about. You needn't worry; I shall look after everything for you, in all conditions."

Radhu returned from her school at four o'clock. After she had taken snacks, the Mother said to her, "Come, I shall braid your hair." Radhu replied, "No, I shall do it myself." As the Mother took a comb to braid her hair, Radhu began to hit the Mother with it. The Mother remarked, "Mad girl! What shall I do with her?" Then Yogin-Ma came and made Pranam to the Mother. Finding Radhu hitting the Mother, she said, "What is this! Why should Radhu hit our Mother? I'll punish her." But Radhu would not stop. Then the Mother said, "I shall call Sarat; I can't tolerate any more pain." Yogin-Ma told Revered Sarat Maharaj, who came out from his room on the ground floor and shouted, "Oh Radhu, don't hurt the Mother." On hearing his voice Radhu was quick to retreat. Kusum-Didi said, "Come, I shall braid your hair." Just like a well-behaved girl, Radhu quietly went up to her and sat very close. At that moment, Radhu's mother came to announce, "Just see, one of your disciples has come with something in hand. If it is a piece of cloth, I shall use it for the top of my mosquito net." Truly, Ni— had come with some fruits, sweets and a cloth. As soon as he saluted the Mother, the latter said, "Ah! The cloth is fine. And the sweets and fruits are very good too. O Golap, take them and keep them ready. When the shrine opens they should be offered to the Master. Ah! My son's face looks dry. Now wash your hands and face and then have some Prasad. May you live long, my son, and may you have devotion. But you shall have to marry." Ni—saluted the Mother and went downstairs. Golap-Ma followed him, carrying the dish containing the Prasad. Then Radhu's mother began to make an importunate demand, saying, "Give me those two Saris. I shall make the top of my mosquito net with them." The Mother said, "How can it be? My son will feel hurt." A little later the Mother said to Kusum-Didi, "Please bring a Sari for me." Yogin-Ma observed, "See how fortunate they are. Who are they, I wonder? In just one day they have received so much of compassion from the Mother. Blessed girl you are! I feel like saluting you." Hearing this I shrank—what is she saying! Then the Mother remarked, "They belong to East Bengal. They have great faith. It is beneficial even to see such people."

Once again I wiped the Mother's feet with a towel. The Mother put on a fresh Sari, sat on the *āsana* for the worship, and began to pray to the Master, " O Lord, look after their welfare. They love you even more than their own lives and so they have come to me from a far away land encountering many difficulties." Later, the Mother called me and asked, "Have you any questions to ask?"

Disciple: Mother, I have been surprised to find young widows here taking fish. In our part of the country it is prohibited by society.

Mother: Do you know what this is? This is but local and regional custom. In our part, young widows are allowed to take fish and wear bordered saris and jewellery. They naturally harbour these desires. If they are restricted from eating fish, they will take it stealthily. When they become convinced that they are doing something against social injunction, they will give it up.

Disciple: Mother, can the desire for enjoyment be given up?

Mother: No, dear, what you say is true. But when people grow up, they see the behaviour of others and feel ashamed of their own conduct. Besides, at the time of quarrels, they have to suffer caustic comments, and so they restrain themselves of their own accord.

Disciple: Well, Mother, you being a Brahmana lady, how could you take rice twice?

Mother: What do you mean, dear? When did I eat rice twice?

Disciple: At the time when you gave Prasad to my son.

Mother: I can do everything for the welfare of my children. There is no harm in it. Besides, in the case of Prasad it is not objectionable to eat even five times! Consecrated food is not like ordinary food. Don't let your mind be disturbed over these trifles. It will make you forget the Lord. Whatever people may say, remember the Master and do what you consider to be correct. The Master used to say, "Look upon people as worms." By this he did not mean all kinds of men. He was referring only to fault-finders and people of mean tendencies.

It was now time for me to depart. A carriage was waiting for me. With tears in her eyes the Mother stroked my head and said, "Come again." I could not bear the idea of departing. I caught hold of the Mother's feet and began to weep. The Mother said, "Don't weep, dear; I am already your own. Come again."

This was my first and the last meeting with the Holy Mother. Her blessings and loving words of consolation are the treasures of my life.

14

(RECORDED BY AN ANONYMOUS MALE DEVOTEE)

Some days after he had received initiation from the Holy Mother, there cropped up in Lalmohan's (Swami Kapileswarananda's) mind a doubt: "What have I done? Alas, I took initiation from a woman." This gradually developed into a severe mental anguish. Finally he decided that he would abandon the Mantra unless the Master resolved his mental conflict in a day's time. The next day Lalmohan, under the instruction of Revered Baburam Maharaj, (Swami Premananda) carried cow's milk to the Holy Mother's house at Calcutta. As soon as he stood up after saluting the Holy Mother, she said to him, "Look, I didn't give you the Mantra it was the Master who gave it." A few days later, this doubt haunted his mind again. An idea struck him now : "I shall believe that the Master himself has given me initiation, only if Haren Babu comes to announce that he has received power from the Mother." Some days later, at the time of the Master's birthday festival, Haren Babu actually came and said, "Today I have been favoured with a special power from the Holy Mother." Then only did all his uncertainties vanish.

Once it was decided for some particular reason that the services of the Brahmana cook in the Udbodhan house should be dispensed with. But because this would cause inconvenience to the Holy Mother, the monastic Head of the Centre did not then carry out this decision. When the matter was reported to the Mother, she remarked, "After all, you are monks. Renunciation is your goal. Indeed, can't you renounce a cook?"

Once a monk of the Belur Math slapped a servant for insubordination. When this news reached the ears of the Mother, she said "They are monks; they are supposed to live under trees. But, now they are having monasteries, buildings and servants. What is more, one of them has gone even to the length of beating a servant!"

Swami Brajeswarananda had gone to ask for the Mother's permission to practise austerities in Uttarakhand. On hearing him, the Mother said, "This is the month of Kartika(October-November);

all the four doors to the abode of Yama are open now. Being your mother, how can I grant you permission now?"

A certain person had committed a contemptible offence. Some people advised the Mother to inflict severe punishment on him. But the Mother said, "I am his mother. How can I do such a thing?"

Once a devotee said to the Mother, "I am very poor, Mother. I wish to come and see you now and then, but as I am not able to bring the offerings I would like, I don't come regularly." On hearing this, the compassionate Mother said affectionately, "My child, don't worry about it. Whenever you desire to see me, bring simply one myrobalan fruit."

A certain devotee had gone to see the Mother. She asked him, "Have you been initiated by me?" The devotee replied, "Yes, Mother. But I am very much tied down to worldly life. I am unmarried, and yet I have to remain busy with many family affairs. What will happen to me, Mother?"

Saying, "Let me see", the Mother stretched out her hand to touch the chest of the devotee, and the latter hurriedly began to unbutton his coat. After she had stretched out her hand to some extent she remarked, "You need not remove your coat. You will certainly achieve the goal, otherwise my hand would not have moved in that direction. I have given you nothing of my own, but only that which I received from the Master. If it doesn't prove efficacious, he himself will have to come to your help."

One day the mother of a monk proposed to the Holy Mother that her son should go back to the worldly life. The Mother said to her, " It is a great fortune to be the mother of a monk. But people cannot give up attachment to even a brass pot; how could they then think of renouncing the world? You are his mother. Why should you worry? Though he has become a monk, he will serve you."

Once in the course of a conversation, the Mother told a certain devotee, "The Master is really God who assumed a human body to remove the sufferings of men. He moved about just as a king walks through his city in disguise, and he left the world as soon as his identity was discovered."

During the Mother's last stay at Jayrambati, one day the woman cook returned at about nine in the evening and announced, "I have touched a dog. I shall have to take a bath now." The Mother said, "Don't take a bath so late in the evening. Wash your hands and feet, and change your Sari." The cook asked, "Will it suffice?" The Mother replied, "Well, then sprinkle a little water of the Ganges on your body." But this suggestion could not satisfy her either. So finally the Mother said, "All right, then touch me."

Now and then Swami Jnanananda used to prepare various kinds of dishes at Nabasan and carry them to Jayrambati. On his way some people of a certain village were surprised at the frequent visits of the Swami, and one day one of them remarked, "Ah, into what delusion he has fallen!" When Swami Jnanananda reported this to the Mother, she animately said, "See, my child, they are very worldly-minded people. They belong to a different class. They will again and again come to the world and go rotting in their worldly life. If at any time they are blessed by God, only then can they be liberated."

A devotee named Rajendralal Dutta asked the Mother, "I am a Kayastha, Mother. Can I offer cooked rice to Sri Ramakrishna?" The Mother replied, "You are his child, my son. What harm can there be if you offer him cooked rice? You can do so without any hesitation."

One day Pitambar Nath, a devotee from Dacca, was talking with the Mother, sitting on the verandah of her house at Jayrambati. The Mother was in her room and said, "My son, come into the room and speak." The devotee said, "Mother, let me sit here in the verandah. I belong to a low caste." At this the Mother replied, "Who says you belong to a low caste? You are my child; enter the room and take your seat."

One day at the Udbodhan house the compassion of the Holy Mother was being discussed. Yogin-Ma, staring at the Mother, said smilingly, "The Mother, no doubt, loves us all very much, but it is not as intense as the Master's was. What concern and love he had towards his disciples! We saw it with our own eyes. Words cannot describe it." The Mother said, "Is it to be wondered at? He accepted only a few select disciples, and that too after various kinds of testing. And towards me he has pushed a whole row of ants!"

One day while speaking about Sri Ramakrishna, the Mother said, "The Master, who was such a great renouncer, nonetheless worried about me. One day he asked me, 'How much do you need for your pocket expenses?' I said, 'Five or six rupees will be enough.'

Next he asked, 'How many *chapatis* do you eat in the evening?' I felt very embarrassed and wondered how I could answer. But as he insisted on a reply, I said, 'I eat five or six.'" One day an enraged Radhu told the Mother slightingly, "What do you know? Can you comprehend the worth of a husband?" On hearing this, the Mother laughingly remarked, "That's true ! My husband was but a naked Sadhu!"

Once in the course of a chat Swami Keshavananda said to the Mother, "After you, Mother, no one will revere goddesses like Sasthi and Sitala." "Why not?" said the Mother, "They are my parts."

Another day Swami Keshavananda said to her, " Either rectify the wrong attitudes of the people of our locality or relieve me of my urge for philanthropic work. None is there to build, they know only how to destroy." At this the Mother replied, " The Master used to say, 'The Malaya breeze transforms all trees with substance into sandal wood.' Since the breeze of divine grace has come, now all trees (meaning aspirants), excepting bamboo and banana, will turn into sandal wood."

Then someone asked her, "Mother, your relations have enjoyed so much of your holy company, still why do they not show the least glimmer of wisdom?" The Mother replied, "They are like bamboos and silk-cotton trees. Even if they grow close to a sandal wood tree, what will it profit them? The trees must have some essence."

Once a woman devotee asked her, "Mother, why can't we realize that you are the Divine Mother?" She replied, "How can everybody recognize divinity, daughter? There lay a diamond at a bathing place. Taking it as an ordinary stone, people rubbed the soles of their feet against it after their bath to remove the dry skin. One day a jeweller went there. Seeing the stone, he immediately recognized that it was a big precious diamond."

Once as the Mother was leaving Jayrambati for Calcutta, her aunt, the mother of Uncle Surya, came to her and said, "Dear Sarada, don't forget us, come back soon." The Mother touched the floor of her room with her forehead and quoting a Sanskrit proverb, said, "One's mother and motherland are superior to heaven itself."

Once a young male disciple of the Holy Mother very unexpectedly received a marriage proposal from the family of a distinguished, wealthy man. He was offered a large sum of money which would remove his pecuniary difficulties for almost his entire life. The young man had secured an M.A. degree and was serving as the headmaster of a school. As his mind was not altogether free from desire for enjoyments, he wanted to learn the Holy Mother's view on the marriage proposal. So he raised the topic before her at Jayrambati. It was May, 1915. Hearing everything, the Mother said, "My son, you are doing fine. Why do you want to get burnt in the fire of worldliness? You are doing a noble work; you are helping many boys to receive education. They will turn out good by their association with you, and that will bring good to you also." The young man said, "Mother, I do not feel quite confident, for my mind at times gets restless and rushes towards enjoyments." At this, Mother said, "You need not entertain any fear. I say, in the Kali Yuga the mental commission of a sin is no sin at all. Free your mind from all such worries. You have nothing to fear." Ever since the devotee heard these words of assurance of the Holy Mother, he never thought of marriage, nor did he feel perturbed by monetary worries.

One morning a girl from the hostel of the Sister Nivedita Girls' School came to see the Mother, who was doing Japa at the time. After a while the Mother asked various questions concerning the girls of the hostel as well as about a boy named Kalu, about what sights the girl saw on her way, etc. When she failed to give satisfactory answers, the Mother said to her, "Look, my daughter, take notice of your surroundings when you move through a place. And you must also keep yourself informed of everything that happens at the place where you live; but you should not gossip about it."

One afternoon the girls of that hostel visited the Mother. Golap-Ma approached the Mother and said, "Mother, please tell them a little about the Master." In response the Mother said, "What shall I say further about the Master? Many important pieces of information connected with him have come out in the *Kathamrita* written by Master Mahasaya. Ah! How many more teachings about the Master would have been published had Master Mahasaya maintained good health! How many people would have been benefited by them! What has already been published is a priceless treasure. Could I realize then that even the casual words of the Master would be comparable to the Vedas? Just see, how beautiful was the way in which the Master taught—see how, recalling his experiences at the Haldarpukur, he used them as illustrations in his teachings! It was his nature to explain his teachings through anecdotes from everyday life."

A devotee asked the Mother, "The Master said, 'Those who come here (meaning those who accept Sri Ramakrishna as the spiritual ideal) will not be born again.' Again, Swamiji said, 'None can have liberation without being initiated into Sannyasa.' Then what is the way for householders?" The Mother replied, "Yes, what the Master said is true, and what Swamiji said is also true. Householders need not have external renunciation. Internal renunciation will come to them of itself. But some people need external renunciation also. Why do you fear? Surrender yourself to the Master and always remember that he is behind you."

In 1910 at Jayrambati the Mother told a monk regarding spiritual practices, "Every morning and evening perform Japa and meditation with a cool brain. It is not an easy task. Compared to meditation, it is easier to till a plot of land." Pointing to a picture of Sri Ramakrishna, she further said, "Nothing can be attained without his grace." When the monk submitted that the work of the monastery kept one too busy to find time for regularly performing Japa and meditation, the Mother said, "Whose work are you doing? It is His work only." She continued, saying, "In time to come, your mind itself will turn into your Guru and advise you."

Once in the course of a conversation the Mother said, "I am the mother of the virtuous as well as the wicked." She used to tell her disciples, "Why should you worry?"

15

(RECORDED BY Dr. SURENDRANATH ROY)

One Sunday, out of a strong desire to see the Holy Mother, I started from my Calcutta residence at half-past two and arrived, profusely perspiring, at the Udbodhan house. On inquiry I learnt that the Mother had only just returned from some engagement outside, and that she would be meeting visitors only a little later. Feeling very impatient, I however, proceeded to go to her. Swami Saradananda, who was standing near the staircase, saw me going, and forbade me. Young as I then was, I immediatately retorted, "Is she only *your* Mother?", and pushed him aside and went upstairs I found the Mother fanning herself. After I bowed down at her feet she inquired about me and said, "How is it that you are perspiring?" I said, "I walked in the hot sun." Taking the fan from her, I began to fan her.

After a while I asked the Mother, "Where did you go today?" The Mother replied, "Kalighat." Then she said, "Take some Prasad, and then I shall talk with you." After taking the Prasad, I asked her, "Mother, what is the difference between man in his real nature and a god?"

Mother: It is man who becomes a god. Everything is possible if one does work properly.

Disciple: What kind of work?

Mother: Observing the rules and injunctions prescribed by the Master, if one calls upon one's Chosen Ideal with steadfastness, one achieves everything.

On this day I could not talk with the Mother any longer; for one or two women devotees came. I saluted the Mother. As I was taking leave of her, I said, "Mother, I have done a great wrong today. While climbing the stairs I pushed Sarat Maharaj aside. How shall I face him again? Kindly pardon me." The Mother said, "What wrong can children do? My sons are not such as to find fault with others. You need not worry about it." Coming to the ground floor, I came across Sarat Maharaj. I bowed down to him and asked his forgiveness for the offence. Sarat Maharaj embraced me and said, placing his hand on my head, "One should have such yearning, indeed!" Then he added "None will obstruct you henceforth." I welcomed his blessings. But after this incident, whenever he saw me he used to laugh heartily.

On another Sunday when I went to see the Holy Mother, I found that some devotees had already arrived and that others were coming. As I made Pranam to the Mother, she said, "Sit for a while." She gave me some Prasad which I began to eat. Then I said to her, "Mother, I don't find a day when I can disclose to you everything that's in my mind."

Mother: I have to attend to the problems of all my children. But you may ask one or two questions. I shall answer them.

Disciple: Mother, there are very poor people who cannot afford to travel to Varanasi or any such holy place. How can they gain the merit which others visiting those places obtain?

Mother: Why, they can gain the same merit by visiting Dakshineswar or Belur Math, provided they have such genuine faith! He for whom one visits Varanasi is present at Dakshineswar and Belur Math.

Disciple: Mother, what is the way for us?

Mother: Why do you fear? The Master himself will do everything for those who have received his blessings or have somehow come in contact with him.

After this I made Pranam to Mother; for I had to take leave. I shall now give a brief account of a conversation I had with her on some later occasion

Disciple: Mother, what procedure should we adopt for doing Japa and meditation?

Mother: Do them as you like, provided you keep your mind steadfast in the Lord. You will attain to your goal in this way. Why do you worry?

Disciple: Mother, I'm not worried, but I want to hear the instructions from your lips.

Mother: Everybody is behind you. The Master is there. And besides, you can see me directly.

Disciple: Mother, I was not fortunate enough to see Swamiji or Sri Ramakrishna.

Mother: Call on Him devotedly; you will attain everything. I say, you are blessed; for you have been born in such an age. This is the time when you can see His divine sport. One can easily understand this divine play if he looks upon it with faith and devotion.

Disciple: Mother, does everything happen and are a man's aspirations fulfilled according to his own wish?

Mother: Only the noble desires are fulfilled.

16

(RECORDED BY SWAMI VISWESWARANANDA)

In the morning the Mother was making arrangements for worshipping in the shrine of the Udbodhan house. In the course of conversation I asked her, "Why do you have so much attachment? Day and night you talk of nothing but Radhu, just like people terribly entangled in the world. Many devotees come to you but you pay no heed to them. Is such deep attachment good for you?" I had spoken to her in this strain several times earlier also. At this, the Mother used to reply humbly, "I am a woman, and I follow my womanly nature." But today the Mother said rather animatedly, "Where will you find another like me? See if you can find my peer. Do you know, those who are much given to contemplation on God develop a subtle and pure mind. Whatever object such a mind takes hold of, it sticks to it tenaciously. That's why it appears like attachment. A flash of lightning is seen in the glass panes but not in the wooden shutters."

Once I said, "Mother, my mind is never disturbed by evil thoughts." Mother immediately became startled and said, "Don't say like that. It is too presumptuous for one to speak in that strain."

Another day I told her, "Mother, you give initiation to so many people, but you never enquire about them. You don't even give a thought about what is happening to them. A Guru keeps a keen eye on his disciple, seeing whether he is developing spiritually. It would be better if you did not give initiation to so many people. You should initiate only as many as you can keep touch with." The Mother replied, "But the Master never forbade me to do so. He explained so many things to me. Could he not have told me something about this as well? I entrust the Master with their responsibility. I pray to him every day, 'Please look after them wherever they may be.' Besides, do you know that the Master himself taught me these Mantras? He gave me Mantras possessing great power."

One day while discussing about *bīja-mantra*,[1] the Mother dis-

---

[1]*bīja* is the seed or essential part of a Mantra, consisting of a mystic syllable.

closed to me many Mantras and remarked, "I have given you everything I had in my bag. Will you give spiritual initiation to others?"

Disciple: No, Mother. I myself haven't achieved anything.

Mother: Well, what's the harm in giving initiation? You can give.

Disciple: Mother, please make me renounce everything so that I don't have attachment for anything.

Mother: You are an all-renouncer already. Will you grow two horns now?

Another day at Jayrambati I asked the Mother, "How can one realize God?—through worship, Japa or meditation?

Mother: By none of these.

Disciple: Then how?

Mother: God is realized only through His grace. Nonetheless, one must perform Japa and meditation, for they remove the impurities of one's mind. One must practise spiritual disciplines such as worship, Japa, and meditation. As one gets the fragrance of a flower by handling it or the scent of the sandalwood by rubbing it against a stone, similarly one becomes spiritually awakened by continuously contemplating on the Divine. But you can become illumined right now, if you become desireless.

One day at Jayrambati after my meal I was about to remove the used plate, when the Mother prevented me, catching hold of my hand, and taking the plate herself. I said, "Why should you do this, Mother? I shall remove it." At this she said, "What, after all, have I done for you? A child, as you know, soils the lap of its mother. And how much more besides! You are indeed a rare treasure even to the gods."

17

(RECORDED BY MAHENDRA NATH GUPTA)

Two or three days after the birth anniversary of Sri Ramakrishna in March 1914, I went one afternoon to the Udbodhan house with a letter of introduction from a certain devotee living at Barisal. Rashbehari Maharaj (Swami Arupananda) read the contents of the letter and then went to see the Mother. On returning, he conveyed to me the following message from her: "The purpose of taking initiation is to try to realize God through simple spiritual practices. It should not upset the livelihood of the family Guru. I may grant the boy's prayer if he will honour his family Guru as much as he will honour me in case I give him initiation, and if he agrees to enhance as much as he can his annual contribution to the family Guru." When I agreed to these proposals, Rashbehari Maharaj escorted me to the Holy Mother. Two days later I received initiation from her, and my mind was absorbed in an indescribable mood for a week after this.

The Mother had asked me at the time of initiation, "Are you a Sakta[1] or a Vaishnava?"[2] On hearing my reply she gave me the Mantra. Seven or eight years later I learnt from my mother that it was the same Mantra as adopted by our family, and the Holy Mother had only added the Bija to it.

Two months after this, my wife became eager to receive initiation, and so I took her to the Holy Mother. The Mother said to her, "From your appearance it seems that you have a suckling baby. With whom have you left him?" My wife said, "I have not brought the infant for fear that he might dirty this holy place." Learning that the child was only three months old, the Mother said to my wife, "Why do you say so? Who told you that the excreta or urine of so small an infant can defile a place? Children are like Narayana and you should take care of them with that attitude. Go home just now, otherwise the baby may be deprived of its mother's milk. Come here after four days. The Master willing, you will have initiation. But don't forget to bring your baby."

---

[1] A worshipper of Sakti, the Divine Mother of the Universe.
[2] A worshipper of Vishnu or God as the Preserver.

As I was waiting downstairs, I thought: "I shall be convinced that the Mother loves me dearly if she shares with me some of the food she eats." Half an hour later I went to bow down to the Mother, when I found her eating a sweetmeat. As her glance fell on me, she said, "My child, eat this sweet first and then salute me." Being favoured with this unexpected Prasad, I forgot to salute the Mother altogether. After a while she herself reminded me, saying, "Now make salutation to me and then go home."

The Mother's instruction to come for initiation after four days made us sad and worried. But on returning home I understood from my wife's health the Mother's foresight in telling her to wait.

We went to salute the Mother before we left for Barisal. The Mother said, "Go carefully. The Master will protect you from dangers on your way." On our journey a severe storm overtook us and our lives were in danger. When we arrived at our destination, every one of us felt convinced that it was only the Mother's blessings which had protected us.

A year later, in the month of Vaisakh (April-May), I saw the Mother again at Jayrambati, and this time I got the opportunity of coming in very close contact with her. Sitting in front of me, the Mother would feed me affectionately, and I would become filled with joy.

Assuming that I would be benefited more if I practised Japa and meditation while living close to the Mother, one day at Jayrambati I performed Japa and meditation arduously. While I made Pranam to the Mother on that day, she said, "You have come to your Mother; what's the need of so much spiritual practice now? I am doing everything for you. Now eat, drink and enjoy yourself, free from all anxiety."

The next day I desired to offer flowers and sandal paste at the Mother's feet. But how was I to procure them in such an unfamiliar place? While I was thinking in this strain, the Mother sent to me a young girl belonging to the family of the Mother's brothers. She was carrying flowers and sandal paste, and conveyed the Mother's message: "If my son desires to offer these, he may come now and offer them."

On the third day the Mother was suffering from pain in her leg. She had a mild fever too. At about ten o'clock another devotee came and, not being aware of the Mother's ill health, saluted her by touching her feet. The Mother said, "I have a severe pain in my leg. Don't salute me by touching my feet. The Master will certainly bless you." Bilash Maharaj, who was present, asked the Mother, "The scriptures, I am told, prohibit making Pranam to a person who is ill or lying down. What really happens if one does so?" Immediately, the Mother said, "Yes, my child, Pranam made in such circumstances fixes the disease in the person. Nobody should be saluted during his illness."

About three years later during the Christmas holidays I saw Mother for the last time. It was the occasion of her birthday celebration. In the morning that day the Mother told me and a certain monastic member of the Koalpara monastery, "Go to Sibu[1] at Kamarpukur. He will purchase a pitcherful of milk and collect some flowers. Bring them here quickly." To this, Bilash Maharaj added, "The Mother has difficulty if she takes her meal late. So you must return by nine o'clock, otherwise you may not get a chance to offer flowers to her." Nonetheless, it became half-past eleven when we returned. I felt very sorry thinking that we had missed the chance of making offerings to the Holy Mother. Bilash Maharaj rebuked me for being late and said, "The Mother is waiting for you." Just at that moment the Mother appeared from somewhere, took the basket of flowers from my hand, and said, "How beautiful the flowers are! You should first worship the Lord with them. Quickly take your bath and come." Bathing over, we came and found that some of the flowers were kept arranged for us to make offerings with. The Mother's incomprehensible affection captivated us.

---

[1]Shortened form of Sivaram, the name of the youngest son of Rameswar and a nephew of Sri Ramakrishna.

18

(RECORDED BY SWAMI TANMAYANANDA)

Once I was suffering terribly from colic. One day I was feeling drowsy, and in that condition I seemed to hear someone telling me to take water sanctified by the feet of my Guru. The next day I went to Jayrambati and drank a little water sanctified by the feet of the Holy Mother. I said to her, "Mother, I had a desire to worship your feet, but now I have drunk water." The Mother said, "What's wrong in that? Come into the room."

After worshipping her feet, I placed them on my head. At this the Mother said, "Ah, foolish child, should you place a person's feet on your head! The Lord resides there."

Disciple: Mother, I have not seen the Master.

Mother: The Master is God Himself.

Disciple: If the Master is God, then who are you?

Mother: Who else am I?

Disciple: If you so wish, you can show me the Master.

Mother: When the Master touched Naren (Swami Vivekananda), the latter got alarmed. Practise spiritual disciplines and you shall see him.

Disciple: What's the need of spiritual disciplines for a person who has you as the Guru?

Mother: Yes, that's true. But the point is this: the house may have all kinds of food-stuff for cooking, but one must cook them and take his meal. He who cooks earlier gets his meal earlier too. Some eat in the morning, some in the evening, and there are yet others who starve because they are lazy and reluctant to cook.

Disciple: Mother, I don't understand what you mean.

Mother: The more arduously one practises spiritual disciplines, the more quickly one will attain to God. Even if he doesn't practise any spiritual disciplines, he will attain to Him at the last moment of his life—he will certainly. But the person who spends his time raising a hue and cry without practising spiritual disciplines will take a long time. You have renounced the world for performing spiritual practices. But as you are not able to practise them always, you should do work, looking upon it as the Master's work. Since you suffer from colic, you should avoid too austere a life.

Take care about your food. This disease is not fatal, but it is painful.

While living at the Koalpara monastery it was my duty to clean the kitchen and scour the brass pots two times daily. It was rainy season. As my hands got often wet by scouring the pots, they became sore. I was suffering. One day I went to Jayrambati. When I made Pranam to the Mother, she enquired, "Well, dear, are you keeping all right?"

Disciple: No, not quite.

Mother: Why? Are you having pain in your stomach again?

Disciple: No, Mother, I'm not suffering from colic now, but my hands have developed sores because of frequent contact with water. I have to scour and clean cooking pots two times a day.

Mother: 'A man eager to keep away from acid food builds a home under a tamarind tree'—so goes the proverb. Whereas you have renounced the world to repeat God's name, you are now entangled in activities. The Ashrama has become your second world. People come to a monastery renouncing their families, but they become so deluded that they don't want to leave the Ashrama. Since you are not keeping good health, you should go to Daharkund. There you should teach the boys as much as you can, and practise meditation and worship.

Disciple: Mother, I wish to go to a lonely place and perform austerities, but I'm not keeping good health.

Mother: Now, keep yourself engaged with some work, and when you feel a strong urge, you may go for practising austerities.

Disciple: I perform Japa but my mind doesn't become steady.

Mother: Whether the mind becomes steady or not, practise Japa. It will be nice if you can perform a certain number of Japa daily.

Disciple: Bless me so that I may have a vision of the Master.

Mother: You have seen him in dream; well, you will have his vision.

Another day on my way to Jayrambati I was thinking that I would be very glad if I could do some personal service to theMother. On arriving at her house, I found her sitting with her legs stretched out. A cup containing massaging oil was kept by her side. I began to rub her leg with the oil. The Mother said, "See, I feel acute pain in this leg. Rub oil on this leg putting some pressure."

I did it for about twenty-five minutes. Then the Mother said, "Are you satisfied, now? I shall go for my bath now, and then I shall have to perform the worship of the Master. Take your food here before you leave."

Disciple: No, Mother, I have to go right now. I shall come some other day.

Mother: No, no, I say. Kedar (Swami Kesavananda), I suppose, has forbidden you. Will you obey me or listen to him? Tell Kedar that the Mother did not permit you to go.

19

(RECORDED BY SWAMI PARAMESWARANANDA)

It was the birthday of the Holy Mother in the month of Pous (December-January). The Mother was sitting on a cot in her room at Jayrambati, keeping Radhu's child in her lap. Everybody was worshipping the Mother by offering flowers and sandal paste at her feet. I put a string of large marigold flowers round her neck and offered flowers at her feet. Then I said, "Mother, today is your birthday. Many devotees wish to see you and worship you, but they are not able to come to such an inaccessible place. On this auspicious day, I pray for your blessings on behalf of everybody. Kindly give your blessings, Mother, for the good of all." The Mother graciously said, "Yes, my son, I pray to the Master for the welfare of all. May he bring good to all!"

As desired by the Mother, I was at this time staying with her. I was kept very busy with many duties like performing the worship of the Master. One day I heard that a few monks of the Belur Math were going out for practising austerities, and so I said to the Mother, "Perhaps it is not good for me to remain confined to all these duties. I want to go and practise austerities. Please give me your permission." The Mother said, "Why so, my child? You are doing my work. You are doing the Master's work. Are these in any way less worthy than austerities? It will be futile for you now to go out. When you feel a really strong urge to practise austerities, well, go for a month or two."

Jayrambati was infested with malaria. Intermittent fever had made the Mother's health very bad. So at the bidding of the revered Sarat Maharaj, no interview with the Mother was permitted for some time. During this period a certain devotee from Barisal came and expressed his great eagerness to see the Mother, but I refused to allow him. And so a heated argument ensued. The noise gradually reached the Mother's ears. She came to the door greatly excited and said, "Why do you prevent him from seeing me?" I said, "Sarat Maharaj has imposed this restriction. If you give initiation when you are ill, your health will deteriorate further." The Mother replied, "Who is Sarat to say that? I am born for this purpose. I shall initiate him." Then the Mother said to the devotee, "Come, my child. Take your meal today. You will have initiation tomorrow." The gentleman, however, had taken the resolve of taking his meal after he was initiated.

One evening the Mother was sitting quietly on the verandah of her new house, when we went to prostrate at her feet. Of her own, she began to say, "Just see. K. . . . says, 'Out of greed for good dishes, the boys (monastic workers) are moving from one Ashrama to another.' Do you see how he speaks? Why should my children—the children of the Master---suffer for want of food? Certainly this will never be. I myself prayed to the Master, 'O Lord, please see that your children never suffer from want of food.' How can he say that the boys move about goaded by gluttony? Why should they not take good food? Only he who has attachment will suffer."

After finishing her worship of the Master, the Mother was sitting quietly in the shrine, when one of my fellow disciples suddenly asked, "Mother, how do you look upon the Master?" The Mother remained silent for a while, and then said solemnly, "I look upon him as my child."

One day the Mother said spontaneously, "Look, do not try to start a sensation by shouting *vande mataram*.[1] Rather you should make looms and weave cloth. I wish to spin thread if I can get a spinning wheel. Do constructive work."

In the course of conversation I said to the Mother one day, "Mother, such is our mental condition that at times our mind becomes so distracted that we are seized with fear lest we should be drowned!" The Mother replied, "How's that, my child? Why should you be drowned? You are the children of the Master; why should you be drowned? No, never. The Master will protect you."

The Mother was then staying at the Jagadamba Ashrama at Koalpara. One day she said, "You see, I saw the Master here today after a pretty long time. He was taking rest after his meal."

One day I asked, "Mother, how does one attain to knowledge of Brahman? In the beginning does one have to practise Sadhana step by step? Or does it come spontaneously?" The Mother replied, "This is a very difficult path. Call upon the Master. He will make you understand this at the right time."

[1]Literally, 'Hail to Mother'; i.e. Motherland. This slogan was used by India's freedom-fighters.

20

(RECORDED BY Dr. UMESH CHANDRA DATTA)

One day at Jayrambati the Mother said, "Look, my child, in my young days I would see a young girl who resembled me moving with me and helping me in all my work. She used to have fun and frolic with me. This continued till I was ten or eleven years old."

One day the Mother said, "Sometime after the passing away of the Master, I began to see the vision of a bearded Sannyasin who asked me to perform *panchatapa*. In the beginning I didn't pay much attention to it. I hardly knew what *panchatapa* was. But the Sannyasin gradually put pressure on me. So I asked Yogin about *panchatapa*, and she said, ' Very good, Mother, I shall also perform it.' Arrangements were made for *panchatapa*. I was then living in Nilambar Babu's house. Blazing fires of dried cow-dung were lighted on four sides, and there was the intense heat of the sun above. After my morning bath I approached the fires and saw them burning brightly. I was seized with much fear. I wondered how I would be able to enter the area and remain seated there until sunset. But repeating the name of the Master, I entered the area and the fires seemed to have lost their heat. I practised this discipline for seven days. But, my child, it made my complexion dark like black ash. After this I didn't see that figure of the Sannyasin again."

Once I asked, "Mother, the Master remarked that those who take refuge in him are living their last birth. Now, what will be the fate of those who take refuge in you?"

Mother: What else will happen, my child? The same is the case here too.

Disciple: Mother, what will happen to those who receive spiritual initiation from you but do not perform Japa and meditation at all?

Mother: What else will happen? Why do you worry so much? The desires in your mind—you must first fulfil them. Later on you will attain to eternal peace in the Ramakrishna Loka. The Master has created a new kingdom for all of you.

A certain devotee forgot the method of counting Japa on his fingers and so wrote me a letter asking me to get it clarified from the

Holy Mother. On hearing this, the Mother remarked, "Is that of much consequence? Well, you can do it just as it suits you. All this is meant for gaining concentration of mind?"

One day I asked the Mother about liberation and devotion. In reply she said, "Liberation may be granted at any moment. But God is reluctant to bestow devotion." And she left the place immediately. She said these words in such a way that it appeared that to grant liberation was in her hand.

As regards purity and impurity, the Mother one day said, "You see, my son, the Master had a weak stomach. When I lived in the Nahabat, I used to prepare for him bitter curry, soup, and other dishes as he desired. When I could not cook for him during those three days a month[1] when women are debarred from cooking, he would get consecrated food from the Kali temple. But that food would invariably upset his stomach. One day he told me, 'You see, as you didn't cook for these three days my stomach trouble is aggravated. Why didn't you cook these days?' I said, 'Women are prohibited from cooking for others when they remain unclean for three days.' Then he said, 'Who told you that? You will cook for me; there is nothing wrong in it. Please tell me what is impure in your body—the skin or flesh, or bones, or marrow? It is the mind that makes one pure or impure. There is nothing called impurity outside the mind.' Thenceforth I used to cook for him every day."

During the Mother's illness at Koalpara I prepared Sherbet for her, and to be sure that the preparation was satisfactory, I tasted a little before I offered it to her. Although the Mother didn't know of this, a few days later she happened to remark, "Look, my son, it is very good to taste the food before it is given to some one you love." Then I said, "Mother, I also tasted the Sherbet I gave you." She said, "You did well, my son. This is how one should offer food to beloved ones. Haven't you heard that the cowherd boys used to taste the fruits before offering them to Sri Krishna?"

I asked her one day, "Mother, sometimes when I see certain persons on the road, I feel that they are well-known to me. Later, on enquiry, I learn that they are either devotees of the Master or of you. Why do they appear so familiar even when seen suddenly

---

[1]A Hindu woman is considered unclean for the three days of her monthly period.

for the first time?" The Mother replied, "The Master used to say, 'Suppose there is a clump of weed; if one pulls at a weed, the whole clump is affected. The weeds are related to one another like the branches of a plant.'"

Another day I asked her, "Mother, all other Incarnations survived their spiritual consorts (Sakti), but why this time did the Master pass away leaving you behind?" The Mother said, "Do you know, my son, that the Master looked upon all in this world as Mother? He left me behind this time for demonstrating that Motherhood to the world."

21

(RECORDED BY NALINIBEHARI SARKAR)

When the topic of Japa and meditation came up, the Mother said, "There should be a regular time for the practice of Japa and meditation. For no one knows when the auspicious moment[1] will come. It comes suddenly—one has no hint of it before hand. Therefore, regularity in spiritual practice should be observed, no matter how busy one may be with worldly matters."

Disciple: The demands of work or illness prevent me from always being regular in my spiritual practice.

Mother: Illness is not within man's control. And if you are really tied down with work, then simply remember God and make salutation to Him.

Disciple: What time should one set aside for Japa and meditation?

Mother: To call upon Him at the conjunction of day and night is the most auspicious. Night disappears and day arrives, or day disappears and night arrives—this is the conjunction of day and night. The mind remains pure at these times.

When asked about the weaknesses of the mind, the Mother said, "Son, it is Nature's law, just as you find the full moon and the new moon. Similarly the mind is possessed of noble thoughts at times and haunted by evil thoughts at other moments."

When the Mother used to go to Baghbazar from Jayrambati, she would ask me to visit Jayrambati occasionally to keep myself abreast of the happenings there. I tried to obey this order as far as practicable. But because of the Mother's absence from Jayrambati I didn't enjoy my visits there and so wrote to the Mother to this effect.

On her return to Jayrambati, in the course of a conversation she said, "Oh N——! listen to what Ranni[2] says." During her last visit to Calcutta, the Mother had retained the service of the female cook and engaged her to assist the eldest aunty Subashini,

---

[1]One day the Mother told this proverb in connection with success in an endeavour. An auspicious moment can do that which cannot be achieved by money or men.

[2]Ranni or Radhuni, meaning 'female cook.'

wife of Prasanna Kumar. It was summer and the female cook slept with the mosquito net fixed in front of the door of the Mother's old house. Now, she dreamt that the Mother approached her after her bath carrying a flower basket in one hand and a water pot in the other. "Get up, get up from here," she said, rebuking her for lying across the door. When the female cook finished recounting her dream, the Mother smiled and said, "Listen, my dear, who knows what she is talking about?"

One day in the course of a conversation I said, "Mother, nothing worthwhile can be achieved in worldly life." In reply she said, "Son, the world is a great mire. If one gets into it, he finds it difficult to get free. Even Brahma and Vishnu gasp in it, what to speak of man! Repeat His name. If you repeat His name, He will take you beyond worldliness. Son, can anyone attain liberation unless He helps? Have deep faith in Him. Know the Master to be your refuge, just as parents are to children in this world."

When one day the topic of faith in God was raised, the Mother observed, "Son, does one acquire faith by mere study of books? Too much study creates confusion. Suppose I write to you a letter asking you to bring such and such things for me. How long would you need this letter? As long as you don't know what it says. As soon as you have known the contents of the letter, what would be the need of it any longer? Then what is required of you is to bring me those things. Without doing so, what would be the good of reading the letter day and night?"

One day I told the Mother passionately, "Mother, I come to you so frequently, and I have received your grace, too. But then, why haven't I achieved anything? I feel that I am as I was before."

In reply the Mother said, "My son, suppose you are asleep on a cot and somebody removes you along with the cot to another place. Will you realize immediately on waking that you have been transferred to a new place? Not at all. Only when the drowsiness clears away completely will you realize that you have come to a new place."

Once I had left home to attend a festival at Belur Math, but *en route* I had got off at Midnapore to attend to some minor work. As I could not catch the evening train, I went back to Calcutta the next day. On reaching Calcutta in the evening, I went to see the Holy Mother. When she saw me, the Mother asked, "Didn't you attend the festival?" "No, Mother, I couldn't attend it," I said, and began narrating my experiences during my journey. On hearing of them, the Mother said, "One should attain his objective somehow or other. You see, my child, you missed seeing so many things. First do the work which you intended to do." Subsequently the Mother said, "Come here tomorrow and partake of the Master's Prasad."

As regards food, the Mother used to say, "First offer to God whatever you are going to eat and then take it as Prasad. This will purify your blood, and purified blood will make the mind pure."

One day, for some reason or other, the Mother became annoyed with her brothers. When I approached her at that time, she told us a few anecdotes regarding the reason for her annoyance. Then she remarked, "My child, they crave for money and money only. They simply keep on saying, 'Give us money, give us money.' Never have they prayed, even mistakenly, for knowledge or devotion. Well, let them have what they seek!"

Once when the Mother was suffering from a dangerous fever at Jayrambati, just prior to her last illness, I was massaging her feet, when she said, "Look, my child, I have been praying for the last few days, but there has been no response. How much I have wept! Even then, nothing happened. At last the Divine Mother Jagaddhatri came today. But Her face resembled my mother's face. Now I shall recover from my illness. Once when I was young, I was travelling to Dakshineswar. On the way I was seized with high fever. I was lying unconscious when I saw a girl with a very black complexion and feet covered with dust enter my room and sit by the bedside. She began to stroke my head. Noticing that the girl's feet were covered with dust, I asked, 'Mother, didn't anybody give you water to wash your feet?' She replied, 'No, Mother, I shall be leaving immediately. I have come to see you. Why do you fear? You will get well.' From the next day I gradually recovered. This time I have suffered very much, my child. Only after much prayer did I see Jagaddhatri today. I am going to be cured this time also. Why fear, my child? If you call upon Him earnestly, He will protect you in all situations."

22

(RECORDED BY INDU BHUSHAN SENGUPTA)

It was in the month of Kartik (Oct-Nov) 1910, a few days before the Kalipuja, that I visited the Holy Mother for the first time at the earnest request of Sri Chandrakanta Ghosh of Shillong. Arriving at Calcutta, I went to the Udbodhan house in the company of one of my friends who had already received spiritual initiation from the Holy Mother. After waiting for a short time, I met the Holy Mother, when suddenly my friend requested her to grant me spiritual initiation. The Mother replied, " All right, he will have initiation tomorrow." Her reply startled me, for I had not even mentioned anything to her regarding my initiation. Nevertheless, I went there the next day at the appointed hour. I saluted the Holy Mother, and when I was about to offer flowers at her feet, she said, " Not now; I shall tell you when to give the offerings." My spiritual initiation over, the Mother sat on the floor with her legs stretched out and said, " Now you can offer the flowers." I offered flowers at her feet and said, "I am offering flowers not from a deep sense of devotion, but because Chandrakanta Babu taught me to do so. I only followed what he told me to do. It is Chandrakanta Babu who sent me here."

Smilingly the Holy Mother said, "Chandrakanta has shown you the right path, son," and so saying, she placed her hand on my head.

Another day I went to see the Holy Mother. In the course of conversation I said, " Mother, various worldly troubles as well as my official duties keep me busy. I am therefore unable to devote time to spiritual practices. I do not also find any improvement in the state of my mind." The Mother immediately assured me saying, " Whatever may happen to you now, the Master will have to appear at the last moment of your life to receive you. He himself said this. Can his words fail in your case? Now, do whatever you like."

Disciple: Mother, is it true that those who have received spiritual initiation from you will not be born again?

Mother: It is true, they will not come to earth again. Know for certain that there is One behind you.

Disciple: Mother, we have found you, so we are protected.

Mother: Why do you worry, child? The thought of you all comes to my mind very often. I do remember you all very much.

Another time when the Holy Mother was at the Koalpara Math, I said to her, "Mother, I am hardly able to do any spiritual practice."

Mother gave me courage as well as assurance, saying, "You need not do anything special. I shall do the needful for you."

Astonished at this, I asked, "Shall I have to do no spiritual practice?"

Mother: None.

Disciple: Will my future progress not depend on my own deeds henceforth?

Mother: No, what will you do? I shall do whatever is necessary.

I was struck dumb by this unrestricted grace of the Holy Mother. The talk next drifted to the pain in her legs. I asked, "Mother, I have heard that you suffer only when certain persons touch your feet."

Mother: Yes, son, the touch of some persons makes the body cool; but the touch of some others feels like the sting of a wasp. But I never give expression to this experience.

Now I began to brood whether I belonged to the group of 'wasps'. The Mother, as if she was indwelling my mind, said instantly, "Son, you are not one of them."

About a month later during the holidays of the Car Festival, I visited Koalpara once again. On the day of the Car Festival I had the following conversation with the Holy Mother.

Disciple: Mother, my strength and hope spring from the grace I have received from you.

Mother: Why do you worry, child? You have found a place in my mind. Whenever I need anything, your thought comes immediately to my mind. I think, 'There are Indu and others; what's there to worry?' You will not have to do any spiritual discipline. I am doing it for you.

Disciple: Do you do the same for all, who have taken spiritual initiation from you, wherever they be?

Mother: Yes, I do it for all of them.

Disciple: You have so many children (initiated disciples). Do you remember all of them?

Mother: No, I do not remember every one of them.

Disciple: Then, how can you say that you do spiritual practices for all?

Mother: I tell beads for all those whose names I can recall. And for those whom I cannot remember, I pray to the Master saying, "Thakur, I have so many children in various places. I cannot remember the names of many of them. You kindly look after them. Kindly look after their well-being."

———

23

(RECORDED BY AN ANONYMOUS LADY DEVOTEE)

After giving me spiritual initiation, the Holy Mother said, "Look, dear, I do not usually give initiation to a young widow. I have given it to you only because you are a noble soul. See that you do not betray me. A spiritual teacher has to suffer for the sins of his disciples. Always repeat the name of the Chosen Ideal like the ever-moving hand of a clock."

Another time when I saw her before leaving for my father-in-law's place, she said, " Don't mix with other people, don't get involved in others' affairs. Say: 'Dwell, O Mind, within yourself; enter no other's home.' The Master was fond of coconut balls. When you go back home, please prepare coconut balls and offer them to him. Increase your service to him as well as your Japa and meditation, and read books about the Master."

One day the Mother and I were alone together; there was none else present. The Mother said, " Look here, don't get too close and intimate with men. You should not do so even with your father or brother; what to speak then of other men?"

She instructed me not to visit frequently the Math or other places where monks lived. She used to say, " You see, you may no doubt be going there with a good heart and with deep devotion, but if your visit affects the minds of the monks, it would cause you harm."

She asked me not to go on pilgrimage frequently or in the company of any and everyone. She told me, " Whenever you have some money in hand, feed some holy men." Pointing towards a woman devotee who was sitting in front of us, the Mother said, " Here is someone who was sorely cheated on her pilgrimage. Going on pilgrimage means courting hazards on the way; be not taken too much with it. Staying in your own home, you can achieve more than you could by wandering. It all depends upon your aptitude."

One day five women-devotees were criticizing another devotee. On hearing this, the Mother remarked, " You must have respect for her. It was she who brought you here first."

I wanted to bring up a child of another family, and asked for the Mother's permission. In reply she pointed to her own wretched condition in having to bring up Radhu and said, "Don't try that by any means. Do your duty towards everyone, but don't bear love towards anyone except God. Loving others brings much misery."

Learning that I had received spiritual initiation from the Holy Mother, our family preceptor had cursed me. I informed the Holy Mother about this. She wrote in reply, "No curse can do any harm to one who has taken refuge in the Master. Be free from all fear."

An old woman devotee told me one day, "There is no charm in the Math or other such places these days." I reported it to the Mother who sat up startled and said, "If there is any true religion, it can be found only here and in the Math."

One day Nalini-Didi[1] and I were discussing the affairs of a woman devotee. We told the Mother, "We do not feel any kind of disrespect for her." The Mother replied, "That's because she calls upon the Master. To one who calls upon the Master, whoever or whatever that person be, none feels disrespect."

---

[1]A niece of the Holy Mother.

24

(RECORDED BY PRAFULLA KUMAR GANGULI)

It was the year 1916. Durga Puja was being celebrated at the Math. The Holy Mother came to the Math on the Saptami-puja day, and was staying in the garden house to the north of the Math campus. On the Ashtami-puja day at about 8 a.m. she came to the Math to witness the worship of Durga. A number of householder devotees, monks, and Brahmacharins, were engaged in dressing vegetables in the hall adjoining the kitchen. On observing them, the Mother remarked, " Well, the boys seem to cut vegetables fairly well." One of the monks, Swami Jagadananda, replied, " The grace of the Divine Mother is our aim, be it through spiritual practices or by cutting vegetables!"

On this day a large number of visitors saluted the Holy Mother. Jogin-Ma, noticing that the Mother was now and then washing her feet, said, "What are you doing, Mother? You will certainly catch cold."

The Mother replied, " What shall I say, Jogin? When some people touch my feet, it produces a soothing feeling, but in the case of some others, their touch is like fire on my body. Nothing short of a wash with Ganges water brings me relief."

Later, one day I asked the Holy Mother in the course of a conversation, " Once during the Pujas I heard you say that when some persons touch your feet you feel a terrible pain."

Mother: Yes, my son, it is so. It is like the sting of a wasp, but I do not give expression to my feeling.

Soon after,she cast an affectionate gaze towards us and added, " Well, dear, I do not mean any of you."

I said, " I am full of fear, Mother; for I feel I have not gained much even under your care."

The Mother said, " Why should you fear, son? Know that the Master is ever behind you. I too am with you. Why should you fear when I, your mother, am with you? The Master has assured me, saying, ' Whoever takes refuge in you, I shall take him by the hand during his last moments and lead him along the path.' Wherever you may go, whatever you may do, the Master will have to come during your last hours to lead you to the Light.

God created man's hands and feet, so it is natural that man will use them. The senses will have their sway."

Once when I was offering food to the Master, I noticed a stream of light falling on the offering. Referring to this, I asked the Mother, "Mother, is that experience of mine a mere fantasy, or is it true? If a fantasy, please do something so that I can be free from it."

The Mother thought over it a little and said, "No dear, these are all genuine."

Disciple: Do you know what I see?

Mother: Yes.

Disciple: Does the Master receive the food that I offer to him? Do you, too, receive what I offer to you?

Mother: Yes.

Disciple: How can I understand this?

Mother: Why? Have you not read in the Gita that God receives the fruits, flowers, water, and other things that are offered to Him with devotion?

Surprised at this reply, I said, "Then, are you God?" On hearing this, the Mother laughed heartily. We too joined her.

25

(RECORDED BY AN ANONYMOUS DEVOTEE)

It was a day in Chaitra of 1321 B.S. (1915) when I went to see the Holy Mother at the Udbodhan house.

Once I had wanted to take my grandmother on a pilgrimage. But as the time was inauspicious, she refused to start. I referred the matter to the Holy Mother for her guidance. She replied, "Son, some say that a man loses the merits he has already earned, if he visits a pilgrim centre at an inauspicious time. But it is wise to perform all holy acts without much delay."

I could not satisfactorily comprehend her meaning, and so expressed my doubt to her once again. I specifically asked her what I should do in my present circumstances.

Mother: People no doubt say that pilgrimages during inauspicious times are prohibited. One can postpone a holy duty out of considerations of time, but look, death[1] (Kala) takes no notice of time. Since death has no fixed hours, one should perform holy duties as soon as an opportunity comes.

* * *

It was Chaitra 27, 1323 B.S. (1917). I was having a chat with the Holy Mother.

Disciple: Mother, everybody says that one who approaches the *Kalpataru* (wish-fulfilling tree) has to ask for something. But I wonder, for what should children ask their Mother? A mother gives to every child according to its need. As Sri Ramakrishna used to say, "A mother serves different dishes to suit the stomachs of her different children." Now please tell me which is the correct attitude.

Mother: How much intelligence does a man possess? He is likely to ask for something other than what he really needs. He may even end up creating a monkey in place of Siva. It is wise to take refuge in Him. He will always give you whatever is necessary. However, one should pray for devotion and desirelessness; for such a prayer does no harm.

---

[1]Kala means 'time', as also the god of death. There is a pun on the word.

Disciple: The Master said, "Those who come here will be in their last embodiment." Again, Swamiji said, "None can have liberation without complete renunciation." What, then, will be the fate of householders?

Mother: Yes, what the Master said is true; and what Swamiji said is equally true. But householders need not renounce externally. They will automatically acquire internal renunciation. However, some need formal Sannyasa. Why should you be afraid? Surrender yourself to Him and live. And know that the Master is always behind you.

Another time when one of my friends died prematurely in a hospital in a miserable condition, I wrote a letter to the Holy Mother. I mentioned my friend's pure character and devotion to God and prayed for his liberation. In reply the Holy Mother wrote, "I bless your friend. May his soul be liberated. Let the Master emancipate him from all bonds."

26

(RECORDED BY AN ANONYMOUS LADY DEVOTEE)

The happiest days of my life were when the Holy Mother was alive. One day when I had gone to see the Mother, she was mixing a quantity of coarse powder of parched paddy in a bowl. She happily put two or three crumbs in her mouth and then distributed the rest in the hands of all the devotees present in the room. I said, "Ah! Mother, you hardly took anything." The Mother replied, "If these girls eat, it is the same as my eating."

Another day I went to see her and found that she had an eruption of patches of nettle-rash all over her body.

Mother: What are these, my child? What's the cure?

Disciple: Mother, people say that one gets cured if he rolls two and a half times on a blanket spread on the floor of a cow-shed.

Mother: Ah! The cow-shed and the Ganges are very pure indeed! Perhaps that's why one gets cured.

One day my seven-year old sister accompanied me to see the Mother. A few days earlier, she had gone to Navadwip and there had started wearing a string of beads made of basil wood. Noticing the string on her neck, the Mother was happy and patted her on the back, saying, "Ah! When did she get this ornament?"

On that day I had left at home in Basirhat my two-month old suckling daughter. I had come by the morning train and intended to return by the night train. I was feeling that milk was about to ooze from my breast, and so I shrank in uneasiness. Observing this, the Mother asked, "Why are you behaving this way?" I told her the difficulty.

Mother: Ah, my child, why have you left behind your two-month old daughter? You could have brought her.

Disciple: Mother, I have not brought the baby lest she makes the place dirty.

Mother: What if she does? (*Repeatedly to all those present*) Ah look! From what a distance she has come leaving her two month old baby at home! And how much she is suffering!

When I asked her for a little earth from the temple of Simhavahini[1], the Mother told her niece to give it to me and remarked, " She (Simhavahini) is a living goddess." Before taking leave, as I bowed down to her, she said, " Come, come again, my child."

---

[1]The deity of a temple at Jayrambati. People believe that earth from the foot of the shrine can cure diseases.

27

(RECORDED BY AN ANONYMOUS LADY DEVOTEE)

One day I told the Mother, " Mother, the day I saw the Master for the first time, there was a lustre radiating from his body. It looked like the glow created by sun's rays falling on a piece of glass." On hearing this, the Mother said, " My child, you have seen correctly. When I used to rub oil on his body, I would occasionally see such a lustre."

Another day the Mother's niece Nalini, being very angry, had fasted the whole day. All attempts of the Mother to induce her to eat failed. At long last the Mother called her and said, " Don't take me to be just your aunt. If I so wish, I can give up this body just now."

While talking about the Master, one day the Mother said to Lalit (Swami Kamaleswarananda), placing her hand on her chest " If ever I attain to the Master, you too will certainly attain to him."

28

(RECORDED BY AN ANONYMOUS DEVOTEE)

The day before the Jagaddhatri Puja of November 1908, I arrived at the Holy Mother's house at Jayrambati to receive initiation from her. When the news of my arrival reached her, the Mother sent word that she would initiate me the next day. Accordingly I received initiation.

Following the Mother's instruction, some of us together visited Kamarpukar and then returned. Unfortunately, during this brief time I had a serious altercation with one Swami over some trifling matter. On our return to Jayrambati, Uncle Varada told the Mother all that had happened.

Elated with joy, I began to sing songs in front of the image of Jagaddhatri. After a while the Mother called me and said, "You have a joyful nature. You will spend your days in such joy. Pass your time joyfully, just as you were doing, by singing songs in front of Mother Jagaddhatri. This monk is of that nature—you should not feel sorry for his words. But you must remember these few things and carry them out in your life. The Master is very compassionate towards you. Therefore you have felt a spontaneous attraction for him from your young days. Know that one has to be careful about these three things: First, a house situated on the bank of a river; any time the river may suddenly destroy the house and sweep it away. Second, a snake; you must be very careful as soon as you see one, for there is no knowing when it will attack and bite you. Third, a monk; you don't realize that one word or thought of his may do harm to a householder. When you see a monk, you should show him respect. You should not slight him with disrespectful retorts." These valuable words of the Mother have remained a part of me all through my life.

29

(RECORDED BY AN ANONYMOUS LADY DEVOTEE)

One day I went to the Holy Mother's house taking my son Haricharan, who was then in a deranged state of mind. Approaching the Mother, he began to address her contemptuously in the language used for inferiors, saying, "I am hungry, give me food", etc. The Mother gave him some consecrated food to eat. While taking the food he began to throw the leavings here and there. Being annoyed at this, I remarked, "This is a shrine, and the boy is making a mess." Immediately the Mother affectionately said, "Let him eat the food. After he has finished, you remove the leavings."

I asked the Mother, "Mother, what's the matter with him? As soon as he sees a Brahmana or a cow he bows down." The Mother remarked, "Compassion for living beings has dawned in him."

On the Kojagari[1] fullmoon day of one year, Haricharan and I fasted and went to the Udbodhan house for offering flowers at the Holy Mother's feet. After the offering, we saluted her. Then, the Mother blessed Haricharan, saying, "May you have good fortune! May you live long!"

The Holy Mother said to me, "I find peace in meeting you all. But I feel sad when I see you, for you have lost your educated son who was maintaining you."

One day I said to the Mother, "Mother, may I have devotion to the holy feet of the Master." The Mother said, "By practising devotional disciplines you can gradually have it." Whenever I visited the Mother in the morning hours, she would feed me with rice after Radhu's noon-meal but before the offerings were made to the Master, saying, "Mourning for your dead son has dried up your heart. You shall take your meal early." I would say, "Our family already suffers from want of food. Should I take my meal before the food has been offered to the Master?" At this the Mother would observe. "You will never suffer from want of food."

---

[1]The fullmoon day in the month of Aswin (October-November).

One day the Mother said, "I have interviewed many a madcap to find out your lost son. I feel that your son is alive. Sarat (Swami Saradananda) too said that he is alive."

When I asked the Mother if my son would return home, she said, "He will come." After this, the Mother held a bundle of sticks[1] in front of the picture of the Master. Many pieces of torn cloth were firmly wrapped around the sticks. She held the entire thing in front of the Master and said, "Please say correctly whether her son will return or not. If you do not, you will get involved in the sin of killing Brahmanas, women, and cows." In the meantime the sticks within the wrappings had become loose and they rose up. As soon as Mother touched them, they dropped down. The Mother said, "Did you see what happened, my child? It showed that your son will return. You may try this yourself at home." According to her instruction I performed the same ritual and it gave the same result.

One day I escorted my mother to the Holy Mother's house with a new Sari for the Mother. I had asked someone to purchase a Sari, but he could not get a good quality cloth. In presenting the cloth to the Mother, I said, "Mother, this cloth is not good. It's not to my liking." The Mother immediately changed her Sari and eagerly put on the new one, saying, "Look, I have put on your Sari. Don't feel sorry. I shall wear this Sari for bathing in the Ganges."

One day I went to see her at Balaram Babu's residence. On that occasion, I saw a person presenting the Mother with some money, saying, "Mother, a certain person is sick. Please see that he gets cured." The Mother replied, "Take back this money. Whoever is born, dies one day. What can I do?" Some days later we heard that the sick man had expired.

---

[1]'*Aag tola,*' which literally means 'to get the first harvest', is a ritual to ascertain the truth of a thing.

30

(RECORDED BY JITENDRA MOHAN CHOWDHURY)

In Jayrambati certain devotees asked the Mother, "When we travel by railway train or steamer, how should we do Japa?" The Mother replied, "You should do it mentally." She said further, "Son, gradually your hands and lips will cease to work and your mind only will repeat the name. The mind will eventually turn into your Guru."

Once in Varanasi the Holy Mother's birthday was being celebrated. On that day Swami Keshavananda's mother was shedding tears on remembering the death of one of her relations. At this the Mother said, "For shame! To weep on this day! It is a day of joy."

On the Rathayatra day at Koalpara, one of my Gurubhais told the Mother, "Mother, my mind is very restless. I can't make it steady by any means." In reply the Mother said, "As a storm blows away clouds, so does His holy name disperse the cloud of worldliness."

On that day I confided to the Mother my mental weaknesses. She said in reply, "Do you think one can get rid of lust altogether? It will be there in some form or other as long as the body lasts. But then, I tell you, it will be reduced to a state comparable to a charmed snake."

The Mother once said, "Why fear? Always remember, there is one person behind you." She further said, "So long as this body (meaning her body) lasts, pass your days in joy."

Once during a conversation the Mother said, "Except for grass and bamboo, everybody will have to come here." Its implication, as I have understood, is that only those who have no substance in them will be excluded, otherwise everybody else will accept the ideas of Sri Ramakrishna. The Mother communicated similar ideas to Swami Keshavananda and Swami Vidyananda also.

A woman devotee asked the Mother, "Mother, many persons perform the worship of Siva. Can we also perform this worship?" In reply the Mother said, "The worship of Durga, Kali, and others can be done with the Mantra I have given you. But if anyone so wishes, he can learn the specific worships and perform them. You needn't do them; they would be a burden for you."

Regarding offerings to be made to Sri Ramakrishna, somebody once said to the Holy Mother, "Mother, I know nothing of the Mantras prescribed for making offerings." At this, the Mother said, "There is no need for so much formality in worship. Everything can be done with the Ishta Mantra."

31

(RECORDED BY LALITMOHAN SAHA)

One day in 1915 I went to see the Holy Mother at the Udbodhan house. When I stood up after saluting her, she said, "How firm was the Master's adherence to truth! How far can we follow his example? The Master used to say, 'Truthfulness alone is the austerity of the Kali Yuga. One attains to God by holding to truth.' "

The following year at Jayrambati the Mother was once discussing a letter from a monastic disciple in which he had expressed his despondency. Suddenly the Mother began to say gravely and emphatically, "How is it, my dear? Is the Master's name a trifle that it will come to nothing? The uttering of his name can never be futile. Those who have come here remembering the Master will certainly have the vision of their Chosen Ideal. Even if one does not have it during his lifetime, he will assuredly have it at least just before his death."

One Sunday in 1918 I suffered from a mental tribulation which made me feel offended with the Master and the Holy Mother and I resolved that I wouldn't visit the Mother any more. But my friends persuaded me to go to the Udbodhan house. There I found a large number of devotees waiting to salute the Mother. They bowed down before her one after another. The Mother didn't speak a word to anyone. But when I made Pranam last of all, the Mother affectionately asked, "Are you keeping well?" I answered emotionally, "Yes, Mother, I am keeping very fine." At this, the Mother smiled at me and said, "How is it, my child? This is the mind's nature. Simply because of it, should you behave this way?"

Another day, when I was studying law, I made Pranam to her and asked, "Mother, you see, this is the condition of my mind. And besides this, I am going to practise law. What will be my fate?" The Mother said with assurance, "Why do you fear, my child? It is nothing more than an occupation."

—

32

(RECORDED BY SWAMI MAHESWARANANDA)

Once on her birthday at Jayrambati, the Mother had been feeling unwell since early morning. She intended to avoid bathing, but lest her attendants should worry on hearing this, she finally decided to take her bath. In the evening, however, she was found running a high temperature. When I went to see her, she said, "My child, obey the dictates of the mind first. The mind is the first Guru. Just see, this morning as I woke up it occurred to me that I should not bathe today, for I was not feeling well. Nevertheless considering various factors, I finally took my bath. And now I am suffering."

In another context the Mother remarked, one day, "The Master used to say, quoting a proverb: 'Eat warm food and lie on a soft bed.'"

One day at the Koalpara monastery, as a distinguished devotee went to salute the Mother, he said to me, "Since touching her feet in salutation causes much suffering to the Mother, we should rather avoid it." The Mother heard this and said, "No, my child, we are here for this purpose only. If we do not accept others' sins and sorrows and digest them, who else will? Who else will bear the responsibility for sinners and sufferers? When some noble devotee touches my feet, I feel no pain. But there are persons whose touch brings an acute burning sensation in my feet. Of course, my child, you will salute me by touching my feet."

—

33

(RECORDED BY SARAYUBALA SEN)

One morning as the Holy Mother and Golap-Ma were getting ready to go for a bath in the Ganges, Golap-Ma said, "Mother, please rub oil on your body." The Mother said, "No, I won't use oil." When Golap-Ma continued to urge her, the Mother said, "One should not bathe in the Ganges with oil on one's body. If I use oil, all others will use it."

One day a certain woman came to the Mother with a repentant heart and said, "Mother, what is the way out for us?" The Mother became a little annoyed at this and said, "You bear children every year; you haven't even a little self-control. What is the good of coming to me and saying, 'What is the way out?'"

After the Holy Mother's return from Rameswar, I asked her one day, "Mother, won't you please tell us what you saw?" The Mother said, "Many people came to see me. The women there are fairly educated. They asked me to make a speech. I told them I cannot make speeches. Had Gaurdasi come, she could have given a talk.'"

One day the Mother remarked, "A great soul is unique. He is of a kind by himself. Gaurdasi is one such soul."

Another day I found the Mother putting an amulet on Radhu for the cure of her illness and keeping aside some money for the guardian deity. I asked, "Mother, why are you doing this? Everything happens by your will." The Mother replied, "During one's illness if one promises an offering to the guardian deity, one becomes free of danger. Besides, everybody should be given what is his due."

Once Gauri-Ma was lying seriously ill with smallpox in the house of a devotee at Maniktala. The devotee's mother and others nursed her at the risk of their own lives. On hearing this, the Holy Mother said, "The mother of A.... will be liberated in this very birth. Not only she, but even anybody who had trimmed the wick of the lamp during Gaurdasi's illness will be liberated."

34

(RECORDED BY PRIYABALA DEVI)

On 12 Pous (December) 1916 I first bowed down at the lotus feet of the Holy Mother and was blessed with initiation by her. As I climbed the stairs to the first floor of the Mother's house along with a sister disciple, I was trembling in excitement. Yogin-Ma embraced me and escorted me to the Mother, saying, "Look Mother! Here is another daughter of yours—how her eyes and face look!" The Mother, who was pealing fruits at the time, said, "Yes, dear, I know her. She is Rama's[1] daughter." I was surprised at this and wondered how the Mother had come to know about me.

The Mother called me to the shrine room and made me sit on an *asana* by her side. When my sister disciple invited me to go for a bath in the Ganges, the Mother remarked, "She does not need to have a bath in the Ganges." She sprinkled Ganges water on my body and then gave me initiation. After telling me a word of the Mantra she remarked, "The Master left for me this part of the Mantra." When I was about to offer flowers and leaves at her feet, the Mother said, "Put the basil and Vilva leaves in my hands but offer the flowers at my feet."

One day while speaking with the Mother, the sister disciple mentioned above said about me, "It will be nice if she is admitted into Nivedita's boarding school." The Mother replied, "No, she need not stay there, but it would be fine if she could stay with me." But I never had the good fortune for this to happen.

One day I asked the Mother, "What shall I do for my spiritual progress? I know nothing at all." The Mother said, "What else shall you do ? Do what you are doing now. Repeat His name everyday in the morning and the evening."

On hearing from a woman devotee that widows in our part of the country are very austere regarding their food, etc., the Mother said to me, "In the night you should take *chapatis* and such other things after offering them to the Master. One should observe the local customs."

---

[1]Ramakrishna Bose, son of Balaram Bose.

THE GOSPEL OF SRI SARADA DEVI
THE HOLY MOTHER

SECTION III

TRANSLATED BY OTHERS

1

(RECORDED BY PRAVRAJIKA BHARATIPRANA)[1]

UDBODHAN:

When I met the Holy Mother for the first time, I was a student of Sister Nivedita's school, at 17, Bosepara lane. One day after the school, Sister Sudhira took four or five of us to the Holy Mother's house. The Mother was sitting in the shrine room. Sister Kusum was reading some book. When we bowed down to her, the Mother said, "Sit down, my dear girl." And she said to Sister Sudhira, "Are you well, my dear? Is your school over just now? Do these girls study in your school?"

Sister Sudhira: Yes Mother, these girls study in our school.

Mother: They are good girls. (*Indicating me*), Where does this girl come from? She seems to be a very good girl.

Sister Sudhira: She is of Brahmana parentage. Her house is nearby only.

After this conversation, the Holy Mother said, "Kusum, you read. These people will listen." Reading began. I think the book was *'Krishna Charita'*. Hearing the description of Sri Krishna drinking all the curds and milk through various strategems, the Holy Mother and all others began to laugh very much. She said, "What a mischievous boy!" Soon after, our vehicle arrived. The Mother enquired, "Will you go just now ? Could you not stay a little longer?" Hearing Sister Sudhira's reply, she said, "Then come in the morning, my dear." After receiving Prasad, we bowed down to the Holy Mother and took leave of her. She said "Come, my dear, come again."

Another evening Sister Sudhira took me to the Holy Mother's house. The Mother was lying on a mat spread on a plain cot. Seeing us, she said, "Sit down, my dear." We made Pranam and sat down.

---

[1] Originally a student of the Nivedita Girls' school, Saralabala Devi became later a disciple-attendant of the Holy Mother, and it was she who nursed the Mother in her last illness. When the Sarada Math and the Monastic Order for women was founded in 1953, she became a Sannyasini under the name Pravrajika Bharatiprana and the first Head of the Order. These reminiscences were recorded by her in her pre-monastic days.

Mother: Is your school over? What is the time now?

Sister Sudhira: Today our school was over in the morning itself. Now it is half past three. And so I came, bringing them with me.

Mother: You have done well.

Later the topic of our conversation turned to a girl. The Holy Mother said, "Just see, my dear. She will not go to her father-in-law's place. She has come to me. She does not like the son-in-law because he is dark. Should she reject him simply because he is dark? He is her husband. What kind of girls these are, I do not know. And I hear that his nature is not good. On that account also she does not wish to go. Even if it were so, he has not neglected her. All said and done, he is her husband. I do not know, my dear, what kind of girls these are! If people come to know of this, what will they think? Let her do as she pleases." Saying this, she went to wash her clothes. At the time of taking leave, we made Pranam and said, "Mother, we are going." She corrected me, saying, "You should not say 'I am going'. You should say 'I shall come'.[1] Come again when you get time, dear."

One Saturday evening Sister Sudhira took a few of us to Dakshineswar and on the way back we went to the Holy Mother's house. The Mother was then lying on her cot. Seeing us, Yogin-Ma said, "Where are you coming from at this time of night?" The Mother enquired, "Who has come?" "It is Sudhira", replied Yogin-Ma. Hearing that, the Holy Mother sat up. All of us made Pranam to her and sat down.

Mother: Where are you coming from at this time of night?

Sister Sudhira: I took these girls to Dakshineswar. After seeing Arati, as we were returning, it was dark. I thought, having come so close, should I just go away? And so I came over here.

"You have done well," said the Mother and lay down again. Sister Sudhira began shampooing her feet. I stood nearby fanning the Mother. Sister Sudhira was speaking with her about Dakshineswar.

Mother: You have seen the Nahabat. Have you not? I

---

[1]In the Hindu tradition it is inauspicious to say 'go' at the time of leave-taking.

used to stay in the lower room of that Nahabat. Under the stairs I cooked.

Sister Sudhira: Yes, Mother, I know that. Even now, the stairs on the front side are walled over with matting. Under the stairs there is a hearth. And the baskets of the fisherwomen are left there in that same verandah of yours. I told these girls about you, how you stayed in that room. Well, Mother, how could you live in that room? Did you not have problems?

Mother: The problem was only regarding the morning ablutions and bath. The want of proper toilet arrangements was another. It affected my health. And those fisherwomen were my companions. They came to bathe in the Ganga, and keeping their baskets in the verandah, would get into the water. How much they used to chat with me! And at the time of going, they would pick up their baskets and leave. I used to hear the fishermen sing while catching fish at night. How many devotees used to come to the Master! How much singing! I used to hear it all and think, 'Were I one among those devotees, I too could have stayed very near the Master like them and how much more could I have listened to!' Yogin and Golap know everything. They would come to me and sometimes stay with me.

The Holy Mother looked at Yogin-Ma and said, "How blissful it was then, Yogin!" Saying this, she became a little absent-minded. Yogin-Ma now remarked, "What an intense bliss it was—can it be described in words? The soul is thrilled to think of it even today." The Holy Mother turned to us and said, "It is night. Won't they at home scold you for being late?"

Sister Sudhira: Yes, they will get a little scolding today. Their people at home are quite angry with the folk here. If they hear that these girls have been to this place, they will bite their heads off.

Mother: That is so, my dear. Poor children, how much scolding they will get! How many kinds of people there are—who can say? For those who live in society, there is no end to their fear. Dear ones, you take leave now. Ah! how much scolding they will get!

Sister Sudhira: If they cannot endure a little, what are they good for? By your blessing they will have nothing to fear.

Mother: By the grace of the Master everything will become easy. If they scold, do not say anything in return. In the world so many kinds of people are there. We have to put up with all of them.

The Master used to say: *śa, ṣa, sa* meaning, he who 'endures' alone will live.[1]

For our sake she folded her hands before the Master and said, "Lord, give us protection." We bowed down to her and took leave.

During the holidays, one day at noon, Sister Sudhira and three of us went to the Holy Mother's house. The Mother saw us and said, "Sit in the shrine. I shall come after making the offering to the Master." A little later, when she returned, we bowed down to her. After enquiring about our welfare, she asked, "That day, did they scold you at home?" "Not much," we replied. "We did not even feel it."

At the end of the meal the Holy Mother gave cooked Prasada to Sister Sudhira. Among us two were widows. Seeing that they were hesitating to take it, the Mother said, "You eat, my dear, there is no objection to taking Prasada."

The Holy Mother rested a little thereafter, asking us to lie down on the floor, spreading a mat. In the evening the Mother gave us some Prasada, and sat in the verandah, talking with Sister Sudhira. One young lady handed over a picture of Gopal in a lace knitting to the Holy Mother, made Pranam and sat down. The Mother looked at it and said, "My dear, did you make this?" "Yes, Mother," replied the young lady. "Ah, it is well done. What a beautiful expression in the face! See how well she has done!" remarked the Mother. Saying so, the Holy Mother showed it to all of us and continued, "It is well done, is it not?" We all agreed. She looked at the picture again, touched it to her head and asked it to be hung up. Later she enquired after the welfare of the lady's family and gave Prasada to her.

The Holy Mother showed the lace-work to Golap-Ma as soon as she came and said, "See how beautiful it is!" Pointing to the lady, she explained, "This young lady has done it." Golap-Ma looked at it and said, "Everything is quite well done. Only the left arm has become a little too thick." We began to laugh. The Mother also laughed and said, "Golap has come and showed up the blemish. Their taste is different, my dear. Golap is the master of many arts and is therefore critical. Her work is always neat. Besides she has many kinds of skills. All the personal requirements of the Master used to be made by her. She makes all kinds of

[1]See the foot note on p. 287.

things—mosquito curtains,pillows,pillow cases etc. She is never idle."

A little before dusk the lady made Pranam to the Holy Mother and was taking her leave. The Mother said, "Come again, my dear." Yogin-Ma came and bowed down to the Holy Mother and sat. After a little conversation the Holy Mother showed her also the picture and said, "See how beautifully it is done! What a beautiful expression in the face!" "Well done indeed! Who has done it? It has come out quite excellently!" exclaimed Yogin-Ma. The Holy Mother told her about the lady and said, "Golap says that the left hand is a little stout." Yogin-Ma replied "O, don't mind her words."

When it was dusk the Holy Mother made Pranam, saying, "Haribol, Haribol, Gurudev, Guru's grace" etc., and bowed down in the direction of the Ganges. She spread her seat in the room and sat down, took a little Ganges water and started doing her Japa. The Arati now started. The room was full of people, of whom many were doing Japa. What a wonderful sight!

On the day of Akshay Tritiya two of my friends took initiation. Unluckily, I could not have it at that time, as I was not then in Calcutta. A little after this, one evening, I went with Sister Sudhira to the Holy Mother's house. The Mother was to have gone to her village but the journey had been put off.

The Holy Mother replied to some questions put by Sister Sudhira and then said, "My youngest sister-in-law has become quite abnormal. She will be better as soon as she goes to the village. And there is Radhu's marriage. Because of all this, I have to go soon. Everything was fixed up for my journey that day. But it was postponed, as the day was not quite auspicious." After Arati, the Holy Mother lay down a little.Sister Sudhira was massaging her feet. The Mother said, "Press a little harder, my dear. Tomorrow is full moon day, and so the rheumatism in the leg is aggravated. Just see, this disease has taken such a hold that there is no sign of its abatement. It started quite long ago, when I was still staying at Dakshineswar."

Gaining a little relief through the massage, the Holy Mother fell into a nap. Our vehicle arrived. We made Pranam to the Master and were leaving, when the Holy Mother woke up and said, "Are you going? Come again." Yogin-Ma told her about my initiation. "Come tomorrow morning," she replied.

Next day morning when I reached the Holy Mother's house,

she had finished the Master's worship and was getting ready to go for her bath in the Ganges. Seeing me, she said, "Come, my dear, I shall initiate you quickly and then go for bath." After the initiation was over, she said, "Offer these flowers at my feet." I was wondering what I should say while offering. The Holy Mother gave me some flowers and continued, " 'Whatever that is mine, I offer unto you' — saying this, offer these flowers at my feet." I complied. Showing me the Master's picture, she said, "He is your all in all. Call upon Him and everything will be yours."

I applied oil upon her feet at her bidding. After the Mother finished her bath, Sister Sudhira said that we should now be leaving. "How can you go away now, my dear?" objected the Holy Mother. "Have your Prasad and go in the evening." When Yogin-Ma came upstairs, the Holy Mother told her, "These people want to go home." Yogin-Ma said: "They should take Prasad, and then go. I have just told the cook about their food."

Yogin-Ma was going home. She bowed down at the Holy Mother's feet. The Holy Mother placed her hand on her head and blessed her and said, "It is quite late in the day. Why don't you take your food here? To cook again after reaching home will be difficult." "No, Mother. My mother is there. She would have made all arrangements. I shall have only just to cook," replied Yogin-Ma. So the Holy Mother hurried her on the journey, saying, "Then don't make any more delay, my dear. The sun is hot and you have to go quite a long distance."

After that, Lalit Babu's wife came, made Pranam and sat down. Her daughters had passed away recently and she was grief-stricken. The Holy Mother consoled her in various ways. Said she, "Ah, all the three passed away! Could not at least one survive? Added to that, Lalit is ill. May he recover by the Master's grace. It will be a great solace if Lalit is saved." She gave her Prasad and continued, "Eat, my dear. How thin you have become!" Taking leave, Sister Sudhira now said to the Holy Mother, "After how many days hence could I hope to have your Darsan?" "I shall return soon," replied the Holy Mother. "Why don't you come to attend Radhu's marriage?" Sister Sudhira did not say anything in reply to this, but said, "For the present I shall take leave, Mother." The Holy Mother gave her blessings and said, "Come again after my return."

After the Holy Mother came back from the village, Sister

Sudhira and I went to the Mother's house one evening and paid our respects to her. Sister Sudhira remarked, "Mother, you have become very dark and lean." "Our village is in open fields, you know," the Mother replied, "and so the complexion becomes dark. In addition I had to work hard too."

Sister Nivedita now came in, bowed down to the Holy Mother and took her seat. The Holy Mother enquired after her welfare, and gave her a woollen fan made by herself, saying, "I kept this for you." The Sister was very happy to receive it. She put it on her head, touched it to her heart and said, "How beatiful, how wonderful!" She showed it to us and said, "Just see how beautifully it is made !" The Holy Mother said appreciatively, "Do you notice her happiness upon receiving some small present! Ah, what simple faith! As if she were a Goddess! How much devotion she has for Naren! Because he is born in this country, she left her all and has come to do his work with her heart and soul. What a devotion to the Guru! What love for this country!"

The Sister was going to Darjeeling. She told the Holy Mother about it. When Radhu came in, the Holy Mother told her, "Radhu, bow down to your sisters." Sister Sudhira protested, saying, "No, no; let her not do so. Why should she salute us?" But the Holy Mother persisted, saying, "You are all her elder sisters. Should she not salute you?" One Brahmacharin now came in and informed the Holy Mother of men devotees waiting to make Pranam to her. "Let them come," she said and sat covering herself with a shawl. Some time later we returned home after receiving the Mother's blessing.

One day Sister Nivedita told us that the Holy Mother would visit our School, and that we should all be full of joy on the occasion. The Holy Mother's carriage arrived only in the evening instead of in the morning. Radhu, Golap Ma and others were with her. As soon as she got down from the vehicle, Sister Nivedita made Sashtanga Pranam (full prostration) to her and led her to the prayer hall. She gave us all flowers to be offered at the Holy Mother's feet. As the girls offered flowers, Sister Nivedita introduced them one by one to the Holy Mother. The Mother asked the girls to sing a little. They did so and recited a poem. The Holy Mother listened to it and appreciated the poem. Then she directed some Prasad to be given to us. A little later Sister Nivedita took her around and showed her the whole house, the handicrafts of the girls, etc. On seeing all that, the Mother was much pleased and remarked, "The girls have indeed got good training." Later on Sister Nivedita took the Mother to her own room for rest.

At the time of Sister Nivedita's passing away, Sister Sudhira too was quite ill. How much the Holy Mother worried for her sake! She would cry, saying, "Oh Master, has Sudhira got to go? How much work she has still to do!"

To the 'aunt at Syampukur' the Holy Mother said, "Could you bring me news of Sister Sudhira, my dear? Ah, how ill she is!" When she agreed, the Holy Mother gave her the Master's Charanamrita, pomegranate etc., and said, "Give these to her, and let me know how she is. I am offering Tulasi leaves to the Master for her sake."

After Sister Sudhira recovered her health, she, I and Sister Christine went to the Holy Mother's house one evening. After Arati we made Pranam to her and seated ourselves before her. "Have you got well, my dear?" enquired the Holy Mother. Sister Sudhira replied that she was much better but that she had still to be careful. "I was greatly worried about you," said the Holy Mother. "You have, however, recovered by the Master's grace. Just now Nivedita passed away and you fell ill right after that—hearing it I wondered, if Sudhira too goes, who will run the school? (*Refering to Sister Christine*) Ah, they were together all the time. Now how much more difficult it will be for her to be alone! Even our hearts are afflicted by her demise, what then to speak of your grief! What a personality she was! How many people weep for her today!" Speaking thus, the Holy Mother began to weep. Later she asked Sister Christine many questions about the school.

Sister Sudhira was to go to Kasi for a change. I was to accompany her. Hearing that from us, the Holy Mother made detailed enquiries about our plan and said, "Start soon, my dear. The body is to be cared for, is it not?"

It was many days later that I went to the Holy Mother next. Mrs———was with me. As Sister Sudhira was not with me that time, I was greatly worried whether the Holy Mother would be able to recognise me. We went to the shrine and saw that the Mother had got up after finishing the Puja. Seeing me, she said, "Oh! my dear, you have come at last? It is many days since your last visit, is it not? How much I thought of you! Where were you?" As I made Pranam, she put her hand on my head and blessed me and enquired about Sister Sudhira. I said that she had come to Calcutta and that I came with her. My soul was filled with bliss at the thought that the Holy Mother could recognise me.

That day there was an invitation from Balaram Babu's house and all were going there. Radhu was not well. So the Holy Mother said referring to me, "She won't go anyhow, not being an invitee. Radhu and she shall remain here."

The vehicle to take the Holy Mother arrived. Before leaving, the Mother told us, "You two amuse yourselves. I shall return quickly." Then she said to Radhu, "Play with your sister, my dear. I shall return shortly."

The Holy Mother came back after four. I, together with others, was to go by the same vehicle. The Mother hastily gave me some Prasad and said, "Ah, my dear, we have just arrived and you are going away immediately. What can be done? You have come with them, and it is proper for you to return with them."

Radhu: Why not let the sister stay?

Mother: How can she stay, my dear?

Radhu: No, let her stay. Let the others go away.

Mother: She (Radhu) is senseless, for sure. If she stays, how can the others go? No, my dear. You get ready quickly, they are calling you from below.

I bowed down to the Holy Mother and took leave of her. She blessed me and said, "How many days you have to stay like this, the Master alone knows. Come again, my dear." She came with me upto the stairs. What a deep compassion of hers I experienced that day, I cannot describe in words. She gave me much instruction, saying "Do this, do that etc."

VARANASI: 1912

During the holidays of the month of Paush (February), Sister Sudhira wished to be with the Holy Mother and went to Kasi, taking along a few of us with her. When we met the Holy Mother, after some talk, she enquired about Yogin-Ma and said, "Ah, my dear, Yogin could not come. She was quite ill. The Master and the Divine Mother saved her. I was much worried over Yogin." After a little conversation, Sister Sudhira and others went to see the house hired for our stay.

The Holy Mother fell asleep a little. The house was almost silent with everybody resting. In that silence a song was heard from the verandah:

Where has my Mother gone?
For many days have I not seen you; Mother, take me in the lap.
What sort of a Mother art Thou, so stony-hearted towards the child!
Grant Thy vision, Mother, and make me weep no more.

The song was sung in such a gentle tone that I felt as though some one was weeping at quite a distance. Suddenly the Holy Mother woke up and said, "Who is singing? Let us go, my dear, to the verandah and see." We went and what I saw struck me dumb with astonishment. One girl was singing the song and her chest was bathed in tears as she sang. As the Holy Mother sat there, the girl bowed down to her and said, "Mother, my heart's desire of many days is fulfilled today. I cannot express the joy that is flooding me today, Mother." The Holy Mother blessed her and asked her about herself.

Girl: I am only a beggar girl, Mother.

Mother: Where do you stay?

Girl: I stay at the gate of Annapurna, near the Behari Baba's temple at the Dasasvamedh Ghat.

Mother: You are well off by taking alms , I hope?

Girl: By your blessing everything goes on well, Mother. There is no worry about daily needs. By the grace of Annapurna, no one has to go without food here, Mother. I am worried about how to get a little Bhakti.

Mother: That will certainly come about, my dear. You stay in such a sacred place. Here Lord Viswanath and Mother Annapurna are reigning actually. By Their grace everything will come about.

The Holy Mother asked her to sing another song. She began to sing:

Mother, may thou be pleased to
keep me as a child!
Let me not grow,
leaving behind the beauty of childhood.
A beautiful simple soul,
unaware of honour and infamy;
It does not know cruelty,
nor censure nor shame nor contempt.

Mother: What a beautiful song!

Girl: I had a great desire for many days to see you. Hearing that you are here, I often think of coming but feel afraid that some one would object.

Mother: None will say anything. Come whenever you like.

The Holy Mother asked Prasad to be given to her. After receiving Prasad the girl was taking leave. The Holy Mother told her, "Come again, my dear." Later she told us, "The girl has great devotion."

During the few days we were in Kasi, we used to go to the Holy Mother everyday, morning and evening. One evening, when we went there,the Mother was going to the Ramakrishna Advaita Ashrama to attend a Bhagavata discourse. Seeing us, she said "We are going to hear the Bhagavata at the Math. Some Pandit recites. Will you come? Why not you come with us?" We went with her. The talk lasted two hours. After the talk was over, the Holy Mother gave a Rupee, bowed down and returned. In the course of a conversation she said, "Ah, what a wonderful recitation! The Pandit has done very well."

One day after dusk Sister Sudhira and I were sitting near the Holy Mother. The Mother then said, "Any one who has once called on the Master, with sincere faith and devotion has nothing more to fear. As one calls on Him, by His grace one gets Prema-bhakti, loving devotion. This love is to be cherished in utmost privacy, my dear. The Gopis of Vraja had this Prema-bhakti. They did not know anything except Krishna. It is said in Nilakantha's song: 'This treasure of Prema must be preserved with the greatest effort.'" Saying this, the Holy Mother sang the song. In what a sweet voice did she sing that day! It is even today resounding in my ears. At the end of the song, she said, "Ah, how excellent is this song of Nilakantha! The Master liked it immensely. While the Master was at Dakshineswar, Nilakantha would come to him now and then and sing songs. How blissful it was! How many kinds of people came to him! It was as if a mart of joy was set up at Dakshineswar."

I went to the Holy Mother's house another day. The Mother was sitting in the verandah and talking with two ladies. The beggar girl mentioned earlier came and bowed down to the Holy Mother. In her hand was a pear. She offered it to the Mother and said, "Mother, I got it as alms today, and so I have brought it for you. But Mother, I cannot muster the courage to offer it to you." "You have done well," assured the Holy Mother. "Ah! give it to me,my dear." Saying this,she took the pear, touched it to her head and said, "The things given as alms are very pure. The Master loved them very much. It is quite a good pear too. I shall eat it now." The girl was deeply touched and said, "I am only a beggar girl, what compassion are you bestowing upon me!" Tears trickled down her cheeks as she said this. The Holy Mother continued, "Your songs are so sweet. Now do sing a song for me."

The girl sang:

Gopal, I shall deck you now.
  Do dance thus and thus, wheel and turn about.
I shall fix up your anklets, my dear,
  They would sound well jingling.
A golden cloth I shall wrap around your waist.
  Gopal, my dear, I shall feed you,
And give you two pairs of golden wristlets.

Concluding the song,she added, "Mother, if this song is sung, the Behari Baba Sadhu of Dasasvamedha Ghat would keep dancing just like Gopal. His nature is exactly like that of a boy."

The Holy Mother said, "Quite a good song, won't you sing another?" She sang another song. The Holy Mother asked Prasad to be given her. Taking the Prasad, she bowed down to the Mother saying, "I shall take leave for the day, Mother." "Come again, my dear, come whenever you like," said the Holy Mother.

One day at about three, the Holy Mother picked us up on her way to the Old Women's Ashrama. When we got down there, a young woman came and took the Holy Mother upstairs. All the old ladies began to offer flowers at her feet and bow down at her feet.

Mother: What is this? These are all dwellers of Kasi. Why then do they make Pranam?

Young Woman: Should they not, Mother? They are all maintained by your food.

Mother: My dear, Lord Viswanath and Mother Annapurna are there. I take it that you are the care-taker of these people?

Young Women: Yes, mother, as you make me do.

Mother: Ah, that is good. If these helpless old ladies are served, Narayana's service is done. Ah, what wonderful work these children are doing!

After that, the Holy Mother made their acquaintance, visited their rooms and returned.

One day after dusk we returned from Sarnath and went to the Holy Mother's house. The Mother was lying down. Radhu was lying by her side. Hearing the description of Sarnath, she asked, "Mother, will you go once to see the place?" "How can that be, my dear?" responded the Holy Mother. "Do I have legs to go round and see? Just look, my dear, I cannot go and have Darsan of Viswanath even. Seeing all these people go, I too get a desire to go and see Lord Viswanath. But I cannot walk. How to go? I cannot do anything. When my legs were in good condition, I walked from my village to Dakshineswar. What a distance could I walk then! After the Master's passing away, I went to Vrindaban. I used to walk from place to place and have Darsan."

Another day one woman and her daughter of ten or eleven years were seated near the Holy Mother. The woman was very poor.

Mother: Where is your husband?

Woman: He became a Bairagi some time back. He went away when this girl was quite young.

Mother: All these days how have you managed without work?

Woman: I did some work and managed with whatever was got. Now this won't do any longer, Mother, I am in great difficulty. If only you could tell them and arrange something, Mother!

Mother: I could put in a word. But they collect by begging. How many people they help that way! They will do as they think fit, surely.

The Holy Mother gave her a rupee and a cloth and said, "Take food here today." The Mother was sitting on the roof. Below, the cooking was going on. The woman said, "Mother, the girl says 'What a fine smell of cooking is coming!' " The Holy Mother said reprovingly, "What is this? Should one say such things? The food is intended for the Master's offering." At the time of taking Prasad the Holy Mother told the cook to serve a large helping of fish curry etc, to the girl. After food, the woman said, "I had a hearty meal, Mother; the girl does not want even to get up." "That's good," said the Holy Mother. "Now that the meal is over, go below and rinse your mouth." When the woman went away, the Holy Mother said, "What poverty! What greed! The girl ate and ate until she was about to vomit! Such a big girl and no sense at all. Nothing will benefit these people. Prosperity will never attend on them."

When they returned upstairs, the Holy Mother gave them betel rolls and bade them goodbye. After they had gone away, the Mother lay down on the cot and was chatting with us. "So many kinds of people live in Kasi," she said. "How many of them come to me and say 'Please tell your children to help us a little.' What could I reply? You just see, they built a home for helpless old women. How hard they have worked for it, and how much service they are doing! A hospital for the sick is there. Their activities for the relief of the poor seem endless. How much the poor children toil! It is all His will, my dear. What He is making us do from where, He alone knows."

One evening when I went to the Holy Mother, she was sitting in the verandah talking with a few widows. One among them was wearing an ochre cloth. She sang a song for the Holy Mother—

'Just you wait, Oh Java, you the beauty of the forest!
Flower of the wild you are, blossoming in the wild.
When I see you on the bosom of Siva,
I think I see the crimson feet of the Divine Mother,' etc.

Golap-Ma: Ah, what an excellent song! Do sing another.

The girl sang another song.

Mother: Have you seen the Sevashrama?

Sister Sudhira: No, we have not seen.

Mother: Then go with Golap and see.

Another evening the Holy Mother was talking of Devavrata Maharaj and Sachin. They went away suddenly because of the Government's objection to their presence on account of their political antecedents.

Mother: Ah, Devavrata went away today. The Company (the East India Company, the old name for the British Govt. in India) offered some help in connection with the acquisition of the land proximate to the Sevashrama. But they raised objection against the stay of these two. So Rakhal told them to go away. Do you know, my dear, they are innocent, but yet a detective is ever after them. Ah, the boys did not even take food before going.

Sister Sudhira: Brother (i.e. Devavrata Maharaj) and Sachin had food with us.

Mother: Ah, my dear, did they have their meal? That is good. I was worried about it.

Sister Sudhira: Wherever brother goes, they keep track of him. So he says 'My father-in-law's people have come. I will go, have a look and return.'

Mother: Father-in-law's people indeed! It was very long ago that they caught him in connection with the Swadeshi Movement. Still they are on his trail. Just see, the whole day my mind was troubled thinking that the boys had had no food. I am, however, at peace now, after learning that they took food at your place.

UDBODHAN, CALCUTTA

It was the day of the Jagaddhatri Puja. Devotees had been arriving from early morning. The Puja was at Yogin-Ma's house. She came in the morning and went back, asking the Holy Mother to go to her house. One devotee came, bowed down, and said, "Mother, be so gracious as to sanctify the house of your worthless son by bestowing in it the dust of your lotus feet." "Well, let me see if I can go in the evening. You come again in the evening. I shall come, if I find it convenient," responded the Holy Mother.

That noon the Holy Mother and some of us went to Yogin-Ma's house, had the Darsan of the Deity and returned. The Holy Mother fasted the whole day as there was Puja in her house. At about four when the Puja was over, she took a little Prasad and rested.

That devotee came to take the Holy Mother. The Holy Mother heard of it and said, 'He pressed me so much in the morning. I'll go for a little while.' Their home was not far away. It was in the Rajvallabhpara. As the Holy Mother got down from the vehicle, they washed her feet and preserved the water. The house was small, and dilapidated. We made Pranam to the Deity and went inside. They spread a seat for the Holy Mother to sit. She spread her seat near the door and said, "I'll rather sit here."

One old lady began to talk with the Mother.

Old Lady: Mother, please bless my boy. He had a great desire to perform the Puja, but we have no house or other facilities. Yet somehow the Mother's worship has been done. He alone did everything.

Mother: Ah! he did well. When Mother has come, then

house and everything else will come. Your boy is very good. He has much devotion.

A little later Prasad was brought and the Holy Mother put a little in her mouth and got up to leave. She put a rupee before the Deity, made Pranam and said, "The image is very beautiful. Mother's expression is wonderful; this is because the worship has been done by a devotee!" Returning home, Nalini began, "What a house, oh Mother! There is no place to sit even. Oh dear, how could he perform the worship in that house." The Holy Mother said, "What can he do? He is a poor man,but very devoted. Ah, he brought the Divine Mother. Out of compassion the Divine Mother came to his house."

A letter came from Jayrambati saying that the worship of Mother Jagaddhatri concluded successfully and that many people had Prasad. The Holy Mother said, "By the grace of the Mother, the worship was concluded auspiciously. I was much worried about how they would manage. Jnan was there, so the Mother's worship was done well."

One day after dusk the Holy Mother was sitting near Radhu, giving her fomentation. Radhu had a pain under her ribs. Now one woman devotee made Pranam to the Mother and sat down.

Mother: Come my dear. How are you?

Devotee: I am well, Mother. What has happened to Radhu?

Mother: Radhu has the same sickness. Just see, the child is exhausted. The wretched pain—wherefrom has it come? So many doctors are attending, and I am making vows of offerings to so many Deities, but all to no effect.

Devotee: She will get well, Mother, why fear?

Mother: Do bless her.

She took Prasad and left after a little chat. I asked the Holy Mother, "How surprising, Mother? How she has changed! It is beyond my understanding."

Mother: How can you understand, my dear? When sin enters, is there a way to protect oneself? She is forbidden to come to my place. And so she comes stealthily at night.

Disciple: I saw her earlier staying with you.

Mother: Yes, earlier she used to be with me in day time and go home at night. How much she served Radhu! Her star turned a little and she has become like this. Coming to me is completely stopped. She has done nothing in this birth, all flow from the past birth only.

Another evening the Holy Mother was sitting in the room. The Master's disciple Purna Babu was quite ill. There was no hope of his survival. His mother came. Seeing her come, the Holy Mother said, "There she comes. How she troubles me coming every day,saying, 'Mother, please bless. Please make Purna well.' I know that Purna will not survive. Still for their sake I have to say, 'He will get well.'" Purna Babu's mother came, made Pranam to Holy Mother and said, 'Mother, make your child well,' and began to weep.

Mother: What can I do, mother? Appeal to the Master. He will set everything right.

Purna Babu's Mother: You can, if only you wish, Mother.

Mother: I for my part can only let the Master know of it.

Later the Holy Mother told us, "The Master had said, 'If you marry him off, he will not live long'. She did not listen then. In haste, lest he should become a Sannyasin, she got him married."

A few days later, the Holy Moter, Yogin-Ma, etc., were lying down after evening Arati. The Mother was drowsing a little. Suddenly she got up, saying, "Is Purna dead, Yogin?" Yogin-Ma was amazed to hear this query and asked, "Who told you this, Mother?" The Holy Mother replied, "I was sleeping. Suddenly I heard some one saying 'Purna is dead'. Yogin-Ma confessed then, "Yes, Mother. Today evening that calamity occured. I did not tell you, Mother." That night the Holy Mother would speak only of Purna Babu. She was quite sorry for his sake.

In Dakshineswar at the time of the Master's illness, the Holy Mother was serving him. Later the devotees took him to Calcutta for treatment. During that time Golap-Ma said to Yogin-Ma in the course of conversation, "Look,Yogin-Ma , perhaps the Master was angry with the Holy Mother and went away to Calcutta." The Holy Mother heard this from Yogin-Ma, and hiring a carriage went to Calcutta. Weeping , she asked the Master, "You have come away, being angry with me. Haven't you?" "No, no, who told you this story?" the Master asked in surprise.

"Golap said," replied the Holy Mother. The Master was enraged to hear this and said, "Is that so? Did she speak thus and make you weep? Does she not know who you are? Where is Golap? Let her come, I'll teach her to desist from telling such stories." The Holy Mother was thus pacified and returned to Dakshineswar. Later when Golap-Ma came to the Master, he scolded her severely and said, "What did you tell her to make her weep? Do you not know who she is? Go this moment and seek her forgiveness." Immediately Golap-Ma walked all the way to Dakshineswar and said to the Holy Mother, weeping, "Oh Mother, the Master was terribly angry with me. I did not realise the seriousness of what I said, and merely blurted out those words." The Holy Mother did not say anything except, "Oh Golap! Oh Golap!" She patted her thrice on the back, smiling. All the grief of Golap vanished that moment, and her mind was restored to peace. This incident was narrated to us by Golap-Ma herself.

Revered Baburam Maharaj was performing Durga Puja at Belur Math and he took the Holy Mother there. The Holy Mother stayed in the garden house north of the Math. One lady devotee suddenly presented herself to the Holy Mother one night. Seeing her intense desire to see her, the Holy Mother said, "Look, if this kind of yearning is not there, can one get Him?"

In the year 1918 Golap-Ma was seriously ill. In that crisis, the Holy Mother was praying to the Master, "O Lord, please heal Golap. If Golap and Yogin are not here, I cannot stay here any longer. With them gone, how can I stay here?" She then said, "Yogin and Golap know all the stages of my life. Ah, Golap has no kind of shortcoming. She does not know anything of pride. And look, Yogin also is like that. In those days Yogin used to meditate with such concentration that even if mosquitoes sat on her eyes, she was unaware of them. Ah, those will be blessed who speak of them."

One day Yogin-Ma complained to the Holy Mother of the licentious behaviour of a devotee and said, "Mother. please warn him a little. Otherwise he will be spoiled." The Holy Mother replied, "My telling won't do, Yogin. If I tell him anything, he would not be able to listen. I am his Guru. If he cannot respect my words, then it would be inauspicious for him." Yogin-Ma did not say anything more.

One evening, after talking about diverse matters, the Holy Mother said, "Look, I suppose everybody says that I am restless with the thought of Radhu, that I am inordinately attached to her. If this little attachment were not there, do you know, this body could not have survived after the Master's passing away. It is for his work that he has generated this attachment for Radhu and detained this body. When my mind withdraws from her, this body will not remain anymore."

In the year 1918 the Holy Mother was once quite unwell at Koalpara. At that time Yogin-Ma and revered Sarat Maharaj were with her. Radhu saw the serious condition of the Holy Mother and yet went away to her father-in-law's place. The Holy Mother did not want her to go. She said to Yogin-Ma, "Look here Yogin! Radhu has deserted me and gone away." Yogin-Ma replied, "Why won't she go, Mother? Did you not walk all the way to Dakshineswar to be with the Master? Do you not remember?" The Holy Mother smiled a little and said, "That is true, Yogin." The Mother recovered from this illness and came back to Calcutta.

At the Udbodhan, she said one day, "Look, when Radhu broke her attachment for me and went away, I thought perhaps this time I would pass away. But I see that still there is more of the Master's work to be done."

Once Yogin-Ma got a doubt: "The Master was a man of such renunciation, and I see the Holy Mother so deeply engrossed in this wretched world, with all her brothers and brothers-in-law and sisters-in-law. I cannot understand this." One day while meditating on the Ganges Ghat, Yogin-Ma saw the Master. He was saying, "Look at that object floating on the Ganges." Yogin-Ma saw a new born baby tangled in entrails and filth, floating past in the Ganges. The Master now asked, "Can the Ganges be polluted by it? Can anything sully its purity? Know her to be like that. Do not doubt her. Know her (the Mother) and this (showing his own body) to be one." Returning from the Ganges, Yogin-Ma bowed down to the Holy Mother and said, "Mother, forgive me." "Why, Yogin? What happened?" the Holy Mother enquired. Yogin-Ma then narrated the incident and said, "I was unfaithful to you. So the Master made it clear to me today." The Mother smiled a little and said, "What of that? Doubts will arise and again faith will come. This way alone faith is strengthened. Gradually, after many such attempts, firm faith will come."

One lady devotee used to come to the Holy Mother at the Udbodhan. The Mother was quite fond of her. She was not of a good character. So among the monks, many used to wish that she did not come there. When the Holy Mother was apprised of this, she said, "On the Ganges so many impure things float by. Does the Ganges ever become impure thereby?"

One devotee asked some questions of the Holy Mother and left. Later the Mother herself said, "Look, my dear, you must surrender and await His pleasure. Then alone will His grace descend."

Once I asked her with regard to Japa. "How shall I do Japa?" The Holy Mother replied, "With whatever thought you do Japa, that thought will take hold of the mind. Think that the Master is always yours." Later she demonstrated the way of doing Japa on the fingers.

While talking of her days in Vrindaban, after the passing away of the Master, the Holy Mother said one day at the Udbodhan, "Look, my dear, I prayed to Lord Radharamana, 'Lord, take away my fault-finding nature. May it be that I never can see anyone's fault.'"

The Holy Mother used to say, "Man is bound to make mistakes. One should not notice them. If one dos not follow this rule, it harms oneself alone. By constantly observing the faults of others, in the end one will become a mere fault-finder." Once she said to Yogin-Ma, "Yogin, never notice anyone's faults; else, you will end up as a fault-finder only."

One night at Jayrambati, the Holy Mother was lying down. As usual, I was then massaging her feet. In the course of conversation, she began to tell how she first gave initiation, "Look, my dear," she said, "I was at Vrindaban after the Master's passing away. Every one was distraught with grief over his loss. One night the Master said, 'Why are you weeping so much? Where have I gone—except from this room to that?' One day the Master spoke of giving initiation to the boy Yogen. Hearing that, I felt a little afraid and also shy. Seeing him the first day I thought, 'What is this? And what will people think? Every one will say that the Mother has already started making disciples.' But the Master repeated this instruction on three days in succession: 'I have not given him Mantra Diksha (initiation). You do it.' He told me which Mantra was to be given as well. In those days, I was not in the habit of speaking directly to the boy Yogen. The Master said that I should speak to him through Yogin-Ma. I then said the same thing to Yogin. She asked the boy Yogen and discovered that the Master had not initiated him. The Master appeared to the boy Yogen also and asked him to be initiated by me. Yogen did not have the courage to speak of it to me. When I saw that the Master told both of us the same thing, I gave initiation to Yogen.

With Yogen's initiation my period of imparting initiations began. He served me unstintedly. No one else could have served as he did. Only Sarat could. And Sarat is serving only after the boy Yogen's demise. To carry my burden is very hard, my dear. Except Sarat, no one can bear my responsibility. Golap and Yogin—if they were not there, it would not have been possible for me to stay at Calcutta."

While the Holy Mother was at Jayrambati, one devotee came to her from Ranchi and said, "I have come to take you to Ranchi for a few days. Accommodation etc. have all been arranged." "Does Sarat know about this?" asked the Holy Mother. "No," was the reply. The Holy Mother continued, "Then I cannot come. Sarat came here and returned. I shall first go to Calcutta. If he approves, then we shall see." The devotee persisted saying, "Mother, we have made all arrangements!" But the Holy Mother was firm. "Why did you do so without letting us know of it first?" she asked.

The devotee left. Later the Holy Mother remarked, "Look, my dear, they think that to take me is very easy. They are led away by popular excitement. Another time in Dacca, they printed pamphlets that I would be going there. Yet I knew nothing of it. Any one can serve for two or three days. Is it easy to carry my whole responsibility? I have not seen that anyone is capable of it except Sarat. He is my Vasuki. With a thousand hoods he is engaged in so much work. Wherever a little water drips,he will hold an umbrella there."

One day a woman devotee told the Mother about her strained relations with one of her friends. Thereupon the Mother said, "Look, my dear, if one loves a human being one has to endure grief and sorrow. If one can love God, one is indeed blessed, one has no more grief or sorrow."

Another day one woman devotee wished to learn the rituals connected with the Master's Puja from the Holy Mother. The Mother replied, "Look, you are in the world. You will not be able to do so much. You have received His name; let me see how much you can do with it. If you could do that properly, everything will be all right."

Once the Holy Mother gave me a silk cloth. Some one objected and said, "Why are you giving the cloth to her only, Mother? There are five more people waiting." The Holy Mother replied, "If I do not give it to her, who else will give? Tell me who else is there for her?"

Because of Radhu's illness the Holy Mother was staying at the rented boarding house of Nivedita's school in Bosepara. I was there to serve her. One day she asked me to make food offering to the Master. I did not know the Mantras etc., for offering food. So I told the Mother, "But, Mother, I do not know how to offer food to the Master." The Holy Mother then explained, "Look, my dear, think of the Master as your own and say, 'Please come, please sit down, please take, please eat,' and you must think that he has come, he has sat down, and he is taking food. Do you need Mantras etc., for your own near and dear ones? All ceremonies and forms are like the honour and respect shown to relatives when they come. With your own people you won't need all that. With whatever attitude you give him, with the same attitude he will take." After that the Holy Mother taught me a Mantra for making food-offering to the Master.

The Holy Mother once said to a disciple, "Look, my dear, it is not that you will not face difficulties. They will arise. But they will not remain. You will see that they pass away like water under one's feet."

One devotee asked the Holy Mother, "I have done so much Japa and austerity, yet nothing has happened." In reply she said, "What you seek—is it any greens or fish that you could buy it by paying so much price?"

In Jayrambati the Holy Mother's close relatives used to harass her in various ways. One day she became so much vexed that she said, "Look here, do not trouble me too much. If the one who is within me once raises his hood, there is none among Brahma, Vishnu or Maheswara that can save you."

In the year 1919 the Holy Mother was at Koalpara. On the day of the Dassera festival some devotees worshipped her holy feet with lotus flowers and left. Later she asked me, "What is the matter today, that all those boys offered flowers at my feet?" "Today is Dassera," I replied. "That is why they did so." The Holy Mother smiled a little and said, "Oh dear, am I Goddess Manasa, then?" And folding her hand in the direction of the Master she continued, "He alone is Manasa, Ganga and everybody else."

Radhu was like a madcap during her stay at Jayrambati because of her neurosis. Many times the Holy Mother used to feed her. Often, she would take food in her mouth and spit it out on the Mother's body. One day the Holy Mother was annoyed and said to me, "Look, my dear, know this body (showing her own) to be a divine body. How much more defilement and insult could it endure? If it is not a divine body, can any human being endure so much? The Master never struck me even with a flower. He never addressed me as *tui* but always as *tumi*. How much he was distressed because once he addressed me as *tui* mistaking me for Lakshmi! Biting his tongue, he said, 'Oh dear, is it you? Please do not take it amiss. I thought you were Lakshmi and so addressed you as *tui*.[1]' But see how these people take the life out of me, my dear. This time if the Master somehow cures Radhu, I will have nothing more to do with them. Look, my dear, as long as I live, none of these can know me. Later they will understand everything."

At the Udbodhan, during the Mother's last illness a certain monk came to see her. The Mother was then sleeping. The monk began to massage her feet. There was no veil over the Holy Mother's head at the time. After the monk went away, the Mother rebuked me, saying, "There was no veil over my head. Why did you not arrange it? Am I dead? Even now you are doing like this!"

At this time the Holy Mother had practically no taste for any food, and could not eat anything. Her food therefore was very meagre. One day while she was taking food, Dr. Kanjilal arrived there. He thought the quantity of the Holy Mother's food was a little too much, and said to me in front of the Holy Mother, "You will not be able to serve the Mother. Tomorrow I will bring two nurses for her service. You need not do anything." The Holy Mother heard these words of the doctor and said later, "Ha! Does he think that I will be served by those booted ladies? That I cannot do. You will attend upon me as you have done. Why does Kanjilal make so much fuss over my eating rice? Am I able to consume rice? He does not know!"

A few days after this, her rice diet was completely stopped. One day the Holy Mother said, "Look, that day Kanjilal was annoyed at my taking rice. From that time on I could not eat any rice at all."

During those days the Mother's nature became like that of a five year old girl. One night at twelve when I went to feed her, she

---

[1]See the footnote on p. 75.

became stubborn. "I will not eat. You know only to say, 'Mother, eat,' and to put that stick(the thermometer) under the arm." Seeing that the Holy Mother was refusing to take food, I said, "Then, Mother, shall I call Maharaj?" Often she would eat at the mention of Maharaj's name. But this time she was totally unwilling. She said, "Call Sarat. I will not eat from your hand." As soon as Sarat Maharaj heard of it, he hastened to the Holy Mother. She made him sit and said, "Just pass your hand over me a little, my son." Then taking both his hands in hers, she continued, "Just see, my son, how they are troubling me! Her constant utterance is 'Eat, eat,' and she knows also to put that stick under my arm. You ask her not to trouble me." Maharaj replied, "No, Mother, they will not trouble you anymore." Pacifying her thus, he later enquired, "Mother, will you now take something?" The Holy Mother replied, "Give me." Maharaj asked me to bring food. The Holy Mother heard this and said, "No, you feed me, I will not eat from her hand." I poured milk in a cup and gave it to Maharaj. He somehow fed a little of it to the Holy Mother and said, "Mother,rest a little and eat." Hearing this, the Holy Mother said, "Look now, what sweet words these are—'Mother, rest a little and then take food!' Do they not know how to say these words? But see, what trouble they have given the poor boy at this time of night! Go, my dear, go and sleep." Saying this, she stroked his body. Later Sarat Maharaj arranged her mosquito curtain and said, "Mother, I shall go now." The Holy Mother said, "Come, my dear, what a trouble we have given this poor boy."

For the last few days before her passing, the Holy Mother would not ask for any news of Radhu. One day she told her, "Look, you go away to Jayrambati. Do not stay here any more." She told me, "Tell Sarat to send them away to Jayrambati." I asked, "Why is she asking them to be sent away? Can she do without Radhu?" "Certainly I can," said the Holy Mother. "I have taken away my mind from her." I repeated these words of the Mother to Yogin-Ma and Sarat Maharaj. Yogin-Ma then came to the Holy Mother and asked, "Why, Mother, do you want them to be sent away?" The Holy Mother said in reply, "Yogin, hereafter they have to stay there only. H—— is going; send them with him. I have taken away my mind from them. I do not want them any more." Yogin-Ma protested,saying, "Do not say that, Mother. If you thus take away your mind, how can we live?"

The Holy Mother replied, "Yogin, I have cut off my attachment; now no more of it." Yogin-Ma said nothing and informed Sarat Maharaj of all that took place. He said, "Then we may not be able to keep the Mother any more amidst us. There is no more hope, now that she has taken away her mind from Radhu." I was standing there. The Maharaj told me, "Look, all of you are with the Holy Mother for long hours. Try and see if you could turn the Mother's mind a little towards Radhu." But all our efforts were in vain. One day she said quite forcefully, "The mind which I have withdrawn will never come back. Know it for certain."

Two or three days before passing away the Holy Mother called Sarat Maharaj and said, "Sarat, I am going. Yogin, Golap and others are here. You look after them."

2

(RECORDED BY SWAMI ISHANANANDA)

It was the month of Jyeshtha of 1316 B.E. (1909). One morning I heard that, on her way to Calcutta, the Holy Mother and her party would be reaching Koalpara that very evening at about four. Arrangements were already made for their reception. The Holy Mother was to be received in the shrine room of our teacher Sri Kedarnath Dutta (Swami Kesavananda), and the others, namely, Revered Sarat Maharaj (Swami Saradananda), Yogin-Ma, Golap-Ma and the rest, were to stay at our school. But even after dusk there was no trace of them. Later we got the news that their cart got stuck up near the river side. Immediately a few of the devotees set off in that direction, and, by and by, all of them arrived at about 10 p.m.

The Holy Mother, properly veiled, got down from the cart and went with Kedar Babu's mother to their shrine room, slightly dragging her feet. After she made Pranams to the Master and seated herself, all the assembled men and women bowed down to her. I also followed suit. Kedar Babu's mother was slightly deaf and so the Holy Mother was talking to the men devotees through me. In the meantimeRevered SaratMaharaj sent word that it was getting late and so the Holy Mother hurriedly finished her refreshment consisting of a piece of Sandesh and some water, and got up, ready for the journey. Along with the others in that crowd, I also hastily made Pranam to the Holy Mother and put my offering, which my father had given me for her, in her hand. The Mother affectionately fondled my chin and said, "My child, whatever is offered must be placed at the feet." She finally got into the cart.

Compared with the taste of her affection expressed through those few simple words, the love of my father and mother even seemed too paltry. I could feel it even at that age.

Once at the time of Jagaddhatri Puja, on her way to Jayrambati from Calcutta, the Holy Mother reached Koalpara Ashrama in the morning. Resuming her journey at noon, she said to the enthusiastic workers of the Ashrama, "Here, you alone are my relatives now. While I a.n in the village I depend only on you. I see, therefore, that the Master is residing here." One by one she blessed us all and said, "Come to Jayrambati now and then. Especially at the time of Jagaddhatri Puja, all of you must come."

And so, on the Jagaddhatri Puja day, the three of us went to Jayrambati, taking a load of vegetables and greens from our farm. The Holy Mother was much pleased to see us all and said, "Here vegetables are not always available. Now and then we are put to much difficulty. I see that the Master himself is arranging everything through you." From that time onwards whenever she stayed at the village, we used to finish our daily tasks at the Ashrama and go to her with vegetables twice or thrice a week either from our garden or purchased from the fair. On some days we reached the Holy Mother's place when she would be lying down and resting. On our making Pranam to her, after disposing of our offerings according to her directions, she would raise her head a little and bless us saying, "May your spiritual consciousness awaken, may you have faith and devotion!" and then ask us to take some puffed rice. We would take that and, munching it on the way, return to the Ashrama sometimes at midnight.

One winter day we took loads of vegetables and cow's ghee on our heads and reached Jayrambati by dusk, streaming with sweat. One of the ladies there who saw our state commented, "How much toil you are in for, as soon as you become a devotee! The poor boys' heads are worn off carrying loads." The Holy Mother heard this remark, and said, "Do they still have their heads? They have given them away to Him (the Master) to whom they belong." After that she placed her hand on our heads most affectionately and blessed us. Later she sent word to the Ashrama that instead of sending such large quantities at a time, we should send them little by little. Otherwise the vegetables would dry up and get wasted. Thereafter we would take small loads and go to her presence much more frequently.

After the Jagaddhatri Puja the Holy Mother was to go to Calcutta. At that time, the Koalpara Ashrama was being stirred by a great wave of Swadeshi Movement and everyone's inclination was more towards handloom, spinning wheel etc. rather than towards worship and meditation, Japa and scriptural study. Hearing that the Holy Mother would be leaving, KedarBabu went to Jayrambati for her Darsan. The Mother said to him, "Look, my dear, you have built a room for the Master and provided a resting place for me on my way. Therefore on my way I shall install the

Master there. You make all arrangements. Worship, food offering, Arati etc. must be done regularly. What will you gain by merely making so much of Swadeshi? Whatever we may be, we are rooted in the Master. He is our ideal. Whatever you do, if you keep a firm hold on the Master, nothing will go wrong." Kedar Babu replied, saying, "But Swamiji exhorted us so much to work for the nation. If he were alive today, how much would he have not done for the country!" Hearing this, the Mother said quickly, "Oh dear, if my Naren were here today, would the Company (meaning the British Government) leave him in peace? They would have locked him up in jail. I could not see it and live. Naren was an unsheathed sword. Returning from abroad, he said 'Mother by your grace this time, instead of leaping across, I went to their country in their own ship. Even there, the glory of the Master is evident in abundance! How many virtuous people came to me and listened enchanted to his teachings and accepted his ideas!' " Continuing, she said "They also are my children. What do you say?"

One or two incidents closely related to this come to my mind. Once at the time of Durga Puja, the Holy Mother gave me the responsibility of buying garments for her nephews and nieces. I bought for them all only Swadeshi (India-made) clothes. The girls did not like this at all and began to order as they pleased. I got irritated and said, "All that is foreign stuff. Do you think I will buy foreign goods?" The Holy Mother was sitting on one side. She said, smiling, "My dear, they too (foreigners) are my children. I have to run the house including everybody. Could I be one-sided? Please bring the things to suit their taste." Subsequently I observed that whenever any foreign articles had to be bought the Holy Mother would get them through others rather than tell me. It was not in her nature to hurt anyone's feelings.

But soon came news of Police high-handedness. Two pregnant ladies, wife and sister of Deven Babu of Yuthavihar village, were arrested in connection with the Swadeshi Movement and were made to walk miles to Bankura Police station. On hearing this the Holy Mother's anger burst forth in blazing fury. At first she shuddered, saying, "What do you say!" Recovering from the shock she continued, "Is this the Company's order or is it the heroics of the Police? We never heard of such atrocities on innocent women under the rule of Queen Victoria. If this act is indeed the order of the Company, their days are numbered. Were there no men there to slap those fellows and release the girls?" She was much pacified a little later by the news that the ladies were released and said, "If I did not hear this further news, I could not have slept at all tonight."

Another day when the Holy Mother was at Koalpara, Rashbehari Maharaj arrived there with some mangoes sent by Revered Sarat Maharaj. Just after his arrival Prabodh Babu also came to make Pranam to the Holy Mother. After enquiries about their welfare, the Holy Mother asked, "What is the war news? What a destruction of humanity has taken place! What all arts of killing men have been invented! Nowadays, there are so many kinds of machines—telegraph etc. Just see, Rashbehari started from Calcutta yesterday and reached here today. In those days with how much difficulty and after how much walking did we reach Dakshineswar!" Prabodh Babu was a little enthused by this. Praising the Western science and education, he said, "Under British Government the country has advanced very much in many fields." The Holy Mother agreed with him, but added, "But my dear, with all those comforts, the scarcity of food and clothing too has increased enormously in our country. Earlier such scarcity of food was not felt."

On her way to Calcutta the Holy Mother enshrined the Master's picture at Koalpara. She herself placed the Master's and her own photos and performed special Puja. The Homa was performed by Kishor-dada. At noon the Holy Mother went walking to Kedar Babu's house with his mother. While she was returning from there, P—— Maharaj requested her to enter the palanquin. A little displeased, she got in. Reaching the Ashrama, she spoke to him, expressing the cause of her displeasure: "This is my own village, and Koalpara is my drawing room. These children are my near and dear ones. I come here and move about freely. Returning from Calcutta, I heave a sigh of relief. There you keep me fenced in. All the time I have to stay there quite cramped. Here, too, am I to come and go at your beck and call? That cannot be. You write that to Sarat." Then in great humility P—— Maharaj began to entreat her pardon and said, "Sarat Maharaj particularly enjoined us to take all care of you. I felt that perhaps it is due to our lapse that you had to walk. But then, Mother, you are free to do as you like."

According to P—— Maharaj's instruction, we were to make

ready their food packets before six in the evening. But, however much we tried, we could not finish it in time. Seeing that P—— Maharaj began to get angry. Brother Rajen said, "All right, you start off with these people according to your schedule. We shall get the food ready and bring it to you on our heads, however far you may have gone." The Holy Mother heard everything and said to P—— Maharaj, "Why do you lose your head and show so much temper? This is my village. Do you think everything will click with the needle of the clock here, as in Calcutta? You see how the boys are breaking their bones since morning! Whatever you say, I will not move from here without taking food." Finally at about eight at night, finishing their meal they started towards Vishnupur in eight bullock carts.

The Holy Mother had just returned to Calcutta from Rameswaram (1911) after her Pilgrimage. We three went to meet her at the Udbodhan house and went upstairs to have her Darsan. We sat down after bowing down to her. She enquired after everybody at Koalpara and Jayrambati and said to Kedar Babu, "Hearing that you are coming, I have kept two photos of Rameswaram for your Ashrama. Take them with you when you go. You may worship them there." Kedar Babu replied, "But there you have yourself established the Master and asked us to worship him as the embodiment of all the deities. Now you are giving all these deities. How many gods shall we worship? We shall not be able to worship other gods." The Holy Mother did not press the matter. "All right," she said. "Have these pictures properly framed and keep them in the shrine room." Kedar Babu enquired about her impression of Rameswaram etc. "My dear, Rameswar is the same as when I kept Him," said the Holy Mother. Golap-Ma was passing that way just then. Hearing these words, she asked innocently, "What did you say, Mother?" The Holy Mother looked startled and said, "When? What did I say? I am saying that I was very happy to see just the same as I have heard from you all." "No, Mother," Golap-Ma continued, "I heard everything and it won't do to try to give the slip now. What do you say, Kedar?" Saying this, she went off from there and started telling Yogin-Ma and others about it.

The Holy Mother continued. "Ah, Sasi had me perform the Puja of Rameswar with a hundred and eight golden Bel leaves. The Rajah of Ramnad, hearing that I was there, sent his minister with instructions to show me the temple treasury. If I had a fancy for any article, it was to be immediately presented to me. What could I say? Unable to decide what to say, I replied 'What do I need? Sasi is arranging for all our requirements.' Again, thinking that they would be hurt, I said, 'All right, if Radhu needs anything, she may take it.' I told Radhu that she could take anything she liked. Then seeing all those priceless rubies and diamonds, my heart went pit-a-pat. Anxiously I prayed to the Master, 'Oh Master, grant that no greed should arise in Radhu's mind.' And so Radhu replied, 'What of these shall I take? I do not need them. But I lost my pencil. Buy me a pencil.' Hearing these words, I heaved a sigh of relief and bought her a two pice pencil at the roadside shop."

Conversing in this manner she got up to make food offering to the Master. We too came downstairs.

Two or three days before Janmashtami (Sri Krishna's birthday) I expressed to the Holy Mother my desire to be initiated by her on that day. Hearing this, Golap-Ma said in her usual loud tones, "Such a little fellow (a boy of thirteen), asking for initiation! He is likely to forget the Mantra in two days. How thoughtless of Kedar! The Holy Mother is from your own village. When she goes there after due deliberation, you can get initiated." Thus remarking, she went away. But the Holy Mother rejoined reassuringly, "Don't you take Golap's words to heart, my dear. If one of your age learns anything well, can he ever forget it? Let the boy do whatever he can from now on. As for the future, I am with you always." And so she initiated me on the day of Janmashtami after the Master's Puja. Demonstrating the manner of doing Japa according to her instructions, she said, "Can you not keep this much in mind? Certainly you can. Later, as and when necessary, I will show you everything." And then she blessed me, touching my head and chest affectionately. Getting up from her seat, she asked me to go with her. I made Pranam to her and followed her into the next room. She took two sweets out of a vessel, bit off a small part of one and gave me the remainder, saying, "Eat." I received the sweets in my hand and out of shyness was hesitating to eat them in her presence. Noticing my hesitation, she said, "Don't be shy. After initiation one must take food," and then gave me a glass of water to drink.

Soon after that, we returned to Koalpara along with Kedar

Babu's mother. (This old lady served the Holy Mother in various ways. At sixty years of age, she felt the desire to read and write and started with the first Reader, and towards the end she was able to read and understand the Ramayana, Mahabharata etc. Even when she accompanied the Mother to Rameswar, she went with her first Reader and a slate. She passed away six or seven years after the Holy Mother's demise). At the time of our departure, the Holy Mother gave some money to Kedar Babu asking him to buy some paddy and make some rice ready.

In the month of Phalgun, the Holy Mother returned to her village. From Koalpara three of us went far ahead early in the morning to receive her. Catching sight of her cart from a distance, the other two went back to inform the Ashrama. I remained to accompany the carts. The Holy Mother spotted me from a distance and was saying, "Who is that? B— is it not?" As I approached her and made Pranam, she enquired after every one's welfare. The carts were rolling on, while I walked alongside. The Holy Mother peeped out of the cart and was asking questions like, "What village is this? Whose pond is that? How far is Koalpara from here," etc. As we left Kotulpur the Holy Mother said, "Why don't you get into the cart? You have walked far enough." But Radhu was in the cart along with the Holy Mother. A little later, the cartman got down from the cart and said, "You please sit in front. I'll walk a little." I then got in front. Seeing me handling the oxen and driving them faster, the Holy Mother burst out laughing, "Ah, you are an expert cartman! It is good to know all trades." In due time we reached the Ashrama. The Mother's was a rather delicate constitution. As she had sat for long cross-legged in the cart, her legs became numb. Kedar's mother helped her to get down from the cart and slowly led her to the shrine room verandah and seated her there. After a little rest, she bathed and said to me, "My dear, I cannot now exchange shouts with Kedar's mother (She was a little deaf). You change your dress and make arrangements for the Puja."

In my ignorance I put on one of the Mother's clothes and was going to pluck flowers. Noticing this, Kedar Babu's mother got quite upset and was saying, "You dunce! You are wearing the Mother's cloth! Leave them immediately. Leave!" But the Mother, said, "What does it matter? He is a young boy. What harm is there, if he wears my clothes? Go, go, bring flowers."

Kedar Babu said in the course of conversation, "Mother, all your children are learned men. Only we few are ignoramuses. Sarat Maharaj wrote a book on the Master and spread his teaching everywhere. Other children are all giving lectures and touring. How much work is going on!" At this the Holy Mother said, "What do you say? The Master himself was not learned. He learned only to keep his mind on God. Through you a great deal of work will be done in these parts. This time the Master has come to liberate all—the rich and the poor, the wise and the foolish. Now there is a splendid Malaya breeze.[1] Just set your sail a little, take refuge in him and immediately you will be blessed. This time anything other than grass and bamboo—whatever has a little core—will surely become sandalwood. What do you think? You are my own people. But do you know, a learned Sadhu is like an elephant with gold-sheathed tusks." Saying this, she got up for Puja. A little after dusk the Holy Mother left for Jayrambati in a palanquin.

The man who was to go from Koalpara as the storekeeper for Jagaddhatri Puja, fell ill. And so in his stead I went to Jayrambati. The Holy Mother said, "It is very good you have come. Today you observe everything. Tomorrow quite early in the morning take bath and come to the store. Attend to the work there, observing all ceremonial procedures. Keep a little distance and carry on the work. Everything will be all right." She said these last words, because in those regions caste restrictions were quite strict.

On the day of the Puja, she came early in the morning to the store and took her seat on a sack, with her feet dangling. When any one came for anything from the store, I showed the required things to the Holy Mother and then handed it over to the person. At the end of the Puja, the Mother bathed and went to the Mandap, taking the aunts with her for the flower offering. She offered flowers thrice at the feet of the Devi, and with hands folded, and the end of her Sari wound around her neck in humility, she sat silently for some time. Puja concluded without a hitch. In the noon many men and women of the village were fed. As I had fever on the second day—for the image had to be kept for three days—

[1]It is a tradition in India that the mythological breeze blowing from the Malaya mountains will turn all trees and plants that have a core, into sandalwood trees.

the Holy Mother herself looked after the store. After evening Arati all the monks and devotees together started singing Bhajans. "Worry not to have the Mother's vision, she is not mere mother of yours or mine alone, She is the Mother of all, of the whole Universe" —thus they sang again and again. The Holy Mother was sitting in the next room with the other women and was listening with absorption. That night she remarked to me, "Ah! The singing was enthralling. What is caste to devotees? All children are one. I feel like feeding all of them from one plate. But in this wretched region they make much of caste.[1] However, there is surely no objection to puffed rice. Tomorrow quite early in the morning you go to Kamarpukur and bring two seers of the Jilapis (a certain sweetmeat)." Next day I returned with the Jilapi by about 9 a.m. The Holy Mother offered them to the Master and arranged them in a big plate around the heap of puffed rice. This delicacy she sent to the devotees. In great joy all of us began to partake of it and the Holy Mother looked on us from the next room.

Once in the rainy season there was an epidemic of malaria and dysentery. The Holy Mother too suffered much for a few days from blood dysentery and recovered through Dr.Kanjilal's treatment Because of constant walking through mud and water in Koalpara, nearly all of us got fever. Noticing that from Koalpara none of us went to Jayrambati, the Holy Mother sent a maid to get news of us. She brought us a letter from the Mother to the following effect: "My dear Kedar, I have established the Master in that Ashrama. He used to take boiled rice and fish also. Therefore I say, you must offer boiled rice and fish to the Master, at least on Tuesdays and Saturdays. Do not offer fish on Sundays. By no means should you offer food to the Master without three curries. If you practise too much of austerity, how can you withstand the malaria of these parts?"

A few days after this, the Holy Mother was speaking to Kedar Babu about Radhu. She said, "She has grown to be such a big girl and yet she has so little sense. What bondage has the Master brought on me through her! After he passed away, when I came to the village, completely indifferent to the world, I used to see a

[1]Once when Sister Nivedita expressed her wish to go to Jayrambati, the Holy Mother said, "No, dear. While I am alive you should not go there. If you do, they will out-caste me."

small girl wrapped about in red clothes, moving about before me." Seeing that Kedar Babu had become absent-minded, she said, "Oh Kedar, are you listening? That was Yoga Maya." Kedar Baba replied, "No Mother, I did not hear everything—please tell me again." Then the Holy Mother resumed: "After the Master's passing away when nothing in the world had any meaning for me and I was panting for release, I used to think, 'What is the point of my living any more?' In that state suddenly I saw a young girl of ten or twelve years dressed in red clothes, moving about before me. The Master showed her to me and said, 'Take her for support and live. Numberless children will come to you.' Next moment he vanished and I could not see the girl also any more. Later on one day I was sitting just in this place. Radhu's mother, my younger sister-in-law, was then totally mad. She was going this way dragging some rags behind her. And Radhu, crying bitterly, was crawling behind her. My heart bled at the sight and I rushed to take her up in my arms. I felt that no one would care for her if I did not. Her father was dead and her mother is that madcap. Thinking thus, no sooner had I taken her in my lap, than I saw the Master in front of me. He was saying, 'This is that girl. Live with her as your support. This is Yoga Maya!' What can I say, my dear! Earlier she was well. Now-a-days she gets all kinds of diseases, and she is married too. I am now afraid, that this daughter of a mad woman might herself turn mad. Have I, after all, brought up a madcap?"

While she was at Calcutta, the Holy Mother had once written to Kedar Babu, "If you could put up a room for me at Koalpara, then when I come to the village, I could stay with you." Receiving this letter, we ourselves constructed a house for her and called it Jagadamba Ashrama. When the Holy Mother came there for the first time, she stayed there nearly a fortnight before going to Jayrambati. Later, a day was fixed for her second visit. We got a palanquin ready. But on that day, right from the morning, it started raining cats and dogs. We got news that the water level in the river Amodar had risen quite high. Yet Kedar Babu said, "You take the palanquin as she has instructed and be present in time. There after you may do as she wishes." We came to the river and found it too deep. Rajen Maharaj swam across and fetched a ferry, and all of us together crossed over with the palanquin and reached Jayrambati at about 3 p.m.

Uncle Kali rebuked us, saying, "In this weather how could you think of taking my sister?" The Holy Mother was much amused. Brother Rajen replied, "We have no power to take her. But we had promised to bring the palanquin today at this time, and so we have come." The Holy Mother on hearing this laughed and said, "You have kept your promise. I too should keep mine. I alone shall come in the palanquin. The others will follow afterwards." Thereupon we came forward, telling, "No, Mother, how can it be? In the rain, nobody is able to step out of their houses. Should we take you drenched in the rain and make you fall ill?" Uncle Kali and the Holy Mother laughed and laughed. Taking the empty palanquin we returned to our Ashrama.

But the Holy Mother fell ill immediately after, and so she could come to Koalpara only after a few months. One morning at about eleven when I went to Jagadamba Ashrama. all the ladies were in great excitement. Kedar Babu's mother said in a hushed voice, "She (the Mother) is in ecstasy. Saying 'Thakur' (the Master), she has just lost consciousness." The ladies attended on her, sprinkling water on her head and eyes. A little later when she recovered, Nalini-Didi asked, "Oh, aunt, what happened?" The Holy Mother replied, "What happened? It is nothing. I was trying to thread the needle and got dizzy." Hearing these words, no one spoke any more on the topic.

Later, during her last illness, the Holy Mother herself told me fully about this incident of ecstasy. That day it was about half past one or may be two. Her fever was rising. I, as usual, sat by her bed and was fanning her and massaging her forehead gently with a wet hand. Patting me affectionately, she looked at my face and said, "If I pass away, all of you will feel very miserable. I can understand that." In gentle reproach I said, "Why do you talk like that, Mother? When the medicine is not showing any effect, why don't you speak to the Master about your body? Everything will get right, if you do that." The Holy Mother smiled a little and said, "At Koalpara I used to get such high fever that I lay unconscious in my bed frequently. Yet when I became conscious and thought of the Master for the sake of my body, immediately I could have his vision. In a very weak state, I was one day sitting in the verandah. Nalini and others were perhaps sewing. There was the burning heat of the sun all around. Suddenly I saw that the Master entered through the main door, sat in the verandah and then stretched himself down to sleep. Seeing that, I hastily went to spread my upper cloth. While spreading, I had a peculiar feeling. Kedar's Mother and others were making all kinds of fuss. So I told them, 'O! It's nothing. While trying to thread the needle, I got dizzy'. For your sake, do I not pray to the Master about my body? I do pray. But now when I think of him for the sake of the body, by no means am I able to get his vision. I feel it is not his wish that this body should remain. Sarat is there." After my return to Koalpara I heard just the same thing from Kedar Maharaj's mother also. She must have heard it from the Mother herself.

Another day at about two in the noon, I reached Koalpara. It was quite hot. The Holy Mother brought me some sweets and water,and was talking,"Oh dear, what a heat! Cool yourself a little. You should not leave before evening. How is Gopesh? What did you eat today? What did you cook? Take some fruits and vegetables with you when you go." I said smiling, "In accordance with Gopesh-da's instructions I mixed together green plantains, potatos and such things and cooked a potato-rice. But as I was not able to make a proper estimate, I prepared food enough for eight or ten people." Hearing this, the Holy Mother had a hearty laughter. As we chatted, the sky became overcast. The Mother said "Ah! a little rain would cool down mother earth." Moments later, strong winds blew and a hailstorm began. Enjoying that, the Holy Mother put one or two hail stones in her mouth. This sudden exposure to chill brought on her a fever, which took a very serious turn later on.

Rashbehari Maharaj and I were sitting on either side of the Holy Mother's bed one day. She placed her hand on my chest and back and said, "Ah! So many women are here, but no one's body is cool. These are boys and their bodies—how cool they are! My hand is soothed." In the travails of illness the Holy Mother used to look for Sarat Maharaj a great deal. Getting the news, Sarat Maharaj arrived there accompanied by Dr. Kanjilal and went straight to the Holy Mother. The Mother was then restless with a burning sensation all over her body and was stretching her arms this way and that. Sarat Maharaj saw that and taking off his shirt sat by her bed. The Holy Mother put her hand on his back and said "Ah, my whole body is cooled. Sarat's body is like a cool slab." Sarat Maharaj said, "Look now, Mother. All of us have come, and now you must get well." In reply the Mother said,

"Yes, my dear; if Kanjilal gives a little medicine I shall immediately get well." Sarat Maharaj was very happy to hear these words. Within a few days, she was free from fever, and she began to take her normal food. One day Sarat Maharaj said, "Mother, this time we shall not leave you here. I would like to take you with me to Calcutta." The Holy Mother also did not seriously object to this but said, "My dear, I must go to Jayrambati and start on an auspicious day." Sarat Maharaj agreed to this and set about fixing the day for going to Jayrambati.

It was during this illness of the Holy Mother that Swami Prajnananda passed away at the Udbodan. Later the Holy Mother came to know that his sister, Sudhira, the head of the Nivedita School, was sitting quietly by his side,fully controlling her emotions. Hearing that, the Holy Mother said, "Oh! It would have been better if she had expressed her feelings through weeping. It would have somewhat assuaged her grief. You please see that she does not fall ill. Already she has a heart complaint."

In this connection another incident comes to my mind. I was then at Jayrambati with the Holy Mother. One day I returned to Jayrambati from Koalpara with an old woman carrying a headload of things for me. The old woman put down her load and bowed down at the Holy Mother's feet. "What is the matter, my daughter?" she said. "You have not come this side for so many days?" The old woman replied in a piteous voice, "Mother, now-a-days I am in great difficulties. Searching for food, I go to different places. And so, when there is an occasion to bring a load here, the gentlemen do not find me in time. A few days back, my young earning son passed away." The Holy Mother was much affected to hear this and her eyes were filled with tears.

"What do you say, my daughter?" she said. On the Mother expressing her sympathy, the old woman gave way to her grief and wept loudly. The Holy Mother was overcome by a wave of sympathetic grief, and she began to lament with the woman, resting her head on a post of the verandah. The other women of the house rushed to the spot on hearing the sound, and stood transfixed there for a minute at the sight they saw. A few moments passed in this way. When the intensity of their grief subsided a little, the Holy Mother asked for some coconut oil. It was brought and she poured it on the old woman's head. After properly oiling her hair the Holy Mother tied a quantity of puffed rice and molasses in her cloth. Bidding her farewell, with her eyes still glittering with tears, the Mother said, "Come again, my daughter." The woman departed, highly consoled by the compassionate conduct of the Holy Mother.

After she recovered the physical strength a little, the Holy Mother went to Jayrambati on the appointed day, accompanied by Sarat Maharaj and others. All men and women of the village came to see her. Some said that they had given up all hope of seeing her again. The Mother replied, "Yes, I suffered very much from illness. Sarat, Kanjilal and others rushed to my help. By the grace of Mother Simhavahini, I was saved this time. Sarat says I must go to Calcutta. If all of you permit me, I shall go and return after regaining my health." Everyone gladly gave her permission, and seven or eight days later the Holy Mother started for Calcutta.

A few months later, I came to Belur Math. Radhu was ill at Udbodhan. She could not stand even a little noise. The Holy Mother therefore took her to the Boarding Home of Nivedita Girls' school. So I used to go there often to pay my respects to the Mother. She was considerably worried and would say, "Well, where can I go with her? The village is quiet enough but there is no medical facility."

On Swamiji's birthday I came to know that the Holy Mother was leaving for her village the next day. In obedience to Revered Sarat Maharaj's instruction I hastily reached the Udbodhan house by evening, ready to accompany the Holy Mother. She was packing a bundle of coir. Seeing me, she said, "I am going to my village taking these endless number of things. What about your coming with me? You boys are my only support there." I bowed down at her feet and said, "Whatever you command will be done. I shall go with you, what difficulty is there?" "That is good, my dear. See to these ropes and things and pack up all other items of luggage. Till now nothing has been set in order. I was waiting for you and packed the ropes." Along with her I packed things until eleven in the night, and quite early next morning we left on our journey.

After resting at Vishnupur for three days, we started again with our six bullock carts. Eight miles further at the Jaypur village, arrangements were made at an inn for cooking. At the time of taking down the pot of rice from the fire place, the pot broke and rice and water got scattered all over. We were stupefied and did not know what to do. But without any hesitation or excitement, the Mother took a broken sherd and separated the water from the rice. She then washed her hands,took out the Master's picture from her box and set it up on one side. Gathering the upper layers of the scattered rice, she arranged the rice and some curry on a leaf plate. With that make-shift offering, she said to the Master with folded hands, "You have willed it this way for today. Please finish your meal quickly while it is hot." All of us witnesed this strange procedure of the Holy Mother and began to laugh. Thereupon she remarked, "We have to adjust our ways to changing circumstances. Now please sit down for your meal, all of you." We sat down in a circle. The Mother served us all and served herself also on one side, sat down cross-legged and started eating. "Quite well-cooked," she said. We finished our meal and the carts moved on again. By eleven in the night we reached Koalpara.

Yet another incident comes to my mind. Once Revered Gauri-Ma was going to Jayrambati to call on the Holy Mother. From Koalpara she took me for company, and we started in the evening. We reached the river bank near Jayramabati while there was still daylight. So Gauri-Ma lingered there. So we could reach the Mother's house only a little after dusk. She asked me to wait outside the gate, and went in. There imitating the beggars, she called out, "O mother, give me alms, mother." Hearing that, the younger aunt came out, enquiring, "Who is that?" Gauri-Ma repeated her cry. The aunt was quite frightened. With a shriek she ran back to the Holy Mother. The Mother, who had heard the shout, came out with composure, and said in a firm voice,"Who is there?" Gauri-Ma once again said from the same place, "Give me alms, Mother, I am a night beggar." The Holy Mother recognised her voice in the dark and exclaimed, "Is it not you Gaurdasi! Come, come, when did you arrive?" Every one had a hearty laugh.

After staying for a day or two at Koalpara, Radhu developed a liking to the place, especially because of its loneliness. So the Holy Mother stayed there with her for six months. Arrangements were made for Radhu's stay in another lonely house, a little away from Jagadamba Ashrama. A thorny thicket surrounded the three sides of her house. One day the Holy Mother said to me, "Now-a-days I find my mind is having a strange power. Whatever thought arises, it comes true, be it good or bad. Radhu likes this forest because it is lonely. For a few days I have been feeling that, wherever you may be during the day time,after dusk you must come here and be with us. I am much afraid, my dear. I told Rajen also. He will come after ten or eleven in the night." From that day, after dusk, I used to keep watch under a tree in front of Radhu's house until eleven in the night. The Holy Mother too would sit up by me and talk with me in a very low voice. One day she remarked, "What a jungle! Any day a bear may pop out." I replied, "Why, Mother, I never saw a bear in these parts." But as a matter of fact one or two days later, word came that about a mile away, in the village Desra, one huge bear did attack and kill an old woman at noon while she was collecting cowdung. The bear too was shot. At dusk the Holy Mother said, "Did you not hear of the bear being on the rampage? It seems it has killed the mother-in-law of Ambika (the watchman of Jayrambati). And you declare there are no bears in this area!"

The Holy Mother used to eat some sweets and have a drink of water at dusk. She used to give me also a portion of it when I sat with her under the tree. She would say, "After the whole day's labour if you eat something and drink some water, the body will be quite refreshed. Thereafter , be it in Japa, meditation or any other work, the mind will settle down quite steadily." One day she said, "While I was staying at the Nahabat for the service of the Master, what hard conditions I had to endure in that tiny room! How many articles and things! I used to keep fish in a pot for the Master and hang it up. But in his service I never felt these as difficulties. The day would go by in inexplicable bliss. Now I am in these straits on account of Radhu. I am sitting here in this jungle with all of you. Good deeds, austerities, meditation—are all no more. Now by His grace, if we come out of the present difficulty safely, we should consider ourselves fortunate. "(Radhu was then nearing her confinement). A little later the lady from Navasan came and said, "O Brother, did you hear? Today at noon the Mother and I were sitting here, quite alone. The Mother was saying, 'Those two crows used to come right at this time, and sitting on that tree caw and caw, to the great annoyance of Radhu. But for the last few days, I do not see them at all. Can you tell where those two have gone?' Even as the Mother was saying these words, those two crows alighted on the tree and began cawing." The Holy Mother too laughed and confirmed her story saying, "Yes, my dear."

Another day, in the early part of the month of Ashadha (June) the Holy Mother and a few of us were seated at the foot of the tree. It might be about 10 p.m. Suddenly the Mother said, "Look, that mad man has not been coming here for many days. He is stark mad, but sings quite well. Yet, my dear, I am greatly afraid lest he should come here and create a commotion." The sister from Navasan protested, "Why do you think of him, Mother? Suppose your thought turns true, and he pops up here at this time of night!" "Who knows, my dear," rejoined the Holy Mother. I intervened and said, "You are merely imagining. In this weather how can anyone cross the river and come here?" Even as these words came out of my mouth, there stood the mad man, with a palm leaf plume on his head and a bundle of *sajina* greens under his arm. "I have brought these greens for you," he said. The sister from Navasan slipped inside, in fright. The Holy Mother said to him, "Go away. Don't make noise at this time of night."

The mad man replied: "How can I go? There is high tide in the river." I intervened saying, "How did you come then?"

The mad man replied: "I swam across."

The Holy Mother now said once again, "My dear fellow, don't make noise." The mad man then went away without a word. For two months the Holy Mother was in this mood often.

On another occasion I was sitting near the Mother in the verandah opposite Radhu's room, writing up the accounts. As a woman devotee passed by carelessly, the end of her cloth brushed my back. The Holy Mother noticed this and was much annoyed. "What is this? This boy is sitting before me and writing; and you are so unmannerly as to go brushing the ends of your cloth against his back! These are Brahmacharins (monastics),and you are women; you should move with due deference towards them. Bow down to him." The Holy Mother said these words in such an irritated voice that all the women of the house, including the woman so addressed, were frightened.

One new Brahmacharin at Koalpara desired to stay with the Holy Mother for a few days. To him the Mother said: "You want to stay with me. But you will have to face many difficulties if you stay here. I have a lot of work, and I am in this jungle with Radhu." But seeing the earnestness of the young man, she continued, "All right; tell Kedar and stay here for a few days." Just at that time, the attendant who looked after Radhu had to go to

Calcutta for a few days. The Holy Mother enquired if the Brahmacharin could manage that work, and when he agreed, she asked him to learn the work from the regular attendant. On the very first day as he was carrying Radhu's food. the vessels slipped from his hands and all the food was spilt . He could not decide what to do. He took the empty vessels to the Holy Mother. The consequence was that Radhu had to go without food that day. The Holy Mother was much vexed. Later she said, "As a monastic this boy may be quite good. But in my establishment I need dexterous workers. My work cannot be done by a 'foot-of--the-tree' monk. And again there are people who perform wonderful deeds under momentary excitement. But a man's true worth can be known only by observing the attention he bestows on his daily inconsequential actions." As the regular attendant returned within a day or two, the Brahmacharin had no chance to stay.

Yet another day one boy of Koalpara escaped from Police observation and came to the Holy Mother at dusk, wishing to be initiated. As the police kept a watch on the Ashrama of that place, the head of the Ashrama told him to go away. The Holy Mother came to know of this and told me,"See, the boy has come with such eagerness, braving so many difficulties. If you could arrange to keep him in somebody's home for this night, then in the morning I shall initiate him and ask him to go." As desired by her, I found him accommodation elsewhere for the night.

Next day quite early in the morning I was going to Radhu's house with the Holy Mother. The boy had bathed in readiness for initiation, and cutting across the fields, approached the Holy Mother. She asked me to bring some water from a nearby pond and I brought a tumbler full of it. The Holy Mother was looking around for something, and I asked her if I could get her a seat. She replied, "Yes. But you need not go again. Bring some hay and we two will sit." I did accordingly. They spread the hay and sat down on the ground. Asking me to move away, the Holy Mother purified herself by sipping water and initiated him.

One day at dusk, the Holy Mother said in the course of a conversation."I can no longer see or hear of anybody's faults, my dear. It all happens according to one's Prarabdha, the effect of past deeds. Where a ploughshare has to hit, at least a needle must prick. They speak of the faults of A—. Where were they at that time? How much he served me! In those days I was boiling paddy in my brother's houses. My sisters-in-law were all too young. Not minding the cold or rain, he used to work with me from dawn to dusk, taking down huge vessels of boiled paddy from the ovens. Now so many come as devotees. Then who was there with me! Are we to forget all the happenings of those days? Besides, what is his fault? In earlier days I also had an eye for people's faults. Thereafter I wept and wept before the Master, praying, 'O Master! I do not wish to see any one's faults' and finally got rid of that habit. You might have done good to a man a thousand times and harm only once; he will turn away from you for that one offence. People see only the faults. One should in fact note the merits."

One day at Jayrambati the Holy Mother said in connection with the evil mentality of some of the attendants, "Look, there is certainly what is called *Sevāparādha*, faults in serving. That means: as one serves, gradually one becomes more proud and egoistic, and then one wants to make a puppet of one's master. Whether the master sits or stands or eats, he must do so at the bidding of the attendant. The attitude of service completely disappears from them. Why should people turn out to be so— people who serve a saint forgetful of their own bodies, and take the master's joy and sorrow for their own? Is there a greater degeneration? Most holy men have an aura of grandeur around them. Attracted by that, many come to serve them and remain intoxicated by that grandeur. That will cause their downfall. How many can serve the holy men with the proper attitude?" The Mother then narrated a story: "Look, the story goes like this. In a tank there was a reflection of the full moon. Seeing that, all the small fish of the tank were immensely pleased. They leaped and splashed and played around the moon, thinking that it was one among them. But when the moon went down, they were the same old lot. All leaping and playing came to an end—they never understood anything." I said, "Kedar Maharaj says that one should not remain long with one's Guru. Seeing the commonplace actions of the Guru, the disciple's faith and devotion may be reduced." The Holy Mother said, laughing, "But, my dear, don't you go spoiling your minds with all those words. If it is true, how can I get on with my work? Do not entertain such a godly attitude, but have a human attitude towards me, and attend to what I say, and carry on with your work. You need have no fear."

There were a very large number of letters from devotees on

one occasion. At dusk I read them all to the Holy Mother. She heard them through and said, "Did you notice how many children have written with how many different desires? Some say, 'I pray so much, meditate and tell so many beads and yet nothing happens.' Others write about the anxieties, fears, wants, diseases and sorrows of this world. I cannot hear any more of this. I say to the Master, 'O Lord! In this world and in the next, you alone have to save them.' Where is the yearning? They speak so much of their devotion and earnestness on the one hand, and on the other they are so pleased with any little enjoyment they come to have and say, 'Ah! How merciful is He!' That is the measure of their devotional hankering. They say, 'How is Radhu's health?' That is to please me—this anxiety for Radhu. As soon as I pass away, no one will even look at Radhu." The sister from Navasan now said, "Mother, for you all children are equal. But to those who want to know the desirability of marriage, you give permission to marry. To those who want to renounce the world, you give instruction praising renunciation. Should you not take them all on the one path that is good for all?" To that the Holy Mother said in reply, "Will they abstain because of my prohibition if their desire for enjoyment is strong? And to those who have understood by virtue of great merit that all this is Maya's play, and believe that God alone is the reality, should I not offer a little help and encouragement? Is there any end to the miseries of the world?"

Nalini-Didi and others argued among themselves for some time and finally asked the Holy Mother, "Aunt, what kind of false description is good?" The Holy Mother, expressing her wonder at the question, said, "False description is by itself bad. In that how can there be good and bad again?" After a little talk of this sort, she said, "But then it is better to be described as a rich man though falsely. If any one were to be told that he is quite rich, whatever humility or displeasure he may show in his face upon hearing these words, in his heart of hearts he will feel quite happy." The Mother now passed on to another topic and said, "Now to another question. Well, let me see if you can tell what object is to be prayed for from God?" Nalini-Didi replied, "Why, aunt; wisdom, devotion, objects that make you happy in life, all these are to be prayed for." The Holy Mother said "To say in one word, we must pray for *Nirvāsanā,* freedom from desire.

Desire is at the root of all sorrows, the cause of repeated births and deaths, and the main obstacle on the path of liberation."

In the month of Sravan, the Holy Mother came to Jayrambati from Koalpara, accompanied by Radhu. At the time, we were fifteen or twenty people in her house. The Holy Mother herself would look after the welfare of every one. One day she told me in the course of a conversation, "My dear, that day, what in the world did Kedar tell me, accusing A—? Kedar after all is a man with a generous heart. For such a generous man it is not at all proper to speak as he did. I understood his mind, and at the time of my departure gave him a binful of paddy for the expenses of the Ashrama. But he did not wish to take it. He discovered his own error and has come to seek my forgiveness." Thus saying, she narrated the whole incident. "That day he (Kedar) came in the morning to make Pranam and said, 'Mother, all these people were quite obedient to me before. But now they have grown 'wise' and do not always wish to respect my words. When they come to you or to Sarat Maharaj, you treat them with great affection and keep them with you. They get nice things to eat also. If you do not entertain them, but convince them of the error and send them back, they will be obedient to me.' I replied, 'What are you saying? Our root is love alone. Out of love alone the Master's family has grown up. And I am their mother. How dare you make spiteful remarks to me about my children's requirement of food and clothing?' Ah, how much I prayed for them, wept for them before the Master! That is how they have today a monastery and such other things by his grace. After the Master's passing away, his children renounced the world and gathered together at one place for a few days. Thereafter one by one they left and were wandering here and there. Then I felt very sad. I began to pray to the Master: 'O Lord, you have come, performed your divine play with these few people, enjoyed yourself and gone away. Is everything finished with that? If so, what was the need for you to come, taking so much trouble? I saw in Kasi and Vrindaban so many Sadhus who live by begging and dwell under the shade of trees, wandering at will. There never was any dearth of such Sadhus. I cannot bear to see my children, who have left everything and come away taking your name, wandering around for the sake of a few handfuls of food. It is my prayer that those who come away in your name should not lack food and clothing, that all of them stay together, taking you, your memory and your teachings for their support; and that those who are scorched by the miseries of worldly existence come to them and obtain peace and solace by learning of your life and teachings. This was the purpose of your advent. It wrings my heart that they should wander here and there shelterless.' Since that time, slowly Naren built up all this."

At the time of Durga Puja at Jayrambati on the Ashtami day a devotee was coming with a basketful of lotus flowers. He saw me at a distance, and raising his hands together with the basket, saluted me. The Holy Mother saw this from a distance. Later she told me, "We cannot worship the Master with these flowers now. Throw them away."[1]

Two of us were wearing borderless clothes. The Mother noticed it and said, "Why are you wearing plain clothes without a border? You are young men. You must wear clothes with nice borders. Otherwise your minds will get old. One must always have enthusiasm," and she gave each of us clothes from her box.

On the same day a little after dusk, Sandhi Puja was performed. Many offered lotus flowers at her feet as Pushpanjali. The Holy Mother said, "Bring more flowers. Rakhal, Tarak, Sarat, Khoka, Yogen, Golap—offer flowers in the names of each of them. Offer flowers for the sake of all my known and unknown children." I did so and with folded hands the Holy Mother sat erect for a long time steadily looking at the Master. Finally she said, "May all be blessed in this world and in the next!"

One morning Kedar Maharaj sat near the Holy Mother at Jayrambati and asked her, "Mother, in our free dispensary those who are fairly well off also come to take medicines. But our dispensary is meant for the poor only. Is it right that such people are served?" The Mother thought for a minute and said, "My dear, in these parts all are poor. Yet, knowing all the details, if they still come to wait for free medicine, you will of course serve them if you can. Any one who comes begging may be considered poor."

Kedar Maharaj asked, "Mother, is it for the establishment of the harmony of all religions that the Master came this time?" The

---

[1] The idea is that when the flowers are shown to some one along with a salutation, they are to be considered as offered to that person. They cannot be offered to the Deity afterwards.

Holy Mother replied, "Look here. I never felt that he practised all the religions with the intention of teaching the harmony of all religions. He was always immersed in God-consciousness. He followed all the disciplines—those of Christians, Muslims, Vaishnavas, etc.—for the sake of God-realization, and he enjoyed the Divine *lila* (play) in different ways,entirely unconscious of how time passed. But still, do you know, my dear, in this age renunciation has been his speciality. Has anyone ever seen at any time that kind of spontaneous renunciation? What you have said of the harmony of religions is also true. In other Incarnations one ideal or another was emphasised over others."

That day after dusk, I went to the Holy Mother as usual, after finishing my duty of baking bread, to read her mail to her. One woman devotee often wrote letters full of praise and glorification of the Holy Mother. I told her its essence. She heard everything and said, "Look, many times I wonder,I am but the daughter of Ram Mukherjee, and many women of my age are there at Jayrambati. How do I differ from them? All these devotees come from various places and bow down to me. On asking them I find that some are doctors, some are lawyers. Why do these people come?" She was silent for a while. A little later I said, "Well Mother, do you not then always remember your real nature?" The Holy Mother replied, "Is it possible always? If it were so, can all this work go on? Yet amidst all this work, whenever the desire arises, inspiration comes in a flash upon a little thought and the whole of the play of Mahamaya comes to be understood." Some one said, "How, Mother, even with so much effort we are not able to understand anything!" The Holy Mother reassured her, "It will come, my dear, it will come. Why are you worried? In due time everything will come." We were talking late into the night. I said, "Mother,KedarMaharaj says,'You exert yourself doing all this work and then what should happen will happen of itself.'" The Holy Mother replied, "You must work, of course. Work keeps the mind in order. But Japa, meditation and prayer are quite essential. At least once at dawn and dusk one must sit down for spiritual practices. It is like the rudder of a ship. When you sit at dusk, you get to think of all that you have done and not done during the day. Then you have to compare the states of your mind yesterday and today. Then doing Japa one has to meditate on the form of one's Ishta. Though in the beginning, one sees only the face of the

Ishta, one must meditate on the whole form from the feet upwards. Along with work, if you do not meditate morning and evening, how can you understand whether you are working on the right lines?" I said, "Some others say that we gain nothing by work,that everything is gained if we can meditate and do Japa all the time." The Holy Mother answered,"How did they know that by this they gain and by that they do not? By meditating a little for a few days, is everything accomplished? Unless Mahamaya opens the way nothing will happen by any means. Did you notice the other day, how one man forcibly did more Japa than he could stand and got his mind deranged? If the mind is gone, what remains? It is like the thread of a screw. If one thread is loose, the fellow becomes mad, or falls into the trap of Mahamaya and thinks himself very clever, that he is doing fine. On the other hand if it is tightened the right way, one goes along the correct path and obtains peace and bliss. One must always remember Him and pray, 'Lord, grant me good tendencies.' How many can do Japa and meditation all the time?

"It may be that one does these for some length of time in the beginning. Because of this one becomes egotistic like N——. Afterwards he fails to do even that, but sits thinking of all kinds of things, which only generates restlessness in his mind. Far better is it to work than to let the mind loose to indulge in riotous thinking. If the mind is allowed a little laxity, it will create such a turmoil. My Naren observed all this and so laid down the foundation of selfless work." Referring to N—-, the Holy Mother continued, "Just see, sitting and sitting, what an impure mind N—— has acquired! The purity-mania alone is on the increase, and there is constant complaint of want of peace. Why so much restlessness? In spite of such experiences, why is it that wisdom does not dawn on him?"

Next day at about ten or eleven the Holy Mother was sitting at the main entrance. We were in the drawing room. Uncle Kali and Uncle Varada were exchanging words over the path between their houses, and gradually it developed from words into an exchange of blows. The Holy Mother could not restrain herself any longer. She rushed towards them. Now she would scold one saying, "It is your fault", and next she would try to drag away the other. She was caught up in the fray. At this juncture we all ran to the spot, whereupon the quarrel subsided a little. Still abusing each other, the two brothers withdrew to their respective houses. Still angry, the Holy Mother too came back and sat down. No sooner had she sat than she burst out laughing. "What a play of Mahamaya! Here is this wide earth, spreading endlessly. This bit of land too remains there always. Puny man cannot understand even this much!" Saying this, she rocked with a prolonged laughter.

Six months had passed after Radhu's child was born but still she could not stand up because of weakness. She could only crawl about. What was worse, she got addicted to opium. The Holy Mother's health too was not good. Now and then she would have attacks of fever. She was trying to wean Radhu away from opium eating. But Radhu was quite cross over it all the time. That morning the Holy Mother was cutting vegetables. Radhu came and was waiting for opium. The Mother understood and said, "Radhu, why don't you stand up? I cannot bear with you any more. For your sake I left all my spiritual practices. How do you think I can meet so much expense?" At this mild rebuke Radhu got angry, and taking a big brinjal from the wicker basket in front, she hit the Mother very hard on the back with it. As I turned my eyes at that thudding sound, I saw the Holy Mother rise, curling her back in pain. Immediately that spot was swollen. Looking at the Master, the Holy Mother prayed, "O Lord! Do not take notice of her actions. She is an idiot." Touching the dust of her feet to Radhu's forehead, she said, "Radhi, never once did the Master speak harshly to this body, and you give me so much trouble! How can you understand where my place is? Simply because I put up with you, what do you think of me?" Radhu burst out weeping.

A few days after this incident one day, Radhu's mad mother, out of some whim, searched for her son-in-law,Manmatha, in many places. She even got into the pond in her search and came to the conclusion that he was drowned, and that it was all the manipulation of the Holy Mother. She then ran to the Holy Mother in her wet clothes, fell at her feet and started shouting and weeping, "Oh dear, Oh sister-in-law, my son-in-law is drowned in the pond. Oh dear, what is to be done now?" This was a bolt from the blue to the Holy Mother. She was upset and called to us, "Come quickly. Just hear what this mad woman is saying." We all rushed there. Hari said that he saw Manmatha playing cards with his friends. "Make haste and bring him here," said the Holy Mother. We immediately left and returned with the son-in-law. Seeing him, the mad aunt was embarrassed and withdrew angrily, pronouncing curses on the Holy Mother.

In the evening the Mother was cutting vegetables for the night. Suddenly the mad aunt came and sat near her and said, "You fed Radhu with opium and disabled her. Thus you keep her in your control. You do not allow my daughter and granddaughter even to approach me." The Holy Mother retorted, saying, "Take away then your precious daughter. She is there lying like a lump. Have I kept her hidden anywhere?" After one or two exchanges like this, the aunt's madness reached its peak. She ran to bring a burning firebrand to beat her with. The Holy Mother shrieked in terror, "Oh, who is there, this mad woman will kill me!" I ran to the spot. I found the mad aunt aiming the blow and the fire brand about to fall on the Mother's head. I snatched it away from the mad aunt and pushed her out of the main door. Shaking with anger, I threatened her and forbade her ever to enter our portals again. The Holy Mother too was quite excited and blurted out these words. "Mad woman! What were you about to do? That hand of yours will rot and drop." No sooner did she say this, than she bit her tongue and shuddered. Turning to the Master, she said with folded hands "O Lord, what have I done! What is the way out now? Never did a curse on any one ever come out of my mouth till now. Finally that too has occured. What more?" I was stunned to see this boundless compassion of the Holy Mother.

A few months before, Sri N—— of Bangalore had come on a short leave to see the Holy Mother at Koalpara. Seeing that the Mother had to incur much expense on account of Radhu, he used to send considerable amounts as monetary offering to the Mother. At the time of his departure he said to the Holy Mother, "Mother, whenever you feel any want of money, please inform me without any kind of hesitation." With the passage of time the expense at Jayrambati had greatly increased. Revered Sarat Maharaj wrote saying that there was some delay in arranging for money and that he would therefore be late in sending it. Listening to this letter, the Holy Mother said, "Then Sarat does not have much money in hand. Otherwise, why would he write like that? N— had offered to help that day. But ah! how can I ask money of him? O Master, can I not obey your last instruction? Radhi, for your sake I am about to lose everything. The Master had said, 'Look, never stretch out your hand for money before anyone. You will not be in want of simple food and clothing. If you stretch your hand for a pice before anyone, you will be selling your head to him. Yet to live on charity is better than to live under another's roof. Wheresoever your devotees may keep you in their homes and look after you, don't you ever lose your own house at Kamarpukur.' "

A boy named Manasa came to the Holy Mother. He wanted to be initiated and become a Sannyasin. The Holy Mother satisfied his desire with much pleasure. He was very glad and sitting in Uncle Kali's drawing room sang the two songs: 'There is nothing in the world, Shyama is the only essence!' and 'I cast your image in the mould of my mind, O Shyama!' The Holy Mother liked the songs very much. Sitting near him Radhu, Maku, Nalini, one or two aunts and many others were listening to the singing. One of the aunts said, "Sister-in-law has made a monk of this boy. Such fine boys she turns into monks. With what difficulty their parents have brought them up, and pinned all their hopes on them! All that is shattered. Now he will either go to Rishikesh and beg for his food, or clean the dirt of patients in the name of service! To marry and set up a family also is a rule of creation. If you keep turning out monks like this, Mahamaya will be angry with you. If they want to be monks, let them do so by themselves. Why should they do so through your agency, aunt?" The Holy Mother replied,'Maku, they are all children of the gods.They remain pure as flowers in the world. Can you tell what greater happiness is there than theirs? You know yourself what happiness there is in worldly life! You know also the happiness of having a husband. Are you not ashamed to go to your husband again and again? What have you learnt, staying with me so long? Why so much infatuation, so much animality? What happiness do you enjoy? If you again approach your husband, I will send you away from here. Cannot a pure thought ever come to your mind even in a dream? Can you not even now live as brother and sister? Do you want to live like a pig? My bones burn in the fire of your worldly life."[1] All hung their heads in shame.

The Holy Mother continued, "Whether a man calls on God or not, if he does not marry, he is already half liberated. When the

---

[1]Some time before this, Maku's baby son had died, and after that she had another son born to her.

mind happens to be a little attracted to God he will progress by leaps and bounds. Family life is the result of demerits. A man involved in it, even if he is inclined to God, cannot do anything about it. He is tied hand and foot."

Of late, almost every day, the Holy Mother was having slight fever. Her body was getting very weak. Revered Sarat Maharaj was trying to take her soon to Calcutta. But he had to go to Kasi on urgent matters. So when it was proposed at that time that she should go to Calcutta, she said, "When Sarat is not there, the question of my going to Calcutta does not arise at all. To whom should I go? When I am there, if Sarat should say, 'Mother, I am going elsewhere for a few days,' then I say, 'Wait a minute, my dear. First I shall move away from here and then you may go.' Other than Sarat who will bear my burden?"

It was winter and the Holy Mother's health was getting very bad. Even then she would, as usual, get up early in the morning at three. Finishing her ablutions, she would sit for some time on her bed, covering herself with her quilt and then lie down again. We used to enter her room, then close the door and sit silent in the darkness. The Holy Mother would perhaps say, "At such and such time, do Japa of such and such a Deity, in such and such a manner" etc. A little later came up the topic of some of our monks going to live with the householders when they fall ill. The Holy Mother said, "Just because of illness why should monks live with householders? There is the monastery. A monk is the ideal of renunciation. A monk should not associate with women. And for monks to accumulate money is absolutely bad. There is nothing that money cannot do—one may lose even one's life on account of it. There was a monk in Puri, living on the seashore. He had a little money. Getting scent of it, two disciples could not control their greed. They murdered the monk and went away with his money."

One day at about nine or ten, the Holy Mother was rubbing oil on her body. An attendant just then swept the place and threw the broom on one side. The Holy Mother noticed it and said, "What is that? The job is over and straightway you threw it off so carelessly! It will take just as little time to keep it properly as it takes to throw it away. Should you neglect a thing because it is small? Whatever you care for, will care for you also. Won't you need it again? That aside, in this family it also is a part. From that angle also it deserves a certain regard. Whatever regard a thing deserves, that must be accorded to it. Even the broom has to be replaced respectfully. An ordinary work too must be done with care and attention."

One day Radhu's dearest cat was lying at the edge of the yard. One woman was standing near by and was petting it with her foot. Gradually she placed her foot on its head also. The Holy Mother noticed it and said, "Oh dear, what are you doing? Head is the seat of the Guru. Should one place one's foot there? Salute it." The said woman responded, saying, "I never knew that, Mother. I came to know of it only now."

Some devotees came from Calcutta one morning, all tip-top. They were dressed expensively. They also brought a lot of fruits and other things for the Holy Mother. In the evening the Holy Mother was talking to herself, "They have taken the life out of me. I cannot bear any more. Some children come and my family is as if filled with peace and bliss. From somewhere vegetables and all other needed things come to hand. I never have to worry about anything. Whatever is ready, they quietly eat and get up, folding up the leaf plate. Ah, their spoken words also are like a balm to my heart. Now look at this! Since morning, I am in a turmoil. They brought a binful of fruits. And half of them are so rotten as to be fit only for manure. Where to throw these? I do not know. They wear such tip-top clothing and yet they say. 'I forgot to bring my towel.' Where should I go to get a towel? Still I procured one. Now my worry is what I shall cook for the night. I learn further that there is no string for their mosquito nets. Hari is now searching for thread. O Master, you look after your family yourself. As for me, I can do no more. On one side is Radhi, and on the other are all these people." I recollect one or two incidents of how some devotees exasperated the Holy Mother.

The Mother was then at Jayrambati. A little before dusk I returned from Shyambazar and saw she was lying on a mat spread in the verandah. As soon as I went, the Holy Mother said with vexation, "All of you are here, but you will have to go out upon works. Today some one came, Sri——, an elderly person. Seeing him from a distance, I went inside and sat on the cot. He made Pranam from the outside. That was all right. But he was anxious to take the dust of my feet. However much I objected and shrank back, he would not desist. In the end, more or less forcibly, he touched my feet and took the dust. Since then my feet are burning unbearably and I have mortal pain in the stomach. I washed my feet three or four times but still the burning sensation does not abate. If you were near, you would understand my sign and could have forbidden him. With regard to devotees, those boys in Calcutta are so strict. It won't do otherwise. How many types of people come! You are young boys, you cannot understand."

Finishing all out-door work, I came to the Holy Mother at dusk. She said, "Today evening B—— brought a high Police Officer (she named him) to me. That man was of a peculiar nature—he came twirling his moustache and bowed down to me. He wanted to take the dust of my feet. I shrank back and could not by any means allow it. What a restless nature! And yet B—— was there in front of me, praising him to the skies to his own face. On my part, I was on tenterhooks, wondering how to get rid of him. Finally I made some Halwa and, giving it to him, sent him away."

One day the Holy Mother got up after Puja at the Udbodhan house. One devotee came with some flowers and went to pay his respects to her. At the sight of this stranger, the Mother covered her whole body with a shawl and sat there on the cot hanging her feet like a new bride. The devotee offered flowers at the Holy Mother's feet, bowed down and sat down crosslegged in front of her. Sitting there like a log of wood, he began Nyasa and Pranayama. Every one in the house was busy and there was none near the Holy Mother. She was sweating profusely. Time passed.

Seeing that the devotee was worshipping the Holy Mother, Golap-Ma had gone elsewhere on some other work. When she returned some time after and saw the same devotee sitting in the same fashion, she could understand the whole situation. Laying hold of his arm, she pulled him up to his feet and said in her natural loud voice, "Are you before a Deity of wood that you are about to enliven it by your Nyasa and Pranayama? Have you no sense? Can you not see the Mother is perspiring and is in great discomfort?"

Once another devotee went to make Pranam to the Holy Mother and knocked his head with force on her big toe. The Mother cried out with pain and stood up. When he was asked why he did so, he replied, "I knocked my head on her foot and pained her. As long as the pain is there, so long will the Mother remember me."

These two incidents, the Holy Mother narrated to us many times, to our great amusement.

As soon as revered Sarat Maharaj returned to Calcutta from Kasi, he sent an escort to bring the Holy Mother from Jayrambati. In due time, one morning she got ready for the journey with all her entourage. After every one had saluted her, K-Maharaj and H- bowed down to her. She gave them a cloth and a wrapper used by her and said, "Keep these." She placed her hand on their heads and blessed them, with tear-filled eyes. Then she started on her journey. I rode a bicycle alongside of her palanquin. On the way, in Sihore, the Holy Mother stopped the palanquin at the temple of Santinath Mahadev and offered Puja to Siva with two rupees worth of Sandesh, sugar and molasses. She then distributed the Prasad to all of us, took a little herself, and tied some at the end of her cloth for Radhu. All of us reached Koalpara in due time. That evening Radhu and other women started in bullock carts for Vishnupur. Next morning at five, when I went to the Mother at Jagadamba Ashram, she had just finished the Master's Puja with sweets and flowers, and was wrapping up his photo in a cloth and putting it in the box. She was saying to the Master, "Please rise. It is time to start." Seeing me, she said, "You have come! You are so late! It will soon be hot. Take this flower for the journey." Saying this she touched an offered flower to her head and gave it to me. Later she bade farewell to all and entered the palanquin. A little farther on she said, "Always keep near me and go attentively. Radhu's and Maku's jewels are all in Maku's palanquin." When we reached Jaypur, the Holy Mother stopped the palanquin. She got down at the inn, at which once we had cooked and taken our food on our way to Jayrambati. Seeing it in a dilapidated state, she said laughing, "Ah, it is that same inn of ours." She spread a blanket near it and sat down. "Feed the bearers with something," she said and had two rupees worth of puffed rice given to them. She then warmed the milk for Maku's son and having washed her hands and feet in the pond in front, said, "Buy me also a pie worth of puffed rice. I'll chew a little. And for you and Maku, see if you can get some puffed rice fried in oil." I brought all these. The Holy Mother ate very little, and gave it away to us, saying, "I cannot chew anymore." After the bearers finished eating, they took up the palanquin. We crossed four miles of jungle and reached Tantipukur where we saw a few labouring class people making a hullabaloo sitting near a small shop. I was thinking that it was best to cross this area as quickly as possible. Two miles farther we could reach a somewhat inhabited area and I could be free from worry to a great extent. But the Holy Mother peeped out from her palanquin, saw the shop and said, "Stop the palanquin a little. Sitting here my legs have become numb. Bring me half a pice worth of oil in a leaf from the shop. I shall shampoo my feet." Hearing this, I was beset with fear. Finally I told her, "Here are some people who seem to be unruly. There is no point in your getting down. Please stay inside, and I shall bring the oil." Maku was saying at the same time, "I am thirsty after eating puffed rice. I want some water to drink." The Holy Mother replied, "Drink. Go to that pond and drink." I protested, "Drink that water! It is not at all good." The Holy Mother said, "So many people drink that water on their way. Nothing will happen, go. You go with her and bring her back." I got the oil for the Holy Mother and accompanied Maku for her drink of water. Immediately on our return we resumed our journey.

At about twelve in the noon we reached Sureswar Babu's house in Vishnupur. Sureswar Babu had passed away a few months earlier. The Holy Mother said, "Ah, whenever I would come here, my Suresh would always stand there with folded hands. Sometimes he could not climb the verandah even. What devotion he had!" That day we stayed at Vishnupur, and next day noon after finishing our meals we caught a train for Calcutta, and travelling third class, reached Udbodhan by about ten at night.

Yogen-Ma and Golap-Ma saw the Holy Mother's condition and exclaimed, "Oh, dear, what a Mother have you brought us! So black in complexion! You have brought us a few bones and skin! We could never imagine that the Mother's health was so bad." From the very next day, Revered Sarat Maharaj made all arrangements for her treatment.

By the treatment of Dr. Shyamadas Kaviraj, the Holy Mother was a little better for a few days. One evening some women devotees came to see her. One among them was quite gorgeous in her dress and ornaments. Referring to her, the Holy Mother said, "For a woman, modesty is her ornament. Flowers are best used in the service of the Lord. Otherwise it is better that they fade away on the trees. I feel very bad when I see foppish gentlemen make sometimes a bouquet of flowers or sometimes casually put a flower to their nose and admire: 'Ah! What fine scent!' Oh dear, perhaps the very next moment they throw it on the floor and trample it with booted feet."

One day Ramlal-Dada, Lakshmi-Didi and Ramlal-Dada's daughter came to the Holy Mother from Dakshineswar. They were on their way to the festival at Entally. Ramlal-Dada bowed down to the Holy Mother and went downstairs to Sarat Maharaj. At the request of the Holy Mother and others, Lakshmi-Didi sang in a low voice and simultaneously mimicked the sound of the play of Khol (a kind of drum) with her mouth, to the amusement of all. After that the following conversation took place about the Master's birthplace, the temple to be built there and connected matters.

Lakshmi-Didi: If it happens (if the temple comes up), it should be under our control, shouldn't it be? Their (Ramlal-Dada's and Sibu-Dada's) children will do Puja etc., and live there.

Mother: How can it be? These are all monks and devotees. Can they observe caste regulations? Ladies and gentlemen of so many countries will come here, stay here, and have their Prasad. We have to do with devotees alone. But you are householders. You have your society. You have to perform the marriage etc., of your children. Would it do for you to live along with them?

After conversing thus for a while the Holy Mother said, "Houses just like those you have now, but with corrugated iron roofing, will be built for you separately in another area, either near Yugis' farm or somewhere on the western side."

Lakshmi-Didi: Then will Raghuvir and Sitala stay in the temple that is going to be built?

Mother: How is it possible? They are your family deities. On festival days your daughters and in-laws will have to worship them. That cannot be. For Raghuvir they will construct another temple. There will be left a small passage on the side so that the women can come and go. You, Ramlal or Sibu, when you go there, will be fed and accommodated in the temple with the devotees. What more worry is there for you?

Ramlal-Dada and others came upstairs to Sarat Maharaj's room. Ramlal-Dada and Lakshmi-Dadi wholeheartedly agreed to the Holy Mother's proposal, and after listening to the whole arrangement, Sarat Maharaj also expressed his happiness.

When Ramlal-Dada and Lakshmi-Didi left, the Holy Mother called me and said, "Look, talking with Lakshmi I forgot to give her a cloth and money. You go with Krishnalal to Entally and see the festival and also give this cloth and money to Lakshmi. They decorate the Deity at Entally beautifully." Saying this, she took out two rupees and a cloth and gave them to me. Later she said, "Lakshmi used to imitate the singers and sing and dance before the Master, displaying all their postures. The Master said to me, 'That is her mood. Be careful that you do not lose your modesty trying to follow her example.' "

From Jayrambati a letter came one day, conveying the news that some native of that place took to robbery and was under arrest. Hearing this, the Holy Mother said, "Oh dear, did you hear? I knew that he was a robber. But with what affection I used to treat him and give him so many things! So he was obedient to me. He would be as harmless as an earthworm with me. I live there with the responsibility of these girls and their ornaments. As for you, there is never any certainty where you will be at any time. Wicked men must be kept at a distance, in whatever manner it may be."

The Holy Mother's illness was gradually worsening. The temperature would rise only to 102° or 102.5°, but because of the burning sensation in hands and feet, there was great restlessness. Regarding it, she had been saying repeatedly, "Take me to the Ganges bank. I shall be cooled on the Ganges bank." Revered Sarat Maharaj wanted to do as she wished. But the doctors forbade all movement in her present condition. One day the Mother told me, "You take Radhu and all their set to Jayrambati and leave them there." Radhu was the Holy Mother's second heart, so to speak. She could not part with her even for a moment. And today in her worsening state of health she was directing them to be sent to Jayrambati. What could be the matter? we wondered. Gradually she was getting so much displeased with them that Nalini-Didi and others were afraid to go near her. Revered Sarat Maharaj tried to cajole the Holy Mother, "They will be unhappy to depart, leaving you in your days of illness. They will go after you get well a little." The Holy Mother replied, "It is better to send them away, so that they may never come near me again. I have no inclination to see even their shadow."

One day at noon Radu was sleeping in a side room. Her child crawled over on all fours to the Holy Mother's bed and was trying to climb on her chest. The Mother looked at it and said, "I have cut off my attachment to you totally. Go now. You cannot bind me any more." To me she said, "Take away this child elsewhere. I do not like all this any more." I took the child in my arms and gave it to its grandmother.

One day at Jayrambati when some one spoke rudely to the youngest aunt, she said, "What is that, dear? Should one speak such words as would hurt the feelings of another? Even if it is truth, it should not be told in an unpleasant manner. Finally, you will end up with that kind of nature. If one's sensitivity is lost, then nothing would control one's speech. The Master used to say, 'If you have to ask a lame man how he became lame, you must only say: How did your leg get bent this way?' "

Towards the end, the Holy Mother became so weak that she could not sit for long. But I noticed that she would be doing Japa even while lying down. Sometimes at Jayrambati I had to wake her up at one or two at night in connection with some work or other. She would respond at the first call. When I enquired if she did not sleep, she would say, "What shall I do, my dear? My children come eagerly and take initiation. But some do nothing regularly; some others do nothing at all. I have taken up their burden, should I not look after them? And so I do Japa for them. I pray to the Master on their behalf, 'Oh Lord, arouse their spiritual consciousness. Give them liberation. This world is a well of sorrow and misery. See to it that they do not have to come to it again.' " Saying this, she would rise very slowly to a sitting position. She would continue, "With so much earnestness they take initiation. But why then are they not practising anything? Is it so difficult to do so? With a little practice one gets such joy! Ah, with what bliss Yogin-Ma and I used to do Japa for long hours at Vrindaban! Mosquitoes would cause eruptions on our faces, but we were unaware of it all."

One day the Holy Mother said, "However much of Japa you do, however much of work you perform all is for nothing. If Mahamaya does not open the way, is anything possible for any one? Oh bound soul! Surrender, surrender. Then alone will She take compassion on you and leave your path open." Saying this, she told an incident in the Master's life at Kamarpukur. "One day in the month of Jyeshta, there was a heavy rain one evening. The whole field was covered with water. The Master was going along the main road near Dompada wading in the water. There, seeing that many fish had accumulated, people were beating them to death with sticks. One fish kept going round and round the Master's feet. Noticing it, he said, 'Hey, do not kill this fish. It is going round my feet, surrendering itself to me. If anybody can, let him take this fish and set it free in the pond.' Then he himself set it free and came home and said, 'Ah, if any one could surrender in this manner, then alone can he find protection.'"
